Images of Eternity

JAMES BENZIGER lived and attended school in
England, not far from Wordsworth's lakes and
the Brontés' moorlands. He later received his
B.A. and Ph.D. degrees from Princeton University, served in the Army Air Force during
World War II, and has taught at Northwest-
ern, New York University, Carleton College,
and, since 1950, at Southern Illinois University.

James Benziger

IMAGES OF ETERNITY

Studies in the Poetry of Religious Vision

from Wordsworth to T. S. Eliot

SOUTHERN ILLINOIS UNIVERSITY PRESS

CARBONDALE

Publication of this book has been made possible
through a special grant from the University.

For my wife

For my wife

PREFACE

A FIRST DRAFT of this present study was written ten years ago. In its broad outlines and much of its detail the work was the same then as now. Professor Carlos Baker was kind enough to read this early draft; he generously praised what was good and suggested ways of strengthening sections that were weak. Professors Douglas Bush, Arthur Mizener, and Vail Motter did almost as much.

In the intervening years many books and articles have appeared which are directly relevant to the matters under consideration. In the text and in the notes I have taken cognizance of many of these. But amidst the abundant writings of our new Age of Criticism several useful commentaries may have been overlooked.

More recently the Southern Illinois University Press requested two scholars to read a revised version of the work. I am indebted to both men for the insight, the learning, and the close attention with which they performed their task.

Finally, I wish to express my gratitude to Vice President Charles Tenney and Vice President John Grinnell, of Southern Illinois University, without whose encouragement this work could not have been completed or published, and to Mr. Alan Cohn and other members of the library staff for their unfailing helpfulness.

James Benziger

Carbondale, Illinois.
Spring, 1962

CONTENTS

Images of Eternity

The Transcendentalizing Imagination

Nineteenth-Century Poets and Eternal Questions

"THAT'S WHAT WE CARE ABOUT," says Ivan Karamazov. "Young Russia is talking about nothing but the eternal questions now. Just when the old folks are all taken up with practical questions. Why have you been looking at me in expectation for the past three months? To ask me, 'what do you believe, or don't you believe at all?' That's what your eyes have been meaning for these three months, haven't they? . . .

"And what do they talk about in that momentary halt in the tavern? Of the eternal questions, of the existence of God and immortality. And those who do not believe in God talk of socialism and anarchism, of the transformation of all humanity on a new pattern, so that it all comes to the same, they're the same questions turned inside out. And masses, masses of the most original boys do nothing but talk of the eternal questions." (Bk. V, Ch. III.) Thus, in *The Brothers Karamazov*, with characteristic intensity, Dostoyevsky goes right to the heart of the matter as it was in nineteenth-century Russia. At the same time he has described the spiritual situation among many of the most "original boys" of nineteenth-century England, especially among the poets. If these poets, now somewhat out

3

of fashion, are to be valued correctly, they must often be understood as men who were talking about the "eternal questions," about "the existence of God and immortality."

It is possible that the nineteenth-century poets are out of fashion partly for the very reason that they are not thus understood. The narrator of Proust's *Remembrance of Things Past* remarks that all of Vinteuil's musical compositions came finally to be apprehended almost as a series of variations upon a single theme. This notion of the fundamental unity of a musician's work is often applicable to a poet's work also. But what if the clue has been lost? What if we no longer perceive the single theme that is being constantly varied? The body of the poet's work will seem confused and weak.

This study is predicated upon the assumption that seeking fresh answers to the eternal questions has been a principal occupation of poetic minds from Wordsworth's time through the rest of the nineteenth century and even up to the present. Formerly men had believed in the existence of God upon the authority of tradition, of the Church, and of the Scriptures. And by such authority they had believed also in God's providence and in the immortality of their own souls. But in the seventeenth, eighteenth, and nineteenth centuries many educated men were finding it increasingly difficult to believe these doctrines on authority. Authority and tradition were being called into question in all other fields, and they must be questioned in religion also. Rousseau in *Émile* had, in effect, asked if it were reasonable to suppose that God, if he wished to communicate with a man living today, would do so by way of Moses. Neither he nor the majority of his readers could truly answer yes. By implication Rousseau was also raising the question of whether it was reasonable for God to communicate with men today through the person of Christ. He presumably felt not. It was common to say in those days that each man could find the answer to important spiritual questions by looking into his own heart. And it was in the desires of their own hearts, in the interaction between these inner desires and the outer world that the great poets of the past century and a half have sought the answers. In short, each man sought them rather in his own experience than in the words of other men who had lived long ago. So also in literary criticism emphasis had shifted from faith in the traditional rules to faith in original genius.

It is easy to establish a *prima facie* case that such an interpretation of more than a hundred years of poetic effort is valid. One of the most ambitious and widely-read poems of the mid-eighteenth century had been Edward Young's *Night Thoughts on Life, Death, and Immortality*. The author depicts a rich young man, supposedly typi-

cal of the time, who has sunk into melancholy and apathy because
he no longer believes in the great truths which Christianity taught.
Many long books of blank verse are filled with attempts to argue
him back into belief. At the end of the same century Wordsworth
was beginning a poetic career dedicated to arousing in men's spirits,
deadened as he believed they were by the conditions of the times,
the old sense of a Divinity within and above things. In *The Prelude*,
Wordsworth celebrates those particular moments of his life to which
he believed he owed his sense of Divinity, and in his *Ode* he touches
specifically upon the question of immortality. *The Prelude* he regarded as too private to be published in his own lifetime, but he did
publish *The Excursion*. The central figure of this poem, the Solitary,
is as deeply sunk in melancholy as Young's Lorenzo, and one of the
principal reasons for this melancholy is his lack of faith in "the
great truths of religion." The exhortations of the other characters
fail to arouse the Solitary—after all, it was characteristic of the period
that it refused to take its beliefs on the authority of others. But a
sequel was intended in which the Solitary would undergo a personal
experience which would restore him to some degree of faith. Wordsworth believed that spiritual despair was characteristic of many of
the finest minds of his time, and he hoped that his poetry as a whole
and his *Excursion* in particular would help these minds.

His hopes were not completely misplaced. Keats, who suffered
from melancholy, expressed deep gratitude for *The Excursion* and
often quoted from the *Ode*.[1] And at a slightly later date young John
Stuart Mill, suffering a sudden and intense attack of despondency,
found strength in Wordsworth's poetry, as he tells the story in his
Autobiography. Mill had not in general concerned himself with
metaphysics but with measures which would bring a more nearly
perfect state of affairs to pass right here on earth—with the metaphysical question "turned inside out," in the words of Dostoyevsky.
For one brief metaphysical moment, however, he had asked himself
whether all further human effort might not seem zestless and without point once the millennium had arrived. The question disturbed
him profoundly, and he remained grateful to poetry for its power
to suggest some value beyond the range of his rational analysis.

In the middle of the century another young man, Matthew Arnold,
raised his voice in thankfulness to Wordsworth. Wordsworth had
just died, the last of three great poetic figures to whom Arnold believed he owed most. Goethe, he says in *Memorial Verses*, teaches a
serene wisdom which will give men fortitude to confront these dark
days when the light of the spirit is extinguished. Byron shows that
sheer energy can also offer help. But only from Wordsworth do we

learn that the heavens we behold are not really an empty void, that the blank dark is but a cloud which has obscured the light; Wordsworth can push aside the cloud and show us that the heavens are still there:

> *Ah! since dark days still bring to light*
> *Man's prudence and man's fiery might,*
> *Time may restore us in his course*
> *Goethe's sage mind and Byron's force;—*
> *But where will Europe's latter hour*
> *Again find Wordsworth's healing power?*
> *Others will teach us how to dare,*
> *And against fear our hopes to steel;*
> *Others will strengthen us to bear—*
> *But who, ah! who, will make us feel?*
> *The cloud of mortal destiny,*
> *Others will front it fearlessly—*
> *But who, like him, will put it by?*

The poetic figure of the closing lines is not fully developed, but its import is unmistakable: a stoical fortitude is a fine thing, but a hope-bearing vision is better. The hope-bearing vision is hard to achieve in the present age, but one great poet has achieved it. This was the opinion of Arnold the poet in his youth. A few years later Arnold the critic was to start preaching similar notions. The old dogmatic religion is dead, he was to say in his *Study of Poetry*, but great poetry will take its place; great poetry will be our surest spiritual stay. He did not mean that great poetry would teach us fortitude only, but in its very grace and perfection would give us vision also— though as to the precise theological meaning, if any, which this vision implied, Arnold was characteristically reserved.

Arnold did not classify Shelley and Keats with Wordsworth as men who had put by "the cloud of mortal destiny." Rather he classed Shelley with Byron and himself and Sénancour among those who merely "grieved" for the loss of the old belief. For all his prizing of the critical intellect, Arnold valued an inner spiritual assurance which he believed Wordsworth's poetry breathed. Yet he ought to have classed Shelley and Keats as men who at least sought to put the cloud by.

Tennyson in *In Memoriam* catches hints of the workings of Divine Providence and of some immortality "behind the veil." So do Browning's characters in many of his most celebrated poems. In America Walt Whitman views death with mystical exaltation in *When Lilacs Last in the Dooryard Bloomed* and *Out of the Cradle Endlessly Rocking*. No more examples need be cited. The opinions of

Wordsworth and Arnold as to the basic problem of the age might alone have warranted the value of such an interpretation as this study will offer. A reading of the poetry of such twentieth-century writers as W. B. Yeats, Wallace Stevens, and T. S. Eliot will further reveal that something of the old imaginative preoccupations have persisted even into our time under altered conditions and in different modes—even, in a curious way, in the case of the frankly antitranscendental Stevens.

Romantic Poets and Modern Criticism

IF THE NINETEENTH-CENTURY POETS were to so great an extent meta-physicians, then should not this fact have been known to writers since Matthew Arnold's time? One might suppose it would need no elaborate exposition at this late date. It has been known. For many decades there have been books and articles upon the "religion" of one or another of the great nineteenth-century poets. Yet these men were primarily poets rather than theologians, and many of the studies which have concentrated almost wholly upon their theology have failed to find readers among those interested more in poetry and the imaginative processes.

This theological interest of the poets has also been known to many whose tastes were more literary. Only a few instances need be given. C. M. Bowra has set the matter forth briefly but perceptively in the introductory essay to his book *The Romantic Imagination:* he writes thus of all the great early nineteenth-century Romantics except Byron: "Each was confident not only that the imagination was his most precious possession but that it was somehow concerned with a supernatural order. . . . They were convinced that, though visible things are the instrument by which we find this reality, they are not everything and have indeed little significance unless they are related to some embracing and sustaining power."

D. G. James's books *Scepticism and Poetry* and *The Romantic Comedy*, G. Wilson Knight's *The Starlit Dome*, and David Perkins' *The Quest for Permanence* are based upon an apprehension of the same situation. So also are many studies of single poets: much of J. Middleton Murry's writings upon Keats, for example, most of the contributions to the anthology *Wordsworth: Centenary Studies*, and David Ferry's examination of Wordsworth, *The Limits of Mortality*. To specialists, in short, the central contention of the following chapters will not be new. Yet a new exposition may be freshly suggestive in its details.

The more general student of literature can certainly profit from a fresh development of the theme. One instance may testify to the need. A few years ago a well-reputed scholar now deceased, not himself a specialist in the Romantics, wrote a long essay introducing an anthology of Victorian literature. Among the quotations used to aid the student's understanding of the period are the lines on Wordsworth from Arnold's *Memorial Verses*. But the last three lines are omitted; the reader never learns that Wordsworth's "healing power," his ability to "make us feel," has some connection with his putting aside the cloud that obscures our mortal destiny. Doubt more than belief may be the resonant note in Arnold, but to ignore the vestigial sympathy with belief is to apprehend the poet incompletely.

The change in spiritual climate is one obvious explanation of why the nineteenth-century poets are thus only partially understood by the nonspecialists. In the *Stanzas from the Grande Chartreuse* Arnold describes Romantic melancholy as the grieving for the decline of the old religion by men who have grown up in the shadow of an abbey wall; such men may not quite believe the old religion, but their imaginations have been fired by it, and by comparison the bright shapes of the merely material world are dull:

> *"Long since we pace this shadowed nave;*
> *We watch those yellow tapers shine,*
> *Emblems of hope over the grave,*
> *In the high altar's depth divine;*
> *The organ carries to our ear*
> *The accents of another sphere.*
>
> *"Fenced early in this cloistral round*
> *Of reverie, of shade, of prayer,*
> *How should we grow in other ground?*
> *How can we flower in foreign air?*
> *—Pass, banners, pass, and bugles, cease;*
> *And leave our desert to its peace!"*

The great nineteenth-century British poets for the most part grew up in the shadow of Christianity. Their education was largely under ecclesiastical auspices, and even Keats is to be found, by readers of his letters, in the position of helping a younger sister learn her catechism. Most modern American scholars have not attended schools where religion was officially supported nor gone to universities like Oxford and Cambridge where an outward alliance between religion and literature still exists. Whatever the cause, modern criticism in the United States is split asunder: Americans of one sort have produced studies of the poets' religious beliefs, while their fellow citizens of another sort have often written wholly secular criticism. And the untranscendental criticism of the secular critics is the dominant voice in the literary world. Few American writers of either variety are quite at home in the borderland between a humanist poetic imagination and a more traditional religious faith. Yet some such land is the Romantic locus. Carlos Baker has recently stressed this fact when writing of Shelley;[2] and those writing on other nineteenth-century poets would usually do well to stress it likewise.

Another difficulty in the way of sympathy is that modern humanism is frequently de-Platonized as well as de-Christianized. Basil Willey contrasts Coleridge, who could use both Plato and Christianity against the eighteenth-century mechanists, with D. H. Lawrence, who in our time could appeal only to "the blood, the solar plexus, and the dark gods of paganism."[3] The poets to be studied here were usually Platonists at heart; but to many of their modern readers the Platonic metaphysic, which sees this world as the symbol of another, or this part as a symbol of the whole, is even less a live option than traditional religion.[4]

In particular we differ from our nineteenth-century forebears in our diminished interest in the question of the immortality of the individual soul. In a biography of a man of a hundred years ago written by one of his own contemporaries, one might read that the deceased had lost his faith in many dogmas but had never doubted his personal immortality. Such a passage strikes the modern ear with an odd ring. Today even the orthodox are likely to pass lightly over the question of how faith can redeem us in eternity and stress rather how it can redeem us here and now.

For this last reason a modern reader may not immediately realize the full significance of such Romantic terms as "hope" and "fear"; these were often intended to suggest specifically hope for immortality and fear of total extinction. The "hope" not without which "we suffer and we mourn" in Wordsworth's *Elegiac Stanzas* is much the same as "the faith that looks through death" in the Intimations *Ode*.[5] And a modern reader coming upon Keats's imaginative presentations of a fuller, richer state of being (as in the *Ode on a Grecian Urn* and the *Ode to a Nightingale*) may overlook the record in the letters of the semitheological speculations which preceded these imaginings; he may read these poems instead as forerunners of the "vacational" poetry which Wallace Stevens recommended as an enrichment of life in merely human terms.[6] Vacational they were, but Keats was also making a last desperate effort to hold onto a view which would see in such imaginings some great symbolic portent.

There is no wish to deny the willingness of modern humanist readers to adjust their minds to worlds not their own. They have often showed themselves willing and able to adjust to writers far more remote. But it is sometimes hardest to sympathize with the recent past. Likewise, the still older writers often took their metaphysics for granted and within the framework of its presumptions were free to concentrate upon moral and emotional issues in which a humanist can easily become engaged; but insofar as the crisis from Wordsworth to T. S. Eliot is often precisely within the domain of metaphysics itself, a humanist when reading these poets may at times find it difficult to feel himself in touch with human reality.

A proper historic understanding of the Romantic crisis in belief, a viewing of it as an episode in the larger and more general crisis in religion, is not made any easier by the tendency of critics, even those who are not wholly secular in their own thinking, to avoid specifically religious terms. There are several reasons for such avoidance. A writer may feel that literary criticism and theological discussion are separate genres, and he may wish to speak a language which secular readers will not find altogether strange. In any event, instead of hearing, in Dostoyevsky's terms, of poets asking questions about the existence of God and the immortality of the soul, we are more likely to read of "the numinous" in Wordsworth, of Shelley's "vision," or of the conflict between "the real" and "the ideal" which Allen Tate says (very correctly) is the basic problem in Keats's poetry.[7]

The reluctance to use specifically religious terms may also be justified on other than tactical grounds. The poets themselves often, though not always, employ more secular phrases because they wish to be true to their own imaginative experiences, which did not come to them in precisely traditional terms. These experiences might be more accurately rendered by Wordsworth's "Presences," his "Infinite," his "something far more deeply interfused," or by the "eternity" which, in the Ode on a Grecian Urn, teased Keats out of thought. To a great extent the more traditional terms, when the poets used them, were, as John Crowe Ransom has noted, intellectual constructs made upon the foundation of the original experience.[8]

But though the desire of one kind of criticism not to distort the poet's basic experience deserves respect, there is yet some need for another kind of criticism which serves as a bridge from the poet's personal consciousness to larger movements of thought. By keeping such terms as God and immortality a little more in the forefront of awareness, one may apprehend the Romantic moments of intimation as what they were historically, derivatives of the whole Western religious tradition. One may see Romantic poetry as leading in one direction into the still more secular and private imaginations of the French symbolists, of William Butler Yeats, and Wallace Stevens, and yet in another direction anticipating such reaffirmations of tradition as Wordsworth and Coleridge made in their own later years and as have been made in our own time by such poets as T. S. Eliot, Allen Tate, and W. H. Auden. If one considers Shelley's starting point, for instance, as Christianity, then one may view his career as part of the great modern falling away; if one views his starting point as the position defined in *Queen Mab*, his subsequent years reveal a movement back towards a partial reaffirmation.

In his 1800 *Preface* Wordsworth said that the poet was "a man speaking to men" and maintained that poetry should so far as possible be written in a language generally intelligible to men. The privateness of the imaginative worlds of Tennyson, Browning, and Arnold were an urgent problem to the poets themselves, as E. D. H. Johnson has recently emphasized in *The Alien Vision;* the same is partly true of the Romantics. Professor Johnson sees the Victorian situation as anticipating the even greater alienation of the modern poet from a large public. His personal regret is that the great Victorians did not take the course of some of their successors and remain within their private worlds untroubled by their inability to communicate with any substantial number of their fellow men. The accommodation of vision often presents a nearly insoluble problem, and the modern course insures an integrity of sorts. The nineteenth-century poets, however, did not take this course. While still cherishing the private quality of their vision, they sought some degree of universality by relating this vision to tradition. A study of their writings may appropriately make about as much use as they themselves made of such intellectual constructs as the ideas of God and immortality, ideas by which they sought to relate their experiences to wider traditions.

One way in which these poets may be apprehended historically is the way of H. N. Fairchild in his many-volumed work *Religious Trends in English Poetry*. Professor Fairchild has seemed ultraorthodox even to some who would class themselves as believers, but precisely because he stands entirely outside the Romantic movement he enables us to view this movement as a whole—though we may not agree with him in his judgment of what he sees.

Fairchild acknowledges that the Romantics were seeking, in their own imaginative responses to experience, replacements for the old Christian beliefs. This fact is the precise grounds of his objection. God has revealed himself to man in the person and teachings of Christ. To pay little heed to this revelation and to seek rather to create one's own revelation by the exercise of one's own imagination is to be guilty of ingratitude and pride. It is also to be doomed to failure. All the Romantics, as Fairchild sees them, declined into some form of spiritual despair. For they were worshipping not the super-natural God, supernaturally revealed, but the creations of their own minds. The Hope or Faith for which, briefly, they seemed to have found some basis in their own experience, is seen in the end to be a mere phantom, the creation only of desire. Fairchild's severity is exerted partly upon the individual poets themselves, but chiefly on Romantic philosophy. He deplores the proud Romantic rejection of the help which men customarily receive from parents and teachers, Church and tradition, the excessive insistence that each man is on his own. He deplores even more the Romantic rejection of the help which, he believes, men have received directly from God himself.

How, if at all, may a Christian disagree with Fairchild's judg-ment? Christian theologians have commonly acknowledged the exist-ence of something they term natural religion. Without any super-natural revelation men have at various times and places held beliefs resembling those of Christianity. But the natural revelation was weak and confused, and thus a supernatural revelation was vouchsafed. Thus far Christian theologians have agreed. But at this point they may diverge. Some have been unfriendly to natural religion because men may seek to make it suffice by itself. Others may be more kindly disposed; they will see a certain corroborative value in its affinities with Christianity.[9]

The Romantics may be termed apostles of this natural religion. Wordsworth, who in the days of his poetic prime was interested only in natural revelations, believed that many conditions of the age had starved men's natural religious instincts. He was right. Conditions which had weakened supernatural religion among certain classes of men and women had weakened natural religion also. Wordsworth believed these conditions had done so primarily because they had stunted the growth of men's imaginations; to restore natural re-ligion to its strength, imagination must be restored, and this was the task of the poet. In effect, all the poets studied in this volume, includ-ing those of the twentieth century, have been in agreement on this point, though the "natural religion" which Wallace Stevens culti-vated was rather more narrowly delimited than that cultivated by Wordsworth.

At any rate, this study is undertaken in a four-fold belief. First, the metaphysically-oriented imagination of the poets from Words-worth to the present is a major moment in man's spiritual history. Second, the full import of this movement of the poetic imagination should be apprehended in relation to what preceded it, surrounded it, and in some cases succeeded it—namely, the larger religious tradition. Third, certain physical and intellectual forces persisting to our own day still stunt the imagination and make us less than whole men. Fourth, the strengthening of the imagination and the making of men whole—merely as mortal men—is a noble task and one that need not militate against religion.

Background—Chiefly the Eighteenth Century

SINCE THE ROMANTIC MOVEMENT was both a development out of the eighteenth century and a reaction against it, a few comments on that age may help place the Romantic metaphysical imagination in clearer perspective. Out of proper deference to those eighteenth-century specialists who point to the richness and variety of their period, let it be conceded in advance that any generalization about an entire period cannot be wholly valid.[10]

The opening of the eighteenth century witnessed the high water mark of the deistical movement in Western Europe. So widespread was its influence upon educated minds that even Swift and Pope, outwardly the enemies of the deistical radicals, often seem scarcely distinguishable from them in their innermost assumptions. Among these educated minds many of the components of traditional religion which had appealed to feeling and imagination, the imagery of the New Testament story and the parables, began to be replaced by mental abstractions. A comparatively concrete and personal God became an abstract Universal Cause; the love of a Divine Father for his children became a principle of Universal Benevolence not always very different in character from the newly understood principle of gravity. The knowledge of the physical sciences was the ultimate model. The New Testament account of the life of a single man lost the concreteness of history and began to take on the partial abstractness of myth. The taste of the age was carried even into the realm of poetry: the abstract and the general came to be regarded not only as more dignified but even as more poetical.

Some such tendency is perhaps inevitable in any age of intellectual enlightenment, and no final assessment of the merits and defects of deism is here required. Suffice it to say that a reaction set in, a reaction in some ways sympathetic to older modes of religious consciousness which deism had lost. In England the Wesleyan movement was the extreme form of the renewal of a religion of emotion and imagination, of conversion as an experience of the whole man, not just a passive acquiescence in a set of intellectual principles.

Among the poets William Blake evidenced the most radical revulsion: in his marginalia to Sir Joshua Reynolds' *Discourses* he affirmed
"To Generalize is to be an Idiot. To Particularize is the Alone Distinction of Merit." At much the same time another poet, William
Wordsworth, was describing metaphysical insight as a concrete event
that suddenly happened; it occurred at a particular moment in particular context of circumstance which somehow seemed to authenti-
cate it. Wordsworth may be viewed as seeking to establish natural
religion more firmly than the deists, to keep its ideas from floating
away into the void by anchoring them to the vital actualities of his
own existence. In this respect the Romantic poets may be said to
recover some of the qualities of traditional Christianity, which in
origin had been less an intellectual system than a set of events: the
life and death of Christ, the sudden flash which struck the Apostle
Paul on the road to Damascus.[11]

Another aspect of the Romantic reaction might at first seem less
congenial to orthodoxy. Much of the revelation of Christianity had
become over the centuries very traditional, very collective and public,
publicly accepted and publicly transmitted like any other general
knowledge of the human race. Deism had at least retained this public
character; it was supposedly a set of ideas to which the common
sense of mankind had universally assented. The Romantics would
have claimed that their own revelations were universally valid, but
these were none the less privately received, freshly original, as one
would expect of an age that extolled "original genius." The critical
side of Wordsworth occasionally uses phrases which concede that
his own metaphysical ideas are part of a collective human inheritance,
but the imaginative effect of many of his most powerful passages of
poetry largely counteracts this concession. In re-creating his celebrated "spots of time," he writes not so much as though the specific
moment of experience had strengthened ideas already weakly planted
in his mind by tradition, but as though the idea itself were originat-
ing at that very moment. J. Middleton Murry has remarked upon
Wordsworth's extraordinary effort to create a religion *"de novo."* [12]
But even from the traditional point of view the intense inwardness
of the Romantics may be seen to supply a deficiency. Christianity at
its most vital had never been so detached as deism; it had been a
continuing interaction between public convention and private experience; organized religion had usually viewed the receivers of private
revelation with suspicion but it had sometimes ended by canonizing
them. (Intellectual history, often adept at discovering ironies, points
to John Locke as one of the progenitors of Romantic individualism.
Himself cool, collected, blandly generalizing, in harmony with the

rationalist temper of his age, he nevertheless focused attention upon the processes by which external circumstance generate ideas within the human mind; thus he appears one of the shapers of those private worlds in which the Romantic poets passionately contemplate their own inner responses—worlds whose whole tone is so different from Locke's own.[13])

Again, in their feeling for the supernatural or numinous, the Romantics appear to be recapturing something which deism had lost. In re-creating his visionary moments Wordsworth often suggests an intrusion from outside the material world, a grace given, a sudden flash from beyond. Subsequent nineteenth-century poets achieve this effect less often and less powerfully than Wordsworth, but achieve it they sometimes do, or appear at least to be reaching towards it. So Shelley, in his *Hymn to Intellectual Beauty*, writes of his own mind not as generating power but as receiving it: "Sudden, thy shadow fell on me."

External nature was the first great region in which deists and Romantics sought images to nourish religious instincts no longer sustained by the Biblical narrative and religious tradition. The contrast between the earlier, more deistical apprehension of nature and the later or Wordsworthian mode may be indicated by quoting Shaftesbury's well-known apostrophe to nature in *The Moralists*:

> Ye fields and woods, my refuge from the toilsome world of business, receive me in your quiet sanctuaries, and favour my retreat and thoughtful solitude! Ye verdant plains, how gladly I salute ye! Hail all ye blissful mansions! known seats! delightful prospects! Majestic beauties of this earth, and all ye rural powers and graces! Blessed be ye chaste abodes of happiest mortals, who here in peaceful innocence enjoy a life unenvied, though divine; whilst with its blessed tranquillity it affords a happy leisure and retreat for man, who, made for contemplation, and to search his own and other natures, may here best meditate the cause of things, and placed amidst various scenes of Nature, may nearer view her works.
>
> O glorious nature! supremely fair and sovereignly good! all lovely, all divine! whose looks are so becoming and of such infinite grace; whose every single work affords an ampler scene, and is a nobler spectacle than all which ever art presented! O mighty Nature! wise substitute of Providence! impowered creatress! Or thou impowering Deity, supreme creator! Thee I invoke and thee alone adore. To thee this solitude, this place, these rural meditations are sacred; whilst thus inspired with harmony

of thought, though unconfined by words, and in loose numbers, I sing of Nature's order in created beings, and celebrate the beauties which resolve in thee, the source and principle of all beauty and perfection.

This is an unusually emotional interlude in the calm pages of the noble earl; the power of Milton's verse rhythms is felt behind the structure of its prose—the same power which also made a contribution to the blank verse of Wordsworth. But concreteness and a radically fresh originality, two qualities most striking in many great Wordsworthian passages, are not sought for or achieved. Neither the moment nor the scene is specific, and when, in the middle of the second paragraph, Shaftesbury moves from praise of nature to praise of its creator, he is not praising a creative spirit whose very existence has at that moment been freshly revealed, but the creator of general human tradition.

In partial contrast to Shaftesbury's apostrophe, such topographical poems as Dyer's *Grongar Hill* celebrated a more specific moment and scene. But Dyer's scene offered no fresh metaphysical insight; it simply harmonized with the poet's already held ideals of innocence, peace, and virtue. A more richly concrete passage from the same general period is the ending of the Countess of Winchilsea's *A Nocturnal Reverie:*

> *When odors which declined repelling day*
> *Through temperate air uninterrupted stray;*
> *When darkened groves their softest shadows wear,*
> *And falling waters we distinctly hear;*
> *When through the gloom more venerable shows*
> *Some ancient fabric, awful in repose,*
> *While sunburnt hills their swarthy looks conceal,*
> *And swelling haycocks thicken in the vale;*
> *When the loosed horse now, as his pasture leads,*
> *Comes slowly grazing through the adjoining meads,*
> *Whose stealing pace and lengthened shade we fear,*
> *Till torn up forage in his teeth we hear;*
> *When nibbling sheep at large pursue their food,*
> *And unmolested kine rechew the cud;*
> *When curlews cry beneath the village walls,*
> *And to her straggling brood the partridge calls;*
> *Their short-lived jubilee the creatures keep,*
> *Which but endures whilst tyrant man does sleep;*
> *When a sedate content the spirit feels,*

And no fierce light disturbs, whilst it reveals,
But silent musings urge the mind to seek
Something too high for syllables to speak;
Till the free soul to a composedness charmed,
Finding the elements of rage disarmed,
O'er all below, a solemn quiet grown,
Joys in the inferior world and thinks it like her own.[14]
In such a night let me abroad remain,
Till morning breaks, and all's confused again;
Our cares, our toils, our clamours are renewed,
And pleasures, seldom reached, again pursued.

One can see why Wordsworth found the Countess such a refreshing exception in an age when observations of nature were usually so generalized and conventional. Her poetry, by harking back to an older, pre-Augustan tradition, manages at the same time to recapture a lost charm. Likewise her accurate observation of the external scene is accompanied by a precise notation of the inner response. In its own minor way this poem reminds one of the Tintern Abbey *Lines*, which tell how the poet, when his body is made quiet by "the power of harmony" becomes a "living soul." And it resembles Keats's nocturnal *Ode to a Nightingale* alike in its sensuous detail and in its half-visionary climax. The poem is a full record of a particular event. The great difference, of course, is in intensity. Lady Winchilsea treats her experience almost lightly, with no claim to portentous insight and no anguish at the moment's passing. As a Roman Catholic, living at the mere dawn of the Enlightenment, she knew no metaphysical crisis and the moment tells her only of a superior world of whose existence she was already informed. But the Romantics, for whom another century of critical thought and the French Revolution had shattered the traditional worlds of belief and imagination, felt compelled to a great effort to re-create new structures almost from the ground up. Hence the great burst of creative effort which the Romantic movement in poetry represented, and hence its extraordinary seriousness.

These introductory remarks have considered English literature first and foremost. But the subject under discussion was not a provincial one and should not be allowed to seem so. The metaphysical crisis affected the whole Western world. Suggestive parallels to the efforts of English Romantics to resolve this crisis are to be found in contemporary German speculations.

Immanuel Kant in his last great work, the *Critique of Judgment*, published in 1790, commented on the imaginative deficiencies of

deism. He had in mind a more purely rational deism than that expressed in Shaftesbury. Such a deism generally claimed to believe in
a Supreme Being, in Universal Benevolence, and in personal immortality. But it would sustain these beliefs without the imagery of
orthodoxy and with less reliance than Shaftesbury upon the beauty
of "all-lovely" nature. Deism, Kant said, insofar as it precludes the
imaginative presentation of its own concepts, "furnishes no knowledge whatever." He felt that contemporary philosophy, more especially his own work prior to his last *Critique*, had arrived at what is
technically known as solipsism, a position in which the mind appears
unable to get in touch with any reality other than itself. The mind
knew directly its own inner aspirations towards a perfect good,
towards a full obedience to the moral law and towards God and
immortality. But what warrant had it that these aspirations were anything more than desires reaching out into a void? (A student of the
Romantics may here recall Shelley's intense aspiration and his anguished concern for the reality of the ideal towards which he
yearned.) The faculty of the mind which Kant called the understanding could not sense the reality behind the outer world of physical appearances; it perceived these appearances as constituting only
a mechanism which in no way corresponded to the soul's higher impulses. But Kant had not yet treated fully an area of knowledge
which was being discussed by many of his German contemporaries,
the realm of the imagination and of the beautiful. Here in this area,
he proclaimed, was to be found the escape from solipsism. The beautiful was somehow the "symbol" of the good; it supplied an intimation that behind the material world was some "supersensible substrate" [God], the nature of which in some mysterious way harmonized with the mind's reaching towards an ultimate good. The moral
sense, so important to Kant as the organ of metaphysical aspiration,
needed to be supplemented by the aesthetic sense; this aesthetic sense
was somehow an organ of metaphysical knowledge—even as David
Hartley in his somewhat earlier speculations upon the imagination
had decided that this faculty in one of its highest forms constituted
the "theopathic power." All these Kantian theories, stemming in part
from Shaftesbury and Leibniz and ultimately from Plato, were the
foundation for much of the German idealistic philosophy that followed and for its nineteenth-century derivatives in Britain and
America. They have also influenced much subsequent theological
thought.[15]

A second area in which the imagination sought intimations was in
the beauty of human art. Art and nature are not wholly separable,
and Kant had considered the beauty of both. In the late eighteenth

century the apotheosis of art was more fully developed in Germany than in England, and many of Kant's successors emphasized almost exclusively the beauty of human creation. The difference between Kant and his German successors is somewhat like that between the Tintern Abbey *Lines* and the *Ode on a Grecian Urn:* though itself a work of art, Wordsworth's poem dwelt upon a beauty not wholly the product of the human mind, a beauty which Wordsworth regarded as half created by man and half perceived by him; Keats's poem, on the other hand, exhibits human art extolling human art. The difference is not without some religious bearing. The artist celebrating art is more immediately open to the attacks of such critics as H. N. Fairchild, who believe that the Romantic poet is not in fact worshipping any power greater than himself but only the power of the human imagination itself.[16]

A third area most suitable for the metaphysical probings was that of human love. Wordsworth extolled the domestic and social affections as supplying a necessary power not found in a life of abstract thought, but in celebrating these affections his poetry was not touched with the mystical exaltation inspired by nature. The supreme imaginative effort of nineteenth-century poetry to find a transcendental significance in human love really starts, somewhat abstractly, with Shelley, and it culminates with Tennyson and Browning. Here again the poets place themselves in the tradition of Plato's *Phaedrus* and *Symposium.* But they are even closer to Christianity: if God's love is considered his chief attribute, if Universal Benevolence is what one most wishes to find exhibited in concrete form, there is perhaps no area which the imagination may more fruitfully explore than that of the love of human beings for each other.

The Scope of the Present Study

As FIRST ENVISIONED, the present study was to have made use of a more secular idiom than it has adhered to. Without frequent reference to the categories of religion, it was to examine in themselves, as it were, those moments and images in which the contradictions and evils of human life are transcended or reconciled. Perhaps some such study should still be made.[17] But even as Wordsworth's and Coleridge's and Browning's secular explorations of imagination became ever more closely involved with traditional religious ideas, so this work has taken a similar course.

Yet something of this original purpose remains. It should give the following chapters a special focus and define their usual limits. Here it may be helpful to describe in advance what matters will *not* be fully canvassed. Religion is a broad subject. After the moment of revelation, says T. S. Eliot in *The Dry Salvages*, "Is prayer, observance, discipline, thought and action." There is no plan to consider at length how the various poets may have felt about all these components of a religious life. Nor how they felt upon the question of sin. Upon this last matter conservatives may deem the Romantics unsound. At times, among the defects from which their imaginations momentarily redeem the world, they are conscious of the moral weaknesses displayed by the generality of mankind more than of those most properly their own. (Here perhaps Coleridge had a spiritual advantage over his fellows since his own special frailties were ones of which a man must always be aware.) However, it is permissible to feel that a writer like Professor Fairchild, in his zeal to discredit Romantic philosophy, exaggerates the personal defects of some of his subjects, particularly Wordsworth and Shelley, and that he pays too little respect to their virtues.

Again, this study will not undertake to determine in each separate case how far the poet's individualism and his discontent with the beliefs of his period and with its social and ecclesiastical structures can be ascribed to personal pride. A man who thinks and feels for himself is bound to be accused of this fault. He should certainly be on his guard against it, but at the same time he cannot allow himself to be paralyzed by this wariness. The question is a delicate one. Even D. G. James, whose discussion of the Romantics as seen from a Christian point of view is far more sympathetic than that of Fairchild, on occasion oversimplifies the issue. He calls the simple acceptance of Blake's *Songs of Innocence* Christian and the critical discontent of the *Songs of Experience* anti-Christian.[18] He also designates the first mood as essentially religious and the second as moral. These second terms are more satisfactory than the first, but they are still not so good as Blake's own terms. Religion and moral criticism cannot be sharply distinguished either in the Old Testament or the New. Again, it is sometimes said that religion stresses only individual morality. But the Gospels with their reiterated criticism of the privileged classes who devoured the substance of widows and orphans certainly by implication criticize the structure of the Jewish church state. By the end of the eighteenth century history had forcefully raised the question of whether the whole social fabric did not require considerable modification, whether it was any longer sufficient simply to preach charity to the rich and patience, frugality, and industry to the poor. Furthermore, in the England of the time, the richest country in the world, in which an immense accumulation of wealth was seen side by side with an ever greater mass of poverty, in which the Church itself seemed part of the privileged Establishment and in which the comfortably beneficed Bishop of Llandaff could counter the new ideas by writing a book on the wisdom of Divine Providence in making men both rich and poor—under such circumstances it was inevitable that revolutionary political ideas should develop, whether logically or illogically, certain religious corollaries.[19] (In the case of one of the poets, an exception will be made to this deliberate limitation of the discussion: Browning himself has much to say upon the question of individual vision and pride in *Pauline, Paracelsus,* and *Christmas-Eve and Easter Day,* and what he says will be noted.)

Where then will the attention of the following chapters be focused? As has already been suggested, they will examine chiefly those images by which the "burden of the mystery" is lifted, those moments of imaginative revelation which, as Eliot says, must precede the observance and discipline and action. Here it may be remarked at once that the poetic imagination of the Romantics often lifted the burden simply by enjoying its own freedom. This freedom does not always suggest any transcendental realm in the usual Platonic or Christian senses. The imagination merely expatiates in its own rich domain, liberated for the time being from all that it finds meager or painful in everyday life. But at other times, on occasions characterized more by intensity and concentration than by relaxed expatiation, the imagination seemed to touch some eternal reality by which the inadequacies of time are redeemed—some God, some immortality. "Vacational" fancies, common enough in most lives, were common in the lives of the Romantic poets, common in the poetry of Keats, and certainly too common in the poetry of Shelley. In *The Fall of Hyperion,* in an agony of self-reproach, Keats has Moneta rebuke him for a mere dreamer and assert that the dreamer and the true poet are distinct. But Keats is himself perplexed upon the occasion. The truth is that the movement of concentration and intensity often seems to rise out of the heart of a movement of relaxation, as in the *Ode to a Nightingale* and in Wordsworth's Tintern Abbey *Lines.* In a somewhat similar way traditional religious consciousness has found itself both soothed and summoned by its mysteries, sometimes chiefly the one and sometimes chiefly the other, and on occasions both almost equally. Without doing literary violence to the complexity of the passages under consideration, a critic of the Romantic poets often cannot discriminate too sharply between times when the poet is simply vacationing from everyday reality and when he feels himself truly beckoned to some reality beyond.

Another way of viewing the complexity of the Romantic moment of imaginative intuition is to cite S. F. Gingerich's brief but
excellent presentation of Romantic philosophy in the introduction to
his *Essays in the Romantic Poets.* This philosophy is seen as a composite of two closely allied beliefs: belief in freedom, including freedom of the will, and belief in what Gingerich terms the "transcendental" principle. This last belief is the conviction that the process
of knowing the human mind is an independent force, not just the
passive product of impressions. (Obviously both these beliefs are
likely to be intimately involved in the poet's awareness of the freedom of his own imagination, even when this freedom finds expression in humble form in relaxed reverie.) Gingerich then adds that
this inner mental or spiritual force, transcending the world of matter, may in turn appear as an "abiding and therefore immortal energy
of soul" and as "an intuition implanted in man by which he perceives
Deity." Such, theoretically, is the full Romantic complex of belief.
It need scarcely be added that upon any single occasion it is possible
that only one constituent element of this complex will make its presence distinctly felt. But one or more of the other elements will very
likely be close at hand in some obscure guise. Gingerich's discussion,
touching as it does upon freedom of the will, immortality of the
soul, and the existence in some form of a Deity, naturally invites a
comparison between Romantic philosophy and traditional religion.

A few further observations will be made in the final chapter upon
the relation between Romantic poetic faith and orthodoxy. For the
time being it need only be said that the present study will usually
be a sympathetic one: it will not stress the divergence between poetic
faith and religion to the disparagement of the former. Since Wordsworth and Coleridge, Browning and T. S. Eliot, men who outlived
their youth, all lived to concede the inadequacy of a merely individual imaginative response to life, there is no need to quarrel with
such a writer as Fairchild when he insists upon this inadequacy with
such eloquence. But a defender of orthodoxy need not go further
and see the whole Romantic movement as a deliberate perversion.
The great intellectual developments of the seventeenth and eighteenth centuries could hardly have been withstood even if one would.
Among minds that felt them most strongly these developments
"called all in doubt," created fissures in mental lives which might
otherwise have seemed whole. Painful readjustments, fundamental
reassessments, fresh syntheses were demanded of those who led any
intellectual life at all. Whether a new faith was to be established or
the old re-established, imaginative power had to be revitalized if
wholeness was once again to be achieved.

Under the circumstances, strengthening men's imaginations, as the poets wished to do, seeking to make them again whole men by whatever means seemed available, was a noble and necessary task. It could not be known in advance whether revitalized men would be better secularists or better Christians; but insofar as the poetic imagination frequently pressed towards some metaphysical solution, it might be regarded as friendly to Christianity, preparatory to it. In this way Wordsworth and Coleridge were inclined to regard it. Here again there need be no quarrel with Professor Fairchild for asserting that Wordsworth was inclined to overvalue the power and certainty of natural revelation, that he overprized the ecstasy with which this revelation had been accompanied in his own case, that as his early feelings fade and he comes to the verge of traditional religion, he does so only as to a last resort, as to something second best, with a continual looking back to something better.[20] Any critic might make much these same observations of the poet's middle and later years. But again one need not go further. Professor Fairchild never actually says that the Romantics could have avoided their anguish and melancholy simply by consulting the nearest clergyman, that the Church had the answer which would have given them assurance. But some such judgment seems to be implied. If so, it is questionable. The poets under consideration did not wilfully involve themselves in uncertainty. Their adult intellectual lives may be said to have started in division and uncertainty. They could not simply accept the clergyman's answer, because the validity of this answer was one of the great points at issue.

Professor Fairchild may feel that he is more anxious to insist upon the wilfullness of the Romantic Movement as a whole than upon the wilfullness of individuals. Some such distinction of thought may be partially valid. Intellectual historians almost inevitably apply such phrases as "wilfulness" to periods and to philosophies. But there is always some risk in so personifying whole movements by employing terms which, in such a context, fall so clearly within the category which semanticists would designate as "fictions."

In examining the intimations and images of eternity as these occur in several poets, one might proceed in two different ways. He could take a single imaginistic pattern or mode and in a single chapter trace it through all the poets, and in another chapter he could trace another pattern. A certain intellectual clarity might be gained, but the results would have some of the inhuman abstraction of Maud Bodkin's *Archetypal Patterns in Poetry*.[21] One of the special merits of literature is its full humanity and concreteness. To retain some of this humanity it has seemed best to follow for the most part a second method: to consider one poet at a time in his individual development and variety. Continuing patterns can be pointed out along the way; they will in any case be apparent to the reader himself.

Again, it might be possible to discuss the different poets primarily in order to note each one's theological position. It might be asked just how far a poet is a pantheist, or how far he is an atheist, or how far his habitual imaginative patterns constitute a religious belief and how far they merely reflect a poetic mode. In relation to men like Wordsworth and Shelley and Keats and the others, such questions have an obvious relevance. In the following chapters they will not be altogether avoided; they may at times even be canvassed more fully than a purely literary taste might wish. However, the aim in each case is not to haggle over the precise terms of a final judgment. First of all, the poets' intense imaginative and intuitive experiences are in the final sense unanalyzable, independent of the schemes of rational thought. When a poet momentarily senses the immediate presence of some transcendent being, is he aware only of a transcendent essence within his own inner nature, his own spark of divinity? Or is he aware of some cosmic Being? If the second is the case, does this great Being transcend only the physical universe, or also the spark of spirit within the poet himself? To such questions the single, unschematic moment of intuition does not give theologically distinct answers. Again, literature itself is more a living presentation than an analysis. This study therefore is intended chiefly as a living presentation; it will attempt to exhibit, in the instance of several poets of the past century and a half, the rise, the development, and in some cases the subsidence of certain imaginative impulses.

But insofar as the discussion of images and of the imaginative contexts of intuition is accompanied by some commentary on a poet's thought, no apology need be offered. In the study of a poet, the development of imagination and the development of thought must, so far as possible, be considered simultaneously.

A Note on Blake and Coleridge

THE ORIGINAL PURPOSE and limits of this study may also explain why there will be no separate chapters upon two great Romantics, Blake and Coleridge. In *Auguries of Innocence*, Blake with beautiful simplicity describes what might appear to be the object of Romantic endeavor:

> *To see the World in a Grain of Sand*
> *And a Heaven in a Wild Flower,*

Hold Infinity in the palm of your hand
And Eternity in an hour.

But such innocence is quite lost during most of his poetic career; also, the unity expressed in the *Songs of Innocence* is not a unity triumphing over discord and division, as will usually be the case in the poems to be studied, but the unity of an undifferentiated consciousness which has not yet experienced discord.

Again, despite Blake's denunciation of rational thought and abstract generalization, and despite his exaltation of the imagination, Arthur Symons was right when he noted years ago that Blake's poetry is "concrete" only in its "form," that is "a poetry of the mind, abstract in substance," that "its emotion is the emotion of thought, its beauty the beauty of idea." [22] Rational thought, Coleridge would say, deals with things as "separates," and with marvellously expressive concreteness of form Blake can present his two separates, the view of innocence and the view of experience. But though Blake felt that these opposites must somehow be united, reconciled, or transcended, his imagination does not effect any such process. His poetry presents no actual moments, substantial in detail and circumstance, autobiographical or semi-autobiographical, like those moments in the Tintern Abbey *Lines*, or the *Ode to a Nightingale*, or *In Memoriam* in which the perplexities are resolved. Neither do his attempts at myth achieve even that modicum of imaginative substantiality and artistic success which characterizes *Endymion*. The Prophetic Books are not myth at all, but only allegory, and unsatisfactory allegory at that. Such concreteness of form as they possess is but an ungainly garb of the thought. This thought is the original, the essential element, for Blake is not solving his dilemmas by imagination but by speculations as abstract as those of his contemporary, the German philosopher Schelling—a man who agreed with him in seeing the universe as an evolution of opposites which it was the function of his system to reconcile. (Here both men, and Coleridge also, owed something to Boehme.)

Another way of observing almost the same fact about Blake is to note his "atheism"; he often appears to envision no God as an independent Being from whom man receives grace; divinity then appears to be no more than that perfection which mankind will achieve by the full exercise of creative imagination. At such times the Romantic exaltation of human creativity attains its most extreme form, when man creates everything and receives nothing. Wordsworth believed that his particular form of imaginative faith required that a certain balance be maintained between receptivity and creativity.

If the supreme task of the imagination is to reconcile opposites rather than merely to express them separately, it might be said that Blake's imagination received virtually nothing from the world around him to help it do its work. If this work is, as most of the Romantics believed, to reconcile the real and the ideal, the imagination could scarcely perform this function for Blake in this receptive fashion since, as he himself says, for him natural objects always obliterated imagination. (Both Wordsworth and Keats record that objects of sense could upon occasion have similar inhibiting effects upon their creative powers, yet both gratefully acknowledge how much these powers owed to the senses in the first instance.) Later in life Blake sometimes seems partially to forsake his advanced and precarious philosophic position and returns to something of his earlier simplicity. But to do this is not to resolve his problems but to relapse to his condition before these problems had sharply presented themselves.[23]

Of Coleridge something more need be said. The poet who felt that his friend Wordsworth was virtually a Spinozist or atheist, and who was a little shocked to note how far the North German clergy were gone in deism, preserved much of his original Christian sensibility all through his philosophic speculations. Coleridge in his Conversation Poems is closer to the pre-Romantics than to Wordsworth, Shelley, or Keats: the beauty of nature may push back the clouds, but only to reveal a heaven which he knew was there all the while. Of course, this pushing back the clouds is in itself of great importance to Coleridge. The beauty of the watersnakes re-establishes communication between the Ancient Mariner and his "kind saint," it reaffirms an essential goodness at the heart of the universe, and thus turns sterile remorse into true repentance for an act which had violated this goodness. Coleridge believed in his heart that a supernatural grace penetrates the world to save the sinner and guard the innocent, and he told his frankly miraculous tales of *The Ancient Mariner* and *Christabel* to "realize" this penetration in poetic terms. For the precise terms themselves he demanded no more than that "suspension of disbelief for the moment" which constitutes a poetic faith. But even by such merely temporary suspension, the imagination would be exercised in that proper sense of the miraculous which the Enlightenment had so diminished; the reader would unconsciously be made aware that there are more things in heaven and earth than were dreamt of in the materialist's philosophy. Such was Coleridge's essentially Christian romanticism.

Less specifically Christian is *Kubla Khan*. In recent decades critics have become increasingly aware of the central position of the imagination in all Romantic thought. Robert Penn Warren has read

The Ancient Mariner as a parable on the imagination and *Kubla Khan* may, even more easily, be read in the same way. The following interpretation is similar to that of G. Wilson Knight in *The Starlit Dome* and, to lesser extent, to that of Maud Bodkin in her *Archetypal Patterns in Poetry*, but without the modish post-Freudian complications favored by both these writers.[24]

Coleridge's sacred river, erupting mysteriously from no one knows where, flowing briefly in the open, and then sinking to the caverns measureless to man, readily suggests the stream of human consciousness. Above this lower realm of time, where life appears to rush toward oblivion, is the realm of eternity. Here the great king, Kubla Khan, has created a radiant palace and garden, a City of God or New Jerusalem, a Platonic realm of the ideal. In this "miracle of rare device," this "sunny pleasure-dome" with its "caves of ice," the opposites of the world of time, light and shade, heat and cold, are reconciled. (The reconciliation of opposites by the imagination was, first and last, a basic principle of all Coleridge's thought.) [25] Below, on the stream of human consciousness, the eternal beauty and unity of the dome was shadowed or reflected in time as it should be according to the Platonic scheme of thought:

> *The shadow of the dome of pleasure*
> *Floated midway on the waves;*
> *Where was heard the mingled measure*
> *From the fountain and the caves.*

But, presumably because this shadow is so unsubstantial and uncertain, the artist is needed; as Shelley says in his *Defence*, "Poetry redeems from decay the visitations of the divinity in man." If Coleridge could once more be filled with joy by earthly beauty (the Abyssinian maid and her song), he would then be able to re-create in his poetry the heavenly beauty of the dome and its wondrous uniting of conflicting principles, so that all men would be filled with awe:

> *Could I revive within me*
> *Her symphony and song,*
> *To such a deep delight 'twould win me,*
> *That with music loud and long,*
> *I would build that dome in air,*
> *That sunny dome! those caves of ice!*
> *And all who heard should see them there,*
> *And all should cry, Beware! Beware!*
> *His flashing eyes, his floating hair!*

Weave a circle round him thrice,
And close hour eyes in holy dread,
For he on honey-dew hath fed,
And drunk the milk of Paradise.

This parallel between *Kubla Khan* and the Romantic theory of the poet as the utterer of heavenly truths obviously does not exhaust the poem's implications. The "voices prophesying war" presumably symbolize some evil which threatens the harmony of Kubla's reign. If the poem is not essentially complete as it stands (as some have maintained); if it had already developed at much greater length in Coleridge's mind, as he thought it had, before he was interrupted by the visitor from Porlock, what the further developments were, whether the war occurred and how it turned out, we shall unfortunately never know.

Elisabeth Schneider, in her book *Coleridge, Opium, and 'Kubla Khan,'* objects to discovering symbolic meanings in a poem when these meanings do not press up from underneath and show themselves on the surface. In this instance, one might say that the submerged meaning presses up so far that in the final lines the hidden and the surface meanings have become identical: both tell of a poet who has had a vision of Paradise. Miss Schneider makes the further point that Coleridge in his own taste definitely favored explicitness and translucence. If upon this occasion, in the first two thirds of the poem, this taste is not in evidence, the reason may well be that the symbolic meaning was partly unconscious—as Coleridge's own account of the genesis of the poem would suggest. Coleridge had been thinking long and deeply about cosmic truths and the function of the poetic imagination; it is only natural that images stored in his mind should combine in such a way as to express his notions about the relation between theology and art. Insofar as the poem may have been in large part the product of unconscious forces coming to fruition in a half-trance, one cannot expect it to be explicit. But it need not therefore be regarded as of any less portent. In fact, Coleridge himself might on this very account have viewed it with unusual interest. He has expressed his respect for the unconscious and for dreams by saying that "the reproductive imagination, unsophisticated by the will, and undirected by intrusions from the sense" may be especially significant in its imaginings precisely because of the freedom which it then enjoys.[26] There was of course an instinct in Coleridge's conscious mind to curb as too audacious, if not downright blasphemous, such unabashed exaltations of the human artist as he was to become familiar with in post-Kantian German thought very soon after he had written *Kubla Khan;* hence perhaps the up-welling in this poem of half-suppressed ideas.

If this book were primarily a study of the Romantic theory of poetry rather than of poetry itself, then Coleridge would certainly be presented as a figure of primary importance. *Kubla Khan,* perhaps a parable of Coleridge's theory, with its expressed wish that his poetic imagination *could* embody its intimation of some ultimate realm of splendor in which the conflicting experiences of mortal life are reconciled and united, might be the more fully examined. For Coleridge not only believed, as he insisted in the *Biographia Literaria* and elsewhere, that the imagination is the "co-adunating" faculty, but he also inclined toward the idea that its co-adunated presentations were of some theological significance. Hence in part the continuous appeal to him of certain aspects of the Platonic tradition. Hence the overwhelming impression made upon him by Schelling's Transcendental Idealism, until a number of years later he decided that its grandiose speculations were in important ways misleading and inadequate.[27] Yet for Coleridge the acceptance of Christianity did not constitute the complete repudiation of the efforts of imagination to take the heavens by storm; his view was rather—as D. G. James presents it in *The Romantic Comedy*—that in the central doctrine of the Incarnation, myth and fact become one. Or, as Browning suggests in *La Saisiaz,* God has responded to man's "best question."

Coleridge's poetic theory, with its emphasis upon the mystical unity of the poem itself, is at times a forerunner of more recent Symbolist theory, a fact pointed out by Frank Kermode in his book *Romantic Image.* Professor Kermode admits that the influence of I. A. Richards, blending with other strains of modern criticism, tends at the present time to deprive Symbolist theory of its older "super-naturalism." He then goes on, without any suggestion of irony, to observe the fact that these same deflators, by studying "the secret lives of words as if they were dreams," succeed in restoring to communication some of the "essential Romantic magic." [28] (An ironical conservative might be reminded of people too enlightened for the old superstitions of religion who take up table-tipping instead.) Like most critics Kermode views Symbolist theory in its relation to the modern preoccupation with the isolation of the artist; hence all that he has to say is relevant to the Romantic isolation already referred to here, and to the pressure upon the individual Romantic poet to half-perceive and half-create a revelation of his own. There will be no extensive attempt in the present study, however, to look closely into Symbolist and neo-Symbolist theory and their connections with the poetic matters which are the immediate object of investigation.

For anyone wishing to examine these connections Professor Kermode's book would be an excellent point of departure. Also of interest is Ernest Lee Tuveson's *The Imagination as a Means of Grace;* this study, a suggestive survey of eighteenth-century English aesthetic theory, pays particular attention to the ways in which this theory towards the end of the period anticipates what might be called Symbolism's half-objective, half-subjective "theology." A still more recent book, Richard Foster's *The New Romantics: A Reappraisal of the New Criticism,* undertakes to point out the Romantic ancestry of the theologically-tinted poetic theory of some of this century's best known anti-Romantics.[29]

ii

WORDSWORTH

W ORDSWORTH'S IMAGINATIVE PERCEPTIONS of a realm of the spirit are so varied and complex that to discuss them intelligibly one must resort to a scheme. Any such scheme is suggestive only, not comprehensive or final. With this caution I should like to present his perceptions as constituting a continuous development through three phases: perception of the vital, perception of the beautiful, and perception of the sublime.[1] As a matter of biographical fact these were not entirely distinct from each other chronologically or qualitatively. Taken together they manifest the poet's evolving awareness of the nature of reality.

According to the announced principle that the development of thought and of imagination should be considered together, the discussion of images and of imaginative awareness will be related to observations upon the evolution of Wordsworth's philosophy and religion.

Vitality and Freedom

WORDSWORTH'S FRIEND Coleridge was fond of denouncing what he termed a "mechanical" view of the universe. The net result of the thought of Bacon, Descartes, Hobbes, Locke, and their successors was, he believed, to present such entities as atoms and planets and even trees and human beings, not as creative forces but as the passive recipients of external influences, influences to which they responded with further reactions strictly determined by scientific laws. This view of the world, what Kant called the World of Necessity, was that afforded by the "understanding" or the mere "reflective faculty." This faculty, according to the *Biographia Literaria*, partakes of "Death." The issue at stake in this philosophical crisis was, Coleridge thought, the very existence of Kant's other world, the World of Freedom—the existence of a vital soul and free will. Coleridge's dilemma was produced in large part by the reading of books and by the reading of other books he sought to resolve it. He drew upon the whole tradition of idealistic philosophy to establish an opposite view: mind and spirit are not a mere appearance produced by certain concatenations of material forces interacting according to scientific law; on the contrary, the material world everywhere operates according to law because it is everywhere the product of creative, organizing spirit. Like Leibniz, Coleridge believed that even the material world below the level of the animal and vegetable was essentially vital in its obscure way. This is the view of the universe presented by the imagination, and in this view Coleridge presumably found "Life."

Both Coleridge and his German contemporary A. W. Schlegel praise Shakespeare for the vital freedom exhibited by his characters. The actions of these characters do not appear to be entirely determined by circumstances operating according to regular psychological laws, but to originate in the characters themselves. "Even as a science," Schlegel said apropos of Shakespeare's living creations, "psychology is not worth much, and in poetry it is death itself, a foul corruption that enters in when the living organism has been destroyed." [2] Recently Leone Vivante has praised Shakespeare's characters for this same reason, and he believes that Shakespeare's works are a bulwark to protect the English-speaking peoples from the soul-destroying effects of deterministic psychology.[3]

When Wordsworth settled with Dorothy at Racedown in 1795 he had himself reached something of an intellectual crisis by the use of the "reflective faculty." After his disillusionment in the French Revolution he had sought to evolve a system of moral and social theory based on what he termed "naked" reason. Insofar as the system was Godwinian, it must to some extent have been deterministic, incorporating Godwin's principle of Necessity. In his later criticism of the system he then embraced, however, Wordsworth points not to the presence of determinism but to the absence of the life-giving qualities of natural piety, love, and imagination. Dissatisfied with his system he abandoned rationalist speculations and temporarily "Yielded up moral questions in despair." [4]

It would be misleading to suggest that Wordsworth's crisis in 1795 was purely an intellectual one. As he was less bookish than Coleridge, so materialistic philosophers were less responsible for his problems and idealist philosophers—except Coleridge, with whom his relations were more than just intellectual—contributed less to their solutions. He was in revulsion against all that London represented to him: the insistent presence of getting and spending, the "socialized" intellectual life with its ephemeral fashions, the fevered concern for the passing political situation, the absence of the calm joy and permanent life of nature in the presence of which his own individualistic spirit could flourish. In the city his spirit's freedom was encroached on less by a necessitarian logic than by the compelling social pressures of a whole way of living. Until his fortunate receipt of Calvert's legacy his life had reached an even blanker impasse than his thinking: he was confronted with the likelihood that he might have to earn a living in the city on the city's terms. In other words, the poet's difficulties could not be solved just by a new system of thought. As R. D. Havens has truly said, Wordsworth's ultimate problems were "not so much thought out as lived out." [5] Thus the opening lines of *The Prelude* celebrate a whole new life, a

> *coming from a house*
> *Of bondage, from yon City's walls set free.*
> (I, 6-7.)

Wordsworth envisages a new, liberated mode of existence, more virtuous, more joyous, more fully devoted to the task of writing poetry.

In *The Prelude* Wordsworth ascribes his recovery from despondency partly to close, affectionate intercourse with two living human beings, Dorothy and Coleridge, but his main emphasis of course is upon the renewed intercourse with nature. In the opening lines of the poem the life of nature seems to be the very symbol or complement of his own inner life, and communion with the outer vitality reinforces the inner. This well-known passage does not present any landscape in the full sense of the word. There is no consciousness of permanent forms of hill and valley underlying the changing face of nature. We read only of living or moving things: groves, streams, a river. And the lines themselves are addressed to that age-old symbol

of life-giving spirit, the breeze. All this animation arouses a sense
of joy:

> Oh there is blessing in this gentle breeze
> That blows from the green fields and the clouds
> And from the sky: it beats against my cheek,
> And seems half conscious of the joy it gives.
>
> (I, 1–4.)

This same breeze is then imagined as arousing by sympathy the
creative force in Wordsworth which produces poetry; this renewal
of creative life, though the season is not spring, suggests the life-
giving power of spring:

> For I, methought, while the sweet breath of Heaven
> Was blowing on my body, felt within
> A corresponding, mild, creative breeze,
> A vital breeze which travell'd gently on
> O'er things which it had made, and is become
> A tempest, a redundant energy
> Vexing its own creation. 'Tis a power
> That does not come unrecogniz'd, a storm,
> Which, breaking up a long-continued frost
> Brings with it vernal promises, and hope
> Of active days, of dignity and thought,
> Of prowess in an honorable field,
> Pure passions, virtue, knowledge, and delight,
> The holy life of music and of verse.
>
> (I, 41–54; I, 33–45.) [6]

It is such imaginative responses to nature as these which help Wordsworth to affirm as he does, a hundred lines or so farther on, that he
has one prerequisite of a poet, the "vital soul." [7]

In the years that followed the move to Racedown Wordsworth
experienced often this sudden sense of nature's life and activity. And
in response he continued to feel, if only momentarily, a renewal
within himself. This inner renewal might be induced by a sudden
patter of hailstones:

> A whirl-blast from behind the hill
> Rushed o'er the wood with startling sound;
> Then—all at once the air was still,
> And showers of hailstones pattered round.
> Where leafless oaks towered high above,
> I sat within an undergrove

Of tallest hollies, tall and green;
A fairer bower was never seen.
From year to year the spacious floor
With withered leaves is covered o'er,
And all the year the bower is green.

But see! where'er the hailstones drop
The withered leaves all skip and hop;
There's not a breeze—no breath of air—
Yet here, and there, and every where
Along the floor, beneath the shade
By those embowering hollies made,
The leaves in myriads jump and spring,
As if with pipes and music rare
Some Robin Good-fellow were there,
And all those leaves, in festive glee,
Were dancing to the ministrelsy.

("A whirl-blast from behind the hill.")

Or it could be induced by a bright morning after rain:

There was a roaring in the wind all night;
The rain came heavily and fell in floods;
But now the sun is rising calm and bright;
The birds are singing in the distant woods;
Over his own sweet voice the Stock-dove broods;
The Jay makes answer as the Magpie chatters;
And all the air is filled with pleasant noise of waters.

All things that love the sun are out of doors;
The sky rejoices in the morning's birth;
The grass is bright with rain-drops;—on the moors
The hare is running races in her mirth;
And with her feet she from the plashy earth
Raises a mist, that, glittering in the sun,
Runs with her all the way, wherever she doth run.

(Resolution and Independence.)

Or the dancing daffodils could stir his spirit to keep them company; or the sights and sounds of the May morning could briefly do the same when his heart, not without some melancholy doubts, is at the "festival" of the shouting shepherd-boy, the bounding lambs, the leaping babe, the flower-gathering children, the whole land and sea that "Give themselves up to jollity." Though these sudden ecstasies

grew less frequent with the passage of time, there is a clear record
of one such moment in the opening lines of the sonnet written in
1812, in recollection of the death of his daughter Catherine:

> *Surprised by joy—impatient as the Wind*
> *I turned to share the transport—Oh! with whom*
> *But Thee, deep-buried in the silent tomb . . .*
>   ("Surprized by joy.")

Thirty years later as an old man Wordsworth mentions no transport, but as he scorns the poet tightly bound by the rules he makes
vigorous use of images of organic nature to reassert his old faith in
free creative spirit:

> *How does the Meadow-flower its bloom unfold?*
> *Because the lovely little flower is free*
> *Down to its root, and, in that freedom bold;*
> *And so the grandeur of the Forest-tree*
> *Comes not from casting in a formal mould,*
> *But from its* own *divine vitality.*
>   ("A Poet!—He hath put his heart to school.")

Here as in the opening of *The Prelude* the sense of life is again a
sense of freedom—a release from the World of Necessity.

It should be noted that just as Coleridge's vitalistic philosophy
pervades more than the growing parts of nature, so Wordsworth's
imagination sees life in more than the obviously moving or growing
parts of landscape. The "Presences of Nature," the "Beings of the
hills," the "Souls of lonely places," and the "quiet Powers," discussed by R. D. Havens in his chapter on Wordsworth's "Animism,"
dwell one supposes among rocks as well as among trees—though
what with the lichens, mosses, and grasses everywhere encouraged
by the damp climate, the rocks of the Lake District do not present
that aspect of total nakedness and deadness found in more arid regions. Havens rightly sees the animistic phrases so frequent in *The
Prelude* as much more than a stylistic device: they betoken a deep-
seated mode of feeling.[8]

Wordsworth's perceptions of the vital in nature may be discussed
more briefly than his perceptions of the beautiful, but they are not
to be regarded as less important. They were perhaps the basic perceptions upon which all else depended. Though they do not seem
fully transcendental in the usual religious sense, one must note that
they make possible a liberation of the spirit, a transcending of the
bonds of a materialist determinism, a sense of freedom of the will.

Beauty, Justice, and God

THE SECOND PHASE of Wordsworth's imaginative awareness may be somewhat arbitrarily designated as his awareness of the beautiful. To some extent beauty had doubtless been present in the vitality already discussed. To Wordsworth this beauty was an intimation of cosmic justice.[9]

Joseph Wood Krutch once commented on the "justificatory" function not of nature but of art:

Milton [he said] . . . set out to justify the ways of God to man, and his phrase, if interpreted broadly enough, may be taken as describing all art, which must, in some way or other, make the life which it seems to represent satisfactory . . . by satisfying the universally human desire to find in the world some justice, some meaning, or, at the very least, some recognizable order.[10]

Krutch here describes one of the great underlying purposes of Wordsworth the poet.[11] In part the "recognizable order" of Wordsworth's own verse served this justificatory purpose; in his "Preface" to the *Lyrical Ballads* Wordsworth himself notes how the regular patterns of meter somehow help the reader to transcend the evil or pain in events which a poem may relate. But it was characteristic of Wordsworth that his imagination seeks the aid of nature as well as of human art. And for justifying the world the poet's sudden awarenesses of nature's vitality are inadequate in important ways. They are too narrow. They are too brief. They are fragmentary manifestations of some goodness and joy, but a goodness and joy perhaps separate from evil rather than encompassing it, comprehending it and triumphing over it. The inadequacy of these fragmentary insights is often noted in the very poems which celebrate the insights themselves. The *Lines Written in Early Spring* hail nature's life and joy only to fail immediately into despondency because this life and joy leave unanswered the questions raised by the existence of social evil, "What man has made of man." The joyous scene when the hare runs over the wet fields is unable to repel the sudden upswelling within the poet himself of a fear of poverty, old age, and death. The still later transport succumbs to the cruel realization of Catherine's death. Against the imperfections everywhere apparent in life, Wordsworth needed some images of perfection large enough, stable and permanent enough, to seem to have a cosmic significance. As R. D.

Havens has remarked, Wordsworth's essentially religious nature compelled him to seek everywhere "the abiding behind the flux," "the perfect behind the incomplete," "the one behind the many." [12] The images which might fulfil this need should have some of the unity in multiplicity, the underlying pattern, order, or formal structure, which the word *beauty* frequently suggests. This beauty is perhaps perceived a little more by contemplation, a little less by the immediate empathy which responds to mere vitality. It is suited to a mind which by continued contemplation has at least half detached itself from those human evils for which it seeks an explanation. Two of Wordsworth's most powerful images of cosmic perfection were supplied by two landscapes which he has celebrated fully, those of the Wye and of Grasmere.

When Wordsworth walked along the Wye once again in 1798, after an absence of five years, he says he owes to the "beauteous forms" of the valley

> *that blessed mood*
> *In which the burthen of the mystery,*
> *In which the heavy and the weary weight*
> *Of all this unintelligible world,*
> *Is lightened.*

Among the evils which constitute the burden Wordsworth makes no mention of death (to which for the moment he may not have been paying particular heed); he mentions only temporal imperfections and against these the beauty of nature will provide a remedy:

> *for she can so inform*
> *The mind within us, so impress*
> *With quietness and beauty, and so feed*
> *With lofty thoughts, that neither evil tongues,*
> *Rash judgments, nor the sneers of selfish men,*
> *Nor greetings where no kindness is, nor all*
> *The dreary intercourse of daily life,*
> *Shall e'er prevail against us, or disturb*
> *Our cheerful faith that all which we behold*
> *Is full of blessings.*

Let us look at the landscape of the Wye whose order and pattern seemed so potent a witness of the goodness of the world. In the very opening passage of the *Lines* Wordsworth calls attention to the particular arrangement of objects before his eyes, especially to all those interpenetrations by which they constituted one closely-knit whole:

> *Once again*
> *Do I behold these steep and lofty cliffs,*
> *That on a wild secluded scene impress*
> *Thoughts of more deep seclusion; and connect*
> *The landscape with the quiet of the sky.*
> *The day is come when I again repose*
> *Here, under this dark sycamore, and view*
> *These plots of cottage-ground, these orchard-tufts,*
> *Which at this season, with their unripe fruits,*
> *Are clad in one green hue, and lose themselves*
> *'Mid groves and copses. Once again I see*
> *These hedge-rows, hardly hedge-rows, little lines*
> *Of sportive wood run wild; these pastoral farms,*
> *Green to the very door; the wreaths of smoke*
> *Sent up, in silence from among the trees!*
> *With some uncertain notice, as might seem*
> *Of vagrant dwellers in the houseless woods,*
> *Or of some Hermit's cave, where by his fire*
> *The hermit sits alone.*

In this scene Wordsworth has found the objective correlative for his philosophy of the period, an image in miniature of that larger harmony which he believed—or wished to believe—the world to be. Every detail in its composition is significant. To realize this fact one has only to think of a contrast, of many south German landscapes for instance, strikingly handsome in their way: all human habitations crowd together into a village and scarcely a tree is left among the houses to bear witness to the persistence of that nature which man has repelled; outside this concentration of masonry are wide stretches of ploughed land without bush, tree, or hedge-row; and then, perhaps a mile away, the forest of evergreens, sudden, dark, ominous, impenetrable—as though civilization and primeval nature were living in an armed truce, each proclaiming to the other, "Thus far and no farther." Such a German scene might make an excellent correlative to another philosophy, perhaps to that of the late Irving Babbitt, but certainly not to Wordsworth's in 1798. To Wordsworth was suited rather the valley of the Wye where all intermingled in harmony and unity: the grass "green to the very door" of the cottages; the plots of cottage ground and orchards losing themselves amid groves and copses; hedge-rows and woodlands uniting; wreaths of smoke (from charcoal burners, probably) telling that man was going about his labors even in the depth of the woods; and lastly—a fact which Wordsworth noted first—the lofty cliffs connecting somehow the living, growing landscape with the "quiet of the sky." [13]

In noting this last-mentioned connection, as in observing all the others, Wordsworth is not observing merely as a painter might, one who wished to create a composition whose diverse elements harmonized easily and gently rather than one in which opposite forces precariously sustained a balanced tension. In his observation upon the cliff and the sky and in all the others Wordsworth is thinking as a moralist and theologian also. The world of man, of pastoral farms and plots of cottage ground, merges gently, through orchards and hedge-rows not too neatly trimmed, into nature's copse and woodland. And the busy growing world of nature, by way of the cliffs, merges gently with the quiet of the sky. This sky is a symbol of the Divine Quiet, of the "Eternal Silence" of the Intimations *Ode* and of *The Excursion's*

> *peace, subsisting at the heart*
> *Of endless agitation.*
>
> (IV, 1146–47.)

Thus, in Wordsworth's philosophy, by way of the world of nature, the human and the divine are connected with each other. Here in the landscape all are visibly "interfused," even as Wordsworth felt they should be. To others the heavens have declared the glory of God; to Wordsworth the valley of the Wye and the sky above it declared this glory, but they declared first and foremost the unity and harmony of the universe.[14]

Here may be seen also how a large and beautiful landscape reaffirms the sense of vitality, but in a larger and more comprehensive way. Vitality here is not a momentary and local presence only, but a permanent, pervasive, all-encompassing power—a power

> *far more deeply interfused*
> *Whose dwelling is the light of setting suns,*
> *And the round ocean, and the living air,*
> *And the blue sky, and in the mind of man;*
> *A motion and a spirit that impels*
> *All thinking things, all objects of all thoughts,*
> *And moves through all things.*

In the Tintern Abbey *Lines* Wordsworth is making some attempt to wrestle not just with his own frustrations but with the world's evils. With the help of the valley's beauty he believes he has solved the problem: what is everywhere vital is imagined as being—in the larger view and despite local wrongs—essentially good and just.

It is interesting to note how other "justifiers" have used what one might call the pantheistic image, the sense of one life working from within, to override the consciousness of particular wrongs. Pope's *Essay on Man* had attempted to "vindicate the ways of God to man," to prove to the reader that "whatever is, is right." Pope first seeks to defend creation against charges of injustice in the court of logical reason: he assures us that our middling powers are suited to our middle state; that if our sense of smell were any finer we might "Die of a rose in aromatic pain"; that if we sought to displace creatures higher on the scale of being those below might seek to displace us. As though sensing some inadequacy in this procedure he procures a change of venue and makes his final plea in the court of the imagination: there he seeks to preclude our considering the possibility of imperfection by stating that the cosmos is pervaded by one great unifying life:

> All are but parts of one stupendous Whole,
> Whose body Nature is, and God the soul;
> That, changed through all, and yet in all the same,
> Great in the earth, as in the ethereal frame,
> Warms in the sun, refreshes in the breeze,
> Glows in the stars, and blossoms in the trees,
> Lives through all life, extends through all extent,
> Spreads undivided, operates unspent;
> Breathes in our soul, informs our mortal part,
> As full, as perfect, in vile man that mourns,
> As the rapt seraph that adores and burns:
> To him no high, no low, no great, no small;
> He fills, he bounds, connects, and equals all.

(Pope's proclamation is of course different from Wordsworth's in that it is presented as a generalization made by the mind itself, rather than as a revelation made to the mind by some external scene.) Similarly, young Goethe, seeking to justify Strassburg Cathedral to an audience disposed to find Gothic architecture ill-proportioned and its details inharmonious, had said that every building should be, as this cathedral was, so filled with the unity of the artist's soul that it will stand forth like the cathedral, "its great harmonious masses filled with life even to the countless small details, like the works of eternal nature, all form, all contributing to the whole, down even to the most minute fiber." [15] And so Schlegel and Coleridge, even as they praised Shakespeare's individual characters for their inner life, used organic metaphors to persuade the imagination of the perfection of Shakespeare's individual plays,

each a little cosmos, as it were, pervaded by the creative energy of
the poet; so Coleridge's marginal note praised *Romeo and Juliet*:

> Whence [arises] the harmony that strikes us in the wildest nat-
> ural landscapes,—in the relative shapes of rocks, the harmony of
> colors in the heaths, ferns, and lichens, the leaves of the beech
> and oak, the stems and rich chocolate brown branches of the
> birch and other mountain trees, varying from verging autumn
> to returning spring—compared with the visual effects from the
> greater number of artificial plantations? The former are ef-
> fected by a single energy, modified *ab intra* in each component
> part. Now as this is the particular excellence of Shakespeare's
> dramas generally, so it is especially characteristic of *Romeo
> and Juliet*.[16]

A number of years ago A. O. Lovejoy commented somewhat ironically upon the "metaphysical pathos" generated by statements of
this sort; [17] in the religious solemnity emitted by the idea of one
pervasive life working from within, the critical faculties and their
fault-finding are momentarily silenced.

A year and some months after Wordsworth had composed his
lines on the Wye, he and Dorothy returned in the middle of winter
to make their home in the Lake District in which they had grown
up. Two months of continuous storms did not mar their quiet happiness. When the first mild days tell that winter is almost over,
Wordsworth's emotion bursts forth in the more than 800 lines titled
"Home at Grasmere," or *The Recluse*. Circled by the surrounding
mountains the vale constitutes a perfect microcosm: the crags, the
woods, the lake and its single island, the church, the cottages of
mountain stone

> *Clustered like stars some few, but single most,*
> *And lurking dimly in their shy retreats,*
> *Or glancing at each other cheerful looks*
> *Like separated stars with clouds between,*
>   (ll. 122–25.)

the industrious dalesmen, the shepherd, the widow in her cottage
under the grove which she and her husband had planted, the crip-
ple and his small grey horse, the owls, the lordly eagles, and the
ever-wheeling flights of gulls above the lake,

> *a mighty multitude, whose way*
> *Is a perpetual harmony, and dance*
> *Magnificent,*
>   (ll. 201–3.)

—all these are felt to be united by bonds of love, to constitute as nearly ideal a society as the present time is likely to show. But it was perhaps the vale's beauty, its perfection of form, which convinced the poet of its goodness even more than the fullness of its life; within its wide compass is

> nothing to be seen but lovely pomp
> And silent majesty.
>
> (ll. 561–2.)

The poet speaks of beauty and love with equal emphasis, as though recollecting Plato's definition of the beautiful as that by which love is aroused. Indeed, to Wordsworth the outward blending of the parts into the whole which the eye perceived was but the true and proper symbol of that mutual love which the heart sensed in this fortunate valley, this "one household under God"; the pleasing fashion in which the cottages, like "stars," some clustered, some single in their shy retreats, glanced "at each other with cheerful looks," presented to the eye a miniature version of that one great "galaxy of life and joy" which Wordsworth's imagination, in its happiest moments, affirmed the universe to be. (And so again, in the last book of The Prelude, beauty and love are seen as related by the imagination. There the faculty of imagination which Wordsworth has been celebrating, which has so often been stimulated by the vitality and beauty of the world around him, is pronounced to be the indispensible moral agent in that growth in love which will alone enable us to play our full part in the great cosmic harmony.)

At this point in The Recluse, a note of critical realism intrudes. Wordsworth admits that evil, though diminished in this fortunate valley, is none the less to be found. And conscience intrudes. To what use can the poet put the strength and joy he feels within himself? Especially what can he do to aid the millions of suffering men living elsewhere,

> the fierce confederate storm
> Of sorrow, barricadoed evermore
> Within the walls of cities.
>
> (ll. 831–33)
> (also "Prospectus" to The Excursion, ll. 78–80.)

The Tintern Abbey Lines had celebrated chiefly private happiness. "Home at Grasmere" professes the dignity and responsibility of the poet's public function, and the style accordingly takes on a more Miltonic ring. The life of mankind as a whole cannot be justified in terms of present actualities but only in terms of a future millennium. Wordsworth sees himself, the poet encompassed by beauty, as the spokesman of

> The human Soul of universal earth
> Dreaming on things to come.
> (ll. 837–38; "Prospectus" to The Excursion, ll. 84–85.)

Of some future justice, towards which life is moving, Wordsworth sees the present beauty as prophetic—even as Keats was at times inclined to see beauty as prophetic or prefigurative:

> —Beauty—a living Presence of the earth,
> Surpassing the most fair ideal Forms
> Which craft of delicate Spirits hath composed
> From earth's materials—waits upon my steps;
> Pitches her tents before me as I move,
> An hourly neighbour. Paradise, and groves
> Elysian, Fortunate Fields—like those of old
> Sought in the Atlantic Main—why should they be
> A history only of departed things,
> Or a mere fiction of what never was?
> For the discerning intellect of Man,
> When wedded to this goodly universe
> In love and holy passion, shall find these
> A simple produce of the common day.
> —I, long before this blissful hour arrives,
> Would chant, in lonely peace, the spousal verse
> Of this great consummation.
> (ll. 795–811; "Prospectus" to The Excursion, ll. 42–58.)

Here we have the age-old human habit of resorting to a vision of the future to justify or redeem the present. Many of Wordsworth's successors resort to a similar vision, in one form or another, to answer the same need.

In the harmonious vale in which he had chosen to live, the life of man and the life of nature interpenetrate each other, even as they did along the Wye. But the connection or merging most clearly imaged is that between the earthly and the non-earthly, the ideal, the eternal. Wordsworth's first description of the scene is climaxed by these lines:

> and the voice
> Of lordly birds, an unexpected sound
> Heard now and then from morn till latest eve,
> Admonishing the man who walks below
> Of solitude and silence in the sky.
> (ll. 129–33.)

In another passage later in the poem another bird seems to perform almost the reverse function, to carry into the quiet of the sky some of the warm life usually associated with earth—much as the woodsmen along the Wye had carried some of the cheerful activity of human life into the "houseless" woods. Also in this later passage the blending of the actual landscape with its reflection in the calm lake affords an image of the blending of the world's actuality with the ideal:

> Behold the universal imagery
> Inverted, all its sun-bright features touched
> As with the varnish, and the gloss of dreams;
> Dreamlike the blending also of the whole
> Harmonious landscape; all along the shore
> The boundary lost, the line invisible
> That parts image from reality;
> And the clear hills as high as they ascend
> Heavenward, so piercing deep the lake below.
> Admonished of the days of love to come
> The raven croaks, and fills the upper air
> With a strange sound of genial harmony.
>
> (ll. 571–82.)

The imagery is complex. The sky above towards which the hills ascend heavenward inevitably carries some of its customary symbolic significance, but the main images of the ideal towards which men aspire and of which they dream are the reflections in the depths. Again, the "days of love to come" are primarily the days of spring, but one must wonder whether Wordsworth has not half-consciously given the phrase a more cosmic suggestion also—as though the raven, having seen the idealist's dream in the reflections in the lake, were a Shelleyan prophet proclaiming to the upper or actual world the millennial vision he has beheld.

The visual blending of the two worlds, real and ideal, was not something just casually noted by Wordsworth on this occasion but was to be habitually close to his heart. In the elaborate set piece at the end of The Excursion, the vale of Grasmere is flooded by the refracted radiance of the sun already set, the "unapparent fount of glory" which symbolizes the Deity "inaccessible to human thought"; on this occasion also the "liquid deep" repeats the splendors of the "heavens" with "unity sublime." (Here the images reflected in the lake do not stand for the idealized world as opposed to the actual, but the lower as opposed to the higher or divine.) And in the Guide to the Lake District, when Wordsworth came to write his frankly partisan comparison of the English and the Swiss

lakes, he dwelt upon these reflections as upon a matter of some importance; the Swiss lakes, we are told, owing to their more opaque
waters and their wider and rougher surfaces, seldom if ever produce this wonderfully harmonized double image. One must conclude that during the intervening years Wordsworth had habitually
nourished his soul by those two blended worlds which he so often
contemplated as he walked about the quiet shores of Grasmere and
Rydal Water. Those who have read Shelley widely may remember
how this poet likewise, or the Shelleyan hero of his poems, hangs
suspended above some pool, held as in a spell, though he may not
know why, by a world which duplicates the ordinary world but
is yet set apart from it by a strange quality of otherness.

The oneness which Wordsworth perceives in *The Recluse* is
now not sensed quite so pantheistically as it had been in the *Lines*.
We read not of one spirit that rolls through all things: the valley
is perceived more traditionally as "one household, under God." Suggestive of tradition also is the sense not so much of one world but
of *two* worlds, perfectly blended though these may be.

Florence Marsh has noted, as others must have also, Wordsworth's general movement from "life-symbols" to "eternity symbols" and to images of art.[18] Though Wordsworth in this poem
does not comment at great length upon the mountains surrounding
Grasmere, except to exclaim

> *Embrace me, then, ye hills, and close me in,*
> (l. 110.)

and to note their images descending below even as far as they
ascended above, yet these mountains are so inescapable a fact at
Grasmere that his consciousness of the "special spirit" of the place
and its "majesty" is certainly largely determined by them.[19] The
landscape perforce had some of the solid, three-dimensional presence of works of architecture or sculpture, and some of their suggestion of permanence—Wordsworth does, in fact, compare the
valley to a temple. And the valley had some of the qualities of a
work of art in another way. Aristotle's comment that a tragedy
should be an independent unity, complete in itself, applies to works
of art in general. Precisely this sort of completeness is found in the
Vale of Grasmere. The outlet of the vale is partly masked; mountains seem to encompass it on all sides so that it does not strike the
eye as a mere appendage of a larger valley. This underlying geo-
logical unity, underpinning the more superficial visual harmonies
of color and texture which Wordsworth appreciated, and enforc-
ing that social unity which to Wordsworth bespoke a "true com-

munity," must have been largely responsible for Wordsworth's sense of the valley's unique perfection: [20]

> *No where (or is it fancy?) can be found*
> *The one sensation that is here; 'tis here,*
> *Here as it found its way into my heart*
> *In childhood, here as it abides by day,*
> *By night, here only; or in chosen minds*
> *That take it with them hence, where'er they go.*
> *'Tis, but I cannot name it, 'tis the sense*
> *Of majesty, and beauty, and repose,*
> *A blended holiness of earth and sky,*
> *Something that makes this individual Spot,*
> *This small Abiding-place of many Men,*
> *A termination, and a last retreat,*
> *A Centre, come from wheresoe'er you will,*
> *A Whole without dependence or defect,*
> *Made for itself; and happy in itself,*
> *Perfect Contentment, Unity entire.*
>
> (ll. 136–51.)

What is it that is, not in image, but in reality, "a whole without dependence or defect, made for itself, happy in itself, perfect contentment, unity entire"? According to traditional theology, it is God; according to Plato it is the One. And this is precisely what Wordsworth goes on to say; this scene, he states, will afford

> *an image for the soul,*
> *A habit of Eternity and God.*
> (de Selincourt's note to line 151.)

These last lines were omitted from the final version of the poem, but they express something of what was in the poet's mind when the experience of the vale was fresh and powerful.

Wordsworth's two great poems on the Wye and on Grasmere taken together constitute an interesting study in slightly different methods of justification. Attempts to present the world as essentially beneficent may be divided roughly into two classes. Men may justify the world in its own terms: they may claim that there is enough happiness on earth to satisfy any reasonable desire, or at least that there will be when men correct their individual faults or reform their social order. Or it may be claimed that this world is radically imperfect, but that it is a preparation for some hereafter, some eternity, in which man's inherent craving for perfection will find its fulfillment. Those who believe there is or can be enough happiness here are philosophical monists; they make no deep distinction between spirit and matter. The others are likely to be dualists; spirit to them is in some way different from matter, and men's spirits are destined to transcend the material world we know. As every student of his poetry knows, Wordsworth moved in the course of his life nearer the partial or modified dualism of traditional orthodoxy.[21]

Even as early as the years between 1798 and 1800 Wordsworth was changing. Something of the change can be seen by comparing his imaginative responses to the Wye and to Grasmere. At the Wye "all that we behold is full of blessings"; though life has its pains and languors, these can be alleviated here and now by the memory of beauty. Wordsworth comes close to justifying life in its own terms. In keeping with his near monism, the beautiful scene before him is regarded not as a mere image of transcendental beauty but as a very part of one great beauty. A spirit or life fills the material world and this spirit is scarcely thought of as existing apart from matter. Wordsworth here comes closest to being, what he has often been described as being, a pantheist: his God, for the moment is more in the world than transcendent, or the transcendence, if believed in, is not stressed.

A year and a half later, as he settles down at Grasmere, Wordsworth's feelings are in the process of change. He would still maintain that this life is good; he says in fact that one does the realities of this world a great injustice in holding them to be cold, cowardly, ready to betray, "stinted in the measure of their grace." He even adds the last argument of the hard-pressed monist, the millennial hope. And yet the whole poem, though it breathes an impassioned gratitude that the poet may henceforth dwell in his chosen valley, is touched by an ominous foreboding. Now that the great boon for which Wordsworth has yearned is granted, he half begins to sense the shadowiness of the very thing which he finally has within his grasp, to be chilled by the transiency of all earthly joy and beauty. The old feeling of a single divine force pervading the world is not entirely gone, but it is not so emphasized. The one Spirit begins to be behind and above its creation. We hear not of the one life that "rolls through all things," but rather of a small part of this earth which is a "counterpart" of heaven, an "image of Eternity and God." The scheme of thought is similar to that of Plato, to whom things in this world were counterparts or images of the only reality, the ideal. And it is the scheme of thought which Christianity has accustomed men to. Hence it is not surprising when, in the magniloquent lines at the close of the poem, Wordsworth speaks not only of "better times" for this world, but also of "worlds to which the Heaven of Heavens is but

a veil"; not only of "hope for this earth," but likewise of "hope beyond the grave." [22]

There have been readers of Wordsworth, more numerous perhaps a generation ago than at present, disbelievers in any spiritual
hereafter, who have resented Wordsworth's increasing dualism.
They sometimes speak as though Wordsworth in the course of time
betrayed his own early philosophy. They find it difficult to imagine
that one who has once known the truth as they see it might forsake
it; they regard Wordsworth's change as proof of weakness, of a lack
of integrity. In order to keep a clear distinction between their own
Wordsworth and the orthodox Wordsworth, and to be able to claim
the best of the poetry for the first, the one who has not yet suc-
cumbed to the great transcendental illusion, they may conveniently
regard Wordsworth as one of themselves up until about 1804; then
the semi-orthodox Ode to Duty and the later stanzas of the Ode:
Intimations of Immortality may be regarded as symptoms of the approaching decline in imaginative power. Such a decline does indeed
set in, quite rapidly, and the humanists would seem to have something of a case. But the truth is that Wordsworth did not lack integrity, there was no betrayal, no inexplicable exchanging of his own
strong thought and weak acceptance of traditional religion. The
Recluse, though not much read, makes clear that the traditional distinction between temporal and eternal is already present as early as
1800—at which time there can be no question of a decline in poetic
power. Furthermore, this distinction is not at this time suddenly bor-
rowed from others, as something essentially alien to the poet's own
apprehension. The Wordsworth of a few years before, of 1797 and
1798, had not been a real monist, but had merely been nearer to monism than later.[23] A careful reading of the poetry of these earlier
years, in conjunction with that which follows, will show that the
transcendental apprehensions which were gradually to emerge more
strongly were there from the start, though only in germ. The Tintern Abbey Lines themselves, for instance, had told how men can
owe to the beauty of nature certain mystical moments of ecstasy
in which

> the breadth of this corporeal frame
> And even the motion of our human blood
> Almost suspended, we are laid asleep
> In body, and become a living soul.

There are still other readers, dualists, believers in sharp distinctions between God and creation, time and eternity, sin and grace,
whose pleasure in Wordsworth is somewhat spoiled by his early

nearness to monism, and by traces of monism they find lingering even to the end.[24] One of the earliest of these critics was William Blake, a poet whose own theology—ironically enough—often seems much further from orthodoxy than Wordsworth's. In his annotations to Wordsworth's poems Blake exclaimed,

> I see in Wordsworth the Natural Man rising up against the Spiritual Man Continually, & then he is No Poet but a Heathen Philosopher at Enmity against all true Poetry or Inspiration.
> There is no such Thing as Natural Piety Because The Natural Man is at Enmity with God.

In Wordsworth's case, as earlier in Marvell's and later perhaps in those of Shelley and Keats and Tennyson, a harmonious arrangement of material forms elevates the spirit until it seems to pass beyond matter as we know it. In Marvell's *Garden* and Keat's *Ode on a Grecian Urn* the spirit passes no further than to some Elysian realm, half-material, still imaginable. The other poets at times feel they have passed beyond the still imaginable sublime, to some immaterial region.

In truth, though beauty may have been to Wordsworth a symbol of cosmic oneness, it seems always to have suggested simultaneously some cosmic division, and thus to have been half metaphysical in its implications. It is as though the mere perfection of beauty itself, so contrary to the general imperfection of life, inevitably suggested a magical other world. This otherness Wordsworth often expressed by the word *dream*.[25] The lines on Grasmere had themselves spoken of the "dreamlike blending" of the landscape. *The Prelude* describes the effect upon the young boy Wordsworth of the evening when he and his companions rowed gently away from one of the islands in Windermere while one of their number, still on the island's shore, played a flute alone upon the rocks:

> *Oh! then the calm*
> *And dead still water lay upon my mind*
> *Even with a weight of pleasure, and the sky,*
> *Never before so beautiful, sank down*
> *Into my heart, and held me like a dream.*
> (II, 176–80; II, 170–74.)

A later moment, during a summer vacation, is recalled thus:

> *O happy state! what beauteous pictures now*
> *Rose in harmonious imagery—they rose*

> *As from some distant region of my soul*
> *And came along like dreams.*
> (IV, 392–95 [1805 version].)

On two other occasions, the beauty of sound accompanied by the whole beauty of the landscape suggests to the poet's consciousness precisely the quality which music lacks, permanence in time. It is as though the sounds, so wholly satisfying in themselves, inevitably imply to the imagination an additional dimension required of perfection and quite contrary to the nature of sound as it strikes the prosaic mind. Describing an earlier afternoon's boating on Windermere, Wordsworth writes,

> *the selected bourne*
> *Was now an island musical with birds*
> *That sang forever.*
> (II, 58–60; II, 57–59.)

The other occasion is recorded in *The Solitary Reaper*. F. A. Pottle, who suggests that the almost visionary power of some of Wordsworth's simpler poems expresses the serious religious quality of the imagination which lay behind them, cites the poem about the reaper as a case in point.[26] It may be noted that even on this occasion beauty justifies; the beauty of the song and of the scene render "welcome" and "thrilling" the tale of "old, unhappy, far-off things" or of some present "sorrow, loss, or pain" which the poet imagines to be the subject of the Gaelic strains. And in addition the fleeting beauty suggests an undying beauty:

> *Whate'er the theme, the Maiden sang*
> *As if her song could have no ending;*

and the poet's memory then does its best to vindicate this intimation of permanence:

> *I saw her singing at her work,*
> *And o'er her sickle bending:—*
> *I listened, motionless and still;*
> *And, as I mounted up the hill,*
> *The music in my heart I bore,*
> *Long after it was heard no more.*

This poised stillness of Wordsworth in the presence of beauty, like that which *The Prelude* records of earlier occasions, anticipates the harkening intentness of many of Keats's figures. And so likewise, again and again, Wordsworth's instinctive reading of beauty as mysteriously symbolic, as betokening something beyond the immediate fact, inevitably suggests the *Ode on a Grecian Urn* and the *Ode to a Nightingale*.

Professor Pottle sees Wordsworth's imagination—with a somewhat less private vision than Blake's—as engaged in the task designated in Blake's quatrain,

> *To see a World in a Grain of Sand*
> *And a Heaven in a Wild Flower,*
> *Hold Infinity in the palm of your hand*
> *And Eternity in an hour.*

Beauty was the great means which his imagination found ready at hand for the performance of this task, though the beauty usually possessed more multiplicity brought into unity, more flux brought into calm, than a grain of sand can offer to the naked eye.

Sublimity and Immortality

THE SUBLIME IN NATURE might be defined generally as that which fills man with a great sense of awe in the presence of the mighty Spirit in the universe. Wordsworth frequently felt such awe and something will here be said of those occasions on which he did so. Fuller attention, however, will be paid to moments in which the poet is less conscious of a transcendent cosmic Spirit than of the transcendent nature of his own spirit. These moments may be viewed as a further development of those perceptions of the vital which were discussed earlier. On the first occasions Wordsworth sensed primarily his living freedom *within* the material world, his freedom of will; on the second he sensed rather that his own spirit, in its innermost essence, was not part of the material world at all, that it existed wholly independently of the usual limits of space and time, that it was *per se* infinite in the precise sense of unbounded, that it was destined, in short, for an immortal freedom. (Theoretically any such sharp distinction between the material world and man's spirit may appear to be inconsistent with the tendency in Wordsworth discussed earlier to regard nature itself as thoroughly animated by spirit—as Coleridge and his favorite idealist philosophers were at times inclined to do. The point is one to be debated by the professional students of metaphysics.)

Following the rediscovery of the ancient treatise on the "elevated" style ascribed to Longinus, the word *sublime* had by the mid-eighteenth century become a commonplace term to designate the

awesomely grand. The influence of Addison had helped to popular-
ize the term and to suggest the range of feeling which it could imply. Edmund Burke's *Philosophical Enquiry* strengthened the tendency to associate the word with the idea of terror. Of the sublime
in the Longinian and Burkean senses Wordsworth offers many instances. Though he did not choose to live in one of the wildest and
most awe-inspiring valleys in the Lake District (such as Borrowdale,
perhaps), the mountains around Grasmere possessed enough mild
grandeur to merit Wordsworth's ascription to them of "majesty."
And the darkness, silence, and solitude, which R. D. Havens and
D. G. James among others have particularly noticed as character-
izing many of Wordsworth's most impressive moments, had been explicitly listed by Burke as related to terror and productive of sublimity.[27]

In *The Prelude* Wordsworth describes himself as having been
moulded by Nature and

> *Fostered alike by beauty and by fear.*
> (I, 306; I, 302.)

Thanks to the beauty he learned to love the world. Thanks to fear
he learned to associate the moral impulse within with some awesome
universal power. One remembers vividly the evening when he rowed
out into the lake in a stolen boat and a great, dark mountain suddenly
seemed to rise up before him as it became visible behind the lower
shoreline; and the time when the mysterious night noises followed
him among the hills after he had stolen the catch of another's traps.
But because Nature was grand and beautiful as well as terrible these
fears induced by conscience were ennobling rather than debasing. For
such experiences he thanks the "Wisdom and the Spirit of the universe":

> *By day or star-light thus from my first dawn*
> *Of Childhood didst Thou intertwine for me*
> *The passions that build up our human Soul,*
> *Not with the mean and vulgar works of Man,*
> *But with the high objects, with enduring things,*
> *With life and nature, purifying thus*
> *The elements of feeling and of thought,*
> *And sanctifying, by such discipline,*
> *Both pain and fear, until we recognize*
> *A grandeur in the beatings of the heart.*
> (I, 432-41; I, 405-14.)

R. D. Havens and D. G. James have done these moments justice and only a little more will be said of them here. Perhaps they do not provide intimations of the existence of God, a Spirit of the universe, so much as they color or modify our relation to that Spirit. They are an important and typical part of Wordsworth's total apprehension of life. Among other things, they suggest the presence in him from the beginning of a certain Old Testament consciousness of the sublime origins of the moral law and of the fear of the Lord as the beginning of Wisdom. In a sense they are antecedents of the feelings expressed in the *Ode to Duty*. This poem, deplored by some liberals on general grounds and, in its final form especially, seriously (and cogently) criticized by N. P. Stallknecht,[28] may indeed be a denial of certain of Wordsworth's earlier and freer impulses. But of other earlier impulses it may be considered an affirmation.

The "sublime" moments of which I should like to speak at greater length are those which recall Immanuel Kant rather than Longinus or Burke. The *sublime*, according to Kant's *Critique of Judgment*, was that which intimated to the human soul its own essentially transcendent nature. S. H. Monk's massively documented study of eighteenth-century aesthetics, *The Sublime*, uncovers almost nothing in England truly equivalent to Kant's use of the term.

As has been noted already, Kant construed the beautiful as the image of the One; it is an appearance in the physical world which accords with the spirit's aspiration towards something harmonious, perfect, complete in itself. Beauty is thus a warrant for the monistic tendencies of religion. But Christianity has always sought to contain within its larger monism a dualism of matter and spirit. Kant was as unwilling as any conservative theologian to blur this traditional distinction. So the *Critique of Judgment* balances its discussion of beauty as intimating an original unity with its discussion of the sublime as intimating a persisting division.

As Kant sees it, the sublime properly considered pertains to spirit only: those objects in nature which we call sublime are not truly so in themselves but only make the spirit aware of its own sublimity. They are so great in extent, or so powerful, that their immediate effect is to awe us into a sense of our own inferiority. But the divinity of spirit will inevitably reassert itself. Be a mountain ever so high, an abyss so deep, a waterfall so stupendous, the soul within us, after a moment's pause, will realize that it is itself infinitely greater. It realizes that it transcends completely the greatest spectacle material nature can offer, that in essence it pertains to the unlimited, the infinite, the immortal. Thus, Kant says, the final effect of the sublime is not depressing but pleasurable.[29]

An experience in Wordsworth's poetry which illustrates perfectly Kant's conception of the sublime is the well-known crossing
of the Alps celebrated in *The Prelude*. Wordsworth and his friend
Jones had climbed up for many miles through heavy mists. As they
proceeded hour after hour, Wordsworth seems to have been awed
by a sensation of the never-to-be-terminated, infinite ascent which
the mountain pass itself afforded. When the ascent was in fact terminated by their unexpected discovery that they had without realizing
it reached the top of the pass, Wordsworth's feeling was one of
anticlimax: even the Alps could not equal the infinite magnitudes
dimly sensed by the mind. So Wordsworth hails his own imagination
thus:

> *Imagination! lifting up itself*
> *Before the eye and progress of my Song*
> *Like an unfather'd vapour; here that Power,*
> *In all the might of its endowments, came*
> *Athwart me; I was lost as in a cloud,*
> *Halted, without a struggle to break through.*
> *And now recovering, to my Soul I say*
> *I recognize thy glory; in such strength*
> *Of usurpation, in such visitings*
> *Of awful promise, when the light of sense*
> *Goes out in flashes that have shown to us*
> *The invisible world, doth Greatness make abode,*
> *There harbours whether we be young or old.*
> *Our destiny, our nature, and our home*
> *Is with infinitude, and only there;*
> *With hope it is, hope that can never die,*
> *Effort, and expectation, and desire,*
> *And something evermore about to be.*
>   (VI, 525–42; VI, 592–608.) [30]

In conjunction with this passage the reader must, in justice to the
complexity and fullness of Wordsworth's imagination, consider the
lines which follow almost immediately. These next lines offer no
clear illustration of the sublime in the special Kantian sense, but they
describe a landscape as terrible and grand as any in Wordsworth.
And in its way the poet's mind in this other passage does rise superior
to the awesome spectacle, not by any sharpened sense of its own
transcendency, but by its ability to recognize the scene as a symbol
of some eternity beyond itself. In this eternity the contradictions in
the world of time, such as decay and permanence, motion and stillness, terror and pleasure, chaos and order, are reconciled. This is

the scene Wordsworth witnessed as he walked down from the pass
into Italy:

> *The immeasurable height*
> *Of Woods decaying, never to be decay'd,*
> *The stationary blasts of water-falls,*
> *And everywhere along the hollow rent*
> *Winds thwarting winds, bewilder'd and forlorn,*
> *The torrents shooting from the clear blue sky,*
> *The rocks that mutter'd close upon our ears,*
> *Black drizzling crags that spake by the way-side*
> *As if a voice were in them, the sick sight*
> *And giddy prospect of the raving stream,*
> *The unfeter'd clouds, and region of the Heavens,*
> *Tumult and peace, the darkness and the light*
> *Were all like workings of one mind, the features*
> *Of the same face, blossoms upon one tree,*
> *Characters of the great Apocalypse,*
> *The types and symbols of Eternity,*
> *Of first and last, and midst, and without end.*

> (VI, 556–72; VI, 624–40.)

This passage recalls Coleridge's notion of the imagination as the
power of reconciling opposites, and his belief (derived in part from
Schelling) that this power was the organ of metaphysical insight.

But to return to the sublime as intimating directly the soul's own
transcendence. Sheer spatial extent, as in the case of the long climb
up the pass, was not Wordsworth's principal source for this particular kind of experience. The most frequent occasion was a return,
after an absence of some time, to a spot known before; what the
mind transcends is not an extent of space but a lapse of time. In a
sense, of course, nearly all Wordsworth's poetry was a revisiting of
the past in imagination, a recollecting in tranquillity. But what will
be discussed here are moments of actual physical return.

The Prelude records Wordsworth's return to Hawkshead after
having been away at Cambridge. Though the evening was chilly, the
poet set out immediately to walk along the shores of Esthwaite:

> *When first I made*
> *Once more the circuit of our little Lake*
> *If ever happiness hath lodg'd with man,*
> *That day consummate happiness was mine,*
> *Wide-spreading, steady, calm, contemplative.*
> *The sun was set, or setting, when I left*
> *Our cottage door, and evening soon brought on*

A sober hour, not winning or serene,
For cold and raw the air was, and untun'd:
But, as a face we love is sweetest then
When sorrow damps it, or, whatever look
It chance to wear is sweetest if the heart
Have fulness in itself, even so with me
It fared that evening. Gently did my soul
Put off her veil, and, self-transmuted, stood
Naked as in the presence of her God.
. . .
I had hopes and peace
And swellings of the spirit, was rapt and soothed,
Convers'd with promises, had glimmering views
How Life pervades the undecaying mind,
How the immortal Soul with God-like power
Informs, creates, and thaws the deepest sleep
That time can lay upon her.
(IV, 127–58; IV, 137–68.)

What Wordsworth believed happened upon this occasion is clear
only after the passage is studied a moment. First, as a mere secondary
circumstance helping to make Wordsworth's perception of his own
spirit's transcendent power more vivid, was the unfavorable weather;
to this in his joy he could rise superior. What furnished the main
part of the total intimation was the return to a beloved spot. Once
before Wordsworth had commented upon what happens on such an
occasion; speaking of his coming again to the valley of the Wye, he
had written:

And now, with gleams of half-extinguished thought,
And many recognitions dim and faint,
And somewhat of a sad perplexity,
The picture of the mind revives again.

The two passages are related. The imaginative memory has summoned to renewed life images sunk almost to oblivion, and this
power of the soul to keep images alive in the sub-conscious and then
to resurrect them is what has given Wordsworth

glimmering views
How Life pervades the undecaying mind.

Though Wordsworth speaks of cherishing the image of the Wye
valley, and though during his months on the flats of Cambridgeshire
he had no doubt cherished memories of the scenes around Esthwaite,

during his absence these memories must have become, to the conscious mind, more and more general and indistinct. The precise details of the landscape, just how this lane curved around a rise of ground or how that tree stood in relation to the cottage beyond—such loved circumstances had seemed lost. But upon returning to the scenes, upon seeing once again the lane and the knoll, the tree and the cottage, the poet recognized that it was even thus and so, that the deepest part of the mind had known it to be thus and so all along.[31]

In respect to circumstance, to immediate cause, such a Wordsworthian moment resembles the experience Proust describes as setting off his entire process of artistic re-creation. Proust's narrator, his "I," has returned to the Hôtel de Guermantes; he tastes again a *madeleine* such as he has eaten many years before. All at once the buried past, the *temps perdu*, lives again. Such experiences are common enough: something one has not tasted for many years, a tune one has not heard since a dance in his youth, bring back the past with miraculous power. It is as though time had been annihilated. But in the important matter of the seriousness with which they took this resurrecting power, Wordsworth and Proust were uncommon. For both of them the soul at times seemed to stand outside the flux of things and to participate for a moment in some eternity. Proust did not describe his glimpse in terms so suggestive as Wordsworth's of the traditional doctrine of the immortality of the soul. But he took the glimpse with an almost religious seriousness, for he felt that the artistic memory which recalled the past so vividly somehow presented life with a truth which no other presentation could equal.[32]

Wordsworth walked again along the shores of Esthwaite in 1787 and he crossed the Alps in 1790. His subsequent interpretations of his feelings on these occasions were written into *The Prelude* probably in 1804. The interpretations are thus somewhat late; they belong to the poet's more dualistic period, while the experiences themselves do not. Is it possible, because of their lateness, that these interpretations are entirely false to the earlier fact? That Wordsworth did not, at the time, have any feelings of the dualism between spirit and matter pervading the universe?

I would not myself concede the point. I have suggested that this dualism was always latent in Wordsworth's consciousness and in his thought; one must grant only that in the statements of 1804 it is more clearly defined, more emphatically explicit than in the earlier imaginative awareness. Wordsworth had experienced from his childhood on certain moments, "spots of time" as he called them, which held for him the deepest significance. He does not maintain that at first he understood this significance; he concedes that the "philosophical mind" comes only with the years. But the philosophical mind would not have come all at once; it would have developed, at least faintly, by the time Wordsworth was a student at Cambridge. At that time he seems to have had no clear-cut or insistent religious doubts, and he must have been conscious in a general way of the idea of the immortality of the soul. He may have wondered a little whether he believed it, and he may have decided he did. He had at the time no passionate interest in this particular question. His passion was for nature and poetry and would soon extend to politics. But various religious sentiments were found together with a love of nature in much of the eighteenth-century poetry which he was reading, and so it was altogether likely that these should all have been associated in his mind.[33]

One should note, in this connection, a distinction which Wordsworth was careful to preserve: *The Prelude*, besides these two experiences of the sublime from his university days reports others from his boyhood. In telling of these earlier moments Wordsworth never hints that he was able to put any interpretation upon them at the time, merely that they were intensely powerful, mysterious, deeply cherished.

Certain of these earlier spots of time deserve particular attention here. For they constitute exactly such sets of two moments at one place as we have found to be especially meaningful to Wordsworth.

The well-known lines "There was a Boy," incorporated into the fifth book of *The Prelude*, are a composite. The first part, purportedly about a schoolmate who mimicked owls, was apparently originally written about the poet himself. Yet the second part, telling of his feelings when he returned to visit the schoolmate's grave, is probably authentic enough, though it is less impressive poetically than the first lines, and though the dead boy may not have mimicked birds. Wordsworth speaks thus of the times when he would pause by the grave when walking along the hillside:

> *I believe, that there*
> *A long half hour together I have stood*
> *Mute, looking at the grave in which he lies!* [34]

Again, while going home for his vacation from the school at Hawkshead, Wordsworth had once waited impatiently, at a particular spot among the hills, for the horses which were to be brought from his father's home to take him and his brother on the last stage of their journey. Only a few days later his father died. Wordsworth says that he would often return to this scene of his impatience and that there his soul "would drink as at a fountain." [35]

Both these sets of moments are associated with death. So also is another moment of return some years later. As a young man he was returning from Cartmel where he had visited the grave of his old friend and teacher, William Taylor. He was crossing the same sands of the estuary of the Leven which he and a group of schoolmates had crossed years before. Suddenly he hears from another traveller of the death of Robespierre. The earlier moment comes back to him, the time when

> *a joyous Crew*
> *Of School-boys, hastening to their distant home,*
> *Along the margin of the moonlight Sea,*
> *We beat with thundering hoofs the level Sand.*
>   (X, 564–67; X, 600–603.)

Wordsworth does not analyse his feelings, but it is clear that his earlier presence at the same place makes some important contribution to the mystery of the later moment. It is though the main emotion, the joy that the Reign of Terror is over, is supplemented by a sense of the continuity of his own being, to be set over against the apparent discontinuity of Robespierre's and Taylor's.

For the time being, perhaps, these experiences themselves were of more interest than any possible interpretation, the sense of mystery than any elucidation. But the mystery could be cherished because, in their elation, the moments carried the conviction that the elucidation, whatever it was, must be an inspiriting one; it would be an occasion for hope and joy. This conviction they had carried from the start, else how could the boy, upon returning to the place among the hills, have drunk "as at a fountain"?

When some degree of elucidation finally came, when in 1804 the "sublime" moments at Esthwaite and in the Alps were finally "written up," one may say that Wordsworth's justification of the universe was substantially complete. First, at the valley of the Wye in 1798, the beauty of the scene expresses some cosmic harmony and, by doing so, has temporarily lightened "the burden of the mystery." In 1800, when Wordsworth at last comes to live in the perfect valley of his desire, true perfection is receding from the material world into the world of spirit, to "Eternity and God." Lastly, as he works on the middle books of *The Prelude* and interprets certain mysteriously vivid moments of earlier years, the poet sees in them a revelation that his own spirit transcends the limits of the material world, that it belongs to that infinity, eternity, and God to which his dream of perfection had been receding.

Of course, a somewhat transcendent Eternity had been on the

verge of consciousness all along, shadowed forth even in the valley
of the Wye in 1798, as the "quiet of the sky" brooding above
the noise and motion of time. And the distinction between his own
mind and matter had been present all along. The development was
only one of clearer awareness.

In the interest of completeness one must cite certain other occasions associated by Wordsworth with intimations of immortality.
The famous *Ode* comes close to exemplifying another of the poet's
physical returns: the reader for a moment may think that the poet
is seeing again the very same Tree and Field that he had looked upon
as a child, though when Wordsworth comes to the Pansy at his feet
it is apparent that only a similarity, not an identity, is intended.[36] The
Elegiac Stanzas, terminating with the mention of the "hope" not
without which we suffer and we mourn, also bears some resemblance
to the poems of return: Wordsworth does not actually visit again the
castle by the sea near which he had as a child spent four happy
weeks, but his stanzas are precipitated by seeing the castle again in
a picture. And finally, in the projected sequel to *The Excursion*,
Wordsworth considered having the Solitary return to his native
Scotland and there among the hills witness again such a religious
service as he had known in his childhood; this return was to succeed,
where all the arguments of *The Excursion* had failed, in restoring to
him a faith in Divine Providence and in his own immortality.

Until the difference between this world and eternity had been
accentuated in Wordsworth's consciousness, there could be no relaxation of the extraordinary tension that is present in the body of
Wordsworth's poetry throughout the years from 1797 until 1804.
(The relaxation, when it did come, probably accounts in part for
the decline in poetic power.) This tension has given rise to a curious
contradiction. There have been readers who blame the Wordsworth
of these years for looking only at the cheerful aspects of nature, for
maintaining a shallow optimism by simply refusing to look at all the
facts. Wordsworth gives some support to this criticism by his own
confessions and recantations in the *Ode to Duty* and the *Elegiac
Stanzas*. Other readers, looking at the poetry of these same years, see
stoicism and austerity as already constituting two of Wordsworth's
main characteristics. One can, in fact, read a dozen individual poems
and find Wordsworth everywhere summoning man to joy; at times
joy seems his favorite word and he himself joy's greatest celebrant.
But one may read as many other poems and find Wordsworth's mind
gripped by those facts which make joy most difficult: young women
are seduced and abandoned; mothers are deserted and abandoned;
wounded veterans wander penniless; old people, after harsh lives,

drag out an even harsher old age, their children dead, or missing, or fallen into evil ways; the child Lucy Gray is frozen to death in a snow storm; the other Lucy, Nature's child, dies at the very commencement of womanhood. Wordsworth asserts in 1798 that Nature's beauty lightens the "burden of the mystery," and he then continues to show himself as sorely pressed as ever by the burden's weight.[37]

There is no cause for unfavorable criticism in this paradox. Poets, and lyric poets especially, are not in the first instance builders of logical systems. First and foremost they record the distinctive and particular quality of the separate aspects of life. And it is often their merit, and part of the merit of all great artists, that their very freedom from system enables them to preserve an unflinching integrity. They do not have to distort the quality of one half of experience to fit it into a system based primarily upon a consideration of the other half. Great art, like experience itself, is an indispensable check upon the arrogance of system-makers. It sacrifices theoretical integrity to integrity of a more important kind. Thus, during his great creative years, Wordsworth constantly records seemingly disparate sets of experiences. Beauty gives him cause for joy, for some deeply significant joy, and to this fact he clings. At the same time, life offers painful spectacles from which he will not avert his gaze. He will not deny either his sense of a cause for joy nor his sense of life's tragedy.

The chief of all the painful spectacles which he confronts during these years is none other than death itself. Poem after poem broods upon death, or upon the very verge of death. The young die. The middle-aged and old wait for death. Time and again Wordsworth contemplates older persons after all life's vital activities, all its prospects, have come to nought; in a worldly sense, they have failed. But they have not failed because of any serious defect in themselves. They are the victims of circumstance—of that same chance, fortune, or mutability which medieval poets had written of when they exhorted us to place our hopes in eternal things (and which are also such obstacles in the way of Shelley's vision of cosmic justice).

Until Wordsworth himself emphasized eternity as distinct from time, what hope could he see for these persons? If their sufferings were unmerited, and if in waiting for death they were waiting only for extinction, what of the justice that Nature's beauty had hinted at? From the first Wordsworth was filled with admiration, even with awe, by those unfortunate older persons who awaited their end with patience. At times he can explain this patience, almost explain it away. For instance, in the fine lines titled *Animal Tranquillity and Decay*, composed in 1798, he says that the young behold with "envy" the calm with which an old man moves toward death; they are envious, presumably, because they cannot imagine themselves facing the end so quietly. Wordsworth, a little wiser than other young people, offers the explanation that Nature has mercifully dulled the old man's feelings. Doubtless Nature often does just this. But, still looking at life unflinchingly, Wordsworth had to face the fact that many such persons are not notably dulled. Upon such persons Wordsworth ponders. The traditional belief in immortality comes more to the forefront of his consciousness. It offers a solution to the "mystery" whose burden he has been carrying so long. It makes the cosmic justice which the Wye valley had imaged somehow rationally intelligible. It suggests a significance in those spots of time whose memory he had cherished.

Death poses the question of cosmic justice with especial poignancy when a man dies in the prime of life. Such early deaths inspired Milton's, Shelley's, and Tennyson's famous elegies. And it was the death of Wordsworth's favorite brother John in February, 1810, which suddenly made the cosmic question a closely personal question also. When Wordsworth wrote to his friend Beaumont on this occasion, it is interesting to note that he employed the same argument to support a belief in personal immortality as Browning was to use years later in *Saul:*

> As I have said, your last letter affected me much. A thousand times have I asked myself, as your tender sympathy led me to do, 'why was he taken away?' and I have answered the question as you have done. In fact, there is no other answer that can satisfy and lay the mind at rest. Why have we a choice and a will, and a notion of justice and injustice, enabling us to be moral agents? Why have we sympathies that make the best of us so afraid of inflicting pain and sorrow, which yet we see dealt about so lavishly by the supreme governor? Why should our notions of right and wrong towards each other, and to all sentient beings, differ so widely from what appears to be His notion and rule, if everything were to end here? Would it not be blasphemy to say that, upon the supposition of the thinking principle being destroyed by death, however inferior we may be to the great Cause and Ruler of things, we have *more of love* in our nature than He has?

One may ask why Wordsworth waited a number of years before incorporating into his structure of justification this belief in immortality. It had traditionally been found indispensable; it lay so ready to hand; in the society in which he lived it was the commonly accepted keystone in any arch of justifying arguments.

The answer involves again the matter of poetic integrity and also the long rhythms often found in human life. Until the time arrived when the belief seemed to him an active and vital truth, it would have been false to include it in a poem of vital personal experience. It is a common occurrence for young people growing up in a society which nominally acknowledges certain beliefs to ask themselves whether these beliefs are in fact true. Often these questions at the time will be asked without any deep concern, even by fundamentally serious natures. To those still on the threshold of life, some of the questions are likely to appear purely theoretical. Soon, in the course of their twenties, they are so taken up with life itself that the matter seldom rises into consciousness. But as time goes on, they may feel that belief has in fact some deep relation to life. They begin to sense not merely a theoretical need, but a practical need to hold some belief. First perhaps, as in Wordsworth's case, there will be a need to believe in some justice, some plan. As time goes on, some men may feel the necessity to posit, as the source and upholder of this plan, a Being not unlike the God of traditional religion. The need for a belief in immortality, which some may never feel at all, may in others be the longest delayed in coming pressingly to the fore. The young live much in expectation, and they still have years of life to look forward to.

By 1796, Wordsworth, the once nearly penniless and homeless orphan, had enough money to set up a frugal household with his beloved sister. By 1800 the wanderer had finally come again to the mountains and lakes of his youth. Shortly afterward he received his long-delayed share of his father's estate and was able to marry. By this time also he had composed a considerable body of poetry, and though the world did not know it, he himself knew that this poetry was great. Then a first child was born. In short, many of life's hopes and promises were already fulfilled. The sense of the ultimate inadequacy of such fulfillment, which had hovered somewhat ominously when his wish of settling at Grasmere first came true,[38] grew still stronger and more distinct. If he had, at that moment, been universally hailed by his fellow countrymen, if he had become the lion of London society, the friend and counselor of statesmen, this life might for a while longer have appeared nearly adequate in and of itself. But it would show a misunderstanding of Wordsworth's deepest nature to suppose that any amount of worldly success could for very long have kept at bay the last and most personal of the eternal questions. Such, perhaps, is the spiritual history of a number of persons, even of many who through their twenties preserve a stronger outward attachment to established religion than Wordsworth did. Presumably even for the orthodox not all the teachings of orthodoxy seem at all times perfectly real; without actually disbelieving them, they hold them in inactive reserve.

The Ennobling Interchange

AT THE END of the next to the last book of *The Prelude* Wordsworth speaks of the "balance," the "ennobling interchange" between the spirit working in nature and the spirit working within our imaginations. It might be said that beauty, as the symbol of cosmic unity, is an expression of the force which, he says, works "from without," while the sublime, the mind's awareness of the superiority to the material, is one expression of the force working "from within." *The Prelude* is a celebration of the alternating flux and reflux in the mind, of the relatively passive receptivity to external images and of a more assertive creation—both artistic and philosophical. In the proper balance of these forces, Wordsworth says, man's "spiritual dignity" originates. If the "Mind of Man" is the "main region" of Wordsworth's song, as he claims, it is the mind of man as the scene of these reciprocating actions.

An essential point which Wordsworth makes is that these two forces are not completely distinct; if they were, how could they be so fitted to each other? The passage at the close of *The Recluse*, which proclaims a sort of pre-established harmony between them, is by implication an argument from design to one supreme Power—the "supersensible substrate" which Kant inferred to lie behind the two worlds of matter and spirit. Hence one might say that the division in man's consciousness of which Wordsworth is so aware, between the inner and outer forces which there meet, is contained in a higher unity. Man's awareness, with its changing ebbs and flows, is like the Alpine gorge where all things were like

> the features
> Of the same face, blossoms upon one tree,
> Characters of the great Apocalypse,
> The types and symbols of Eternity,
> Of first and last, and midst, and without end.
> (VI, 568–72; VI, 636–40.)

In fact, the seemingly different presences and influences in this gorge were, as Wordsworth notes, like "the workings of one mind."

This underlying unity reaffirms what was suggested at the beginning of this chapter, that the beautiful and the sublime are not en-

tirely separable from each other (or from that element of the *vital*
with which they are both charged).[39] Both are moments in the growth
of a living mind, moments to which both inner and outer forces con-
tribute but in different degrees. Hence the scenes which were important to Wordsworth and his own response to them constitute a complex whole. The Vale of Esthwaite, which upon that chilly evening
intimated sublimities, must also have possessed a sober beauty. The
Vale of Grasmere, whose beauty was so lovingly recorded in *The
Recluse*, is described again in *The Prelude* in a passage which offers
a particularly fine example of that interchange of which Wordsworth
speaks: the beauty of the landscape to which Wordsworth has now
returned fills him with a vivid sense of the harmonious life or lives
pervading all things, and in this totality of living he is almost immersed; but then a resurgence from within bears witness to the special nature of his own mind and the result of the interaction of the
two awarenesses is a heightened sense of the "dignity" of man:

> *There came a time of greater dignity*
> *Which had been gradually prepar'd, and now*
> *Rush'd in as if on wings, the time in which*
> *The pulse of Being everywhere was felt,*
> *When all the several frames of things, like stars*
> *Through every magnitude distinguishable,*
> *Were half confounded in each other's blaze,*
> *One galaxy of life and joy. Then rose*
> *Man, inwardly contemplated, and present*
> *In my own being, to a loftier height,*
> *As of all visible natures crown; and first*
> *In capability of feeling what*
> *Was to be felt; in being rapt away*
> *By the divine effect of power and love,*
> *As, more than anything we know, instinct*
> *With Godhead, and by reason and by will*
> *Acknowledging dependency sublime.*
> (VIII, 624-40; VIII, 476-94.)

In the *Ode: Intimations of Immortality* both qualities are again
present and are obviously interrelated. The first sections of the poem,
written in 1802, proclaim the beauty of the external world and note
that when the poet was young this beauty had possessed for him a
dreamlike glory, a supernatural aura (even such a quality as Plato
had conceded to beautiful images). Then the later sections, composed
a few years after, suggest that the supernatural glory has not be-
longed to the external world so much as to the poet's own spirit,

freshly arrived from Eternity and as yet undimmed. In the ninth section, in fact, Wordsworth all but completely forgets nature's beauty and concentrates upon the moments of complete abstraction from physical reality which had been frequent in his childhood. And in his own note to the poem he describes how as a child he had sometimes sensed the "indomitableness of the spirit" within himself; such immediate experiences, he says, had given substance to the abstractions of traditional doctrine, and he "used to brood over the stories of Enoch and Elijah" and half persuade himself that he too would be translated to heaven. Wordsworth's note then returns, as the poem itself returns, to the seemingly supernatural beauty of external nature which, he feels, had given his soul its first intimations of its own true character.

The interrelatedness of the beautiful and the sublime is again apparent in the Snowdon scene which Wordsworth reserved for a climactic place in the last book of *The Prelude*. Only a simplified account of this passage will be offered; an examination of all its complexities would be excessively long, partly so because of the changes made between the early and later versions. In this scene Wordsworth stands above the clouds, between earth and heaven, poised like the human race between time and eternity. From below, through a rift in the clouds, mounts the roar of earth's innumerable streams and torrents. Above is the quiet vastness of space and the radiance of the moon. Yet despite the division, the whole scene is a living unity, "shaped for admiration and delight." Wordsworth is emphatic upon this point. As in the valley of the Wye and the vale of Grasmere, there is no clear-cut line of demarcation. At Wordsworth's level, the level of human consciousness, the influences from above and below, the moonlit heavens symbolizing eternity and the voices of the many waters of earth rising through the rift, interact with "interchangeable supremacy." [40]

The division between temporal and eternal does not appear the same as the division between outer and inner. Yet as Wordsworth sees it in the spectacle before his eyes it is an analogous division somehow shifted. In the first version of the passage the intermingled roar of waters, mounting through the rift and at times predominating over the middle scene, is compared to mysterious imaginative forces rising within the depths of human nature. Over against this is the outer world of infinite space; it too at times asserts a dominance at the level of human consciousness and elicits "recognitions of transcendent power."

After presenting the scene, Wordsworth then returns to a more explicit discussion of the inner and outer forces. The external Power,

he says, upon such occasions as this moment atop Snowdon, vouch-
safes to our eyes a vision of how it pervades, unifies, vivifies the
whole cosmos; this vision can be so powerful that even the

> *grossest minds must see and hear*
> *And cannot chuse but feel.*
> (XIII, 83–84; XIV, 85–86.)

Comparable to this unifying Power in the cosmos is the inner Power
of man's imagination, especially of a poet's imagination; this too can
pervade, unify, and vivify its own creations. These two forces,
Wordsworth says, are "Counterparts"—though this phrasing is toned
down in the later, more orthodox version, even as Coleridge seems
later to have crossed out in his own copy of the *Biographia* the
statement that man's primary imagination is "a repetition in the finite
mind of the eternal act of creation in the infinite I AM." (Since
Christian children are taught that men are made in the image and
likeness of God, one wonders whether Coleridge need have felt any
qualms about this celebrated passage—if he did feel them—and
whether orthodoxy really required that Wordsworth modify his
original phrasing.)

In the *Ode* Wordsworth appears to have arrived at a form of
Christian Platonism. According to this general scheme of thought,
the two forces are indeed counterparts in a sense. For the human
spirit was presumed to be a spark of, or to have been created in the
image of, the Divine Spirit. Just as the one breathed life and harmony
into the cosmos but was somehow transcendent to it, so the other
breathed life and harmony into its own body which it likewise transcended.

The Prelude has fewer affinities than the *Ode* with traditional
Christian and Platonic thought, and it expresses much more of
Wordsworth's own private character. A stubborn, stoical independence and pride were notable traits of this character. Thus *The Prelude* has something of a split personality. On the one hand, even in
the early, more spontaneous version, there are moving passages expressing gratitude to some higher power, even specifically to "God,"
and Wordsworth repeatedly creates a strong impression of the human
soul developing through the interaction of inner and outer forces
both of Divine origin. But over against these are feelings less traditionally humble and creaturely: the poem particularly admires "spirits
which are their own upholders," and in the final book the poet upon
occasions is so filled with awe at the creative spirit within himself
that the "Spirit of the Universe" is for the time being forgotten.

This second and more egotistical side of Wordsworth may understandably displease several sorts of readers, but it must be accepted as an inseparable part of the man as he was. It does not alter certain facts: that the human mind appears to be the scene of just such an interaction of inner and outer forces as Wordsworth describes, that no one has presented certain aspects of this interaction with more vividness than Wordsworth, and that no one has so eloquently re-created the sense of the miraculous which this process can sometimes inspire.

This ennobling interchange, this wedding of our mind to the "outward frame of things," as it is called in the Prospectus of *The Excursion*, is described by Wordsworth even as early as 1805 in words which suggest the orthodox definition of a sacrament: it is the means by which men "hold communion with the invisible world," by which they experience the "highest bliss" of which they are capable, the "consciousness of Whom they are," and

> *The feeling of life endless, the great thought*
> *By which we live, Infinity and God.*
> (*Prelude*, XIII, 183–84; XIV, 204–5.)

Philosophically Wordsworth's belief in the substantial reality of this interchange is of great importance. This faith is, as it were, the remedy against one of the great diseases to which the Romantics and some of the moderns have at times been prone. One scholar has said, in partial support of Professor Fairchild's position, that the Romantic mind often verges on solipsism, the belief that the mind really knows only itself and its own aspirations. Faith in original genius, the break with tradition, a fondness for solitude could all strengthen this tendency. Blake, who claimed that in his case external objects obliterated inner imaginative power, often seems to be something of a solipsist. So also is Shelley upon occasion, both in moments of despondent isolation and at times when his strongly intellectual bias inclined him towards a Berkeleian idealism without Berkeley's firm faith in a God who could serve as a warrant of the objective validity of his subjective perceptions. So also—most radically—is the poet Wallace Stevens, whom this study in due course will consider as a modern instance.

Wordsworth recognized in his own case that external objects, including beautiful ones, could temporarily obliterate his sense of the creative imagination within. But he believed that such experiences of passivity were right and proper and indispensable to the growth of the imagination itself. Not being a solipsist, he did not view the imagination as a growth entirely from within, but as a symbiotic relation between outer and inner in which first one and then the other would dominate with "interchangeable supremacy." Even in such a manner on the top of Snowdon the scene is dominated alternately by the sounds rising from within the gap in the mists, as from the subconscious, and by the external influences of the moon and the bare heavens. And even so in the landscape of the Wye the human world thrusts out into the realm of external nature in one way while in another this realm of nature penetrates even to the "very door" of the human world.

Immanuel Kant gave the term "constructive imagination" to the process by which the categories of the inner mind give form to the sense data of the outer world. But Kant's first view of the matter, in the *Critique of Pure Reason*, actually bears some resemblance to solipsism, as he himself recognizes in the *Critique of Judgment*. Then, in what he says about beauty and in his criticism of deism, he arrives at a final position a little closer to that of Wordsworth. For to Wordsworth in *The Prelude* some of the principal categories of the mind are not inherent only in the mind itself: they have developed in the mind's interchange with the outer world, partly by those very experiences when the sense of inner activity has been dominated by influxes from without: to such experiences it owes its "under-sense of the greatest" even among least things, its "feeling of the whole" amid a multitude of parts; these derive in part from "converse with the works of God," chiefly where these works strongly exhibit "simplicity and power";

> By influence habitual to the mind
> The mountain's outline and its steady form
> Give a pure grandeur and its presence shapes
> The measure and the prospect of the soul
> To majesty; such virtue have the forms
> Perennial of the ancient hills; nor less
> The changeful language of their countenances
> Give movement to the thoughts, and multitude,
> With order and relation.
>   (*Prelude*, VII, 721-29; VII, 745-61.)

This particular passage, which makes mind out to be the almost wholly passive product of landscape, is cited as expressing almost the opposite of the view of the *Critique of Pure Reason*, since in it the categories of landscape seem to give form to the mind. But actually these lines express only half of the interchange which Wordsworth speaks of. According to his complete view those harmonious and grand landscapes which so moved him are, as he says succinctly in the Tintern Abbey *Lines*, half-created and half-perceived.

Philosophy, which used to teach how to live wisely and perhaps even joyfully, has often in recent years narrowed itself down to the endless refinement of epistemology. Is it possible that *The Prelude*, besides all that it contains of philosophy in the older and fuller sense, is closer to the mysterious truth even within the domain of epistemology than is the *Critique of Pure Reason* taken by itself alone? The particular terms in which Wordsworth's own view is expressed, of Welsh Border and Lake District scenery, should not blind us to the general philosophic significance of his observations on the growth of the human mind.

iii

SHELLEY

"POETRY," SAID SHELLEY IN HIS *Defence*, "redeems from decay the visitations of the divinity in man." By these visitations he meant primarily those moments in which man's imagination affirmed that there was some Power at work in the world to assure an ultimate justice: justice to society by bringing its evils and sufferings to fruition in a millennium of love; justice to those individuals who helped create this millennium by promising that their own lives would not end in utter extinction.

In 1816, at the threshold of his mature creative years, Shelley composed the *Hymn to Intellectual Beauty*. No poem expresses more compactly so much of his political and semi-theological aspiration. In the *Hymn* Shelley tells how he has pondered mysteries of life: how can men, who have such a capacity for "love," live in a society which evidences so much "hate"? and how can men with so much "hope" so often find themselves deep in "despondency"? Shelley's imagination, like Wordsworth's, is able to "justify" the cosmos, to affirm its benevolence, by means of the inspiration received from beauty. The beauty of nature is here manifested in the spring of the year, always to Shelley the symbol of life reborn and of hope victorious over despair. No doubt the mere exuberant vitality of nature on such occasions filled Shelley, as it did Wordsworth,

72

with an immediate, uncritical joy. But the beauty of the moment, as is often the case with poets, is for Shelley a symbol of something more—in this case of some "unseen Power." The Spirit of Beauty, the emanation of this Power, touches Shelley in his despondency; "Sudden thy shadow fell on me," he exclaims. In a flash of vision he knows that men in this world will not always continue in "dark slavery," and that their graves are not in truth the "dark reality" which, without this revelation, they appear to be: in short, society will be redeemed and the spiritual principle in the individual man will survive.

The *Hymn to Intellectual Beauty*, like many of Shelley's poems, presents few circumstantial details; it is not at all in the tradition of the topographical poem. Partly for this reason some readers may find the revelatory moment less substantial than its counterparts in Wordsworth; the supernatural revelation may seem less a biographic fact and more a matter of mere poetic mode, the mode of the hymn (whether Homeric or Christian). This suspicion is confirmed by the dedication "To Mary" which introduced *The Revolt of Islam*. Here what appears to be very much the same moment is described with no theological overtones: there is no revelation as from a Divine power behind the everyday world; the hopes are principally or wholly terrestrial ones.

The old question of whether Shelley was basically a materialist or a transcendentalist still occasionally vexes criticism. The usual answer of the past is still valid: increasingly with the years his imagination sought transcendental realms.[1] With how much power to convince himself and others, each reader must judge for himself. Here in the *Hymn*, at approximately the midpoint of his career, this imagination perceives or conjures up, somewhat tentatively, both a Divine power and a triumph over death. Much can be discovered about Shelley by examining the several ways in which his poetry imaged these two suppositions.

The Unseen Power

SHELLEY DID NOT ALWAYS FEEL HIMSELF in so warm and almost personal a relation to the "unseen Power" of the universe as he did in the *Hymn to Intellectual Beauty*. If one side of his nature, particularly in his later years, looked to the Divine Love of the Platonic tradition, another side had earlier hailed a Godwinian "Necessity." Godwin had regarded his Necessity as benignant, as Shelley did also in *Queen Mab*, but this deterministic concept is so akin to the laws of physical science and to the materialist's "dialectic of history" that it can easily appear alien to human sympathy. Indeed, this inhumanness accounted for part of its appeal to Shelley, convinced as he was that the ascription of personality to Deity had filled the minds of men with the image of a Being as limited in benevolence as themselves. Thus in *Queen Mab* he had addressed Necessity in these terms:

> *all that the wide world contains*
> *Are but thy passive instruments, and thou*
> *Regard'st them all with an impartial eye*
> *Whose joy or pain thy nature cannot feel,*
> *Because thou hast not human sense,*
> *Because thou art not human mind.*
>
> (VI, 214–19.)

Interestingly enough, the cosmic Power in this same austere necessitarian form was addressed by Shelley in a poem written during the same period in which he composed the more "human" *Hymn*. But the circumstances were different. According to Mary Shelley's note, the *Hymn* was conceived during a voyage around the Lake of Geneva. The ruggedness of the higher mountains was a distant background only; the foreground presented a cheerful scene of town and village and farm set among richly cultivated hillsides. But in the poem *Mont Blanc* Shelley stands on a bridge over the rushing Arve in the primordial chaos of a high Alpine valley. The scene was less beautiful than sublime in the common sense of the word, and Shelley himself describes it by the latter term.

Mont Blanc is not an easy poem; Shelley himself says it is "undisciplined" like the scene it describes, and F. R. Leavis believes it exhibits a scattered imagination unfortunately typical of Shelley.[2] The confusion (as in Wordsworth's first version of the Snowdon passage) rises in part from the poet's attempt to read the scene as an image of the mind and also of the cosmos, and from an inability to bring the two readings together. It will be sufficient, for the moment, to explore only the second reading.

The torrent of the Arve is the cosmic force operative in our lower world as it "comes down" from its "secret throne." This lower world is a mixture of light and shade; though the wind in the pines may now and then make a "solemn harmony" and a rainbow sometimes glorifies the waterfall, these evanescent graces cannot counteract the dominant sense of chaos and destruction:

> *but a flood of ruin*
> *Is there, that from the boundaries of the sky*
> *Rolls its perpetual stream; vast pines are strewing*

Its destined path, or in the mangled soil
Branchless and shattered stand; the rocks, drawn down
From yon remotest waste, have overthrown
The limits of the dead and living world,
Never to be reclaimed. The dwelling-place
Of insects, beasts and birds, becomes its spoil,
Their food and their retreat forever gone;
So much of life and joy is lost. The race
Of man flies far in dread; his work and dwelling
Vanish, like smoke before the tempest's stream,
And their place is not known.

(ll. 107–20.)

Thus the foreground was the world as Shelley in his pessimistic moments saw it—one great march to destruction.

How can such a world be presented as benignant? Shelley's mind notes that the destructive Arve in its lower reaches becomes the "breath and blood" of distant lands, as it forever "Rolls its loud waters to the ocean waves." But this fact his eye cannot see and his imagination does not dwell upon it. Neither does he consider any process by which (as in *The Cloud*) the water may remount to its high source; such a process is not visible to his eye either, and in this poem the poet's eye is to an unusual degree fixed on the object, one might almost say "bound" to it. The imagination is caught by what the eye sees when it is raised above the "dark mountains" of the middle distance. Here is the mighty peak of Mont Blanc itself, pure white in contrast to the nearer mingling of light and shade, "still" and "serene" in contrast to the nearer noise and chaos. While all things near at hand are being riven and swept away, the mountain appears eternal: "Mont Blanc still gleams on high." The entire landscape expresses a Platonic contrast between the ever-changing Many and the unchanging One:

All things that move and breathe with toil and sound
Are born and die, revolve, subside and swell;
Power dwells apart in its tranquillity,
Remote, serene, and inaccessible.

(ll. 94–97.)

Charles H. Vivian has written understandingly of this poem and he also views the mountain as a sort of Platonic eternity symbol.[3] But in the scene before Shelley's eye there is little visible evidence of any Divine Love radiating downward from above, nor for that matter of any mortal love aspiring back toward the eternal. It is pyramidal in form, like the Platonic scheme, with a radiant summit, but there is not the right interplay between the different levels. The river that is rushing down appears an irresistible "Power" only, not a "Spirit" creating life and forming beauty. The mountain is, as the poem itself says, a symbol only of the "law" that "governs" the universe. Hence, I. J. Kapstein, against whom Professor Vivian argues, sees Mont Blanc as embodying primarily the necessitarian aspects of Shelley's thought.[4]

It is not strange that the poem should give rise to divergent critical interpretations. Professor Vivian himself concedes that the mountain does not solve the philosophical difficulties by which Shelley was perplexed, but rather speaks mysteriously of some solution toward which he is still working; the poem, as he interprets it, is confusing precisely because it expresses Shelley's thought when he is halfway between a material empiricism and a transcendental idealism. The confusion, however, must not be attributed only to Shelley's thinking, but also to the configurations of the scene itself. It does not supply a suitable "objective correlative" of the solution which Shelley craved. In some respects the sea would have furnished a more satisfactory eternity symbol than the mountain: from it come the waters that bring life and beauty to the "dull, dense" earth and to it they return. This is the great image of the cycle of life which Wordsworth uses in the River Duddon sonnets and, briefly, in the Intimations *Ode;* it is the image in which Shelley himself was later to find consolation, when he focussed not upon the sea, the eternal source, but upon the cloud, the half-temporal, half-eternal transmitter from that source. Looked at another way, Mont Blanc and the destructive river Arve may perhaps be termed the "objective correlative" of Shelley's somewhat ambiguous philosophic position in the year 1816 (this is essentially Professor Vivian's point), and if this is so, they supply us with vivid evidence of why this position proved unstable.

But even the cold, lifeless mountain offers Shelley some alleviation. It is one manifestation of human religious consciousness to worship the remote and serene just because it is remote and serene, uninvolved in man's storm and stress. Also, as Kapstein has pointed out, both Godwin and his predecessor D'Holbach had remarked the tranquilizing effect upon men's minds of viewing life under the aspect of necessity. Thus, though the remote majesty of the mountain does not visibly irradiate with light the darker parts of the ravine or perceptibly order its chaos, yet Shelley can at least say that it teaches men an "awful doubt" (a doubt perhaps invigorating rather than enervating because of the somewhat pleasurable awe involved in it), or it teaches them a

faith so mild,
So solemn, so serene, that man may be
But for such faith, with nature reconciled.

(The Boscombe manuscript reads, "In such a faith with nature reconciled." The "But for," if intended, must mean "If only for" and
not "except for.") Shelley continues:

> *Thou hast a voice, great Mountain, to repeal*
> *Large codes of fraud and woe; not understood*
> *By all, but which the wise, and great, and good,*
> *Interpret, or make felt, or deeply feel.*

(ll. 77–83.)

The poem itself tends to validate the claim of Necessity to tranquilize
and to "repeal" woe. Though *Mont Blanc* has none of Shelley's ecstatic hope, neither does it exhibit his intense despair. The ravine in
which "So much of life and joy is lost" is contemplated with an
unusual calm.

Many years ago George S. Woodberry noted that the remote,
irresistible eternity of Mont Blanc foreshadows the mysterious figure
of Demogorgon in *Prometheus Unbound*.[5] Demogorgon in his unconcern does not desire the redemption of the world but merely
permits it to be accomplished in due course by the love of Asia and
Prometheus: it is the Power; they are the Spirits. These two latter
beings, half-human, half-divine, somehow seem less primordial than
Demogorgon; they may be supposed to have emerged in the course
of a cosmic evolution.

There had been a similar distinction in popular Greek mythology
between the Fates and the Gods. Every cosmology, after all, must
offer some explanation of the refractoriness of things. Somewhat
similar distinctions are detectable in Platonism and Christianity: between the remote One and the more immediately operative Heavenly
Love, between the Father on the one hand and the Son and Holy
Ghost on the other. But these latter distinctions need not be so great
as that between Demogorgon and Asia; for they do not carry the
burden of the explanation. Platonism and Christianity ascribe the
delay in the triumph of good not to the remoteness and unfeeling-
ness of an ultimate unseen Power but to the recalcitrance observable
immediately at hand in brute matter and in the stubbornness of men
endowed with free will. Hence in Christianity love and concern may
be attributed to the Father as well as to the Son.

The general trend of Shelley's thought is a return to the main
Western traditions. In *Adonais* the transition is substantially com-

plete: there is no longer any reluctant unseen Power far removed
from the struggle to redeem the world, only the "one Spirit" whose

> *plastic stress*
> *Sweeps through the dull dense world, compelling there*
> *All new successions to the forms they wear;*
> *Torturing the unwilling dross that checks its flight*
> *To its own likeness, as each mass may bear;*
> *And bursting in its beauty and its might*
> *From trees and beasts and men into the Heaven's light.*
>
> (xliii.)

Even in *Prometheus* the change is well under way. The unconcerned Power does not dominate the poem as fully as Mont Blanc
had dominated the landscape. The focus is principally upon a warm
and vital Spirit that overcomes the inertness of things. In the middle
parts of the poem Shelley has created a triumphal march of Love and
Life that transforms the surface of the world and the hearts of men.
These well-known and sometimes very beautiful Shelleyan passages
need little comment. The basic or archetypal image is that of the
progress of Spring in nature, and this image as always spoke powerfully to the poet. But once Shelley's own Promethean imagination
has been released from the bonds of present actualities, no "given"
image supplied by the world as it is could be wholly adequate. He
must perforce create images of his own to express the intensity of his
idealism. It was not enough that the surface of the earth be transformed in the familiar manner. Brute matter must be made completely translucent or transparent; the earth is envisioned as perme-
ated by light even to its dark core. As Shelley's imagination ranges
still more widely, the cosmic triumph of Love becomes so total that
even the cold moon is quickened to life, the spheres are smitten by
love for each other, and all creation joins in a universal dance and
song. The vision which Wordsworth had tersely expressed in the
phrase "one galaxy of life and joy" is expanded by Shelley in *Prometheus* to a full-length symphony and ballet. C. S. Lewis believes that
no other passage in English poetry so nearly expresses the beatitude
of Dante's *Paradiso*.[6]

Of particular interest to an understanding of Shelley's thought
is the vision of Asia's sisters, Panthea and Ione, in which the coming
bliss is foreseen as the reunion of similar but divided forces. This
vision may furnish a most significant complication of the impression
made by some of the other passages: two forces, which had once
been united but have since become separated, the one divine perhaps and the other earthly or human, are now rushing together to

effect that transformation of the universe which is the theme of the play. The two sisters stand symbolically on an island made by two rivulets which have parted temporarily only that they may experience again the joy of reunion. They see rapidly approaching each other from opposite directions two transparent spheres. The first sphere, predominantly white though touched with azure and gold, has no name; Shelley could scarcely name it the "Spirit of Heaven" since the term "heaven" in the earlier part of the play had been identified with Jupiter's despotism. In the center of this sphere a babe, radiantly white and winged, is carried in a chariot towards the destined rendezvous. The second sphere is more multicolored, like earth itself. In this sphere another babe, the "Spirit of Earth," winged also but with wings furled, smiles in its sleep as it dreams of things to come. The latter half of the vision is described thus:

> And from the other opening in the wood
> Rushes, with loud and whirlwind harmony,
> A sphere, which is as many thousand spheres;
> Solid as crystal, yet through all its mass
> Flow, as through empty space, music and light;
> Ten thousand orbs involving and involved,
> Purple and azure, white, green and golden,
> Sphere within sphere; and every space between
> Peopled with unimaginable shapes,
> Such as ghosts dream dwell in the lampless deep;
> Yet each inter-transpicuous; and they whirl
> Over each other with a thousand motions,
> Upon a thousand sightless axles spinning,
> And with the force of self-destroying swiftness,
> Intensely, slowly, solemnly, roll on,
> Kindling with mingled sounds, and many tones,
> Intelligible words and music wild.
> With mighty whirl the multitudinous orb
> Grinds the bright brook into an azure mist
> Of elemental subtlety, like light;
> And the wild odor of the forest flowers,
> The music of the living grass and air,
> The emerald light of leaf-entangled beams,
> Round its intense yet self-conflicting speed
> Seem kneaded into one aërial mass
> Which drowns the sense. Within the orb itself,
> Pillowed upon its alabaster arms,
> Like to a child o'erwearied with sweet toil,

On its own folded wings and wavy hair
The Spirit of the Earth is laid asleep,
And you can see its little lips are moving,
Amid the changing light of their own smiles,
Like one who talks of what he loves in dream.
                                        (IV, 236–68.)

(The thought that even the unconscious parts of creation looked forward to the moment of salvation had once moved another poet, Henry Vaughan, to write one of his half-homely, half-mystical lyrics, a poem without title, prefaced only by a quotation in Latin from the Epistle to the Romans: *Etenim res creatae exerto capite observantes expectant revelationem Filiorum Dei.*)

Some of the products of Shelley's idealizing mind may be dismissed by the unsympathetic as imaginatively slack; the elopement at the end of *Epipsychidion* is thin and trite enough in a number of its details, and many readers will feel that even the latter parts of *Prometheus* might with some advantage have pulled together more tightly. But this passage describing the imminent union of the two separate spheres is in the main a genuinely original and deeply suggestive poetic creation.

There is some resemblance between the union of the two similar babes which Shelley foresees and the harmonious interplay which Wordsworth describes between those two "Counterparts," the spirit working in the universe at large and the spirit working in man. Those who are conservative in their theology will see certain dangers in Shelley's thought. But some old and deep-seated human wish or intuition is expressed in Shelley's embleming of heaven and earth reunited. The neoplatonic and mystic traditions had often interpreted with some boldness the notion that the life in the creature was cognate to that in the Creator; Christ himself had reminded the Jews that, according to their own scriptures, those to whom the word of God has come "are gods." During the Romantic period itself the post-Kantian idealists in Germany, especially Schelling, were viewing the cosmos as the product of two forces forever dividing and forever reuniting at higher levels, mind and matter, subject and object, the conscious and the unconscious.

Whether or not this passage does, in fact, complicate the main impression made by the play as a whole depends upon the impression the reader receives.

If one wishes to be favorable, one may say that the drama's final triumph of good over evil is purely ideal and not bound by any laws but those of the poet's own imagination. If one were less well disposed, he might apply to the workings of Shelley's imagination in this instance the terms which Keats, in his epistle *To J. H. Reynolds, Esq.*, once applied to the workings of his own:

is it that Imagination brought
Beyond its proper bound, yet still confin'd,—
Lost in a sort of Purgatory blind,
Cannot refer to any standard law
Of either earth or heaven?

Much of the morality of *Prometheus Unbound* is thoroughly traditional—in particular, its usual Shelleyan emphasis upon love and forgiveness, patience and hope—but the theology of the poem is uncertain and this uncertainty perhaps finds expression in the work as a whole. Is the total redemption which the play celebrates accomplished within the limits of the world of time as we know it or is it accomplished beyond these limits? Is it accomplished in considerable measure by the assistance of some ultimate Power, or does this power merely permit the redemption to be achieved in due course by human endeavor? Those without theological interests may be inclined to dismiss both questions as unreal in themselves and irrelevant to the poem. But they were not unreal to Shelley, as a reading of all his prose and poetry clearly indicates. And—what is more distinctly the point to be made here—they are not irrelevant in the terms of the poem itself.

Bennett Weaver, one of the most sensitive interpreters of the poetic text, believes that, when the redemption comes, time is finally blotted out in the white radiance of eternity.[7] There is much in the text to support this view. But Demogorgon in his final chorus-like speech, delivered when the redemption is complete, considers the possibility that the new felicity may be temporary only, that in the course of time the tyrant Destruction may once again break loose and ravage the world; once again Gentleness, Virtue, Wisdom, and Endurance may be needed to bring him under control. In other words, despite the transcendent radiance of imagery, the salvation which the poem has been praising has been chiefly that temporal and political one dreamt of by the political philosophers.

Again Weaver stresses the fact that when Asia and Panthea visit the cave of Demogorgon, though they cannot see any substantial shape betokening the presence of this mysterious power, Panthea is yet able to say, "we feel it is / A living Spirit." (II, iv, 6–7.) But is it not a singularly inactive, unoriginative spirit? And are not those right who have felt that in Demogorgon there still survives much of the character proper to the Necessity of *Queen Mab?* He seems at times as indifferent as the Fates, as immutable as the laws of the physical scientist. It is true that *Prometheus Unbound* is not precisely an atheistic poem; it is not confined entirely within the limits of a secular humanism. Asia, for example, when she apostrophizes the beautiful mountain scene which she passes on the way to Demogorgon's Cave, wonders if this scene may be "the shadow of some spirit lovelier still." When on this same journey she passes through a dark forest, we are assured, "Beams fall from high those depths upon." [8] Bennett Weaver in his interpretation of the landscape regards this light as symbolic and compares it to that which shines down upon Dante as he stands at the foot of the mountain of Purgatory. [9] But the fact that Demogorgon does not come part way to meet the sisters, that they must come all the way to him, is equally fraught with symbolic portent. Dramatically speaking there is nothing equivalent to Francis Thompson's patient, pursuing Hound of Heaven, nothing comparable to the father who hastens forth from his house to meet the prodigal son, to the Deity of religion who descends to earth in human form, seeks man out to save him despite himself. At the end Demogorgon proclaims,

> *Love, from its awful throne of patient power*
> *In the wise heart, from the last giddy hour*
> *Of dread endurance, from the slippery, steep,*
> *And narrow verge of crag-like agony, springs*
> *And folds over the world its healing wings.*

These lines, while retaining some of Shelley's special virtues, seem at the same time to take on a Miltonic massiveness; Shelley never wrote anything rhythmically more magnificent. But in the context of the poem the Love whose throne is the wise human heart does not seem to be quite the same as Milton's Spirit which preferred "Before all temples th' upright heart and pure." [10] Shelley's Love in this instance seems to be almost wholly and solely human love. For Love does not characterize Demogorgon, who is apparently the ultimate power in the poem. Prometheus and Asia are primarily symbols of intelligence and love, of patient hope and of the ideal hoped for, as these dwell in man's mind. Only Prometheus and Asia are genuinely active; it is their final conjunction that coincides with the redemption of the world. There would be nothing wrong with this plan and very much right with it, if the play had been for the most part confined within the usual human limits of the drama. But Shelley's imagination is insistently cosmic, his social fervor inevitably takes on theological tones. No one will quarrel with a conviction that social fervor and theology should be related to each other, but Shelley's imagination after its usual fashion tends to blur the two concerns together in such a way that each loses much of its own special quality. The result is some degree of artistic confusion.[11] Perhaps it was a growing awareness of this imaginative uncertainty which later caused Shelley himself to be dissatisfied with his most ambitious work.

Upon the assumption that this judgment of the drama is correct I have ventured to single out for special comment Panthea and Ione's vision of the two spheres and suggested that it complicates the general effect of the whole. In the play in general mankind seems to be moving itself from within, redeeming itself in the presence of a merely permissive Eternity; in the vision of the spheres, the Divine moves as rapidly as the human, and more consciously, towards the destined rendezvous.[12]

It would of course be wrong to give any definite doctrinal significance, of an orthodox sort, to these two spheres. The poem, for all its theological suggestions, is in the quality of its hope still too earthly and political; several more years were to elapse before, in the final section of *Adonais*, Shelley was to express an almost medieval *contemptus mundi*. Moreover, one can well imagine the poet, speaking in his capacity of sceptical philosopher, remarking that both spheres simply stand for two different aspects of human consciousness.

Yet the complication is there to be pondered. Both of the opposite but complementary ideas embodied by the two spheres are often inherent in human nature and both were inherent in Shelley. Along with the Promethean instincts, rebellious, aspiring on their own in a virtually "atheistic" universe, Shelley's imagination knew more passive, receptive moments when heaven's light rather than the light of his own aspiration was irradiating the world. As was fitting and proper, the landscapes or images expressive of these more worshipful moments were not created solely by the artistic imagination; they were in a sense "given." In their presence Shelley's aspiration was momentarily calmed; his imagination steadied; he was content, like Wordsworth, to feel the gratitude of a heart which "watches and receives."

Several times such images came to him during his years in Italy. One such occasion was the walk through the pines and by the sea which produced the poem *To Jane:* in the section titled "The Invitation" Shelley notes, "all things seem only one / In the universal sun." The word "seem" denotes some reservation. A broader and richer landscape is found in the poem with the Wordsworthian title, *Lines Written Among the Euganean Hills.* Shelley does not explicitly say that the perfection of the day prefigures an ultimate triumph of

good, but the beauty of the scene decidedly softens his contemplation of the Austrian tyranny which oppresses the cities scattered
over the plain before him. The whole landscape is rendered almost
transparent, etherealized, by the combination of sun and autumn
mist, even as in Wordsworth's Vale of Grasmere the sharp demarcation between the substantial and the unsubstantial had sometimes
been lost. The melting frost, gleaming in the sun, imparts a liquid
brightness to the ground close at hand. In the mist are "dissolved"
the "fragrance" of earth and the "light" of heaven. (Even so, when
Panthea and Ione had witnessed the approaching union of the two
crystal spheres, the "odor of the forest flowers," the "music of the
grass and air," and the "emerald light of leaf-entangling beams" had
seemed "kneaded into one aerial mass.") Here in this actual Lombard scene the mist blurs the sharp line of the horizon. To the south
it relieves the chain of Appenines of their earthy grossness, so that
they seem to float above it "dimly islanded." At an even greater distance, far to the north, the snowy peaks of the Alps rise above the
clouds, themselves almost another bank of clouds bright in the sun.
Even the blades of grass growing out of the nearby tower, "pointing" in the "windless air," seem to express some union. The "trellised lines" of the cultivated vineyards in the middle distance, "piercing" the "dark-skirted wilderness," image the same fusing of wild
and humanized nature which Wordsworth had noted along the Wye.
Shelley does not comment on all these visual fusions; he is content
to note them lightly in his rapid tetrameters. But the symbolic quality of the landscape as a whole is summed up by the lines at the end
which note how every part of the scene, including his own "darkened" spirit, is "interpenetrated" by the light, the "glory of the sky."
In this complete penetration visible to him on this actual afternoon,
Shelley has had *given* to him—or half given—an image of that same
total blending of the earthly and heavenly which, in *Prometheus Unbound*, he strives to express in imagery largely of his own creation.[13]

There is a difference between the images created and those at
least partially perceived. In the Lombard scene, despite such details
as the pointing grass, the glorious light of the sky is felt to be the
principal active force blending and etherealizing all things. In the
woodland scene in *Prometheus* the earthly and the heavenly spheres
had both been active as they rushed toward each other. In a sense,
this episode in *Prometheus* may be said to represent the middle
ground in the total spectrum of Shelley's consciousness, even as its
mode, the allegorical, represents a middle ground between the intellectual and the imaginative. Shelley at his most purely intellectual, as
the radical child the Enlightenment, speaks as though the evils of

earth will be redeemed entirely by earthly and human forces, there being presumably no other forces which could redeem them. But at the other extreme, on this day among the Euganean hills, when he is being highly imaginative and almost religious in his receptivity, some divine glory, some radiance outside and above his own darkened mind, is effecting the redemption.

Here is the passage in question:

Noon descends around me now.
'Tis the noon of autumn's glow,
When a soft and purple mist,
Like a vaporous amethyst,
Or an air-dissolved star
Mingling light and fragrance, far
From the curved horizon's bound
To the point of heaven's profound
Fills the overflowing sky.
And the plains that silent lie
Underneath; the leaves unsodden
Where the infant frost has trodden
With his morning-wingèd feet,
Whose bright print is gleaming yet;
And the red and golden vines,
Piercing with their trellised lines
The rough, dark-skirted wilderness;
The dun and bladed grass no less,
Pointing from this hoary tower
In the windless air; the flower
Glimmering at my feet; the line
Of the olive-sandalled Apennine
In the south dimly islanded;
And the Alps, whose snows are spread
High between the clouds and sun;
And the living things each one;
And my spirit, which so long
Darkened this swift stream of song—
Interpenetrated lie
By the glory of the sky.

(ll. 285–314.)

In this poem, which with copious amplitude describes the rise, the zenith, and the decline of a natural sun over a natural scene, Shelley seems for the moment to have captured the mood which Keats so desired and so seldom found, the mood "Rich in the simple worship of a day." Nor is evil escaped from as in *To Jane*, but comprehended within a larger scheme: The broad panorama includes in its total glory the oppressed cities which Shelley sees. For the moment Shelley's imagination seems satisfied; he appears to be accepting the day and the scene as a grace. In his *Defence* Shelley says that poetry is "the interpenetration of a divine nature through our own," and here on a day among the Italian hills he has witnessed as it were the poetry of the cosmos itself—not just his own efforts to reproduce, or produce, that poetry. (So the city of London, so potent a symbol to Wordsworth of man's need for some redemption, had been visually redeemed and "justified" early one morning as he beheld it from Westminster bridge penetrated by the river, its own "towers" penetrating the sky, and its outskirts intermingling with the suburban fields.) But in Shelley's mind arises the epistemological question which is likely to disturb any poet who combines with his imagination a strongly critical intellect: in the very next lines Shelley says that he does not know whether the unity which he perceives is the product of the "soul of all" or of his own mind. For the immediate present this uncertainty has little effect upon the poem itself, but in Shelley's life taken as a whole the effect was great.

The question itself, of course, is the same as the one which Wordsworth answered by saying that the unity was half-created, half-perceived in the "ennobling interchange" between man and nature.

Immortality

SHELLEY CONTEMPLATED DEATH even more continually than did Wordsworth. As students of his poetry have observed, the subject had for him an almost obsessive fascination. Shelley may denounce death as the one unanswerable outrage to all man's loftiest aspirations, or he may hail it as the glorious moment when man's questing spirit, finally released from material bonds, discovers the Truth behind the mysteries. These opposite views and other intermediate ones change with the mood of the moment. But underlying the short-term fluctuations is a slower, more permanent change of emphasis.[14]

In an early letter to Elizabeth Hitchener, Shelley tells how he had confided to Southey his speculations that the universe was no more than the sum total of animation ever evolving toward some higher state; since he supposed that this evolution might be infinite, he could at this time envision no terminal goal and suggested that this might be an argument against a transcendent God distinct from the sum total of intelligence.[15] The accompanying notion of immortality, the idea that spirit in general is eternal rather than spirits as individuals, accords with one part of the poet's own nature; in some respects Shelley was a singularly unselfish man dedicated not to his own individual triumph but to the triumph of certain general principles. Something of this early impersonality tends to persist in Shelley's thought till the end, along with the "atheistic" pantheism which he sees as its logical counterpart. Both the denial of individual survival and the pantheism are highly unorthodox; yet it should be noted that the imagery in which Shelley expresses these ideas sometimes has distinctly orthodox affinities: the seed must die if the new plant is to germinate; the cloud must be dispersed if the earth is to be watered and a new cloud born; in *The Revolt of Islam* truth has its martyrs. In somewhat similar fashion orthodoxy affirms that it was expedient that one man die that many might live and that he who loses his life shall find it. T. S. Eliot has recently noted, presumably with approval, the marked persistence of such attitudes in Shelley.[16] C. S. Lewis, perhaps partly for this reason, has declared that Shelley's sensibility was far more Christian than that of his fellow Romantic radical, William Blake.[17]

But even in his early days, supposedly under the sway of materialism and pantheism, Shelley falls into the common human habit of assuming that individuality itself survives in one mode or another. In another letter to Miss Hitchener, Shelley makes implicitly the assumption which Browning makes explicitly: that in each incarnation, whether in a flower or in a man, the individual particle of the spiritual principle will develop its own particular potentialities, potentialities for which a properly economical universe will necessarily find a subsequent use; Shelley then repeats the age-old speculation that men may be reincarnated in such new forms as they have fitted themselves to animate.[18] Shelley, the young radical, in his preoccupation with cosmic justice, is making use of some venerable metaphysical assumptions.

Equally early Shelley expresses his yearning for an ultimate transcendence of matter, an escape from an endless succession of reincarnations. Even in *Queen Mab*, where he is describing a semi-earthly millennium, Shelley can remark, "The chains of earth's immurement / Fell from Ianthe's spirit." (I, 188–89.) And in *Prometheus Unbound* Shelley sees men, even after the millennium has arrived, as

> *Not yet exempt, though ruling them like slaves,*
> *From chance, death, and mutability,*
> *The clogs of that which else might oversoar*

> *The loftiest star of unascended heaven,*
> *Pinnacled dim in the intense inane.*
>
> (III, iv, 200–04.)

The reader infers that an ultimate liberation from matter is to be expected—though the last line, so typically Shelleyan, might well persuade one to cling to one's earthly clogs.

For all Shelley's impersonal and unselfish devotion to general ideals, the thought of final justice for the individual, a final individual satisfaction, keeps coming back throughout his life; something very like traditional notions of immortality inevitably recur. In his last years Shelley read a passage in which Wordsworth expresses the feelings of a young revolutionary liberal:

> *this earth*
> *Which is the world of all of us, and where*
> *We find our happiness or not at all.*

Shelley's sensitivity was so outraged that in a letter to John Gisborne he described these lines as nothing less than "demoniacal." [19] If the universe is not to be accepted as devilish, apparently we must posit something very like the traditional notion of personal immortality.

But the purpose of this study is not chiefly to discuss Shelley's theology in the abstract but to examine how his theologically-oriented imagination expresses itself in his poetry. So relentless is Shelley's preoccupation with the mystery of death, that several score passages might here be closely scrutinized. It will be the better part of valor to look only at *Alastor* and *Adonais*.

A first reading of *Alastor* leaves one with a sense of unrelieved blackness. The long passage at the close, one of Shelley's most powerful utterances, expresses the intensest anguish that a pure poetic spirit has been extinguished. So terrible is the thought of such extinction that even the blighted earthly immortality of the Wandering Jew appears preferable:

> *Oh, for Medea's wondrous alchemy,*
> *Which whereso'er it fell made the earth gleam*
> *With bright flowers, and the wintry boughs exhale*
> *From vernal blooms fresh fragrance! Oh, that God,*
> *Profuse of poisons, would concede the chalice*
> *Which but one living man has drained, who now,*
> *Vessel of deathless wrath, a slave that feels*
> *No proud exemption in the blighting curse*
> *He bears, over the world wanders forever,*
> *Lone as incarnate death! Oh, that the dream*
> *Of dark magician in his visioned cave,*

Raking the cinders of a crucible
For life and power, even when his feeble hand
Shakes in its last decay, were the true law
Of this so lovely world! But thou art fled,
Like some frail exhalation, which the dawn
Robes in its golden beams,—ah! thou hast fled!
The brave, the gentle and the beautiful,
The child of grace and genius. Heartless things
Are done and said i'the world, and many worms
And beasts and men live on, and mighty Earth
From sea and mountain, city and wilderness,
In vesper low or joyous orison,
Lifts still its solemn voice: —but thou art fled—
Thou canst no longer know or love the shapes
Of this phantasmal scene, who have to thee
Been purest ministers, who are, alas!
Now thou art not! Upon those pallid lips
So sweet even in their silence, on those eyes
That image sleep in death, upon that form
Yet safe from the worm's outrage, let no tear
Be shed—not even in thought. Nor, when those hues
Are gone, and those divinest lineaments,
Worn by the senseless wind, shall live alone
In the frail pauses of this simple strain,
Let not high verse, mourning the memory
Of that which is no more, or painting's woe
Or sculpture, speak in feeble imagery
Their own cold powers. Art and eloquence,
And all the shows o'the world, are frail and vain
To weep a loss that turns their lights to shade.
It is a woe "too deep for tears," when all
Is reft at once, when some surpassing Spirit,
Whose light adorned the world around it, leaves
Those who remain behind, not sobs or groans,
The passionate tumult of a clinging hope;
But pale despair and cold tranquillity,
Nature's vast frame, the web of human things,
Birth and the grave, that are not as they were.

(ll. 672–720.)

The total desolation of these lines is especially notable in a poet whose life itself, as one critic has noted, was a pursuit of death.[20] Mary Shelley's note to *Alastor* recalls that a few months before composing the poem Shelley had been told by a physician that he was dying of consumption. Though his health had suddenly improved, *Alastor* was written in the shadow of this doom; this circumstance must have contributed to the personal intensity of this great closing outburst.

In view of the despair of this final passage, what is to be made of Mary's other remark that in *Alastor* the death which Shelley had frequently been contemplating is represented "in such colors as had, in his lonely musings, soothed his soul to peace"? First, as W. H. Hildebrand has truly pointed out, the final lines are in a sense dramatic, the imagined expression of the grief of this world from which one particular poetic spirit has departed.[21] Furthermore, the lines are generally allegorical: somewhat like Wordsworth in his *Ode*, Shelley is contemplating a condition of life from which the prophetic power of the Romantic imagination has departed; he is concluding that "there hath passed away a glory from the earth." Even in the more optimistic *Hymn to Intellectual Beauty* Shelley had stressed the fleetingness and infrequency of those flashes of imaginative light which alone brought hope to our darkness. Apparently the dead hero of *Alastor* had afforded the world such flashes. So long as he lived the weight of the unintelligible world had been less oppressive; "nature's vast frame," "the web of human things," "Birth and the grave," which since his death have again grown black, had momentarily been brighter. He had known those "visitations of the divinity in man" which Shelley later speaks of in his *Defence;* but though a gifted spirit, he had presumably composed no poetry which would "redeem from Decay" these visitings. Hence the total darkness in which his death leaves the world.

In contrast to the gloom which the visionless world sees, what had the hero's own poetic spirit seen in death? His own views are imaged by the last stream whose course he pursues and the final landscape which his eyes behold. This stream, in its unknown source and its mingled light and shade, the hero sees as a type of his own life; he adds that he can as well tell what will become of his thoughts after death as the ocean or the air can tell what will happen to the stream's waters. Just before the end the stream emerges from a forest's checkered canopy to flow under a "uniform and lightsome evening sky." This sky retains its light even as the waters flow into a black and rocky gorge expressing the approach of death. At the end of the gorge the whole landscape suddenly drops away; over the precipice the stream

> *Fell into that immeasurable void,*
> *Scattering its waters to the passing winds.*
>   (ll. 569–70.)

In a quiet windless nook at the edge of this abyss the hero dies. The waters of his spirit (like the atoms of his body) are diffused rather than extinguished.

But this abyss is not the edge of the world. Beyond and beneath the poet-hero beholds an immense landscape:

> wide expand
> *Beneath the wan stars and descending moon*
> *Islanded seas, blue mountains, mighty streams,*
> *Dim tracts and vast, robed in the lustrous gloom*
> *Of leaden-colored even, and fiery hills*
> *Mingling their flames with twilight, on the verge*
> *Of the remote horizon.*
>
> (ll. 553–59.)

Though in this instance nothing whatever of individuality survives the plunge over the ledge, the waters of the spirit from this and other streams appear ultimately to recombine; new incarnations of the life principle, still within the material frame of things, may be traced through a new landscape; this new scene may be more spacious than the old, but it still resembles the old in its combined lustre and gloom. The whole evening landscape in its uncertain light recalls precisely those poetic imaginations which Shelley was later to attribute to Keats:

> *Splendors, and Glooms, and glimmering Incarnations,*
> *Of hopes and fears, and twilight Phantasies.*
>
> (*Adonais*, xiii.)

This Purgatorial chiaroscuro makes these lines an interesting contrast to two notable poems by other poets on the same theme. These two poems contemplate separately the two images which Shelley combines, the waterfall and the evening sky. Henry Vaughan's *The Water-fall* is pervaded by the cheerful homely light of day. His stream falls over a smaller cliff; it emerges from the turmoil at the bottom to continue its own course "more bright and brave." Christianity and a touch of Platonism then combine with Vaughan's knowledge of the meteorological cycle: Vaughan is assured that the stream is returning to the "sea of light" whence it came. By carefully contemplating the image before his eyes and then in imagination going a little beyond, Vaughan has found what was for him a satisfying emblem. He has not pushed his analogy so far that his orthodoxy is disconcerted: he does not note that a stream loses all individuality once it enters the ocean, nor that some of its waters will be reabsorbed into the atmosphere and thus commence their cycle all over again. The other poem is by Wordsworth. The sunset towards which Wordsworth is walking in *Stepping Westward* strikes him as a "heavenly destiny." It is far more ethereal than Shelley's landscape: though behind Wordsworth is the gloom of life, ahead of him appears nothing but boundless radiance. Vaughan's and Wordsworth's poems, both brighter than Shelley's passage, likewise are both closer to the real world, less the products of pure fantasy. The waterfall is just such a one as Vaughan must have paused beside on his walks amid the Welsh hills; the sunset was an actual one which William and Dorothy walked toward one evening on their tour of the Highlands. Yet both poems, founded in external fact, are instinct with mystery and awe.

Shelley's climactic poem on the subject of death is *Adonais*. In it his imagination makes its supreme attempt to throw off the last shackles of mortality, to pass beyond those material bounds of time and space which in *Alastor* still hem it in. Since Earl R. Wasserman's lengthy article upon this poem, it is impossible to write upon it without duplicating something of what is there said about the logic of its imagery and the "progressive revelation" of its method.[22]

The first part of *Adonais* is the traditional lament that Keats is dead, that he will not wake; the second part is the almost equally traditional proclaiming that "He lives, he wakes—'tis Death is dead, not he." In the earthbound first part the presiding powers are Urania and Death. Urania, though a spirit of love, beauty, and imagination, is unable to counteract the power of Death. Her spiritual son Keats, had been able to brighten life only by "glimmering . . . Fantasies," like the glimmering landscape which the hero of *Alastor* beheld beyond the precipice, and now that he is gone Urania's world is as dark as the world was at the end of that same poem when it had been deprived of the hero's "surpassing spirit." Urania cries,

> *"Leave me not wild and drear and comfortless,*
> *As silent lightening leaves the starless night!"*
>
> (xxv.)

Urania laments that she cannot follow Keats because she herself is "chained to time"; she envisions him as sunk in a timeless sleep because without his poetic imagination her own spirit's sky is overcast, "starless."

Yet this first part of the poem uses the words "eternal" and "immortal" as readily as the latter part; in conjunction with them it employs an imagery not unlike the ethereal light and star of the later stanzas. It is part of the "progressive" movement of the poem's revelation that initially these terms and images are still bound to earth; at most they can be regarded as no more than prefiguring the more transcendental meaning which they will later bear. The "firmament" in which the dead poets shine in these first stanzas, their "serene abode" is no more than the worldly fame which Browning was to describe ironically in *Earth's Immortalities*. The thought of fame brings the mourners little comfort—as it brought little comfort to Browning's Saul. Even Shelley's elected symbol of hope, the beauty of the spring, offers no encouragement; Grief, noting that all nature is reborn, asks,

> Shall that alone which knows
> Be as a sword consumed before the sheath
> By sightless lightning?

and the only answer is,

> th' intense atom glows
> A moment, then is quenched in a most cold repose.
> (xx.)

How does Shelley push beyond this earthbound sphere? The crucial stanza in which the poem first begins to soar shows that the immediate impulse is a moral one. Shelley's sense of justice demands an eternity which will right the wrongs of time; different fates must be meted out to the lofty spirit of Keats and to the low-thoughted critic who had supposedly slain him. The critic is addressed in these words:

> Thou canst not soar where he is sitting now.—
> Dust to the dust! but the pure spirit shall flow
> Back to the burning fountain whence it came,
> A portion of the Eternal, which must glow
> Though time and change, unquenchably the same,
> Whilst thy cold embers choke the sordid hearth of shame.
> (xxxviii.) [23]

To image the beauty of the home to which Keats' spirit has returned no earthly beauty is wholly adequate:

> Rome's azure sky,
> Flowers, ruins, statues, music, words, are weak.
> The glory they transfuse with fitting truth to speak.
> (lii.)

As Kant had noted, no material appearance can properly image to the soul its own immateriality. Thus if any image dominates the last stanzas it cannot be an image supplied by the material world but by the mind itself. It is in a sense not an image at all; it is the One of Platonic theory which "remains" while the many "change and pass," a pure Eternity whose noblest earthly manifestation is, by contrast, stained. It is, in short, a mental construct. Peripheral or subsidiary to this central construct, seeking to express the relation between it and the universe, are images of more material substance: a burning fountain, a dome of glass, a star. But essentially the One transcends them all. This transcendence is expressed by two latent or half-developed images: the One transcends the many even more completely than the sun transcends those obscuring clouds of our mortality which it will one day burn through; it transcends them even more completely than the sphere of fixed stars in the Platonic-Ptolemaic tradition transcends the lower spheres of those bodies in our planetary system which are ever moving and changing. It is right that these latter images should not be fully developed, for at the climactic moment they have lost all substantiality. As Shelley's own spirit, in the last stanza, fearfully sails its bark out into the unknown, his body's eye beholds nothing: no rift in the clouds, no sun, no star; but the eye of the mind sees even the last veil of the "sphered skies" rent, and beyond all, like a star beyond all stars, the "soul of Adonais" beacons.

The fact that Shelley, like Wordsworth, reconstructed something roughly approximate to the traditional doctrine of immortality, should not obscure the great difference between the two poets. Wordsworth's conscious mind later interpreted earlier visionary moments as being most fully explicable in the light of traditional assumptions, and these early occasions in at least two ways gave Wordsworth's total experience a solidity which Shelley's never had. Wordsworth's most vivid moments, even those in which the mind seemed aware primarily of its own immaterial nature, were so rooted in external circumstance that the intuition they embodied appeared warranted by some reality other than the poet's own mind. Again, many of these moments had occurred years before Wordsworth was deeply engaged in seeking theological answers to life's mysteries; therefore the answer was in a sense given before it was sought and the poet had less occasion to fear that it was merely a case of wishful thinking. But at the end of *Adonais* Shelley is not interpreting a given vision; he is as it were pushing himself to vision. This pushing from within is clearly expressed in the poem itself:

> *Oh, come forth*
> *Fond wretch! and know thyself and him aright.*
> *Clasp with thy panting soul the pendulous Earth;*

As from a centre, dart thy spirit's light
Beyond all worlds, until its spacious might
Satiate the void circumference.

(xlvii.)

Such lines, of course, are made to order to support the criticism that Romantic religion is no more than the worshiping of one's own powers of aspiration. Presumably even for the orthodox the idea of God is in a sense a hypothesis, but it does not ordinarily seem so desperate and tenuous a hypothesis as does Shelley's One when his consciousness is pushing out "Far in the Unapparent." Yet for the very reason that Shelley's faith in the traditional sense is weak, his desire appears the stronger. Herein lies the individual character of his poetry, its distinctive quality. With nothing but his own aspiration and the Platonic hypothesis to rely on, he dare not in fully serious moments relax. The individual Spenserian stanza in Spenser's hands had tended to be static and self-contained, but here in *Adonais* Shelley's imagination is working at such intensity that a score of Spenserian stanzas combine into one great surge. A scattering of earlier images are pulled together, transfigured, and fused into one vision. It is as though hope can triumph over despair only if desire and will keep the mind incandescent. The result is a burst of poetry in which the underlying tension is far greater, or at least far nearer the surface than is usual in Wordsworth.[24]

Even Shelley could not sustain such tension through his day-to-day life. In his poetry a black despair and a flaming hope rise from time to time as from the subconscious to grapple in mortal combat for the dominion of the world, like his two allegorical figures in the opening vision of *The Revolt of Islam*. In the intervals of this recurrent struggle, Shelley the poet could relax, sometimes too much, in dreaming paradisal dreams. And Shelley the man living in the world, conversing and writing letters, could compromise on a middle-of-the-road philosophy which a man of the world would not find strange. In politics, Shelley's letters and prose reveal him at times as a moderate and sensible meliorist. And in theology he could arrive at a mildly optimistic scepticism: he could say, for instance, that as regards the solution of life's mysteries which man might discover in death he had "no fears and some hope." [25] The letters also show how much of the early opposition to religion as an organized whole still survives, even when the poetry in its imaginative sympathies approaches Christian theology at a number of points. In Shelley's case the letters and the prose are particularly necessary to a balanced view; the poetry alone, wavering as it does between the extremes of slackness and of an almost inhuman intensity, supplies a very incomplete picture.

The Personal Image

IN THE PREFACE to *The Cenci* Shelley wrote, "Imagination is as the immortal God which should assume flesh for the redemption of mortal passion." It may be ironic, it is certainly understandable psychologically, that the Romantic poet who most insistently rejected the anthropomorphic deity of tradition should most frequently imagine his own lofty ideal embodied in the persons of fellow mortals, usually women.

According to Ellsworth Barnard, Shelley may be said to believe in a personal deity because he ascribes goodness and love to his supreme power.[26] Such an ascription of desirable attributes to an abstraction, however, cannot quite fill the loneliness of Shelley's cosmos. This loneliness had traditionally been filled by the concrete images of Father, Lord, King, and Shepherd, which helped to give substance to the notion of an emotional link between Creator and creature. Shelley, feeling as he did about parental and regal tyranny, could not easily find satisfaction in most of these terms. But his difficulty was the effect also of wider causes which this study has touched on earlier. Behind him lay the whole tendency of rational deism to suppress the imaginative, and the tendency of eighteenth-century diction to favor abstract words. This depersonalizing of the universe had gone farthest among the educated and the scientifically minded, men who in the course of their lives were less likely to be awed by men in superior positions, and more likely to be impressed by the impersonal principles which their intellects discovered to be operative in the universe. Of this phase of the Enlightenment Shelley on one side of his nature was very much the heir.

Doubtless many men have found themselves supported by beliefs generally religious in nature but disassociated from ideas of a personal deity. Wordsworth—who had early struck Coleridge as being practically an atheist—was such a man. Even as Wordsworth outwardly moves towards Christianity, the inner man in many ways remains a Stoic. Shelley, however, even from his childhood had displayed a stronger than average craving for human sympathy. He may even be viewed as a successor of the eighteenth-century sentimental tradition of intense personal attachments. Such attachments, usually colored by his need to personify his ideals, his imagination generated at Horsham, at Eton, at Oxford, and evermore thereafter. If one can imagine the unlikely possibility of Shelley's being fully within the fold of traditional Christianity, he appears as a man to whom the doctrine of Incarnation would have been especially meaningful.

Again and again, as the poetry and the life reveal, a fellow human being could (very temporarily) help to solve Shelley's basic problem, to convince him of the reality of the ideal. Shelley and the Shelleyan heroes are lonely beings. Like Laon in *The Revolt of Islam* they have formed the loftiest notions from the beauty of nature, the writings of the poets, the marbles of antiquity. But the very loftiness of the ideal increases their alienation from men as a whole; few men seem either to embody the ideal or to aspire to it. Then Shelley or his hero encounters the friend, the beloved. At the humblest level mere physical beauty is a revelation: the "breathing marble" of the sleeping Ianthe's "glowing limbs" in *Queen Mab* images the ideal of mind or spirit utterly pervading and vitalizing matter; it helps the lover who gazes upon it to envisage the millennium when love will have thoroughly pervaded man's social order and his natural environment. Beyond this the beloved will have a more than physical beauty, a radiancy of total being such as is ascribed to Cythna:

> She moved upon this earth a shape of brightness,
> A power, that from its objects scarcely drew
> One impulse of her being—in her lightness
> Most like some radiant cloud of morning dew
> Which wanders through the waste air's pathless blue
> To nourish some far desert; she did seem
> Beside me, gathering beauty as she grew,
> Like the bright shade of some immortal dream
> Which walks, when tempest sleeps, the wave of life's
> > dark stream.
> > > (II, xxiii.)

The immediate effect is to illuminate with a stronger and steadier light the poet's own glimmering aspirations:

> As mine own shadow was this child to me,
> A second self, far dearer and more fair,
> Which clothed in undissolving radiancy
> All those steep paths which languor and despair
> Of human things had made so dark and bare,
> But which I trod alone.
> > (II, xxiv.)

The beloved's radiance is most effective not when dissipated impartially in all directions but when focussed on the hero; the poet hero is warmed by the beloved's sympathy for himself personally and for his lonely hopes and fears which are unheeded by the world.

In his *Defence* Shelley states that our human weakness is that we lack the creative faculty "to imagine that which we know"—in other words, we cannot give substance and reality to our dimly apprehended ideals. To this spiritual weakness the beloved brings strength precisely because she is a "realization" of these ideals; she arouses our latent knowledge to action. Harriet and Mary, according to the poet's own prologues, give Shelley the power to depict the millennium in poetry; [27] Cythna's union with Laon, Asia's unity with Prometheus, transform the world.

But the illusion of total perfection and sympathy which Shelley craved in the beloved cannot last. Poetic creativity, which the illusion stimulates, will subside; Laon and Cythna's revolution proves abortive; even the cosmic transformation wrought by Prometheus and Asia may, as Demogorgon's final speech concedes, prove only temporary: the serpent of tyranny may once more be loosed upon the world and have to be caught once more and confined to the pit.

Shelley himself was finally to confess in a letter to John Gisborne: "I think one is always in love with something or other; the error, and I confess it is not easy for spirits cased in flesh and blood to avoid it, consists in seeking in a mortal image the likeness of what perhaps is eternal." [28]

Here again, as in his statement that imagination is "as the immortal God which should assume flesh for the redemption of mortal passion," [29] Shelley is thinking, as of the boon most greatly to be desired, of precisely some such embodiment of the Divine in the human as Christianity has always claimed as its central mystery. Yet he cannot give serious consideration to the claims of this mystery. Rather it must be such incarnations as his own poetic imagination can create which must be relied on to effect mankind's redemption. One sometimes wonders, however, whether the same influences which had cut him off from so imaginative a religion as Christianity had not also weakened the imaginative power of much of his own poetic creation. Imagination, by his own definition, imparts flesh and blood and of this flesh and blood many readers have always felt his poetry has too little. Imagination is perhaps also the faculty by which we are sharply aware of the existence of personality or personalities other than our own, and here again Shelley's poetic world, when compared with Chaucer's or Shakespeare's or even Wordsworth's, sometimes seems as depersonalized as the cosmos of his philosophy. Professor Barnard defends Shelley's tendency to view both Deity and immortality in impersonal terms, pointing out that for Shelley

the notion of personality was inseparable from the notion of limitation. Shelley's insistent effort to transcend such limitation, which is
not without counterpart in the more mystical traditions of religion,
is perhaps related to his deep response to the scene among the Euganean Hills: here, as much as in some of Wordsworth's scenes, was
expressed the sense of the "infinite," the breaking down of sharp
internal barriers, as each part of the landscape appeared to fuse with
others and all with the whole. At the end of *Adonais*, however,
Shelley's imagination does not conjure up a vision of Keats's spirit
losing its identity in a sea of light: whether impelled by the inherent
logic of his imagery or by some other reason, he imagines him only
as another bright star taking its place among the galaxies.

The Treacherous Likeness

IN THE LAST THREE LINES of *Mont Blanc*, after having been all but
overpowered by the majesty of the mountain, Shelley's mind recoils
(as Kant had said the mind must recoil) from abasing itself before
mere material size and power. Shelley addresses the mountain in these
words:

> *And what were thou, and earth, and stars, and sea,*
> *If to the human mind's imaginings*
> *Silence and solitude were vacancy?*

But these lines imply a little more than the superiority of mind to
matter; in a Shelleyan modification of Berkeley's idealism, they seem
to question whether the material world has any objective reality independent of the human mind. This is Berkeleianism without Berkeley's mind of God.[30]

Here is one of the roots of Shelley's dilemma. Despite the essentially worshipful bent of imagination which Shelley could display
towards the one "white radiance" and towards the various feminine
semi-deities which embody this radiance and preside in his poetry,
he repeatedly found himself face to face once more with the loneliness of his own cosmos, his own "atheism." In his *Defence* Shelley
exclaims, "What were virtue, love, patriotism, friendship; what were
our consolations on this side of the grave, and what were our aspirations beyond it,—if poetry [i.e., man's imagination] did not ascend
to bring light and fire from those eternal regions where the owl-
winged faculty of calculation dare not even soar?" Shelley laments
that as a result of recent developments in the intellectual world poets
have been challenged to resign their crowns to "reasoners and mech-

anists." Now the reasoners and mechanists of the Enlightenment had
been active in philosophy and psychology as well as in the physical
sciences. For a century or more British and continental writers had
been studying what may be termed the naturalistic origin of man's
more fully developed ideas. There is always some danger that what
has been explained may appear to have been explained away. Part
of Wordsworth's peculiar strength, during his greatest period, was
that he could so well digest the psychology of the day; he could
record the natural occasions of his imaginings and yet feel that these
imaginings were miraculous still. But the difficulty in digesting the
age's psychological observations was great. It reduced Hume to complete scepticism. Kant thought he had solved the problem once for
all, but perhaps the thinkers of each age must solve it for themselves.
Shelley may even have thought he had conquered the difficulty. But
there are indications that he had not. The result of a century's attention to the relation of the mind to the external world, and of the
mind's more advanced ideas to its more primitive impulses, was in
Shelley a kind of scepticism. He could not see a mountain as something beautiful in itself. He could not even accept a woman as beautiful and good in herself. So aware was he of the mind's power to
see what it wants to see that Laon acclaims Cythna as his "own
shadow" and his "second self"; and in *Epipsychidion* Emily has no
reality independent of Shelley's own mind and is termed "a shadow
of some golden dream" and a "soul of my soul." Similarly a century
of critical rationalism had marked indelibly upon Shelley's mind the
fact that mankind had in a sense created God in its own unworthy
image; thus when Shelley's imagination sought "to ascend" and bring
light and fire from the eternal regions, he can never escape the realization that this light and fire may exist only in man's own desire.
Hence the special poignancy of the moment when the hero of
Alastor, shortly before his death, looks into the dark depths of a
still fountain: in this mysterious region as in the world beyond death
he beholds no light except the reflection of his own eyes,

> *as the human heart*
> *Gazing in dreams over the gloomy grave,*
> *Sees its own treacherous likeness there.*
>
> (ll. 472–74.)

In other words, if he were to plunge through the film that separates
life from death, the light which he thought he detected on the other
side might prove to have been only an illusion. No lines in all of
Shelley are a more moving commentary upon the philosophical uncertainty of his idealism.[31]

If man is to vivify the ideal by the help of the imagination, he will presumably do so with more assurance if he regards the materials with which the imagination builds—the majestic mountain or the radiant woman—as objectively real. To Bishop Berkeley the material world was the language of God; God was the warrant of its existence and of its value independent of the human mind. Shelley was inclined at times to see the world only as the language of the human mind. In such a case, a man who listens for voices can never hear more than an echo of his own voice; his worship may be a form of spiritual solipsism. The problem of solipsism, lurking everywhere among the Romantics, is in Shelley especially acute. The strong sense always persists that the "circumference" toward which the spirit pushes is indeed "void." [32]

Shelley's dilemma must not of course be viewed simply as a result of his philosophical background. Some inner quality in his own personality made it difficult for him to see people as they were when his deepest emotional needs were involved. His immediate impulse was to idealize a woman to the point where her image bore little resemblance to the flesh and blood creature whom the world knew. This impulse found exaggerated expression in his poetry, partly because of his theory that poetry in its proper nature should be "ideal" in his own extreme sense of the word. He usually did not find it possible to idealize objects, or more especially persons, while looking at them clearly and steadily. Wordsworth, with that total "collectedness" of imagination which F. R. Leavis admires,[33] could see his wife as at once a creature of earth with all earth's duties and tasks, and yet

> A Spirit still, and bright
> With something of angelic light.

Shelley's skylark, as has often been noted, simply soars, while Wordsworth's, remembering its nest in the very midst of its soaring, remains "True to the kindred points of Heaven and Home!" Wordsworth's ability to hold fast to external reality, to receive as well as create, gives his work its greater assurance and solidity.

Within the political and humanist sphere Shelley's almost purely creative imagination has an important, if limited, validity. It may be currently fashionable to maintain the contrary, but time has proved that Shelley and his fellow radicals were often correct prophets. Though the solving of old problems may have brought new ones, it is unjust to deny that time has softened many of those hereditary harshnesses of power which Shelley longed to see softened and said would be softened: the dominion of king or noble over commoner, rich over poor, master over servant, priest over layman, husband over wife, and parent and teacher over child. The modification has often proceeded further than any but the most visionary of Shelley's contemporaries could have imagined, much less imagined possible. And it has come about very largely as Shelley said it would. Pioneers preach the desirability and feasibility of a new order until gradually numbers of men begin to wish for what now seems possible though before scarcely thought of. In this practical sphere, admittedly, the most rapid advances are often effected by men of a pragmatic disposition urged more by immediate fact than by vision; but such a consideration does not eliminate the importance of more originative minds. Thus much of Shelley's loneliness was the loneliness of a pioneer very much in advance of the line of settlement.

In the sphere of metaphysics, however, Shelley's dominantly creative imagination raises certain difficulties. His strong emphasis upon human creativity and his unwillingness to concede to the ultimate Power some equivalent of man's personality harmonize philosophically, as has been noted, with a pantheistic view, a view which sees the universe as developing entirely from within and which regards man's mind as the highest manifestation of this cosmic growth. If Shelley had been content with such a philosophy one might say well and good. But something within him recurrently demands an Absolute beyond the sphere of change. This Absolute, unlike certain developments within the heart of man and within the social system, cannot be conjured up by desire. Either it is a fact or a phantom, something "given" or a "treacherous likeness" of one's own wishes. A more receptive imagination might have given Shelley more metaphysical assurance.[34]

But philosophic consistency and a satisfied imagination do not necessarily constitute the one supreme good in a poet. With these attributes Shelley's poetry could scarcely have had also the special quality of its best passages. And even those readers for whom the best passages are few, who find a certain poetic thinness the radical and pervasive defect, are still confronted with Shelley the man. Few poets have so hungered and thirsted after justice. A reading of a life of the man by such a biographer as Newman Ivey White, neither rhapsodic in praise nor narrow in condemnation, may substantiate some unfavorable judgments, but it leaves one with a sense of awe.

KEATS

K EATS'S POETRY HAS GIVEN PLEASURE to many who have found in it
no serious meaning. Amy Lowell insisted that *Endymion* is not
allegorical, that it is in essence a poem of young love.[1] H. W. Garrod
has viewed Keats as primarily a poet of rich sensuousness touched
by imagination, one to whose genius serious thought was alien and
to whose art it was harmful.[2] H. N. Fairchild, testing Keats by his
own conservative religious standards, concludes that as a seeker of
ultimate answers he deserves little respect.[3] Such opinions may perhaps be explained by Keats's instinct to preserve a fundamental unity,
to save speculation from abstraction by keeping it as close to imagination and sense as possible. Yet these judgments are surely wrong.
The poems themselves decide the case against Mr. Garrod if they
are read sympathetically in their entirety without preconceived notions that certain parts of them may be dismissed because in them
the *true* Keats, simple and sensuous, is not speaking. The letters
decide the case even more clearly. C. D. Thorpe, Douglas Bush,
D. G. James, R. H. Fogle—these, to name just a few, have seen the
whole Keats in all his aspects, a poet in whom lofty imaginings rise
naturally out of earthly aesthetic perceptions, while at the same time,
in spite of his endeavor to minimize division, they often seem to
stand over against the earthly perceptions.[4] The reconciliation of the

real and the ideal is everywhere a problem for the Romantic poets;
it is, as Allen Tate has observed, particularly and insistently a problem for Keats.[5]

Even among those who value the more thoughtful side of Keats
there is further difference of opinion. In his last years Keats often
showed an increasing scepticism about the immortality of the soul
and about the existence of any supernatural truth. Partly for this
reason some modern humanists are likely to find him a man after their
own heart. C. L. Finney, in his two-volume study *The Evolution of
Keats's Poetry*, sees Keats's whole career as a shedding of idealist and
transcendental illusions in favor of a sound "empirical humanism." [6]
J. Middleton Murry urges the opposite view. He believes that Keats
was mortally stricken not when he had come to rest in a philosophy
which satisfied him, but when he was on the verge of finding such
a philosophy, or—more precisely—when he was on the verge of finding religion; Middleton Murry believes that at the end Keats was
very nearly a Christian.[7] It can never be proved what Keats was on
the verge of, and such a difference in judgment will inevitably recur.
Yet Professor Finney perhaps fails to take into full account the extent to which Keats's early patterns persist to the end.

Endymion

Endymion, THE FIRST MAJOR POEM, suggests ample reasons for diverse interpretation. R. D. Havens once wrote an article titled "Unreconciled Opposites in Keats," [8] and in *Endymion* many oppositions
are fully apparent: between ecstacy and melancholy, between flesh
and spirit, between the isolation of a nympholept dreamer and the
useful activity of a humanitarian. Endymion himself, from the time
of his first serious vision until just prior to his translation to some
other sphere, is troubled by these conflicts. The implication of the
poem seems to be that the pangs caused by these divisions must simply be borne. Such a view Keats came to early, and it is commonly
regarded as a mature one. But as was only natural in one who arrived at this opinion while still young, the urge to escape the strain
of inward conflict continued to make itself felt. Again and again
Keats contemplates the possibility of achieving a harmonious wholeness not in death but in the living of life itself. (The resemblance is
here striking to the Matthew Arnold of the poems, and to Yeats and
and Wallace Stevens as their ideals are vividly expressed in *Among
School Children* and *Sunday Morning*.) Thus, besides the conflict
between the real and the ideal, the poems and letters reflect the re-

lated conflict between accepting an inner division as an inseparable
part of this life and seeking to eliminate such a division.

Nowhere in English poetry has a simple Arcadian society been
more finely described than in the passages of *Endymion* which immediately follow the induction. Keats's art achieves just such a naturalism as he often yearned for, a naturalism suffused by imagination
without being disturbed by it, even as the life of the shepherds is
suffused but not disturbed by their pastoral religion. Yet the poem
is not about the simple shepherds. It is about their king who has
grown up among them but who has early felt himself distinct from
them: he has been devoted to the heavenly moon-goddess Cynthia
while they are devoted to the earth-god Pan.

Endymion's worship does not radically dislocate the course of his
life until it culminates in a moment of vision. This vision, as is so
often the case in Keats, comes in the form of a dream. Endymion's
sister Peona concludes that from her brother's subsequent melancholy and perplexity that he must have received knowledge of

> *things mysterious*
> *Immortal, starry; such alone could thus*
> *Weigh down thy nature.*
>
> (I, 506-8.)

The brother then confesses what has befallen him. In a dream he had
been contemplating the starry spheres; he sensed that these spheres
were gliding away from him; he could not keep them in view. As he
relaxed his efforts and allowed his eye to drop to the horizon, the
moon arose in full loveliness. This also his eyes followed until it disappeared into a "dark and vapoury tent." Then suddenly he has to
strain his aspiring spirit no longer. For a radiant form comes sailing
down to earth, so bright that he must at first cover his face:

> *Whence that completed form of all completeness?*
> *Whence came that perfection of all sweetness?*
>
> (I, 606-7.)

The form is that of the goddess Cynthia. When only the most preliminary embracements have been accomplished, Endymion dreamed
that he himself had swooned into sleep; the revelation was too great
to be accepted all at once. But in a subsequent dream, which befell
him when he had left his sister and his shepherd subjects to wander
on a quest, the interrupted union is completed.

Keats's efforts to hold together the two worlds of earth and
heaven are most apparent at the end of the poem. Endymion has by
this time loved the mortal Indian maid, but his love has been marred

by a sense of guilt for having betrayed his goddess. As he returns
with the maid to his home on Latmos, he feels a sudden revulsion
against his metaphysical aspirations:

> *O, I have been*
> *Presumptuous against love, against the sky,*
> *Against all elements, against the tie*
> *Of mortals each to each . . .*
> *There never lived a mortal man, who bent*
> *His appetite beyond his natural sphere,*
> *But starv'd and died.*

(IV, 638–48.)

These lines express just such an empirical humanism as Professor
Finney would recommend; now Endymion might presumably be
ready to settle down among his own people to lead a life of mortal
love and mortal usefulness. Yet events turn out otherwise. Endymion
is again overcome by a sense of dedication to a higher love. He tells
the maid that they cannot live together. But the moment they are
separated he relents and wishes to see her once more. As she returns toward him on his sister's arm, her dusky earthly countenance
is transfigured into the radiant "spiritualiz'd" countenance of Cynthia. Then, perhaps because any sustained earthly union between the
divine and the human is unimaginable, the two lovers bid Peona fare-
well and the poem abruptly ends:

> *They vanish'd far away!—Peona went*
> *Home through the gloomy wood in wonderment.*

Rehearsing this familiar tale may be an imposition upon a reader's
patience, especially since there is perhaps less disagreement upon the
meaning of its central allegory than might be inferred from the volumes of explication which have appeared in print. It may be best,
however, to comment a little further upon this allegory in view of
the objections to Keats which persist in some persons of orthodox
belief or sensibility. Granted only two assumptions, one might almost ask the question, what more could orthodoxy possibly wish
from a very youthful poet handling this myth? One assumption must
be made: the poet must be granted a certain independence and integrity; he must be allowed to contemplate life in the terms of his
own fable and in the light of his own experience. The second assumption, meaningless perhaps to some, is pertinent precisely to the
orthodox tradition. Both Shelley and Keats regarded the poetic imagination as prophetic, not only in the sense of uttering some divine
truth but in the sense of anticipating some fuller revelation. Wordsworth and Coleridge, as has already been noted earlier in this study,

were inclined to regard the imagination as anticipating and prepar-
ing for the truths of Christianity; with the increased study of comparative religion, some such thought has become a theological commonplace. Applying such notions to *Endymion*, and relating them to
those problems of belief which had become especially acute in
Keats's time, what does one discover that the poem has to say? The
human soul aspires to some ethereal truth. In response to this aspiration the stars, pinpoints of light very remote and without distinct
form (as ultimate truth must necessarily appear to pure reason), seem
to recede even further. Then, to an aspiration less rational perhaps
and more imaginative, the divine appears a little closer and in a form
more distinct, like the moon. But this vision is present only for a
while and is soon veiled in uncertainty. Now full faith, orthodoxy
has always maintained, cannot be created by aspiration alone; it is
a gift from heaven. At this juncture, when striving and seeking are
momentarily in abeyance (as Keats and Wordsworth thought they
often should be), the divine suddenly descends of its own accord, as
a human being of flesh and blood. This fuller revelation, which is in
a sense the answer to the yearning, yet serves to intensify yearning;
it sets up tensions which cannot be wholly resolved in this life. In
his perplexity man must not neglect the ties of mortals "each to
each." Nor need he be afraid of these ties; provided he does not forget his commitment to a higher love, he will gradually find that his
natural affections have been "spiritualiz'd."

When the poem is interpreted in this way, Keats almost reminds
one of such a famous apologist for Christianity as Browning himself,
especially when, as in *Saul*, *Cleon*, and *A Death in the Desert*,
Browning is striking a blow at those modern gnostics who would
reduce the flesh and blood of historic Christian truth to pale abstractions. Even more official guardians of tradition than Browning
might vouchsafe *Endymion* a guarded *imprimatur*.

To read a possibly orthodox sensibility into *Endymion* ("meaning" might seem too definite a word) is not to claim that Keats saw
himself in alliance with religion. That he did not do so is a matter
of clearest record. It is also understandable that some may feel the
poem to be designed as a protest against all worship directed towards a world other than this one. But if one considers the poem itself in its own terms, rather than any supposed intent, such a reading
will not do. The Transfiguration at the end is not an obliteration of
the divine, but an elevation of the human to union with the divine.
There is also every reason inherent in the story of the poem to suppose that such an experience would not be vouchsafed at all except
to one who, like Endymion, had been enamored of the divine; and
this union, followed immediately by the translation of Endymion

and his beloved, is apparently not a condition that can be sustained on this earth.

Also, to see such a traditional meaning in *Endymion* is not to pronounce the poem a complete artistic success. As Keats knew, it had serious defects. It is too unrelentingly luxurious. It is too diffuse: its long suggestive episodes, though related to the central meaning, mar the simple form of the story as story. The poem cannot solve the difficulties of its species or kind—the myth developed into an extended allegory. A myth, one supposes, is a story rich in meaning but unconscious of that meaning. Keats's poem has lost its primitive simplicity and has attained self-consciousness. In this new condition it is obligated to distinguish between the imaginative impression of the hero's union with Cynthia and his union with the maid. Since it is partly the function of poetry to give sensuous substance to the unsubstantial, this distinction is difficult to make at best. In some respects Keats scarcely attempts to make it at all; the notorious "slippery blisses" are enjoyed not with the mortal love but with the immortal. Despite its strongly allegorical design, the poem in execution often seems no more than the dream love-story of a passionate young man in love with love. This last Keats doubtless intended it to be also, but he must have wished for a more satisfactory union of the literal and the symbolic than he achieves.

Yet the difficulties which the allegory experiences are in a sense the difficulties of life itself. They do not prove that Keats was being false to himself in attempting to express a serious meaning. He chose the story of Endymion rather than one less rich in metaphysical suggestion precisely because it corresponded to problems which were strongly asserting themselves in his awareness. These problems are perplexing and Christian tradition itself may be said to speak with two voices. Apropos of the imperfect distinction between the sensuous and the spiritual, one voice might admonish Keats that those men are blessed who have not seen and yet have believed. The other might urge that belief in the communion of spirit and flesh is precisely what distinguishes Christianity from gnosticism, that according to Christianity itself the whole *raison d'etre* of the Incarnation was to save the human race from continuing forever, as Dante says, "in desire without hope," from endlessly wanting to believe but never seeing.

The Teased Spirit

KEATS HAD NOT BECOME AWARE ALL AT ONCE of those beckonings, as by a force outside himself, which *Endymion* tells of, or of the impulses within which responded. Students of Keats are fortunate in that the very earliest poems offer a remarkable record of the first manifestations and steady growth of this relationship, an "ennobling interchange" such as Wordsworth had spoken of. In this interchange Keats experienced emotions akin to worship and his vocabulary reveals some degree of affinity between this private devotion and traditional religious devotion.

In his first poems Keats writes as though his spirit has heretofore lived without vision. Now, suddenly, he discovers the beauty of art and the beauty of nature, the enjoyment of each assisting the enjoyment of the other. Both the sights of nature which he beholds in his rambles outside London and the poems and romances which he reads suggest realms very different from the narrow city-pent life of a medical student which was his own. His imagination expands; his spirit has vistas, indefinite but awe-inspiring. In the *Epistle to George Felton Mathew*, Keats complains of living in the dark Borough, where he has often wondered if he would ever see the "roseate dawn" and the sun again, and where his faculties have been "in thrall" and incapable of producing poetry. In a sonnet he expresses his wish to escape from the congested buildings and to climb a little hill from which the dell below "may seem a span." Another sonnet gives thanks for an actual escape from the Borough to the freedom of spirit which nature and literature afford: Keats may now look into "the fair and open face of heaven," and then, after a while, he will sink into the grass and read a "gentle tale of love and languishment."

New and profounder reaches of the mind are suggested by the sea; Keats's response is recorded in the sonnet *To My Brother George*, which speaks of

> *The ocean with its vastness, its blue green,*
> *Its ships, its rocks, its caves, its hopes, its fears,—*
> *Its voice mysterious, which whoso hears*
> *Must think on what will be, and what has been.*

With an appreciation of the grander aspects of the physical world comes a loftier ideal of poetry. In *Sleep and Poetry* Keats says he would at first be content, in some bowery nook, to write of flowers and nymphs

> *many a verse from so strange influence*
> *That we must ever wonder how, and whence*
> *It came.*

> (ll. 69–71.)

(Even this unpretentious poetry will bespeak some mystery.) But he then proclaims that later, in some spot of more awesome beauty, he would write poetry of a loftier strain:

> *The events of this wide world I'd seize*
> *Like a strong giant, and my spirit teaze*
> *Till at its shoulders it should proudly see*
> *Wings to find out an immortality.*
>
> (ll. 81–84.)

As a symbol of the nobler poetry which he will one day write, Keats then describes a mysterious heavenly charioteer who alights on earth. Surrounding this charioteer are shapes which act out the mysteries of life and death, but Keats does not understand the significance of what he sees:

> *Most awfully intent*
> *The driver of those steeds is forward bent,*
> *And seems to listen: O that I might know*
> *All that he writes with such a hurrying glow!*
>
> (ll. 151–54.)

And again,

> *though I do not know*
> *The shiftings of the mighty winds that blow*
> *Hither and thither all the changing thoughts*
> *Of man: though no great minist'ring reason sorts*
> *Out the dark mysteries of human souls*
> *To clear conceiving: yet there ever rolls*
> *A vast idea before me, and I glean*
> *Therefrom my liberty; thence too I've seen*
> *The end and aim of Poesy.*
>
> (ll. 285–93.)

The end and aim of poetry is some vast idea that would clarify the dark mysteries of human souls; this vast idea, dim and indistinct though it is, sets Keats free.

The most famous poem of this early period, and artistically the most wholly successful, is the sonnet *On First Looking into Chapman's Homer.* Here again the wonder with which the grandeur of nature can fill the soul is equated with the wonder which art can inspire. Keats, able for the first time to sense the breadth of Homer, feels like the discoverer of a new planet, or like the discoverer of the Pacific, "Silent, upon a peak in Darien." A new and unexpected world has been opened to Keats's spirit, characterized like the heav-

ens and the distant Pacific by its "wide expanse" and its "pure serene."
Not only in extent but in quality it differs from life as he has
known it, perhaps even from literature as he has known it. This
is as much as Keats can say at this time; he cannot, while remaining
true to his experience of nature and art, go further and add an interpretation more suggestive of the transcendentalism of traditional
religion or of Platonism.

Yet these early poems, though they offer no metaphysical speculation, hover on the verge of it. The "mysterious" voice of the sea
speaks of what has been and what will be; lofty poetry suggests some
vast liberating idea that will solve the "dark mysteries"; the Pacific,
and perhaps Homer, fills one with a "wild surmise." [9]

The first poems in which Keats's liberating idea begins to take
on more distinct metaphysical suggestions are the two sonnets inspired by the sight of the Elgin marbles. The first sonnet, addressed
to Benjamin Haydon, praises him for having been one of the first
to respond to these marbles as to a divine revelation:

> *For when men star'd on what was most divine*
> *With browless idiotism—o'erwise phlegm—*
> *Thou hadst beheld the Hesperean shine*
> *Of their star in the East, and gone to worship them.*

The adjective *divine* by itself might be dismissed as a mere con-
ventionalism. But the last lines are more original and forceful. They
do not refer to any trip which Haydon made to see the marbles in
Greece before their arrival in England, for Haydon made no such
trip. They express a half-conscious analogy between the marbles and
Christ: as Christ to the Christian is the Divine word made flesh, so
to Keats the marbles are some idea of the spirit embodied in physical form; as the three kings, having seen the star in the East, had
come to Bethlehem to worship Divinity incarnate, so Haydon had
come to worship the marbles. The word *Hesperean*, of course, assures that the Christian symbolism will be taken for no more than a
figure of speech.

This sonnet to Haydon was written to accompany another sonnet
more immediately and fully expressive of Keats's own response to
the marbles. This second sonnet, *On Seeing the Elgin Marbles*, is
perhaps Keats's first poem of intimation in the full Romantic sense:
it celebrates a single moment's vision of eternity and this moment
is inspired by one particular experience. The first part of the poem
may not be immediately clear. Keats himself longs to create works
as godlike as the Phidian marbles, but the labor of such creation

appals him and for the present he would rather confess failure than make the effort. The "dim-conceived glories of the brain" are the dimly imagined works which he himself would write. Only the last four lines of the sonnet apply directly to the marbles themselves.

> My spirit is too weak—mortality
>   Weights heavily on me like unwilling sleep,
>   And each imagin'd pinnacle and steep
> Of godlike hardship tells me I must die
> Like a sick Eagle looking at the sky.
>   Yet 'tis a gentle luxury to weep
>   That I have not the cloudy wind to keep
> Fresh for the opening of the morning's eye.
>   Such dim-conceived glories of the brain
>   Bring round the heart an undescribable feud;
>   So do these wonders a most dizzy pain,
>   That mingles Grecian grandeur with the rude
> Wasting of old Time—with a billowy main—
> A sun—a shadow of a magnitude.

Are these lines, one may ask, definitely metaphysical in their suggestion? Is Keats thinking of an immortality or eternity such as religion teaches? Is he not thinking merely of such earthly immortality as great poets and artists have achieved? No, not merely. This is one of those moments when the two sorts of immortality are almost inseparably mingled in his consciousness. He very definitely wishes he might give form to the dim-conceived glories of his imagination and thereby achieve fame. But the climax is not in the lines concerned with his own artistic creation. It is in the final lines describing the sculptures. As these lines show, the immortality of art, the grandeur of these marbles *almost* unaffected by time, is not the sum total of all the immortality and grandeur that is in his mind. They merely suggest some expanse, some glory, which other things not works of art have also suggested: the sea and the sun. This sea and sun are wonderfully apt here, as though Keats cannot forget that the proper setting for the marbles was not the interior of a gallery in a murky northern city, but atop the Acropolis in Athens, where they had been within sight of the sea and illuminated by the clear Mediterranean sunlight. But they are apt in another way too. The sea had always suggested to Keats's imagination some mystery, some unlimited expanse. And the sun has long symbolized divine life-giving power. These images are then climaxed by an extraordinary phrase, "shadow of a magnitude." It reminds one of the climax of Shelley's *Hymn to Intellectual Beauty;* in the midst of the physical beauty of the spring Shelley suddenly feels that he has been touched by the "shadow" of some great spiritual beauty. Shelley and Keats alike are as it were echoing Plato, to whom all the objects of this world were but images or shadows of the other world, the real, the ideal, the divine.

Platonizing in response to beauty had been common for over two thousand years and had often been merely conventional. But the four last lines of this sonnet could not be accused of conventionality. The experience is original, intense, personal, reported as honestly as the poet can report it. A measure of the honesty and truth of the vision is the comment on "the rude wasting of old time." The Elgin marbles are wonderfully fresh to this day. A more conventional poet would perhaps hail them as immortal, as conquering time. But Keats sees them more accurately: they are merely resisting time and time in the long run will win. Such duration as they have can best be but a "shadow" of some state truly transcending time.[10]

This something capable of truly transcending time is imaged by the marbles and the sea and the sun, but besides imaging it Keats wishes to designate it by a name of its own. He can find nothing better for his purpose than the abstract term "magnitude." Such an abstraction may recall the abstract terms *One* and *many* at the end of *Adonais*. But there is a difference as well as a similarity. Shelley in *Adonais* is dissatisfied with the actual and the issue at stake is precisely whether beyond it there is a realm of the ideal. The world, including art, offered Shelley no actualities which could satisfy his imagination and he falls back upon language as abstract, so to speak, as his ideal has long been. Keats on the other hand begins with the actual marbles. His only anxiety is whether he will himself be able to create works equally expressive of the ideal; he has no anxiety as to whether this ideal is a reality or illusion. He is for the moment too filled with the wonder of the images themselves to be so concerned. Yet despite this comparative unconcern with metaphysical ideas, nature and art have for some months been suggesting some such ideas. Up to this moment his poems have not sought especially to relate these to the ideas of any particular philosophy or religion, and thus to appear to give them some more definite intellectual form. Finally, almost of their own accord, they begin to take on such form by merging with certain traditional ideas. Keats suddenly discovers, at the end of these two sonnets, that the "vast idea" which has been floating before him can achieve some more distinct shape by being related to the two great sources of transcendentalism available to a young Englishman, Christianity and Platonism. The Elgin marbles are like Christ, the finite embodiment of the infinite; they are the "shadow" of some Platonic essence. After the more concrete descriptions and images the single climactic word "magnitude" is felicitous. It suggests not merely the indefinite extension of such things as we know on earth, but some mode of being different qualitatively from things we know here; though some things here, the sculpture, the sea, the sun, somehow speak to us of this different mode of being, they are not properly of that mode.

The sonnet on the Elgin marbles is in some respects the high water mark of Keats's early poetry. There will be many who prefer the sonnet on Chapman's Homer, but a distinction which Hegel and other German aestheticians were making during these years may apply here. Hegel believed that Greek classic art was perfectly beautiful because the conceptions of the artists themselves were not very transcendental and therefore put no great strain upon the material medium in which they were expressed. He believed that the art of the Christian era, in which he included his own time, was less beautiful but compensated for this deficiency by its sublimity. Perhaps Hegel might have termed beautiful the sonnet on Homer and sublime the sonnet on the marbles, with its suggestion of a world of spirit which matter can at best but imperfectly symbolize.

If such is the case, how could a supreme example of classic or beautiful art, the sculpture of Phidias, inspire a poem which was not so much beautiful as sublime. As was noted in the case of Wordsworth, the two experiences of the beautiful and the sublime are not always wholly separable. Perfect beauty, such as that of the Vale of Grasmere, seems itself to partake of the sublime because it suggests something so different from the imperfection which is the common lot of this life. So also perhaps eighteenth-century music, with its perfection of poise, is at least as suggestive of a metaphysical reality as nineteenth-century music in which the composer seems to strive harder and to put something of a strain upon the medium he is employing.

In any event, Keats's experience of the marbles partook of the sublime in another way also; despite the obvious damage which the centuries had done, the marbles were still fresh and glowing enough for Keats to feel his spirit in the presence of the great spirit which had created them over two thousand years before. His own spirit by this means effected something of the same conquest of time which Wordsworth effected by his "returns." It is possible to maintain that in the presence of an ancient work of art one should not complicate the pure aesthetic response by too much awareness of the work's great age, that one should view it rather as an ancient contemporary might have done. But Keats did not feel this way about the marbles any more than he felt this way about the urn. That these creations, though still so fresh, were yet so old, was precisely one of the facts which Keats wished to feel most intensely.

Elysiums

SHORTLY AFTER WRITING HIS SONNET on the Elgin marbles Keats began *Endymion*. Following the prolonged effort which this poem required, Keats's poetic imagination, to judge from the works it composed, relaxed for many months while gathering force for the next and final great effort which was to produce the two poems on Hyperion, the great odes, and *Lamia*. (In the letters his speculative mind is still vigorously active and in his personal life he was oppressed by Tom's lingering death.) In its poetic relaxations Keats's imagination continued to luxuriate in reverie, in the fabrication of richly sensuous elysiums. Serious students of Keats must give these elysiums their attention. They must do so because Keats himself took them a little more than half seriously. He suggests in the oft quoted letter to Bailey of November 22, 1817 that the preternaturally luxuriant yet delicate scenes which the imagination can conjure up are anticipations of some half-supernatural state to which the soul is destined. He even decides that if a man is to come to this state he must prepare his soul beforehand by allowing it to create and enjoy such anticipations. If such indeed be the road to salvation, then his friend Bailey, ceaselessly striving after the truth of reason, is not on the right road. Keats supposes that just as the delicate re-enactment of sensuous experience in the imagination gives that experience a "finer tone," spiritualizes it to "essence," so the experiences of this life may be more delicately re-enacted in another. The passage in the letter has been quoted often, but it is so basic that it must be quoted again at least in part:

> What the imagination seizes as Beauty must be truth—whether it existed before or not—for I have the same Idea of all our Passions as of Love they are all in their sublime, creative of essential Beauty. . . . The imagination may be compared to Adam's dream—he awoke and found it truth. I am the more zealous in this affair, because I have never been able to see how anything can be known by consequitive reasoning—and yet it must be. Can it be that even the greatest Philosopher ever arrived at his goal without putting aside numerous objections. However it may be, O for a Life of Sensations rather than of Thoughts! It is "a

Vision in the form of Youth" a Shadow of reality to come—and this consideration has further convinced me for it has come as auxiliary to another favorite Speculation of mine, that we shall enjoy ourselves hereafter by having what we called happiness on Earth repeated in a finer tone and so repeated. And yet such a fate can only befall those who delight in Sensation rather than hunger as you do after truth.

(By "Sensation" Keats appears to mean an imaginative apprehension or re-creation of sensuous experience rather than mere sense perception in itself.) Earl R. Wasserman, in his book *The Finer Tone*, has shown how thoroughly Keats's poems and letters are pervaded by such patterns of thought or—if one wishes—patterns of feeling.[11]

Keats's speculation on these subjects may seem childishly trivial to many readers, the mere rationalization and self-justification of a naturally languorous young man. Like *Endymion* itself, with which it is closely interwoven, the speculation may be dismissed by a stern reminder that "eye hath not seen nor ear heard" the delights of the hereafter. But, as has been suggested, traditional religion may also take a more sympathetic view. Religion has suffered severely in the past few centuries from that ceaseless striving of intellect which Keats's faith in imagination sought to counter. Christianity itself has always had, at least in abeyance, its own doctrine of the ultimate "resurrection of the body," presumably in some spiritualized form. If there is any future life, any "immortality," if man is to preserve any of that individual personality which religion has insisted he does preserve, such a future is hardly to be imagined without some equivalent of his present corporeal existence as we know it. If religious faith is reduced to a set of mere abstract clichés, which in the age of the Enlightenment was increasingly its fate among the educated, such necessities of the imagination might seem of little importance. But to Keats, as to Immanuel Kant, the abstractions of deism, offering nothing to the imagination, might truly be said to have offered nothing at all.[12] Hence in part that unwillingness which Professor Wasserman emphasizes in Keats to aspire beyond "heaven's bourn," a borderland between the corporeal and the purely spiritual. Further aspiration was indeed not just a matter of unwillingness for Keats, it was to him an impossibility. One might further argue that this condition of Keats's mind was in some respects more congenial to orthodox tradition than Shelley's occasional too lofty soaring towards some ultimate truth wholly transcendent and wholly abstract. The traditional doctrine of an historic Incarnation offered such a point of meeting between the corporeal and the wholly spiritual as Keats sought. For that very reason orthodoxy may feel some sympathy for Keats's instinctive insistence upon the "imaginableness" of truth.

The moralist may still regret the lack of earnest moral striving, or striving of any kind, when Keats is exercising his elysian imagination. But to the Romantics in general and to Keats especially the problem of belief was more basic and more urgent than the problem of moral endeavor. The Victorian period, in which an intensification of moral endeavor sometimes went hand in hand with a decline in belief, suggests that the two are at least partially separable. Religion has in fact often discovered that ceaseless moral effort, like intellectual effort, will not in itself produce faith. It may lead to a self-absorbed pursuit of a self-set goal, to pride perhaps, and ultimately to despair. Something of this sort has been illustrated historically by the instance of Luther in his youth, and poetically by Arnold's Mycerinus. Wordsworth found in his own case that effort and relaxation alternated; he believed such alternation was natural and proper. Likewise, in Wordsworth's scheme, the richly harmonious scenes of nature, which relaxed spiritual tension and developed a faith that "all which we behold is full of blessings," were a necessary counterpart to those other configurations of human life and the natural world which by their "discipline of pain and fear" developed a sense of moral urgency. To Wordsworth, as to Coleridge's ancient mariner before he is aware of the beauty of the sea-snakes, the discipline of pain by itself alone could serve no good purpose.

It is important that a hastily erected moral criticism not deter the reader from heeding all that Keats has to say upon the imagination, including what he has to say upon elysian reveries. By listening to Keats, we can better understand and partially reconcile the contradictory opinions which have been held of the great odes. These odes certainly derive in part from Keats's habits of reverie. Yet they command respect from many readers because they no longer appear merely indulgent and evasive as some of the early reveries had been; in them freedom and restraint appear to have achieved a balance.

Keats' vagrancy of imagination, which in due time was to be concentrated and curbed, is early apparent in "I Stood Tip-toe on a Little Hill." (This is in sharp contrast with that "collectedness" of Wordsworth [13] which is so manifest even in his youthful poem *An Evening Walk*.) After only the briefest consideration of the scene before him, Keats decides that it does not offer enough to satisfy him. So his fancy proceeds to heap up images of things not actually there:

> And many pleasures to my vision started;
> So I straightway began to pluck a posey

Of luxuries bright, milky, soft, and rosy.
(ll. 26–28.)

This posey, or mixed bouquet, as readers of Keats know, is a charm-ing one. Delightful detail after delightful detail, of stream and fish, of tree and grass and flower, of light and shade, is set down with fine accuracy to the physical fact and to the very inner quality or essence. As Keats's imagination moves from one object to another, the reader beholds each as with the fresh wonder of a child. But the whole bouquet, like any bouquet, is a mere assemblage, an aggregation of separate things, not a living unity; the details do not add up to any single scene, or even to any one season or mood.

In *Endymion* the enrichments of a luxuriating imagination are in part germane to the poem's serious purpose and in part controlled by it, but at other times the purpose is overwhelmed. Similarly, as Arnold noted, the richness of *Isabella* and *The Eve of St. Agnes* is not achieved without a loss of simple human feeling.

Late in 1818 Keats wrote two poems which show a certain prog-ress in control. The very lightness of the mood in which the little elysiums are now presented indicates that Keats is capable of a certain detachment, of being a little amused by his own most deeply in-grained habits of mind. In *Fancy* he tells how fine it is, sitting by the fire in winter, to imagine all the pleasures of spring, summer, and autumn assembled all together at once. Why should we be content with only the flowers of one season at a time! Also, reality is not only more meager than fancy, but it is "spoilt by use." In the little *Ode* addressed to the "Bards of Passion and of Mirth" Keats touches half humorously on one of the themes of the letter to Bailey. He tells us that by enjoying the delights of the poems which the bards have left behind them, we are finding our way to the region where they are now:

> *Seated on Elysian lawns*
> *Brows'd by none but Dian's fawns;*
> *Underneath large blue-bells tented,*
> *Where the daisies are rose-scented,*
> *And the rose herself has got*
> *Perfume which on earth is not.*

Just as the sensuous delights of earth take on a finer tone when dis-tilled to essence in poetry, so the daisies of this world will be rose-scented in Elysium. When Keats presents his favorite speculation in this very light way, he is showing an awareness that before it can

become a serious metaphysic it must submit to some stern modification.

The Odes

IN TWO GREAT POEMS of the following spring, the *Ode on a Grecian
Urn* and the *Ode to a Nightingale*, such stern modification is
already at work. The tragic circumstances of Keats's life intensify
the seriousness of a poet already serious in the main. The prophetic,
visionary imagination no longer ranges so lightly. The reverie is concentrated, the art disciplined. Both odes thus impress most readers as
being something more than just pleasant reveries. This more powerful effect, at least of the first ode, was described many years ago by
W. P. Ker: in Ker's words, the play of Keats's imagination upon the
urn is not simply "a transformation of sober reality into a pleasantly
lively vision—it is a raid into the eternal world." [14]

Before discriminating between the two odes, one should note
broadly some of the significant ways in which they are alike.

First, both poems still exhibit some of the avoidance of actual
sensuous experience characteristic of the earlier reveries, an avoidance
which had been half-humorously justified in the poem *Fancy*. In the
one ode the exquisite songs piped by the figures on the urn are "dit-
ties of no tone"; the physical passion is never consummated—though
in view of the circumstances of the poet's life at the time one would
say that consummation and relaxation, in the natural cycle, rather
than an eternity of tension, was the condition to be desired; the poet's
and the reader's feeling for the beauty and sweetness of human life
attain climactic poignancy in the contemplation of a scene which is
not depicted on the urn at all, the "little town" which is off stage
and whose precise site, whether upon a mountain or by the sea,
Keats can therefore never know. In the second ode Keats's ear is
not conscientiously attentive to the exact patterns of the bird's song
as Coleridge's ear was in his poem *The Nightingale;* here is Coleridge's very different account:

> *But never elsewhere in one place I knew*
> *So many nightingales; and far and near,*
> *In wood and thicket, over the wide grove,*
> *They answer and provoke each other into song,*
> *With skirmish and capricious passagings*
> *And murmurs musical and sweet jug jug,*
> *And one low piping sound more sweet than all.*

Also Keats does not take an actual glass of wine to see how effectively it could transport him; he does not go across the lawns into the actual grove where the bird is singing.

But Coleridge had said that the poetic imagination "dissolves, diffuses, dissipates" in order to re-create.[15] What are the chief characteristics of Keats's re-creations?

First, the beginning in everyday actuality of sensuous fact, the step-by-step rising to ecstasy in the central stanzas, and the final subsidence—all this dramatic framework gives to both visionary poems the concreteness, fullness, and complexity of an actual event. This impression of imaginative solidity is reinforced by one important condition: through all the imaginative transfigurations of the middle stanzas the physical facts from which the poems start, the marble urn and the actual bird's song, continue as underpresences. Like Donne's travelling compass point, like Wordsworth's skylark never soaring out of sight of its nest, Keats's imagination never completely cuts the bond that ties it to a central point in the actual world, though the actuality of the urn is only assumed for dramatic purposes.

Again, the visionary climaxes of both poems, though approached in different ways, are in themselves similar. Here we come to the essential theme of both odes, to which other subordinate themes attach themselves. A casual inspection may suggest that the central themes are different: in the first instance, the permanence of art contrasted with the impermanence of life; in the second, the fullness and beauty of non-human nature contrasted with the miseries of man's lot. But both present a perfection which, properly speaking, exists neither in works of art nor in works of nature; both in their different ways present a "completed form of all completeness," a "perfection of all sweetness" which belongs simply to the imagination. As Cleanth Brooks emphasized a number of years ago, the urn is not perfect: it may be semi-permanent, but it is lifeless and "cold." [16] As other readers have long observed, the nightingale is not perfect: it may be warm, living, and joyous, but it is not deathless. Yet both deficiencies are made up: Keats's imagination, in its interchange with the object at hand, partly perceives and partly creates perfection. The cold figures on the urn, retaining their permanence, briefly become living, "forever warm." The bird, while yet living and singing, becomes "immortal." The odes are, in fact, fine illustrations of Coleridge's notion, derived in part from Kant, that the imagination is the presentational faculty allied with the Kantian "reason," the faculty which apprehends things under the aspect of fullness and totality.

The final important resemblance between the two poems is that in both instances the joy which accompanies the visions of perfection serves a justifying purpose: it reconciles the poet to sorrow caused by mutability—chiefly by the brevity of actual beauty and love in the first ode, and by the brevity of human life itself in the second. Both poems are, of course, dramatic presentations of the imagination not designed to appeal to the theological intellect; they offer no very clear system of ideas according to which this justifying process can be logically understood. One is none the less reminded of Coleridge's idea (and Schelling's) that the tentative union of opposites accomplished symbolically by the imagination intimates the permanent union of such opposites in eternity. For both poems retain, in however brief or truncated a form, echoes of the "speculation" in the early letter to Bailey. In at least partial accord with this early pattern of thought and feeling, the blended *Beauty* of life and permanence created by imagination in the ode on the urn is *Truth* in some mysterious, ultimate way. In the ode to the nightingale the fullness expressed in the climactic stanzas is perhaps a "vision" of some such ultimate reality and our present life may be a "sleep" from which we will one day waken to a fuller consciousness. Here, of course, the opposite possibility is likewise considered: this life may be all the reality there ever is for us; we may be as awake as we will ever be; and any imaginative presentation of a more fully satisfying reality may be only a "waking dream," in other words, an illusion or will-o'-the-wisp.

Wordsworth was only half right when he remarked upon the similarity between Keats's *Ode on a Grecian Urn* and his own sonnet addressed to the art of painting:

> *Thou with ambition modest yet sublime,*
> *Here, for the sight of mortal man hast given*
> *To one brief moment caught from fleeting time*
> *The appropriate calm of blest eternity.*[17]

For the full truth is that Keats's imagination was also bringing to the calm abstraction which must characterize the merely intellectual concept of eternity something akin to the flesh-and-blood warmth of the life we know.

A crucial critical question is how far Keats's raids "into the eternal world" appear to be successful. Do the two odes effect in the imagination of readers some such juncture of the temporal and eternal as they seem to speak of?

Keats has sought to accomplish this juncture by pure imaginative "empathy," as R. H. Fogle says[18]—by a *feeling into* the very heart of an intense aesthetic experience. This imaginative empathy, in accordance with Keats's own ideal, manifests a *unified sensibility* but a unity different from that ascribed to the early seventeenth-century poets by T. S. Eliot: in these older poets thought and feeling appear to be intimately fused and yet the thought retains its characteristic structure. But in these two odes of Keats, just as direct physical sensation is often transposed into an imaginative key, so the semi-theological thoughts of the letters are likewise adapted to harmonize with the dramatic and imaginative setting. Particularly in the case of the *Ode on a Grecian Urn,* this adaptation involves a drastic curtailment of the schematic fullness which had originally made the thought rationally intelligible even to those who might not find it convincing. One is reminded of Coleridge's belief that the imagination at its fullest included all of man's modes or powers of cognition, but also of *Kubla Khan,* in which the "thought" is so fully subsumed into the imaginative whole that most readers would feel it has virtually ceased to exist. How far such a form of unified sensibility is fruitful is a difficult question, whether the sensibility is operating in the theological sphere or elsewhere. Yet precisely within the realm of a mystical religious awareness, a substantial tradition would be at least partly sympathetic to Keats: according to this tradition, the discursive intellect can do little more than talk about eternity, and if this eternity is to be experienced in any more immediate way it must be apprehended at moments which have "teased us out of thought."

But let us return more precisely to the question of how far a critic will judge Keats's raids to be successful. Perhaps both poems must inevitably be devoid of any profound significance to those who have lost even the last vestige of philosophical idealism and also to those others, like Professor Fairchild, who feel that no important religious truth can be effectively perceived by one so earth-bound as they suppose Keats to be. But between these two extremes are the many critics who, whatever their disagreements about the relative felicity of individual parts of the odes, agree in taking the poems as a whole seriously. The humanist is likely to retain, in however shrunken a form, some of the old sensibility, and he is likely to find the poems to be "friends to man," even as Keats would wish, because they suggest some consolatory, fortifying truth: the anti-transcendental Professor Finney finds them expressions of the finest humanism; the non-transcendental Professor Thorpe finds them "rather like a revelation of a principle of existence . . . an insight into the universal human heart." [19] Professor Thorpe explicitly says that the poems are not the expression of a "religious idea." In a sense he is right; in the odes Keats's speculations would certainly be deemed by

most readers to exhibit less of the distinctive quality of religious *idea*
than they had in the early letter and less than they later show in the
anguished cry to Charles Brown:

> *Is there another Life? Shall I awake and find all*
> *this a dream? There must be—we cannot be created*
> *for this sort of suffering.*[20]

But then the two odes in a sense are not presentations of clear, conceptual *ideas* at all, but rather of imaginative experiences from which
ideas might be derived. In any case, for such humanist readers as
Finney and Thorpe the two odes are successful raids into the eternal
world only so long as the eternal world is defined as the permanent
not-too-metaphysical, non-religious truths of the human heart.

The reasons for the ambiguity of these two odes, their hesitancy
as public statements in pressing too distinctly into the realm of metaphysics or religions, are to be found in Keats's own nature, in his
ideas upon the modesty that becomes both a man and a poem. These
attitudes are well expressed in that letter to J. H. Reynolds, of February 3, 1818, in which he contrasts his own ideals with Wordsworth's: "Every man has his speculations, but every man does not
brood and peacock over them till he makes a false coinage and de-
ceives himself.— Many a man can travel to the very bourne of
Heaven and yet want confidence to put down his halfseeing. . . .
Poetry should be great and unobtrusive."

But for a critic whose own definition of eternal world would include more than this, or who feels that Keats's sensibility—for all its
strong inclination to remain within a humanist's limits—does in fact
include more than this, a judgment upon the poems is likely to be
a little more uncertain though not necessarily adverse. Among such
critics is Allen Tate; indeed, within the framework of the assumptions of this study, he is perhaps the truest and best of all the critics
of the odes. He relates Keats's attempts to synthesize the eternal and
the temporal to the two greatest relevant Western traditions. He sees
Keats, the young Romantic working on his own, at something of a
disadvantage when compared with the fully Christian poets of the
seventeenth century. He also finds him at a disadvantage because he
has apparently never read those great passages in Platonic dialogues
in which Socrates conducted his own raids on eternity by a combination of soaring imagination and rational dialectic. Yet Tate does not
complain that the odes are not something different from what in
fact they are. He has great admiration for the *Ode to a Nightingale*
and examines it seriously as a poem that "at least tries to say every-

thing that poetry can say." [21] Tate's admiration mixed with uncertainty as to the poem's success as a "raid" is close to the general attitude of D. G. James towards the Romantic imagination in general. Professor James, with a somewhat Kantian sense of the limitations of human knowing, treats the Romantics with great sympathy and concludes that imagination cannot lead to belief but only to scepticism.[22] This scepticism he sees not as disbelief but as a wavering between belief and disbelief, an uncertainty which he judges to be the sign of a serious mind rather than of a frivolous one. In this sense both poems may be defined as sceptical. Precisely because the *Ode on a Grecian Urn* is wholly serious Keats is more reluctant than in the earlier letter to Bailey to give to his identification of Beauty and Truth a distinctly supernatural implication, yet at the same time he does not expressly preclude the possibility of some elysian existence after death in which men will be happier than in the life that we know now. In a limited sense this poem is affirmative, but it is also sceptical in that the locus of the elysium which it presents remains wholly uncertain: it may be no more than a region in the mind of the poet himself to which he can briefly repair when wearied by the pangs of life. The *Ode to a Nightingale*, perhaps an even more serious poem, concerned with death rather than with love, is sceptical in a different way: it does not remain uncertainly poised on some indeterminate middle ground of imagination, but poses two distinct alternatives, the belief that man's only life is his present mortal one and the belief that there is another fuller life which in moments of beauty man can anticipate; then the poem remains quite uncertain as to which of these beliefs is the true one.

Heretofore we have tried to see these two odes as largely similar. But now, in distinguishing between the two modes of their scepticism, we have come to an important differentiation. Earl R. Wasserman has sensed this difference, but has, I think, interpreted it misleadingly. Professor Wasserman finds the *Ode to a Nightingale* far less successful than the *Ode on a Grecian Urn*, and he describes its relative unsuccess in terms taken from Keats's epistle *To J. H. Reynolds, Esq.* The *Ode to a Nightingale*, he says, conforms to no "standard Law," it exists in a spiritual no-man's-land that is neither earth nor heaven.[23] Now in this epistle to Reynolds, written over a year earlier, Keats is expressing a wish that the soul's "dreamings" might be all of the "material sublime" (as opposed presumably to the more immaterial sublime of religious tradition), that things could "to the will be settled." But Keats senses that perhaps things cannot be so settled, that in seeking a synthesis of earth and heaven the imagination may be brought

Beyond its proper bound, yet still confined,—
Lost in a sort of Purgatory blind,
Where it cannot refer to any standard law
Of either earth or heaven.

In other words, in writing his epistle to Reynolds, Keats is still wishing, as he had done in the letter to Bailey of November 3, 1817, for a "Recourse" or "Remedy" against the evils of human life which would be, if not wholly earthly, at least "somewhat human," somewhat "independent of the Great Consolations of Religion," imaginings of "the Beautiful" which would be still "within the pale of the World," or at least no farther removed than heaven's bourn. But in the epistle he is considering that such a realm, not wholly of earth nor wholly of heaven, may be without substantial reality, that instead of being a true discovery of the imagination it may be only a dead end.

Now insofar as the vision of the *Ode on a Grecian Urn*, for all its intensification, still is in part a development of Keats's elysian imaginings, still an example of the "material sublime," on the outer fringes of the World, where Keats would wish it to be, rather than wholly beyond it—insofar as these things are so, the elysium of the urn is precisely that middle ground which Keats in his epistle to Reynolds had earlier decided might be no real ground at all. In that case it is this ode on the urn, rather than that to the nightingale, which conforms to no *standard* law of earth or heaven, though, with its vision of love forever panting and forever young, it does conform to the personal, idiosyncratic, elysian law of Keats's imaginings while he still hopes that things can "to the will be settled."

This last law of Keats's personal elysium is precisely the one which Professor Wasserman deserves such credit for exploring fully, and it is to this law only that the *Ode to a Nightingale* does not conform. For when closely examined the poem to the nightingale turns out to be less idiosyncratic than that on the urn, more traditional. It conforms very well to the law of the earth, though of an earth to which "high Heaven doth chime," as Henry Vaughan had said in his poem *The Night*. The grove in which the nightingale sings is not an epitome of elysium but of the earth itself at a time when anguish is briefly forgotten. The poem does not seek to effect any such protracted consubstantion of heaven and earth as the ode on the urn imagines, but rejoices in the richness of earthly beauty as it actually is: flowers in bud, flowers full blown, flowers dying, each succeeding the others. The grove is rightly nocturnal since *vis-à-vis* heaven the earth is as a night. But unlike the "Purgatory" into which

Keats sometimes felt his elysian imaginings to be leading him, the night is not wholly "blind," not without vision of something beyond itself: it is a night into which the unseen moon, like a transcendent Deity, sends from above occasional flickers of uncertain light; it is a night through which the unseen nightingale, like Deity working in the world, sustaining the succession of mortal beauty, pours his pulsating song. If one of Keats's theological problems, like one of Shelley's, is at times an inability or reluctance to separate his earth and his heaven (as Keats himself in the epistle to Reynolds so clearly acknowledges to be the case), then in the poem to the nightingale he may be said to have achieved separation without producing any total cleavage.

In other words, what Keats's imagination momentarily glimpses in this ode is a perfection, but not perfection just of heaven or of elysium; rather it is a perfection of a whole cosmos, with three levels of existence, as this cosmos is seen from within the sphere of earth: a mortal world; a half-divine, immortal agency pervading this world; and beyond an eternal Divinity itself. For a moment he catches the chime which three make in harmony and his heart is cheered. When he can hear the chime no longer, he is back in the one-dimensional world where dying men must sit and "hear each other groan."

A simple but important point should be made about this brief cheering. The statement at the beginning of the last stanza that Fancy "cannot cheat so well" is not, as it is sometimes interpreted to be, an admission that the imagination as an organ of vision has definitely failed. It has failed only as a means of providing a prolonged escape from sorrow to a man still in the midst of mortal life. But the Romantics at their most serious do not consider imagination simply as the means of achieving such an extended vacation. They consider it as suggesting some consolatory hope beyond the sphere of mortality as we know it. Upon the imagination's ability to present such a hope, the last two lines of the poem make their judgment: as has been noted, it is a judgment poised between disbelief and acceptance.

Here again, not argumentatively but as a means of describing the poem accurately, I should like to point out that the darkness of the climactic scene in the grove does not express, as Professor Wasserman suggests, any bewilderment or despair that no more light is to be had, that Keats cannot "see" what flowers are at his feet. The whole grove is a beautiful embodiment of earth precisely as Keats would have it. As it is, he apprehends the fragrance of the flowers more richly and mysteriously than he ever could if he were in an open meadow, under a full moon which almost blotted out the earthly presences which he loved. He wants a heavenly light but he wishes it filtered: an immediate and powerful a sense of Deity, as *Endymion* makes perfectly clear, is too disturbing. Humanly enough, Keats wished to be spared if possible the anguish which a fuller and more insistent revelation brought upon Endymion—"Lest, having Him, I must have naught beside," as Francis Thompson was to say in *The Hound of Heaven*. Browning also, as we shall see, felt that men developed better if God stood at least a "handbreadth" off.

Two further facts should perhaps be noted about this ode. Unlike Wordsworth on occasion and unlike Byron's Manfred, Keats claims no direct intuition of his soul's own immortality. The immediate intuition is simply that this earth, however oppressive its misery often appears, is in fact sustained, penetrated, and blessed by some Beauty from above, and in the immediate presence of this intuition Keats himself, who a moment earlier had been bitterly regretting that men die young, now contemplates death with satisfaction.

The quality of Keats's sensibility here will not be scorned by those theologians who regard as primarily Platonic and stoic a strong emphasis upon the immortality of the soul *per se*, who find more in accord with the original spirit of Christianity a faith in a miraculous rebirth after death, a rebirth achieved only by the grace of God. This second view, as firmly based in tradition as the first, is found in John Donne's well-known sonnet, in which even the soul itself is raised from death:

> *Arise, arise*
> *From death, ye numberless infinities*
> *Of souls, and to your scattered bodies go.*

Now the *Ode to a Nightingale* does not present any divine agent which can miraculously re-establish in an eternity of bliss a John Keats who has become a "sod"—unless the bird itself can be said to operate upon the imagination almost in this way when it suddenly becomes an immortal heavenly power. Keats's imagination does not offer any clear and strong image of a Divine rescuer from death until the *Fall of Hyperion*, presumably written some months later. Hence perhaps the sense of discontinuity which some careful readers have felt in this ode.[24]

It is difficult for one who has read even a small fraction of the explications now in print to recall the first, fresh impression which the *Ode to a Nightingale* made upon him. Yet I do not remember being troubled by such a discontinuity, any more than one is troubled by hearing at a burial service such words as "Dust art thou, and to dust thou shalt return" followed by other words of more optimistic import. In any case, such a discontinuity is no mark of poetic failure. It has been said that it is the function of literature to put the questions, not necessarily to answer them. It is not surprising that Keats should experience simultaneously a sense of sinking into insensibility and a hint of some half-hidden secret source of joy. No more was it surprising that Wordsworth, at a comparable stage in his own development, should have brooded so deeply upon death and deprivation at the same time that he too felt so powerfully hints of some cosmic joy. It might be proposed that the very dramatic presentation of this discontinuity in the ode prepares for the tentative "answer" embodied a little later in the figure of Moneta. But any such supposition, though relevant to the study of Keats as a whole, is peripheral to our judgment of this one poem. At the time Keats wrote this ode, he felt life itself to be a perplexing enigma, sorrowful in the main and yet, briefly and mysteriously, intensely joyful. Such was the situation, such is the poem. Any too distinct integration imposed upon the materials by his imagination at this time would have been dishonest.

The comparison with Wordsworth suggests another observation. Wordsworth—as has been noted—in his ecstatic moments sometimes intuits an infiniteness of the spirit within himself, and sometimes feels overwhelmed by a power greater than himself; at times both experiences even come at once. Just as Keats does not share the seeming sureness of Wordsworth's first feeling, neither is he likely fully to experience the second. Yet there is, even in the *Ode to a Nightingale*, something of Wordsworth's sense of being "summoned" by some external power. The delays of the first few stanzas may be said to express the difficulty which this external power must inevitably encounter in an effort to "transport" out of his "sole self" one so self-centeredly sunk in the miseries of his life as Keats; the drowsy "aching" with which the poet first listens to the happy bird (the occasion, perhaps, of some excessively subtle criticism) may be no more than a dramatically appropriate description of a half-painful awakening which anyone deeply depressed might respond to a particularly beautiful piece of music, as the dormant or sluggish faculties needed for transport are roused a little at a time. On the other hand, the rhetorical devices which Keats employs, especially the "Away! away! for I will fly to thee," and the quite explicit desire to be freed of "The weariness, the fever, and the fret" both strongly suggest the old Keatsian habit of deliberately embarking upon a voyage of fancy. Hence the partial justification of F. R. Leavis's description of the poem as an "indulgence." [25] Yet the grove to which Keats flies is a very real one: some flowers die while others are being born. Thus the imaginative impression made by the poem as a whole is extremely complex, combining the sense of transport induced from without with that of a transport willed from within.

Here again the complexity of mood should perhaps arouse sympathy more than disapproval from those who, morally or theologically, find themselves in sympathy with religious tradition. This complexity is a very paradigm of the similar duality expressed in the orthodox doctrine that salvation is in the first instance a grace from without, but a grace with which man from within himself must at least in part co-operate. Beauty here, as so often in the Romantic tradition, affords the grace and in response to it Keats briefly succeeds in escaping from his despairing "sole self."

As for the sensuousness of the *Ode to a Nightingale*, some may be disturbed by it in direct proportion to the poem's presumed seriousness. They will not be able to respond sympathetically to the seventh stanza, in which Keats imagines himself lying down with Death the lover to experience simultaneously the greatest intensity of bliss and the transition into the insensibility of death. But here as elsewhere the sensuousness is part of the poem's general character, passive in the main though not entirely so. Like Donne in his sonnet, "Batter my heart," which makes use of far more vivid amorous imagery, Keats feels himself almost powerless to save himself; he must first be powerfully acted upon from without. Hence the unsuitability upon this occasion of any such imagination soaring as that manifest in the *Ode on a Grecian Urn*, ascending as it were to some elysium at the very gates of heaven. The senses are a more humble faculty than the imagination. Perhaps the *Ode to a Nightingale* should be viewed with sympathy by those who complain that Romantic imagination is in general too uncreaturely, too prone to try and save itself by creating a heaven according to its own tastes.[26]

This same uncreatureliness might be blamed for the Romantic confusion of earth and heaven which displeases conservative critics such as T. S. Eliot. Yet by being more sensuous and less insistently imaginative, the *Ode to a Nightingale* keeps these two regions more separate than the *Ode on a Grecian Urn*.

Two other great odes, the *Ode on Melancholy* and *To Autumn*, are relevant to the separating out of earth and heaven. In their acceptance of the evanescence and decay of earthly life both poems express moods of which humanism will approve.[27] The first poem declares for the acceptance. The second witnesses its fruits: the beauty of autumn can now be enjoyed in itself, without any excessive chariness of direct sensuous experience and without the pushing to vision which Keats had been evincing a little earlier. In its fine objectivity *To Autumn* represents a great accomplishment; it expresses just that piety "rich in the simple worship of a day" which Keats in the *Ode to Maia* had ascribed to the old Greek poets. The landscape around Winchester, when Keats walked through it on that late September afternoon, one of the last fully happy moments of his life, furnished him with a more-than-elysian perfection. It even mutely imaged an eternity after its fashion: in the course of the first two stanzas, during those hours when an observer would not be sharply conscious of the sun's descent toward the horizon, the scene exhibits that same poised fullness which Keats's imagination had always cherished; the onrush of time is at it were momentarily suspended, not by Keats's fancy but by nature itself. Then, when the sounds and movements of the last stanza break up the sculptural calm, the death of the day comes richly. In keeping with this objectivity Keats does not note explicitly that the full-grown lambs will be next year's sheep, that the gathering swallows will return in spring, or that the redbreast in the garden-croft will whistle all through the winter. Such a philosophy of earthly contentment as the poem expresses, congenial as it is to humanism, is not however entirely uncongenial to traditional religion. It need not preclude heaven and may even be the natural reward of recognizing that earth is earth and that heaven, if it exists, is something different. It represents a maturity and a partial disillusionment at which Keats's early half-metaphysical instincts would have had to arrive whether they were to fade out altogether or, on the other hand, re-establish themselves in some manner more wholly serious than that exhibited in the facile speculations of the letter to Bailey.

The Two *Hyperion*'s

C. L. FINNEY, in *The Evolution of Keats's Poetry*, influenced in part perhaps by his conviction that the general movement of Keats's thought was away from transcendentalism, argued that *Hyperion* was written after *The Fall of Hyperion*. His suggestion has not won general acceptance. But even if *Hyperion* were the last of Keats's important poems it might still afford evidence that Keats's imagination is as deeply involved in transcendental patterns as ever. The poem reveals Apollo at a moment of transition from a lower spiritual state to a higher: at this point he feels as though he is passing from death to some higher life or immortality, and in this higher life, the conflicts of mortal existence are somehow resolved. Just before the scene opens Apollo has felt some stirrings of the higher life within him, like Coleridge's air-sylph first sensing its nascent wings while still in the cocoon: [28] he has been asleep, dreaming of a goddess and of some revelation to come. He awakes, as it were breaking out of the cocoon, and the goddess is there—in short, the pattern is like that described in *Endymion* and in the letter to Bailey. It may be said that Apollo himself is also a god, but in his relation to his goddess Mnemosyne he is as a mortal. And indeed even his goddess turns out to be a deputy deity only and therefore his aspiration reaches still further:

> *"Where is power?*
> *Whose hand, whose essence, what divinity*
> *Makes this alarum in the elements,*
> *While I here idle listen on the shores*
> *In fearless yet in aching ignorance?"*
>
> (III, 103-7.)

The phrase "on the shores" suggests that to Keats the sea is still a symbol of eternity. The goddess Mnemosyne or Memory has come across this "unfooted sea" as though she alone, like the soul's subconscious memory in Platonic myth, maintained some mysterious bond with the "power" beyond. Also Mnemosyne cannot speak, even as the Platonic memory cannot enunciate its mystery in any distinct terms. But looking into the countenance of the goddess, Apollo can read there the image of some immortal knowledge which comprehends the conflicting "Majesties" and "agonies" of the world, the "Creations" and the "destroyings." In the presence of this knowledge Apollo undergoes a transfiguration part painful, part glorious:

> *Most like the struggle at the gate of death;*
> *Or liker still to one who should take leave*
> *Of pale immortal death, and with a pang*
> *As hot as death's is chill, with fierce convulse*
> *Die into life.*
>
> (III, 126-30.)

In *Hyperion*, in short, there still survives much that does not immediately fit into the category of "pragmatic humanism."

In *The Fall of Hyperion* the elements of religious sensibility are even more pronounced. The cosmogony of the poem, supplied by the classical myth with which Keats is now for a second time trying to work, is not reconcilable with traditional Christianity in every respect. Yet if one considers primarily Keats's own imaginative posture in the scene in which he himself appears, it is apparent enough how

The Fall may be rich in meaning to any reader who is inclined to regard Keats as being in some ways an *anima naturaliter Christiana*.

First of all, the face of the goddess Mnemosyne-Moneta, here more fully described than in *Hyperion*, offers a deeply moving image. F. R. Leavis has greatly admired this description as an expression of the tragic view of life, a view which for many modern secularists expresses the equivalent of certain aspects of traditional religion. The scene as a whole, however, is more religious than secular. The person who reads the goddess's face is now no longer Apollo, ostensibly a young deity in the presence of an older deity; he is quite frankly a mere mortal, John Keats himself. But the confrontation scene must be considered from its beginning. Once again in a dream, Keats has found himself in a richly sensuous nether world, and then in a somber and massive antique shrine where the "black gates" are "shut against the sunrise evermore." His spirit is still shut in, in the cocoon as it were, or, more precisely, in a place very like that "Purgatory blind" which he had envisaged earlier in the epistle to Reynolds. In spite of its subterranean gloom, this shrine is not without splendor and is pervaded by "Maian incense." Thus it would not in itself have been entirely uncongenial to Keats, just as earth itself viewed even as a dead-end offered much to gratify his senses. But then the shrine turns out not to be a dead-end after all, not entirely visionless. For at the west end Keats sees the goddess, and this goddess (though veiled at first and even when unveiled seemingly blind) offers to man a vision of divine suffering and saves him from death. It is interesting that the goddess in the later version, unlike her predecessor in *Hyperion*, has the power to speak to men: in this as in her more manifest suffering she is more closely akin to the Divine Redeemer of Christianity. Also in the second version she is usually called Moneta rather than Mnemosyne, perhaps because the Latin term, though cognate with the Greek, carries more suggestion of an admonition. Thus to Keats her voice comes as a warning:

> "If thou canst not ascend
> These steps, die on the marble where thou art.
> Thy flesh, near cousin to the common dust,
> Will parch for lack of nutriment—thy bones
> Will wither in few years, and vanish so
> That not the quickest eye could find a grain
> Of what thou now art on that pavement cold.
> The sands of thy short life are spent this hour.
> And no hand in the universe can turn

Thy hour glass, if these gummed leaves be burnt
Ere thou canst mount up these immortal steps."
(I, 107–17.)

At this moment cold death starts to creep up through the poet's body from the chill marble floor. After an agonizing effort he succeeds in touching the lowest step of the altar just as the cold is reaching his very heart. Immediately life pours into him. He exclaims,

"What am I that should be so sav'd from death?"
(I, 138.)

The conversation which follows between poet and goddess depicts Keats in an agony of uncertainty and perhaps of repentance. In the early letter to Bailey, Keats had applied the terms *dream* and *vision* indiscriminately to his imaginings and he had used both favorably. In the *Ode to a Nightingale* the truly prophetic *vision*, in touch with some substantial truth, is distinguished from the mere illusory *dream;* Keats was uncertain which he had experienced. Here at Moneta's altar Keats fears that he may be merely one of the "dreamers weak." The dreamer, as Keats now sees him, has two defects. He is deprived of action, and as such he is inferior to those who love mankind and labor actively for their good. ("His benevolence was great but inactive," Dr. Johnson had remarked of the poet James Thomson; and one recalls also the humility which Keats himself was soon to feel in the presence of the simple and devoted Severn who nursed him in his last months.) Again, the dreamer is deprived of truth, and thus is inferior to the true poet who in his own way can help the world.

In these deeply felt lines Keats brings to focus doubts which had been disturbing him with increasing frequency, doubts about what was to him the very essence of his being, his character as artist. The passage is one of complete seriousness and integrity. Repentance can itself sink into a luxury of sentiment, a mere beating of the breast. But Keats does not wallow in self-accusation. The warning voice sternly raises the question whether he is not a mere "dreamer," a "self-worshipper": he himself feels that he may be, but he is perplexed—it is just possible that he has been a real poet whose imagination has expressed some truth. A more striking example of Keats's serious "scepticism" in D. G. James's sense would be hard to find. His judgment upon himself and upon his vision is also very close to the sympathetic but uncertain judgment which Allen Tate passes upon the *Ode to a Nightingale*. (So Tennyson, when he flees from his dreamer's palace of art, yet refrains from destroying it.)

Keats's stern discipline of his imaginative perception of life and of his art was in fact a moral discipline also. Within the passage of a very few years he simultaneously becomes more sharply aware that the true poet must present action as action (not just as the motions of a man walking almost in his sleep, like Endymion) and that the true man should also seek an outlet in action. But the peril of action is that those too deeply involved in it may lack vision (as Matthew Arnold was frequently to point out later) and Keats is reluctant to deny that the dreaming, imagining, contemplating side of his nature (which is the part that has so far found most complete expression in his poetry) has been without its own element of truth. Again, though the immortality which the goddess bestows upon him is still in part the earthly immortality of a true poet, the passage strongly suggests that Keats is concerned with something more than art. The harsh circumstance of Keats's last years were leaving him increasingly uncertain of the value *in itself alone* of his "Beautiful," his remedy too much "within the Pale of the world." More than a year before he wrote *The Fall of Hyperion*, in the same epistle to Reynolds in which he had wished that his "Sublime" might be "material," that things "could to the will be settled," Keats's awareness of the ruthless destruction always present beneath the beautiful surface of life had already given him pause. Pause so serious indeed that despite his tendency, as a product of the Enlightenment, to regard religion as comprising chiefly "Superstition" and "Bishops," he could at least consider the possibility that he might in the end be reduced to the "remedy" which Christianity offered:

> 'Twas a quiet Eve;
> The rocks were silent—the wide sea did weave
> An untumultuous fringe of silver foam
> Along the flat brown sand. I was at home,
> And should have been most happy—but I saw
> Too far into the sea; where every maw
> The greater on the less feeds evermore:—
> But I saw too deep into the core
> Of an eternal fierce destruction
> And so from Happiness I far was gone.
> Still am I sick of it: and though to-day
> I've gathered young spring-leaves, and flowers gay
> Of Periwinkle and wild strawberry,
> Still do I that most fierce destruction see,
> The Shark at savage prey—the hawk at pounce,
> The gentle Robin, like a pard or ounce,

Ravening a worm—Away ye horrid moods,
Moods of one's mind! You know I hate them well,
You know I'd sooner be a clapping bell
To some Kamschatkan missionary church,
Than with these horrid moods be left in lurch.

Note the extremely austere form of Christianity which the last two lines present.

As Keats originally planned *Hyperion,* his first version of the myth, it must have been envisioned in part as an attempt to "justify" suffering and tension and displacement. To Keats suffering was an inseparable aspect of growth; as to Wordsworth, pain as well as joy made this world a "vale of soul-making." Pain is presumably inseparable from "civilization-making" also, since *Hyperion* for Keats is clearly a myth about the development of cultures as much as a myth about the development of individuals. His description of the fallen Titans—noble, a little more than life-size, with an undivided wholeness of their own—is a little like Henry Adams' account in his *Autobiography* of the impression which the son of Robert E. Lee, personifying the culture of the ante-bellum South, first made upon his more complex Harvard classmates; like some admirable Southerners, the Titans revealed only one defect: their limitations of imagination and intellect were such that they had no awareness that the world was not static, that it was constantly evolving new forms. Now when this succession of new forms was a succession of modes of a civilization, the justifying of the suffering may seem to satisfy the imagination: the sufferings of a civilization are after all somewhat impersonal and remote and when they have been endured civilization is still there in its new stage to enjoy the fruits earned by the sufferings. But Keats was fundamentally less interested than Shelley in developments within society as a whole; he was concerned more with the development of different stages of being which he could sense within himself. With respect to these painful changes, the crass questions are more likely to arise, "To what end all these agonies of soul-making? Where will John Keats be a few decades hence to enjoy their fruits?" To the lofty idealist, such questions may express spiritual immaturity; but if this be the case, we must just accept the fact, which the letters make plain, that Keats was not at all times mature in this particular sense. One of the reasons for the uncompleted state of *Hyperion* may be that the political theme of successive social orders, which the myth was best suited to express, was not close to Keats's own heart; even in first handling it, he reveals his interest in the more personal or religious question of stages of individual development. In his second version, instead of trying completely to unite both themes in his treatment of one myth, he separated them out into the myth proper of the fallen Titans and the now quite distinct dream-vision of John Keats and Moneta. This separation left the myth with less meaning for him than it had at first, and it is hard to see how he could ever have finished *The Fall of Hyperion* satisfactorily even if his final decline into death had not set in so soon.

Keats never recanted his faith in beauty and imagination (they were all he had, all of which he could be sure), but his own seriousness and pressure of circumstance in his last years appear to have been forcing him to make a choice, against his will: to abandon the semi-metaphysical speculation with which he had early surrounded beauty and to accept beauty simply as a good within a wholly naturalistic scheme of things, or else to see it as prophetic in a more serious and challenging way than he had quite bargained for, and as mingling a warning along with its prophecy. Much within his nature still urged him towards the first choice, the simple naturalism. But the ravin in the world which had destroyed half his family was soon destroying him. The wish that there might be a remedy above the ravin was inescapable.

Keats's life was an unusually harsh one; the view, which at times overwhelmed him, of this world as a mere vortex of destruction is a partial view only. Those who cherish Keats principally for his leanings toward naturalism may dismiss his continued awareness of supernatural possibilities as merely the human weakness of a man condemned to an early death; according to the old adage, "Hard cases make poor law." But if they dismiss this awareness out of hand, they are being more single and certain in their own philosophic outlook than Keats ever was in his.

By critics of a quite different sort Keats's continuing philosophic perplexity might be ascribed to his insistence upon keeping his imaginings close to sensuously perceived earth. Shelley's greater eagerness to soar no doubt suggests a spirit in sympathy with the emphasis which Christianty has always placed upon hope and upon faith in things unseen. Keats, more like Thomas the doubter, when he has not seen does not believe. Yet by staying closer to the concrete, he gains in steadiness. He oscillates less wildly between Shelley's "twin torturers," Hope and Despair. Though there is always likely to be some prejudice against sensuousness when combined with seriousness, the prejudice may be unfortunate. Upon this question each reader must form his own opinion.

Yet, as has already been noted in an earlier chapter, it is an undeniable fact of intellectual history that Christianity originally presented itself not as a system of intellectually grasped ideas but as Truth Incarnate. During its first few centuries it resisted the tendencies of the sophisticated and enlightened Alexandrian schools to refine it into an idealistic philosophy and it resisted pressures from Manichaean modes of thought which would have led it to identify good with spirit and evil with matter. The rationalism of the Enlightenment and perhaps a continuing puritanical strain in English Christianity had long been exerting similar pressures when Keats first began to think about Truth. He was, of course, not concerned with preserving religion. But his poems and letters alike reveal how strongly he was seeking to preserve some incarnate Truth. As a result, his sensibility at times is extraordinarily close to some basic Christian traditions. According to the New Testament, Christ appeared semi-corporeally after his resurrection. Again, the Gospels' most striking expression of the relation between the earthly and the heavenly is not a Shelleyan image of the soul shedding its material encumbrances. It is an image of the material transformed rather than cast off: when Peter, James, and John went up the mountain they say Christ "transfigured" so that his countenance and his garments shone "as white as snow." This is the exact equivalent of the Indian maid's transfiguration into Cynthia at the end of *Endymion*. It suggests something like the *etherealization* of earth which Keats hoped for in Elysium. It is very similar to the transformation, at once physical and spiritual, experienced by young Apollo in *Hyperion*. In view of these similarities there is perhaps some irony in Keats's conviction that the immateriality of the Christian ideal was the chief cause of his own lack of sympathy.

Something of the change which had been brought about during the preceding period may be suggested by going back to 1709, to *Spectator* No. 580. Addison could offer to his readers a thought which was almost exactly Keats's own "favorite speculation," without feeling that he was threatening his own orthodoxy or that of his readers:

The senses are faculties of the human soul, though they cannot be employed, during this our vital union, without proper instruments in the body. Why therefore should we exclude the satisfaction of these faculties, which we find by experience are inlets of great pleasure to the soul, from among those entertainments which are to make up our happiness hereafter?

$\mathcal{V}$

TENNYSON

T̲HE̲ C̲AMBRIDGE̲ "Apostles," the group of which Tennyson and his friend Hallam were members while at the university, undertook upon occasion to discuss such topics as "the origin of evil" and "the personality of God." [1] Hallam himself sought to justify the universe in his *Theodicea Novissima*. The young men in this group were perplexed, willing to believe, but reluctant to shut their eyes to those obstacles in the way of belief which life itself suggests and which had been further magnified by recent rationalist and scientific thought. Such a group early strengthened in the poet a lifelong habit of pondering ultimate religious questions.

Evolutionist, Mystic, and Platonist

T̲ENNYSON̲ I̲N̲ H̲IS̲ O̲WN̲ W̲AY̲ was an evolutionist a score or more years before the theory of evolution was confirmed by Darwin's explanation of its mechanical processes.[2] General human history and the history of fossils suggested to him, as it did to others, that life was evolving toward higher forms. His imagination was committed to two different modes of progress: the continued development of the human race as the earthly species which we know and the destined

138

ascent of the individual through a succession of higher and more spiritual states. In his imagination, as in Shelley's, these two forms of progress were not always sharply distinguished. Such blurring of the usual categories of theology was, as T. S. Eliot has noted, typical of the age.[3] It is also to be found in the great vision at the end of Browning's *Paracelsus*. Equally undifferentiated perhaps had been the sudden consciousness, experienced by Wordsworth when crossing the Alps, of "something evermore about to be."

In this cosmic march onward and upward, the postulate of human immortality seemed necessary to Tennyson not so much that the good might be rewarded and the evil punished, but that God might not be open to the charge of wastefulness. He felt that suffering and love and other human experiences developed individual souls, and presumably this spiritual development was for some use, to some end. He says in section 82 of *In Memoriam*:

> Nor blame I Death, because he bare
> The use of virtue out of earth;
> I know transplanted human worth
> Will bloom to profit, otherwhere.

Tennyson's justifying arguments, like Browning's and perhaps like most such arguments, are based upon the old philosophical principle, "*Natura* (or *Deus*) *nihil agit frustra*"—nature, or God, does nothing in vain. Reliance upon such a principle was, of course, a deliberate act of faith, or will; as *In Memoriam* itself testifies, nature appears to be very wasteful indeed, both of individuals and of whole species. The early death of Arthur Hallam, with his potentialities only partly developed and very little used, raised this question of waste with particular insistency.

So pervasive in Tennyson was the common nineteenth-century progressive or evolutionary cast of thought that he could, almost simultaneously, declare Christianity to be a divinely revealed truth and regard it as being outmoded or outdated for advanced minds. In section 36 of *In Memoriam* he says that though the cosmic truths are "deep-seated" in man's "mystic frame," they reside there only darkly; therefore we must yield "all blessing" to Him who in the actions of His life and death expressed these truths so simply and clearly that all could understand. In the following section the heavenly Muse rebukes the poet for presuming to darken the sanctities of revealed religion with his song; his humbler task, within the province of the earthly Muse, is to record truth as it is written in man's heart. But just four sections earlier—with trepidations at his own boldness and warnings to himself of the danger of pride—he suggests that in his religion of the human heart he may have arrived at a more spiritual belief, beyond the forms and types of Christianity. He is addressing himself and contrasting his own faith in the face of Hallam's death with that of his own sister, who was to have been Hallam's bride:

> O thou that after toil and storm
>   Mayst seem to have reach'd a purer air,
>   Whose faith has centre everywhere,
> Nor cares to fix itself to form,
>
> Leave thou thy sister when she prays
>   Her early heaven, her happy views;
>   Nor thou with shadow'd hint confuse
> A life that leads melodious days.
>
> Her faith thro' form is pure as thine,
>   Her hands are quicker unto good.
>   O, sacred be the flesh and blood
> To which she links a truth divine!
>
> See thou, that countest reason ripe
>   In holding by the law within,
>   Thou fail not in a world of sin,
> And even for want of such a type.
>
> (#33.)

(Tennyson calls his sister's heaven "early" because, in his liberal equivalent of the old belief in Purgatory, he held that men would "close with God" only after many intermediate stages—in a final union which, one gathers, might entail some loss of identity as this is generally thought of.) [4]

There are those who feel, like E. D. H. Johnson in his study *The Alien Vision,* that Tennyson exaggerates the diffidence with which he holds his own natural religion; that he is speaking only with his "public voice" when suggesting that it is only holy awe which deters him from further celebrating Christianity; that in manifesting so tender a concern for pious sensibilities he endangers his own integrity. In any event, the faith advanced in the greater part of *In Memoriam* and in Tennyson's poetry generally is that of the natural inner light, the Romantic faith in individual feeling and imagination. Many Victorian readers were pleased precisely because this was so. Some more orthodox readers were perhaps gratified only because the piety of tone somewhat obscured for them the naturalistic heterodoxy of

idea. Other orthodox readers in Tennyson's own time objected to the
naturalism even as some of their successors have done since.

Tennyson's faith in the inner light was not a matter of cold
demonstrable logic. Quite the contrary. In *The Two Voices* he
speaks of "the heat of inner evidence," and in section 124 of *In
Memoriam* the heart's final answer to doubts raised by "freezing
reason" is simply the ardent assertion, "I have felt." Certain parts
of *In Memoriam* might be said to "argue" in favor of faith by chains
of reasoning derived from the basic assumption of an unwasteful
cosmic purposefulness, but it is the heart or imagination that demands
this assumption. Tennyson himself later stated that these argumentative parts were more affirmative than he felt they should be; he
thought he should have shown that the arguments were "about as
good on one side as the other," and thus thrown the reader wholly
upon "the primitive impulses and feelings." This rather Kantian judgment was perhaps right for Tennyson; the more discursively reasoned
sections of the poem are not the best.

Religion of the inner light, if intensely enough felt and culminat-
ing in moments of especially vivid awareness, takes on the aspect of
mysticism. That Tennyson was something of a mystic has long been
a critical commonplace, a commonplace supported by the poetry,
by the *Memoir* written down by his son, and by other records.

In one of his best-known short pieces Tennyson proclaimed that
if he truly understood the "Flower in the crannied wall," he would
understand "what God is and what man is." But the unit of cosmic
life which he could come closest to understanding was not a flower
but himself. Hence in section 36 of *In Memoriam* he says we find the
truth in our own "mystic frame." Hence also the statement of the
Seer in *The Ancient Sage:*

> *If thou wouldst hear the Nameless, and wilt dive*
> *Into the temple-cave of thine own self,*
> *There, brooding by the central altar, thou*
> *Mayst haply learn the Nameless hath a voice,*
> *By which thou wilt abide, if thou be wise,*
> *As if thou knewest, tho' thou canst not know.*
>
> (ll. 31–36.)

—Even so Keats, searching within himself, had by the central altar
of a temple-cave, heard the voice of Moneta.

In its deepest self-awareness, the soul recognizes itself as belong-
ing to an order of reality higher than the physical world. In *The
Voice and the Peak* the soul illustrates Kant's sublime by refusing
to be overawed by the magnificence of nature:

> *The Peak is high and flush'd*
> *At his highest with sunrise fire;*
> *The Peak is high, and the stars are high,*
> *And the thought of a man is higher.*

This poem is a rhetorical and "public" one and thus reflects a philo-sophic position more than a moment's insight. The thought, of course, is reminiscent of Wordsworth's sense of his own soul's tran-scendence, its sublimity. Furthermore, Tennyson was sustained in his philosophy by moments of vision like those which Wordsworth reports from his own childhood, those moments when Wordsworth was so immersed in himself that he lost all touch with the everyday physical world, or when, at any rate, that world ceased to be appre-hended as the most real of things. In the *Memoir,* for instance, Ten-nyson reports times when, oblivious of all else, he had an intensified consciousness of his own individuality, followed ultimately by a sense of losing that individuality not into extinction but into true life. There was nothing peculiarly Christian about such moments. In the *Idylls,* however, owing to the demands of dramatic appropriate-ness, they are given an orthodox coloring; at the very end of *The Holy Grail,* in lines which Tennyson regarded as the spiritual center of the entire larger work, King Arthur is telling of those visions to which man may give himself more freely when his earthly duties are done:

> *Let visions of the night or of the day*
> *Come as they will; and many a time they come,*
> *Until this earth he walks on seems not earth,*
> *This light that strikes his eyeball is not light,*
> *This air that smites his forehead is not air*
> *But vision—yea, his very hand and foot—*
> *In moments when he feels he cannot die,*
> *And knows himself no vision to himself,*
> *Nor the high God a vision, nor that One*
> *Who rose again.*

(The physical world is here termed "vision" in a sense different from the way the word "visions" is used at the opening of the passage; in accordance with the more or less Platonic metaphysic expressed in *The Higher Pantheism* and elsewhere, Tennyson is proclaiming that the material world is but an *appearance* of the spiritual or divine. So Shelley had thought that earthly beauty might be but the "shadow" of some "unseen Power.")

One special mode of Platonic thought suggests not just that the soul is aware of the higher realm to which it belongs but that it *remembers* that realm. Wordsworth, because of the fame of his *Ode*, is especially noted for celebrating this remembrance. The truth is that Tennyson experienced such a feeling more habitually than Wordsworth. Also he expresses it without any such apology to the orthodox as Wordsworth subsequently published with his *Ode*. In a very early poem, *The Two Voices*, Tennyson asks,

> *how should I for certain hold,*
> *Because my memory is so cold,*
> *That I first was in human mould?*
>
> (ll. 340–43.)

and a few lines farther on he continues,

> *something is or seems,*
> *That touches me with mystic gleams,*
> *Like glimpses of forgotten dreams.*
>
> (ll. 379–81.)

Section 44 of *In Memoriam*, in lines quite reminiscent of Wordsworth's *Ode*, says that as man is immersed more deeply in this present world he forgets his earlier existence, except when

> *the hoarding sense*
> *Gives out at times—he knows not whence—*
> *A little flash, a mystic hint.*

And much later, in a passage which Tennyson says was written out of deep personal feeling, the Seer of *The Ancient Sage* exclaims,

> *To-day? but what of yesterday? for oft*
> *On me, when boy, there came what then I call'd,*
> *Who knew no books and no philosophies,*
> *In my boy-phrase, "The Passion of the Past."*
> *The first gray streak of earliest summer-dawn,*
> *The last long strife of waning crimson gloom,*
> *As if the late and early were but one—*
> *A height, a broken grange, a grove, a flower*
> *Had murmurs, "Lost and gone, and lost and gone!"*
> *A breath, a whisper—some divine farewell—*
> *Desolate sweetness—far and far away—*
> *What had he loved, what had he lost, the boy?*
> *I know not, and I speak of what has been.*
>
> (ll. 216–28.)

Tennyson refrains from making his cosmology as definite as Plato's hypothetical scheme in the *Phaedrus*. These evocative passages in Tennyson do not always suggest that some divine good has been lost, just some earlier good.

Tennyson's deep commitment to these latter lines is related to that pervasive nostalgia which critics have noted in his work. W. H. Auden sees Tennyson as being, like Baudelaire, an exile "from a lost paradise." [5] And Douglas Bush says that the actual world inspired in Tennyson "a temperamental melancholy, a brooding, a wistful sense of the past, an unappeasable desiderium . . . a cry of profound sadness and bewilderment." [6]

In Memoriam: The Glory of Nature and the God in Hallam

THE PHYSICAL WORLD may lose its substantiality to men of mystical imagination. But to Tennyson (as to Marvell and Wordsworth and others) the beauty of this world was often the occasion of those very moments when the world was all but forgotten. Even more so, this beauty was the occasion of those moments when the world seemed transfigured. The best place to study Tennyson's use of intimating moments is *In Memoriam*.

In section 56 Tennyson confronts the problems of evil and death. The natural world appears "red in tooth and claw," devouring without compunction the individual life which we cherish. In the face of this heartlessness, man has yet trusted and praised God and "battled for the True, the Just." Can it be that man's ultimate fate is to be

> *blown about the desert dust,*
> *Or seal'd within the iron hills?*

This section of the poem gives no answer. But the phrasing of its final stanzas suggests that any satisfying reply will come not from reason but from the aesthetic sense which is repelled by the disharmony between man's aspiration and a mere dusty fate. If man and his hopes are doomed to extinction then he is by nature a creature more "monstrous" than the hideous creatures of the prehistoric world:

> *A monster then, a dream*
> *A discord. Dragons of the prime,*
> *That tare each other in their slime,*
> *Were mellow music match'd with him.*

Tennyson longs for an answer from "behind the veil" of surface appearances, an assurance that the ultimate law is not ruthlessness but "Love."

What is it that intimates to Tennyson that the primary truth may be melody or love, not discord? At the unconscious level the harmonies of Tennyson's own verse may serve, as Wordsworth says they should serve, as a powerful indirect "acknowledgment of the beauty of the universe." But at the conscious level Tennyson in *In Memoriam* will say no more than that the making of verses is soothing; nowhere in this work does he claim that the beauty of a merely human art is an occasion for joy, exaltation, vision. Stronger intimations are supplied by the beauty of nature. In section 88, the bird's song is expressly felt as the symbol of some cosmic good:

> *Wild bird, whose warble, liquid sweet,*
> *Rings Eden thro' the budded quicks,*
> *O, tell me where the senses mix,*
> *O, tell me where the passions meet,*
>
> *Whence radiate: fierce extremes employ*
> *Thy spirits in the darkening leaf,*
> *And in the midmost heart of grief*
> *Thy passion clasps a secret joy;*
>
> *And I—my harp would prelude woe—*
> *I cannot all command the strings;*
> *The glory of the sum of things*
> *Will flash along the chords and go.*

The spring of the year had been unable to counteract Tennyson's depression in the earlier part of the poem, that part corresponding to the years just after Hallam's death. But in later years, just preceding Tennyson's hearing the "wild bird," its triumph over winter seems an irresistible revelation. Spring has on this occasion been long delayed; Tennyson had even dreamed it would never come again. Then late one afternoon, after a storm, the sun comes out. Suddenly, spring is at hand. Section 86, celebrating this occasion, has been regarded by one of Tennyson's most distinguished commentators, A. C. Bradley, as the climax of the poem: [7]

> *Sweet after showers, ambrosial air,*
> *That rollest from the gorgeous gloom*
> *Of evening over brake and bloom*
> *And meadow, slowly breathing bare*

The round of space, and rapt below
Thro' all the dewy tassell'd wood,
And shadowing down the horned flood
In ripples, fan my brows and blow

The fever from my cheek, and sigh
The full new life that feeds thy breath
Throughout my frame, till Doubt and Death,
Ill brethren, let the fancy fly

From belt to belt of crimson seas
On leagues of odor streaming far,
To where in yonder orient star
A hundred spirits whisper 'Peace.'

These stanzas, literally interpreted, are not a record of a gift of grace but a prayer for grace. Yet the movement of the language is such that the reader feels the prayer is answered even as it is uttered. —Tennyson's poetic style does not always have the celebrated matter-of-factness of Wordsworth's, and the question arises how far these stanzas on the spring are the record of an actual moment. No reply is possible beyond noting that the lines, according to the *Memoir*, were composed in the spring at Barham.

These parts of *In Memoriam* are often very reminiscent of Shelley. The "secret joy" of the bird recalls the skylark which sang rapturously because it knew something of death about which men were ignorant. Similarly reminiscent is the beauty of the spring, with its "leagues of odours," which brought peace to the poet's fevered cheek. The final focussing on the orient star is similar to the end of *Adonais*. More closely still, section 121, which notes that the Evening Star and the Morning Star are the same, recalls the Greek epigram with which Shelley prefaced his elegy. To Tennyson, as to Shelley, the star suggests some persistence of individuality, at least until a final absorption into the divine.

Like Shelley's poetry, *In Memoriam* is haunted by the spectre of solipsism, the fear that the ideal towards which men yearn has no objective existence or warrant and is merely the phantom creation of our desires. Yet fear appears less powerful than in Shelley's case. More frequently than Shelley Tennyson is able to respond uncritically to the beauty of the world, to accept it quite simply as the authentic revelation of some ultimate Goodness. Here Basil Willey, for all the excellence of his discussion of *In Memoriam*, may be a little misleading. He comments upon this section of *In Memoriam* hymning the return of spring as though it were no more than an exercise in self-expression, a mere utilizing of the outward symbols of nature to give artistic form to the feeling of renewed life which the poet now feels within.[8] Such in part the lyric undoubtedly is, and in the first years after Tennyson's loss the annual rebirth of nature had been insufficient to counterbalance his inward grief. But as the immediate intensity of sorrow subsides, the outer world slowly resumes its legitimate power. Certain phrases in Professor Willey's discussion, such as the Coleridgean description of the moment as the "coalescence of subject and object," would certainly seem to concede as much. Yet other parts of his discussion suggest that we are here concerned with a wholly subjective event. In this same connection one might at least qualify Professor Willey's statement that Tennyson felt "that the whole spectacle of Nature was somehow irrelevant to faith." [9] In a sense this again is true. Considering the ruthless mechanisms of its processes, Tennyson found nature "red in tooth and claw," bespeaking no benevolent First Cause but affording merely that same spectacle of all-destructive ravin which upon occasion had so appalled Keats. Like Immanuel Kant, Tennyson was dissatisfied with the traditional argument from design. But also like Kant he was in practice inclined to make something of an exception in the case of the imaginative perception of nature's beauty. Here, both men somehow felt, was a moment of direct intuitive cognition when the soul escaped the trammels of logic and felt itself in touch with some ultimate realm of spirit akin to itself. In other words, while distrusting the intellectual argument from design, they trusted what appears to be its more imaginative counterpart or equivalent. —In its ultimate origins the argument from design had perhaps been as much imaginative as logical; more recently, the progress in the physical sciences had helped to separate man's response to nature's mechanisms from his response to its beauty.[10]

The point is an important one. Despite the fact that *In Memoriam* speaks of the "heat of inward evidence" which begets religious faith, the poem taken as a whole, together with the rest of Tennyson's poetry and his life, makes it clear that this inward evidence developed in very close conjunction or "interchange" with a partly objective, outward beauty. Tennyson in this respect differs from Wordsworth less than Professor Willey believes. To point out this much is perhaps no more than to repeat what was said earlier: that poets are inclined to be Platonists. The crucial question for Wordsworth and Tennyson, and perhaps for Shelley and the others also, was not whether there is an ultimate Power but whether this Power is one to which man can be related by love. Love, as Plato noted, is the response to beauty even as beauty is the begetter of love.

But the existence of another human being whose grace can arouse
our love can prompt us to faith at least as powerfully as the existence
of a beautiful landscape. In accord with the general Victorian tendency to stress human love as the agent of divine power, Tennyson
finds his strongest intimations not in images of landscape but in the
image of a fellow man, Arthur Hallam, and in Hallam's love for him
and his for Hallam. In this emphasis Tennyson appears to mark a
change. Though *Resolution and Independence* and a few other poems
might be cited as minor exceptions, Wordsworth leaves the impression that he scarcely even contemplated such an experience as Tennyson's with Hallam. Keats may appear to be contemplating it at the
end of *Endymion*, but in actual life his personal relations took on no
strongly metaphysical overtones. Shelley craved some such relationship, but the beloveds of his verse, as has already been noted, have
little substantiality. *In Memoriam*, however, which is as much a love
poem as a religious poem, convinces us that Tennyson loved and
grieved for Hallam the man, not just for Hallam the occasion of
imaginative concretings of the abstract. Hence Tennyson's intimations strike one as being more solidly based than Shelley's.

For five years Tennyson had known Hallam intimately, not as a
living statue, and not as pure spirit, but as living body, mind, and
spirit, constituting in all as full an earthly image of divine perfection
as Tennyson craved.[11] As Wordsworth in the presence of landscape
felt himself in the presence of an immanent divinity, so Tennyson,
listening to Hallam discourse, had seen

> *The God within him light his face.*
> (#87.)

As Wordsworth had seen the divine and the material united before
his eyes in the valley of the Wye or at Grasmere, so Tennyson had
caught an expression in Hallam's eye in which

> *God and Nature met in light.*
> (#111.)

Even as Wordsworth, separated from the Wye, had turned to it in
spirit, in like manner Tennyson, separated from Hallam by death,
repeatedly turns to him in spirit for comfort. The climax of Wordsworth's relationship with Wye valley was his actual return to it. The
climax of Tennyson's relationship with Hallam is similar but more
complicated: back again on the lawn where he and Hallam had spent
many summer evenings, all sensuous desire lulled by the richness of
the night (as Wordsworth's hunger of the "eye" had been made

quiet by the power of visual harmony), Tennyson takes out and
reads again the letters in which Hallam had spoken of doubt and faith;
suddenly Hallam, as it were, touches him again and through this return of his friend Tennyson momentarily stands in the presence of
eternity: [12]

> A hunger seized my heart; I read
>   Of that glad year which once had been,
>   In those fallen leaves which kept their green,
> The noble letters of the dead.
>
> And strangely on the silence broke
>   The silent-speaking words, and strange
>   Was love's dumb cry defying change
> To test his worth; and strangely spoke
>
> The faith, the vigor, bold to dwell
>   On doubts that drive the coward back,
>   And keen thro' wordy snares to track
> Suggestion to her inmost cell.
>
> So word by word, and line by line,
>   The dead man touch'd me from the past,
>   And all at once it seem'd at last
> The living soul was flash'd on mine,
>
> And mine in this was wound, and whirl'd
>   About empyreal heights of thought,
>   And came to that which is, and caught
> The deep pulsations of the world,
>
> Æonian music measuring out
>   The steps of Time—the shocks of Chance—
>   The blows of Death. At length my trance
> Was cancell'd, stricken thro' with doubt.
>
> Vague words! but ah, how hard to frame
>   In matter-moulded forms of speech,
>   Or even for intellect to reach
> Though memory that which I became;
>
> Till now the doubtful dusk reveal'd
>   The knolls once more where, couch'd at ease,
>   The white kine glimmer'd, and the trees
> Laid their dark arms about the field;

And suck'd from out the distant gloom,
A breeze began to tremble o'er
The large leaves of the sycamore,
And fluctuate all the still perfume,

And gathering freshlier overhead,
Rock'd the full-foliaged elms, and swung
The heavy-folded rose, and flung
The lilies to and fro, and said,

'The dawn, the dawn,' and died away;
And East and West, without a breath,
Mixt their dim lights, like life and death,
To broaden into boundless day.

(#95.)

Besides their literal meaning, do the East and West in the last stanza
symbolize for Tennyson, as they sometimes do for Browning, the
religious intuitions of the Orient and the scientific knowledge of the
Occident? Are these to combine into the fullness of truth? After the
momentary lifting of the burden by his mystical experience, Tennyson might hope that such an eventuality will come to pass. In any
event, this ending is notably different from that of Keats's *Ode to a
Nightingale:* when the nocturnal ectasy has passed and the poet is
once again in the natural world, this world does not so much put the
validity of Tennyson's vision in doubt as it confirms it—as the coming of morning and the awakening of life confirms the vision of
David in Browning's *Saul.*

The experience recorded in these stanzas is more out of the ordinary than the earlier responses to the bird and to the coming of
spring. It is as mystical as anything in Wordsworth. And like Wordsworth's return to the Wye, Hallam's return promises strength for the
future:

the face will shine
Upon me, while I muse alone,
And that dear voice, I once have known,
Still speak to me of me and mine.

(#116.)

There is the same drawing upon past strength by both poets, but the
past that Tennyson draws upon is the bond of love with another
man, not the bond with nature. In *In Memoriam* this love is, in
Tennyson's words, his "Lord and king," and because this love guards
him he knows, through the long night of life, that "all is well."

The actual climax of Tennyson's vision, it must be noted, is not just the renewed sense of Hallam's presence, any more than the resurgence of past images was the culmination of Wordsworth's return to Esthwaite or the Wye. Tennyson had originally written that when the dead man touched him from the past, "*His* living soul was flashed on mine" and "mine in *his* was wound, and whirl'd." Upon reconsideration he rephrased these line (perhaps a bit clumsily): "*The* living soul" and "mine in *this*." He felt that in the sequel to the revivifying of the personal bond his imagination had perhaps been lifted to some realm beyond individual personality, beyond that which develops to that which "is." The simple present tense suggests the Old Testament's "I am" and Christ's "Before Abraham was, I am," as well as the obvious parallel of Plato's realm of being beyond the realm of becoming.

In other words, Tennyson's moment of mystic vision on the lawn, which began, like Wordsworth's moment described in the Tintern Abbey *Lines* and Marvell's in *The Garden*, in the appeasement of the half-physical faculty of imagination by the rich harmony of the material world about it, terminated in a moment of sublimity when the soul seems to stand outside the material flux, aware of its bond with some eternal realm of spirit.

As a result of this total experience, Tennyson felt that the universe was in a sense "justified." Chance and Death, the same recalcitrant facts which to Shelley suggest blind ruthlessness rather than ordered benevolence, now seem less discordant: for a fleeting moment some eternal music assimilates them into its harmonious "measure." The basic image, derived from the aesthetic response to art, is the same as in Wordsworth's *Lines*, where the beauty of the landscape has transformed the harshnesses of life into "music," cadences "still" and "sad" perhaps, but withal music.

As has already been remarked by critics, this catching of intimations from man's relations with his fellow man is not peculiar to Tennyson among the Victorians. Rather, it is typical of the age. Browning is celebrated for it. Arnold's *Rugby Chapel* is an instance. Rossetti in *The Blessed Damozel* sees an imaginary man's love for a woman as his only claim to salvation. In *The House of Life* his own love for Elizabeth Siddal takes on religious overtones: he asks what life would be like if he were never to see her again:

> *How then should sound upon Life's darkening slope*
> *The ground-whirl of the perished leaves of Hope,*
>   *The wind of Death's imperishable wing?*
>
>   (#4.)

And when she dies the latter part of the sonnet sequence becomes another *In Memoriam*. Similar also to Tennyson's detecting the God in Hallam is Carlyle's habit of examining the countenances of friend and acquaintance for outward signs of an inward divinity. Meanwhile in America Walt Whitman was combining his love of the man Lincoln with the symbols of the lilac blooming again in spring, the bird's song, and the western star into a triumphal chant which at once accepts death and seems to transcend it—though in Whitman, of course, there are few if any traditional suggestions of individual survival or of an eternal Platonic One. Not until the later *Passage to India*, do the terms of his thought come close to those of religion or idealistic philosophy.

This difference between the impersonal images of the Romantics and the more personal ones of the Victorians is related to other literary facts. There is the comparative weakness of the Romantics in dramatic writing, their rather limited success in creating characters independent of themselves; we must rely heavily, when we would measure them at their greatest, upon those great lyrics in which they speak directly of the movements of their own souls. By contrast, in the Victorian age there was Browning's notable dramatic power. Tennyson himself instinctively turned to the dramatic monologue or dramatic stream-of-consciousness from the very start, though rather more often than in Browning this seems but a thin disguise. Also, in comparison with the earlier period, the middle and end of the century showed a greatly increased activity in the novel and finally a revival of the drama itself.

In any event, when reading *In Memoriam* one is powerfully reminded of the affinity between Tennyson's personal way of receiving revelations and the personal way of Christianity. This similarity is consciously pointed up in the Prologue addressed to the "Strong Son of God, Immortal Love." But this prologue and other more explicitly Christian passages are in one sense almost extraneous to the core of the poem. In that core the note of reverence to a person is sustained toward Hallam rather than Christ; Hallam takes the place of Christ. He becomes the chief witness for the belief that there is some divinity in men, that they are in some sense "children of God." It is in Hallam that "God and nature met." It is not in Christ's words in the New Testament that God speaks, but in the remembered discourses of Hallam when the "God within him" lighted his face. To the Christian, Christ's resurrection from the dead is the warrant of human immortality; in *In Memoriam* this warrant is the return of Hallam's spirit as Tennyson reads the old letters.

In keeping with Hallam's Christ-like position are Tennyson's prayers to his spirit, so evocative of traditional prayers and hymns that many unwary readers must have been misled:

> *Be near me when my light is low . . .*

> *Be near me when the sensuous frame*
> *Is rack'd with pangs that conquer trust . . .*

> *Be near me when my faith is dry . . .*

> *Be near me when I fade away,*
>   *To point the term of human strife,*
>   *And on the low dark verge of life*
> *The twilight of eternal day.*

(#50.)

And a little farther on,

> *I cannot love thee as I ought.*

(#50.)

(In Tennyson a liberal nineteenth-century Protestant appears to have come full circle back to the Roman Catholic practice of the invocation of the saints.) Equally confusing to some readers, perhaps, have been the lines in which Hallam is addressed not as a sort of God-Man but as a deity immanent in all creation; like Wordsworth's spirit that "rolls through all things":

> *Thy voice is on the rolling air;*
>   *I hear thee where the waters run;*
>   *Thou standest in the rising sun,*
> *And in the setting thou art fair*

> *What art thou then? I cannot guess;*
>   *But though I seem in star and flower*
>   *To feel thee some diffusive power,*
> *I do not therefore love thee less.*

(#130.)

Tennyson's love for Hallam has passed into worship.

The semi-religious emotions of humility, reverence, and awe, which Tennyson felt incipiently for the living Hallam and more strongly for Hallam dead, remind one that Shelley never knew anyone in whom for any length of time he recognized any great personal superiority, intellectual or otherwise. This matter is perhaps of some importance. Tennyson's contemporary, Carlyle, built a political and social philosophy on the basis of men's need to have a leader they can look up to. There is evidence that Shelley did not welcome his own exalted isolation: in the person of Beatrice Cenci he portrays the terrifying despair which finally overcomes a noble spirit who can find no one to venerate: Beatrice's father is the personification of evil and all the others whom she knows are either evil or base or weak. Keats at the end may have been moved to admiration by Severn's unwearying devotion, as Wordsworth was moved by the leech-gatherer's courage, but neither of these had Tennyson's chastening experience of living close to one whom he felt his superior in personal grace, in moral power, and in intellect. To Tennyson's credit, he seems not to have felt envy, only love and admiration. Tennyson's consciousness of his own superior poetic power may have helped him to maintain his self-respect, but he was aided by two other qualities also: a certain simple generosity which was his by nature and the feminine strain in his personality which is expressed in *In Memoriam*, somewhat to the amazement of a modern reader, by the imagery in which Tennyson is a bride and Hallam the groom— even as in the language of religious devotion the soul is the bride of Christ.

These observations are not intended to praise or disparaise any of the poets, or to prefer one before the other. But they do cast light upon the poets' psychological situations and their poetry, and upon the inescapable connection between secular emotional patterns and religious ones.

The Child Fixed in Truth

SOME READERS MAY SPECULATE whether some connection is not discernible between the personal sources of Tennyson's intimations and the inferior quality of his poetry. It is widely believed at the present time that *In Memoriam* is inferior to the best poetry of the Romantics. It may be felt also that the earlier men were not only greater poets, but greater minds: that Tennyson was never more than what he had early termed himself, a "second-rate sensitive mind." Plato after all has said that those whose love is focussed upon individual persons are only a few steps up from the bottom of the ladder of love; he believed that the greatest minds rose to apprehend reflections of the One in more and more abstract forms; at the top or near the top of his scheme was nothing so concrete and personal as the Lord or the Christ of traditional religion. The supreme power of the universe is not, some may feel, truly, or at this late date fruitfully, to be regarded as a person. Those inclined to hold such views may see only superior intellectual honesty in the inability of the great Romantics to find any such comfortable spiritual resting-place as the "court" where Tennyson slept, watched over by Love, his Lord and King, which whispered in the night that "all is well." Such speculation would place both Tennyson and the traditional religious imagination in an inferior position. Such judgments may well color certain critical evaluations of Tennyson.

Yet there is no inevitable connection between the inferiority of *In Memoriam* and the personal mode in which it is cast. This inferiority—if it is a fact—may be the result not of any particular forms in which Tennyson's imaginings work themselves out but of the comparatively weaker impulse behind these imaginings. Tennyson's metaphysical Despair is never great enough, one might say real enough, to generate a really powerful urge to find a ground for Hope. Near the end of the poem Tennyson acknowledges as much:

> *Yet Hope had never lost her youth,*
>   *She did but look through dimmer eyes;*
>   *Or Love but play'd with gracious lies,*
> *Because he felt so fix'd in truth.*

(#125.)

This stanza, though distressing in its tenderly mannered style, is fine in its candor. But it reveals why the most satisfying parts of *In Memoriam* are usually those which tell of love and grief with a minimum of cosmic speculation. When Tennyson deals with his despair in the face of the mystery of the universe he is by his own confession playing with the mystery. This is something the great Romantics did not have to do. This mystery was in their case compulsive; it drove their imaginations into action. Their poetry did not have to tease the mystery into life in order to have a worthy topic upon which to exercise itself.

It would not be true to say that Tennyson had no doubts of the rightness of the religious instinct in general. He had many. But they were perhaps largely of the intellect; since like most poets and most men he was not primarily an intellectual, these did not shatter his being to the core. His innermost faith, half-instinctive, half-traditional, was perhaps never shaken for long. Such a faith, once established, is perhaps seldom destroyed by intellectual doubts alone, such questions as circulated among the young Apostles at Cambridge and were combatted by Hallam. The deepest desolation which Wordsworth, Keats, and Shelley knew was not the product of mere intellectual processes. The cataclysmic events in Europe at large and the harshnesses which buffeted them in their own youth made them feel more abandoned, more cut off. The truth seems to be, to judge from Tennyson's own admission, that the loss of Hallam did not strike him so low as the loss some years later of his money. But he unexpectedly got his money back, and his life once more knew its even tenor, its comfortable security. One cannot help feeling that his religious faith itself was shored up by the persistence of comforting externals: his mother and her quiet faith, his sisters and their faith and their music, comfortably situated friends and their comforting praise, pleasant country houses, even pleasanter lawns and gardens, old churches and settled rectories and vicarages, and around all, like a glory, the loveliness of the countryside.[13] Tennyson's imaginative life, like that of most men, was based upon the facts of his own everyday life. At the time, to the class of readers to whom *In Memoriam* most powerfully appealed, these particular facts seemed a secure foundation.

Be these things as they may, Tennyson's encounter between hope and despair is something of a mock battle. He was, as he says, fix'd in truth." Or, as another of his revealing phrases expresses it, he was

> *a child that cries,*
> *But, crying, knows his father near.*
> (#124.)

Not such cries as these are heard in the terrible closing lines of *Alastor,* or in the anguish of the scene with Moneta in *The Fall of Hyperion.*

It must be said in defense of Tennyson that he nowhere makes any effort to deceive others about the true state of affairs. The truth does not wait till such passages as those just quoted from the end of the poem. Even in the middle sections he no sooner voices his fears than he denies their validity. He does not cry for some faith, any faith, so much as for a stronger faith. And many of his doubts are not about the ultimate question, whether there is an afterlife of the soul, but about the subordinate question, whether that afterlife will be satisfying in precisely the way we mortals might wish it to be: whether, for instance, we shall continue to love our friends and be loved by them. Tennyson acknowledges his own frailty in asking such a question. Also, repeatedly in the poem itself and in his reluctance to publish it, Tennyson showed what may have been a sincere modesty. He regarded his "elegies," as he called them, as a cry of weakness, not the pillar of strength which many readers soon found them.

If any such strength was actually there, it was not to be found
in original imaginative power but in the eloquent affirmation of the
traditional position, of the fact that man is not saved just by striving
upwards from below but is aided from above: so Tennyson prays in
the prologue:

> Forgive these wild and wandering cries,
> Confusions of a wasted youth;
> Forgive them where they fail in truth,
> And in thy wisdom make me wise.

This judgment upon Tennyson, that he exaggerates somewhat his
religious despair (though not his sorrow or his temperamental melancholy) and that in him the instinct to believe in a providentially
ordered universe was rather securely implanted, would appear to be
at odds with the opinion of T. S. Eliot. Eliot calls the faith of *In
Memoriam* a "poor thing," and he is impressed by the poem's "religious despair." [14] Since he also deplores the failure of Tennyson to
develop any further after *In Memoriam*, he is perhaps impatient with
him for failing subsequently to push on to such a fuller acceptance
of Christianity as Eliot himself would recommend. Once again we
are face to face with the question of how orthodoxy is to regard a
merely natural religion and a merely natural mysticism. Basil Willey,
though perhaps in agreement with Eliot on the inadequacy of
Tennyson's faith from a Christian point of view, is none the less far
more sympathetic in his interpretation of the historical significance
of the limited spiritual security which the poem represents. Professor Willey remarks,

> In spite of the Prologue, 'Strong Son of God, immortal Love'
> (which was in fact composed at the end), *In Memoriam* is not a
> distinctively Christian poem. The doubts, misgivings, discourage-
> ments, probings and conjectures which make it humanly moving
> could not have existed in a mind equipped with the Christian
> solutions. It is well to remember, sometimes, how much in litera-
> ture as a whole presupposes a suspension, not of disbelief, but of
> belief. Most of literature lives on the level of Nature, not of
> grace. And thus *In Memoriam* is not concerned with the impact
> of the Zeitgeist upon Christian doctrine or apologetic, nor does
> it proffer Christian consolation. It goes behind Christianity, or
> passes it by, confronting the preliminary question which besets
> the natural man, the question whether there can be any religious
> interpretation of life at all. What made the poem acceptable even
> to the Christian reader in the Victorian age was that having,

though with diffidence and humility, vindicated the believing temper, accepted the reasons of the heart, Tennyson had opened a door which gave access to the Christian territory.[15]

A critic contrasting the pallid faith of *In Memoriam* with the warmer and more solid assurance of Hopkins or of Francis Thompson, may perhaps see in this pallor a measure of the desperateness of Tennyson's religious position. But this would be different from asserting that Tennyson himself deeply felt any such desperateness. Given his temperament and the circumstances of the times he seems to have been reasonably content to "faintly trust the larger hope." Some may feel he ought not to have been so easily satisfied, but this does not alter the facts. It is perhaps best to accept Tennyson's own word for it that all the *arguments* for despair which abound in *In Memoriam*, however much they may have affected other Victorians, had never in Tennyson's case penetrated quite to the quick; that at its deepest core his heart had in fact been that of a child who knows his father near.

The Moated Grange

THERE ARE OTHER WORTHY POETIC ENDEAVORS besides the Romantic quest for metaphysical vision. Many eighteenth-century writers, for all their differences from Tennyson, were in his situation: they were a little embarrassed by some aspects of religion but not aware of any desperate metaphysical insecurity. Two of the greatest of these, Swift and Pope, used their imaginations passionately and successfully not in the sphere of religion or metaphysics but in the sphere of morals.

In his later career Tennyson did seek to create a great masterpiece of the moral imagination, *The Idylls of the King*. He failed. The ambitions and vanities and snobbishnesses which Swift and Pope satirized they wholly understood; they had not only closely observed them in others but had felt them in themselves. Such an inner understanding Milton also had of Satan's pride and ambition. But of such persons as the Lancelot and Guinevere of his legend Tennyson could know nothing. One critic has remarked that the *Idylls* are weak because their author, to have told the story with power, should at least have had the potentiality for a great lawless physical passion.[16]

Tennyson did have moral problems which were more immediately his own. They were the problems of the lethargic. His was the lethargy of a poet prone to sensuous reverie. Of this lethargy Words-

worth had known something; and Keats and Thomson, the author of
The Castle of Indolence, had known a great deal. Tennyson's lethargy was also that which may oppress a man who feels that circumstances have cut him off from life. Tennyson's gentle birth and his
temperament cut him off from such working participation as an
ordinary man is likely to know. His comparatively narrow means cut
him off from the full social and political life of the English gentleman, and for many years cut him off from marriage also. With
somewhat similar straitenings Wordsworth and Keats had been familiar. But the problems posed by the situation seem to have been
unusually acute in Tennyson's case. From the first they are treated
symbolically or dramatically in his poetry: in *Mariana*, *The Lady of
Shalott*, *Oenone*, *The Palace of Art*, *The Lotus-Eaters*, *Ulysses*, *Ti-
thonus*, *Locksley Hall*, and *Maud*. The last two deal more particularly with the problem of the impoverished gentleman; the recur-
rence of this theme, and the personal quality of these poems (which,
despite Tennyson's protests, the reader cannot help feeling) indicate
the deep insistency which the matter had. Now all these poems may
not often, if ever, reach great heights. But they have a certain authenticity. It is significant that Tennyson's favorite among his own
works was not *In Memoriam* or *The Idylls of the King*, but *Maud*.

This primacy of *Maud* confirms what a reading of the poet's life
strongly suggests. The earliest and deepest roots of Tennyson's
melancholia are not to be found in the Victorian religious situation.
They are to be discovered in his sense of the social and domestic
wrongs within his own family: the half-disinheriting of his father
by his worldly and tyrannical grandfather; the entailing of the estate
upon the arrogant and worldly uncle; his father's deepening bit-
terness.

The full effect of environment is impossible to measure. Some
readers will dismiss all excuses for Tennyson and say that his poetic
weakness is the natural result of a nature not passionate, or deep, or
powerful enough to produce poetry any better than it did produce.
Here, however, Hugh l'Anson Fausset pleads in extentuation: he believes that in Tennyson's case an undeniable native weakness was
made worse rather than better by many circumstances.[17] More particularly, he believes that Hallam's early death cut the poet off from
one who might have energized and goaded him. In death Hallam was
a source of metaphysical assurance to Tennyson; living he might
have been a symbol and source of life itself to one only too inclined to exist, like the Lady of Shalott, in a world of shadows.

Tennyson sought to put into practice his belief that a man must
move from his private world of imagination and take action in the

world of men. He sought to do so principally by becoming less of a private poet and more of a public one. Perhaps such a solution is an inadequate compromise, and in any event his more public poetic voice is not today listened to with admiration by many critics. Yet his inner urge to action is in itself important and every bit as valid as the similar urge expressed by Keats in *The Fall of Hyperion*. In their fears lest their poetic natures cause them to be mere "dreamers," both poets reveal their awareness of a central moral truth.

The Tennysonian Style

IT MIGHT BE MAINTAINED that nowhere in Tennyson's case did circumstances more clearly augment inherent weaknesses than in the matter of poetic style. If Keats had never written, if Tennyson had been exposed more to Homer and the Attic tragedians and less to Ovid and Virgil, modern dissatisfaction with the Victorian laureate might be considerably less. Insofar as his ideas may be considered apart from the tone which his style imparts, they do not differ greatly from those ideas of his contemporaries which, when presented in a more masculine idiom, can still command respect even when they fail to win agreement.

Tennyson's life and letters and the *Memoir* often suggest that the poet possessed a simplicity of nature, even a noble simplicity. For example, there is the unself-consciousness of his remark to a friend with whom he was walking on the hills: "God is walking with us now on this Down, as we two are walking together, just as truly as Christ was walking with his disciples on the way to Emmaus. . . . To feel that he is by my side now, as you are, that is the very joy of my heart." [18] For a man who could speak thus in prose, an essentially simple poetic style might, one supposes, have been appropriate. But there was the other side of his nature, the languid luxuriance. While he was still a young man his friend Hallam classed him as essentially a "picturesque" poet, who moved us by his charming images, who sought not to convince but to enrapture, by the "fairy fineness of his modulations." Such tendencies were strongly reinforced by the example of Keats; like him Tennyson tried to "load every rift with ore," the ore being usually wrought to a dainty filagree. H. M. McLuhan has recently emphasized that Tennyson's poetic ancestry is to be found not in the high classical tradition but in the late classical idyll and romance.[19] More robust poets like Chaucer have taken Ovid's prettinesses in their stride, but upon Tennyson the effect was perhaps debilitating. In Tennyson Virgil's famous "tears of things"

still fall, in a minor key and to a daintier sadness. In his fine tribute
Tennyson hails Virgil as the

> *Wielder of the stateliest measure*
>   *ever moulded by the lips of man.*

But two other lines reveal that Tennyson found in his Mantuan master other qualities of style which confirmed his own inclinations towards the ornate and towards a lovely wistfulness somewhat re-
lentlessly pursued into the smallest details of diction: he found in him

> *All the chosen coin of fancy*
>   *flashing out from many a golden phrase,*

and

> *All the charm of all the Muses*
>   *often flowering in a lonely word.*

These descriptions of style suggest what should perhaps be regarded as a concession. Tennyson's ceaseless quest for a style which
would flash golden splendor as from some mysterious source is probably related to his most deeply stirring apprehensions of beauty, precisely to such moments of mystical insight as are the subject of this
study. For in these moments the beauty of the world itself seemed
to flash light as through some aperture, or—as Wordsworth said—
to penetrate to the soul with gleams as from "the flashing of a shield."
Beauty to Wordsworth, as has already been noted, inevitably suggested some spiritual otherness, some quality which he could best
designate by the term *dream*. Keats too on such occasions felt he had
had a vision or a dream:

> *Whence that completed form of all completeness?*
> *Whence that high perfection of all sweetness?*
>   *(Endymion,* I, 606–7.)

To the poets such beauty seemed not wholly of this earth—where
had it come from? In an effort to capture some of this rich otherness
which had been their profoundest imaginative experience, no wonder
that Keats and Tennyson tried to make their poetry golden in a
world of brass.

Here, however, certain differences at once suggest themselves.
Keats, for all his luxuriousness, was more masculine and his aureate
style is likely to seem sturdier. Even more significant is another fact:
whereas moments of beauty would often fill Tennyson with an un-

appeasable desire to return to something lost, as to a past, Keats's instinct had from the beginning interpreted them as prophetic of some state still to come. Speculations as to the causes of this difference must perhaps lead to the deepest parts of both men's personalities and the very mysteries of their lives. Here there is time to point to only one set of facts. Keats had grown up in a city which he found not beautiful and sometimes oppressive. Tennyson's early years had been passed in a countryside of mellowed loveliness, enriched by traditions, untouched by the ravages of industrialism. His "believing temper" was closely associated with these childhood scenes, and his dread of the new era—democratic, urban, seemingly chaotic—was doubtless intensified by the threat which it posed to a beloved landscape. Thus in Tennyson the bard of "bower" and of "hall" one feels—far more than in Keats's *The Eve of St. Agnes* or his idealizations of ancient Greece—a neurotic dread sapping some vital bond with the present world, a dread which allies him in spirit to the Pre-Raphaelite painters.[20]

Tennyson's art was greatly admired by Mallarmé; the French poet, I believe, termed it "noble." Perhaps others have noted a certain resemblance between a frequent manner of Tennyson's and the Symbolist obsession with style, with creating an artefact as richly and mysteriously wrought as possible. Arthur Hallam had early perceived that his young friend's poems were in their essence rather like the magical incantations towards which Symbolist art ultimately tends. Tennyson's delicacies of style may be viewed as the expression of an imagination seeking to reconcile itself to a world which in large part it found crude and distasteful. So two notable modern works, *Ulysses* and *Finnegans Wake*, resort to even more powerful incantatory devices in order that Joyce may symbolically say "Yes" to the life of Dublin from which he had, in fact, felt compelled to exile himself forever.

Be that as it may, Tennyson's very real sense of "otherness," his unappeasible "desiderium," seek appeasement in the creation of a second world in which the sturdy reality of this world is often not so much ennobled as refined away into a semi-somnolent daydream. No "Æonian music" measures out the shocks of chance and death, but delicately fingered cadences caress themselves to the point of weariness. The result is well-known: the influence of the poet laureate's style, working upon an age already inclined to turn its back upon much that is vigorous in life, produced especially among the weaker imitators a new poetic style and diction as false as that which Wordsworth had attacked at the opening of the century.

It is no wonder that Matthew Arnold in his 1853 *Preface* should have revolted against what he felt to be the Shakespearean and the Keatsian tradition; that he should have wished a poetry more intent upon the strong outlines of its action; that he feared, some years later, that he had himself not wholly escaped the infection and that his *Sohrab and Rustum* was less strong and simple than he wished. In due course Arnold felt it necessary to rebuff the suggestion that the blank verse of *The Idylls of the King*, with its delicate and melancholy measures, was a suitable medium for translating the vigorous and straightforward verses of Homer; he had earlier remarked that Homer's style was naturally simple in its movement, and he then was compelled in his final essay in *On Translating Homer* to declare that such simplicity as Tennyson appears to achieve is of a very artful kind, "*simplesse*" as the French would say, not the true "*simplicité*." [21]

But no man should be judged by his weaknesses only, or by his most regrettable influences upon others. When what might be termed the special Tennysonian effects are appropriate, they can display a fine perfection of craftsmanship that is almost awesome; the sensitivity of the poet's ear has been praised even by such modern advocates of a more astringent style as Eliot and Auden. In contrast, when almost opposite effects were deliberately sought, the poet was able on two occasions to produce the astonishingly earthy Northern Farmer poems. Lastly, in *Crossing the Bar*, simple feeling is expressed in verse simple enough, both in movement and diction, to have pleased even the taste of Matthew Arnold had that exacting critic still been alive to read it.

BROWNING

Dᴜʀɪɴɢ ᴛʜᴇ ʏᴇᴀʀs when Browning was growing up as artist and man, he wrote three long poems about the psychological and spiritual difficulties along the road to maturity. All three are about "crises of mood," as he termed them in the introduction to *Paracelsus.* Seldom in these poems does the hero experience moments of transcendental revelation in the fullest sense, intimations of some religious truth as vivid as such later Browning characters as David and Abt Vogler will receive. Yet these three poems are of profound interest to the student of Romantic intimations for two reasons. First of all, Browning did not believe that moments of revelation suddenly arrive without any preparation. They are, rather, the culmination towards which the human impulse to worship naturally tends; in the earlier stages of development a man may simply worship images he knows not why, without any intellectual or imaginative appreciation of the fact that he is, according to Plato's scheme, worshipping them because they are images of the One. Of some of these earlier stages of worship both *Pauline* and *Sordello* supply an interesting account. Thus they may be considered as parallel to those early poems in which Keats worships beauty in nature and art without quite knowing his reasons, sensing dimly that it points to the solution of life's mystery. Again, as one might expect in Browning,

164

the crises in mood which all three poems explore are evaluated according to traditional Christian doctrines and standards, and thus the poems may be regarded as more or less orthodox critiques of the whole Romantic tendency to worship images. In this respect, however, *Paracelsus* is different from the other two long poems. There is no question of its hero worshipping images too much. On the contrary, his crises are due in considerable part to his worshipping them too little: in Platonic terms his devotion to ultimate truth, to the One conceived intellectually, is too little supported by devotions to such imperfect but solid images of the One as the beauty of the world and the goodness in its people may supply. The result is a precariousness which Browning did not regard as either psychologically or religiously desirable.

Pauline and Images

OF THESE THREE EARLY WORKS *Pauline* holds the greatest interest for the general reader because of its manifestly autobiographical character. John Stuart Mill's easy penetration of the poem's fictional guise disconcerted the young poet; seldom if ever again was he to reveal his inner life so frankly and fully.[1]

Pauline may be compared with those parts of *The Prelude* in which Wordsworth tells how the imagination is impaired and restored—though, as Mill pointed out, the restoration is probably not so complete at the end of the poem as the poet himself seems to think. In both Browning's and Wordsworth's poems the critical intellect and its attendant pride are principal villains. Yet *Pauline* must be interpreted more broadly also: it records such general feelings of alienation as any man, even one never strongly influenced by intellect, is likely to experience as he moves away from childhood and youth.

The speaker of the poem at times views his crisis as a religious one. The phrases which reveal this fact are sometimes brief, but their implications would have been intelligible enough to contemporary readers. It was customary for the Victorian woman to have a serene religious faith and for the man to be afflicted by doubt. Therefore the young poet, addressing Pauline herself, regrets those "wild thoughts"

> *which, but for me, were kept*
> *From out thy soul as from a sacred star!*
>
> (ll. 14–15.)

Other passages are fuller, unmistakable in their import. He describes the moment when he became aware of his intellectual powers in these terms:

> *My powers were greater: as some temple seemed*
> *My soul, where nought is changed and incense rolls*
> *Around the altar, only God is gone*
> *And some dark spirit sitteth in his seat.*
> *So, I passed through the temple and to me*
> *Knelt troops of shadows, and they cried "Hail, king!*
> *We serve thee now and thou shalt serve no more!*
> *Call on us, prove us, let us worship thee!"*

    .   .   .   .

>   *And I said "Ye will worship*
> *Me; should my heart not worship too?" They shouted*
> *"Thyself, thou art king!" So, I stood there*
> *Smiling—oh, vanity of vanities!*
>
>   (ll. 469–88.)

But this immediate sense of the power of his own mind does not last. The young man must believe in and worship something other than himself. For a while he sees his religious belief as a mere "prejudice" of childhood and upbringing, but he will take even prejudice so that he be not "loveless." Then the sense that such belief is mere prejudice passes away; he returns a penitent and supplicant to the emotionally still very real God of his Chapel-going youth. The soul, he says, sickens of commanding and can only rest

>   *beneath*
> *Some better essence than itself, in weakness.*
>   (ll. 818–19.)

He continues:

> *My God, my God, let me for once look on thee*
> *As though nought else existed, we alone!*
> *And as creation crumbles, my soul's spark*
> *Expands till I can say,—Even from myself*
> *I need thee and I feel thee and I love thee.*
> *I do not plead my rapture in thy works*
> *For love of thee, nor that I feel as one*
> *Who cannot die: but there is that in me*
> *Which turns to thee, which loves or which should love.*
>   (ll. 821–30.)

In order to keep alive within himself the sense of love and worship the speaker determines to stay close to Pauline, who will shut him in from "fear." In other words, the love and worship of Pauline and the love and worship of God are viewed as mutually reinforcing rather than antagonistic; indeed, they seem but modes of one and the same feeling. Students of Browning have long known, and Betty Miller in her biographical study has recently emphasized,[2] the strong and intimate connection between Browning's love for his mother and his love for the God of the theologically simple and happy religion which she had imparted to him. Thus the protective figure of Pauline, when it hovers over the young poet and helps him to feel once more a "contented lowness," stands in his imagination in place of his mother. When many years later Browning was planning to marry, he expressed regret that the marriage would inevitably entail some loss of filial closeness. As Betty Miller shows, with the persistence of a Freudian enthusiast, Browning then stubbornly sought to worship Elizabeth Barrett and to continue to enjoy, now in respect to her, the old "exquisiteness of being transcended." (Elizabeth, needless to say, was not altogether pleased.) Despite brief periods of feeling alone, Browning managed to avoid being weaned psychologically even after his mother's and his wife's death. All during the composition of *The Ring and the Book*, as he told the story of Pompilia and worshipped the memory of his wife, he continued to enjoy some of the old content. Afterwards, except upon occasions, the memory must have become less vivid, and he probably experienced more continuously than in his youth that difficulty which is a recurrent theme in his first three poems, the lack of anyone "higher" than himself to look up to. Hence in part perhaps the aridity of much of his later work.

Betty Smith, for all her implied disapproval of the prolonged bond between Browning and his mother, concedes that the relationship did the poet no permanent harm. The reason why it did none is readily discoverable. In *Christmas-Eve* Browning says,

> *God, whose pleasure brought*
> *Man into being, stands away*
> *As it were a handbreadth off, to give*
> *Room for the newly-made to live,*
> *And look at him from a place apart,*
> *And use his gifts of brain and heart,*
> *Given, indeed, but to keep for ever.*
>
> (ll. 289–95; Sect. v.)

If the young poet's image of the universe had been completely dominated by his mother, and if his religion had remained wholly that of
the chapel to which she took him, there would have been some
stifling. But though Sara Ann Browning was always there, she seems
to have been a happy woman, liberal by nature, with no unnatural
urge to tyrannize; she stood "a handbreadth off" and Browning had
room to grow. This growth involved the straining of old pieties,
but perhaps because they were free to bend they did not break; and
the poet's development involved also the addition of new pieties corresponding to the growing range of his interests.

Thus it is that *Pauline,* for all its brief moments of desolation,
is not mainly a record of a loneliness of heart and an impoverishment
of worship. Rather it records the turbulent succession of stirring and
brilliant images which an eager young man, worshipful by nature
and habit, finds available for awe and wonder. Like Wordsworth and
Coleridge Browning pays tribute to those tales of the marvelous
which first rouse the child's sense of wonder. Later the same sense is
stirred by poetry and by music,

> *which is earnest of a heaven,*
> *Seeing we know emotions strange by it,*
> *Not else to be revealed.*
>   (ll. 365–68.)

One remembers Keats's account of how poetry had early filled him
with wonder and a sense of mystery; Browning's youth repeats the
same story over again.

All this enthusiasm finally focussed, as the poet says,

> *Not so much on a system as a man.*
>   (l. 404.)

The habit of worshipping persons was deeply ingrained in Browning,
and the figure of Shelley, now dead for ten years, becomes to him
even such a demigod as Hallam became to Tennyson. The first and
longest of the poem's tributes to Shelley begins in language which
echoes *Alastor* and *Adonais,* but the living presence of Shelley's
works, now coming into posthumous fame, precludes any sense of
desolation:

> *Sun-treader, life and light be thine for ever!*
> *Thou art gone from us; years go by and spring*
> *Gladdens and the young earth is beautiful,*
> *Yet thy songs come not; other bards arise,*

But none like thee: they stand, thy majesties,
Like mighty works which tell some spirit there
Hath sat regardless of neglect and scorn,
Till, its long task completed, it hath risen
And left us, never to return, and all
Rush in to peer and praise when all is vain.

(ll. 151-60.)

First, as is natural, Browning had been caught by the mere splendor of the poetry (as Wordsworth had first been caught by everything in nature that appealed to eye and ear). Browning then received some inkling of a meaning; the words

seemed
A key to a new world, the muttering
Of angels, something yet unguessed by man.

(ll. 414-16.)

A fuller understanding of Shelley's devotion to liberty and of his dreams of a millennium followed. But the final image remained the man. As Tennyson longed to see the dead Hallam once more, Browning longs to see Shelley:

To see thee for a moment as thou art.

(l. 205.)

Among Browning's "wild thoughts" had apparently been some doubts about immortality; now, half in prayer for strength and half in gratitude for strength received, Browning exclaims to Shelley:

Remember me who set this final seal
To wandering thought—that one so pure as thou
Could never die.

(ll. 207-9.)

In other words, the purity of Shelley's spirit put an end to those wandering thoughts in which young Browning had doubted the immortality of the soul. (Soon afterward Browning seems to have become aware of some limitations of the Shelleyan temperament, but the sense of awe in the presence of a personal radiance persisted at least as late as the writing of the moving *Memorabilia*. This veneration was seriously impaired only at a later date still, when Browning came to believe that he may have been wrong in assuming that Harriet had been unfaithful before Shelley left her.) [3]

All this worshipping of strange gods sometimes seemed to the young poet to be a betrayal of the simple faith of his fathers. Yet penitence for backsliding into polytheism is not the final note of the poem. Browning is already engaged upon his lifelong habit of "case-making." W. C. DeVane has said that after *Pippa Passes* Browning's central preoccupation is justifying the ways of God to man;[4] but the full truth is that Browning was a theodicist from the beginning, finding an ultimate good in as many things as possible. Here he is making a case for the young man in a confused state of seemingly divided loyalties. He finds no insurmountable difficulty in the way of his undertaking because he is naturally a Platonist; like Plato he sees divers manifestations of the good and beautiful as all revelations of the One. Hence all devotions to these manifestations are but forms of aspiration toward the One. So long as he is loving and admiring something which seems better than himself, and (he adds here a human and specifically Shelleyan touch) so long as he feels himself loved, he knows no "fear" and feels all to be subsumed into one great saving scheme of hope and love. In attracting him to the varied manifestations of divinity the young poet's "imagination" has been an ever-present "angel";[5] he has not gone far off course because he has always been guided by a "lode-star," by

> *A need, a trust, a yearning after God.*
> (l. 295.)

Thus it is that at the end of the poem Browning restates rather than repents his love of Shelley—even as Tennyson reaffirms his almost religious veneration of Hallam:

> *Sun-treader, I believe in God and truth*
> *And love; and as one just escaped from death*
> *Would bind himself in bands of friends to feel*
> *He lives indeed, so, I would lean on thee!*
> *Thou must be ever with me, most in gloom*
> *If such must come, but chiefly when I die,*
> *For I seem, dying, as one going in the dark*
> *To fight a giant: but live thou forever,*
> *And be to all what thou hast been to me!*
> *All in whom this wakes pleasant thoughts of me*
> *Know my last state is happy, free from doubt*
> *Or touch of fear. Love me and wish me well.*
> (ll. 1020–31.)

Interestingly enough, Pauline herself is not directly mentioned in this last hymn to God, truth, love, and Shelley; perhaps she has been absorbed into the larger category of "love." Just before these lines she had been addressed in a long Shelleyan passage. Her love is indispensable, the poet tells her, to his own spiritual life. The two will go off (like Shelley and Emily) to an earthly paradise. She will enable him to understand the message which music is trying to utter to his soul; she will be the mystery's "solution, no mere clue." And together they will be able to read the meaning of the seasonal renewal of life:

> *when spring comes*
> *With sunshine back again like an old smile,*
> *And the fresh waters and awakened birds*
> *And budding woods await us, I shall be*
> *Prepared, and we will question life once more,*
> *Till its old sense shall come renewed by change,*
> *Like some clear thought which harsh words veiled before;*
> *Feeling God loves us, and that all which errs*
> *Is but a dream which death will dissipate.*
>
> (ll. 971–79.)

But it was proper that this Emily-Pauline should fade out. Though elsewhere in the poem Pauline is unconsciously an image of the poet's mother, she is here more directly the symbol of the woman he expects one day to fall in love with; at this early stage, Browning's picture of connubial life, only faintly stimulated by his friendship with Eliza Flower, was not very real or vital. John Stuart Mill astutely suggested that the young poet's spiritual confusion would clear up when he met and fell in love with a real Pauline.

When Sara Ann Browning went to buy her son a copy of "Mr. Shelley's Atheistical Poems: very scarce," the bookseller sold her Keats's works as well. In *Pauline* Browning displays some of the strengths of these two poets without the weaknesses which partly explain their anguish. In style, he has much of Keats's solidity without his occasional sense of being drugged; in substance, he embraces the good of the natural world without feeling shut inside a "Purgatory blind." He has something of Shelley's rapidity of style without his occasional thinness and shrillness; in spirit, he aspires like Shelley to the white light beyond the dome of many-colored glass, but his aspiration is less fevered, partly because with his strong traditional sense of deity he has no fear that what he hopes to discover there is no more than a phantom of the human mind. In the meantime he is also much more contented with life under the dome. *Pauline* already shows the vigor and, for all its turbulence, some of the poise which are to prove characteristic of its author. Also, though it shows most of the imaginative patterns of the Romantic convention, its diction is usually free of those easy Romantic poeticisms which occasionally had become a mere bad habit with Keats and Shelley. Browning was too young to have developed yet any of those special mannerisms which in due time could become his own bad habit. The poem in fact shows, as Mill realized, considerable promise.

Pauline already contains most of Browning's later philosophy. Human love and human art are already being subsumed into a theological pattern without losing their earthly reality. The developmental cast of thought is already justifying earthly incompleteness: man's sense of this incompleteness, so painful to some writers, is already hailed rather than deplored; human love, though temporarily "chained" to earthly objects, is envisioned as ultimately outdistancing reason and as "companioning the seraphim."

By conservative religious standards Browning's acceptance of human good may, in fact, seem too complete. But though he sees a continuity between the natural and the supernatural, Browning in *Pauline* also acknowledges a "chasm." Furthermore, he sees this chasm as bridged by a supernatural deliverer. His Christian consciousness has blended in imagination with the mythological picture upon the wall of his study and he feels that the human soul on earth resembles Andromeda on the beach, "naked and alone," but

> *secure some god*
> *To save will come in thunder from the stars.*
> (ll. 666–67.)

This sense of miraculous redemption was to persist through the greatest years, through *The Ring and the Book*. The question is whether it faded out afterwards.

Pauline has these merits and this interest. It should be read more often. Yet it is not likely to be. Though much shorter than *Paracelsus* and *Sordello*, it is long for a poem whose only action is psychological. Though curiously attractive if read as an adolescent confession, its attractiveness will escape anyone who judges it by the standards of maturity. Most important, it is difficult because it appears chaotic. Its chaos is, indeed, richer and more varied than this short summary can suggest. It contains many striking passages upon art and landscape, upon human love and religion; it shows insight into the growth of imaginative patterns, into the breaking up of these patterns, into spiritual hiatuses, and into the beginnings of new patterns of growth. *Pauline* has captured the welter of an adolescent mind and, as it were, brought it back alive. Its constant shifts never fall into such mechanical, metronomic oscillation between extremes as makes a poem like Pope's *Eloisa to Abelard* easy to grasp but a bit dead, especially to a layman not used to sharp monastic dichotomies. The lack of any such sharply delineated pattern in *Pauline* perhaps warrants the poem's authenticity as biographical revelation, as a picture of sacred and profane love partially in conflict but vitally interconnected.

Amid the shifting phantasmagoria of his mind, it may be noted that Browning derived strength and a sense of continuity, somewhat as Wordsworth derived them, by returns to his youth, by reaffirmations of his love for Pauline (as mother-image) and for the suburban home of his childhood and, especially, its garden:

> the old trees
> *Which grew by our youth's home, the waving mass*
> *Of climbing plants heavy with bloom and dew,*
> *The morning swallows with their songs like words,*
> *All these seem clear and only worth our thoughts:*
> *So, aught connected with my early life,*
> *My rude songs or my wild imaginings,*
> *How I look on them—most distinct amid*
> *The fever and the stir of after years!*
>
> (ll. 132–40.)

Paracelsus, Evolutionary Anticipations, and Pride

IN *Paracelsus* the poet who was sometimes to achieve such rich compression first shows that garrulousness which would on occasions prove so tedious; the poem is much too long. It is empty of external action, and though a drama of the mind, it is curiously empty of thought itself.

Paracelsus is presented at the very start of the poem as a man who feels he has a mission "to know"; he expects to effect a complete intellectual revolution. To this mission he deliberately sacrifices everything: imagination, pleasure, human affection. Certain medical knowledge which he achieves incidentally to his larger enlightenment brings him fame, envy, and finally disgrace; but these things happen off stage and we only hear about them. Not until the very end are we ever told what it is that Paracelsus *knows*, and then we learn none of the processes by which he came to the knowledge but only his final summation. The poem is a little like a life of Charles Darwin which told nothing of the researches and speculations which led up to his conclusions.

The historical Paracelsus had, after the manner of other men of his day, mingled theosophy with science. Upon the basis of this fact, Browning presents his hero, in his great speech on his death-bed, as a pure Browningesque theologian. The branch of theology he specializes in concerns the nature and destiny of man. His mode of apprehension is evolutionary. All imperfections are justified—much in the manner of Tennyson—as but stages in a great progressive "tendency to God" developing throughout the cosmos; "progress" is the "law of life." And continuity also, for even volcanoes in their joy and vigor are seen as anticipating the more conscious joy of life in higher forms. The animal world offers rude beginnings of faculties that reach greater fullness in man. Humbler men show the beginnings of qualities more completely manifested in the best men. The best men of the present prefigure the perfection which all mankind will one day reach at the Shelleyan millennium. As in some passages in Shelley and Tennyson, it is not entirely clear whether this progress will one day pass beyond the natural sphere. But man's imagination assures him that some great progress will come: just as in the lower ranges of life "prognostics" tell of man's "near approach," so in man himself

> *arise*
> *August anticipations, symbols, types*
> *Of a dim splendor ever on before*
> *In that eternal circle life pursues.*
> (V, 774–77.)

Such occasions are, of course, the Romantic moments of intimation. These few lines, both in style and content, are particularly close to Wordsworth's passage on crossing the Alps: when the long material ascent was completed, Wordsworth had suddenly felt within his own spirit the possibilities of a far greater ascent, in fact, of an ascent ad infinitum.

(Georg Roppen, in his study *Evolution and Poetic Belief*, has noted that Tennyson's and Browning's evolutionary thought is essentially pre-scientific, in a tradition that goes back through such eighteenth-century poets as Akenside and Pope all the way to Plato. Browning at first hailed the work of contemporary scientists as confirming his own beliefs. He knew less about science than Tennyson and cared less; he was slower to sense some of its implications. Only belatedly did he realize that many of the protagonists of science envisioned a cosmos completely without a supernatural. Then his fundamental theism asserted itself; he could never seriously consider the possibility of a universe wholly the product of internal forces.)

In the absence of any preliminary dialectic leading up to Paracelsus's closing summary of his belief, what was there to hold the readers' interest for many thousands of lines? Something there must have been. The poem was the best received of Browning's early works; the total number of readers may have been few, but these readers presumably found a significant theme. They found in fact a study of the problem of *hubris*, of the unusually self-confident man daring to set himself apart from his fellow men. Since for four long acts the hero scarcely tells us what his revolutionary thoughts are, it might at first seem that the issue of a man's right to think for himself is being treated too abstractly to hold anyone's attention. But in moments of loneliness Paracelsus, like the young poet in *Pauline*, expresses repentance *vis-à-vis* God. The Victorian reader would soon gather that the intellectual revolution would be at least partly in the realm of theology. He might well find himself involved. At the time even young men so little radical by temperament as Tennyson and Hallam were working out new theologies. By adopting evolutionary and optimistic patterns of thought perhaps man could solve the problems still faced by those clinging to the older patterns, problems like the conflict between the Book of Genesis and the new scientific knowledge, or between the new humanitarianism and the idea of eternal damnation. Browning and Tennyson considered the possibility of an infinite progression in which nothing good, not the smallest good in the worst of men, would be lost; it could survive and develop.

But until the end of the poem the focus is entirely upon the psychological accompaniments of pioneering thought, not upon the thought. Paracelsus, whose first confidence in his own intellectual knowledge is followed by despondency, learns from a poet named Aprile that man must also love. But Aprile's love is a generalized, Shelleyan love of the principle of beauty in all things, an aspiration towards the infinite.[6] Browning feels (as Tennyson feels in *The Palace of Art*) that man must also feel a simple affection for concrete things and individual people. Paracelsus had earlier had such an affection for his friends Festus and Michal. At the end, again depressed by despondency, he is rescued by a reunion with Festus. As he lies dying in Festus's arms, he in a sense "returns" to the simple affections of his youth; the long lost scenes of that period live again as Festus sings "Thus the Mayne glideth," a vividly sensuous evocation of the river pastures which the two men had walked through years before. These returns produce a healing: after periods of deficiency has come a sense of fullness, continuity is re-established after many dislocations, a sense of union has driven away loneliness. Most of all, those Romantic desiderata, faith and hope, have been restored: loving and being loved, Paracelsus is able to utter his vision of the cosmos. Then, troubled no longer by the fact that he has been unable to communicate his vision to mankind in general, he dies with the confidence of a typical Browning hero; he knows that we fall but to rise, fail but to succeed:

> *I press God's lamp*
> *Close to my breast; its splendor, soon or late,*
> *Will pierce the gloom: I shall emerge one day.*
>   (V, 901–3.)

W. O. Raymond, who has written of Browning with sympathy and insight, remarks that in *Pauline, Paracelsus,* and *Sordello* the poet has "probed with an unsparing hand the cancer of romantic egoism." [7] This statement is somewhat misleading if it is intended as an expression of Browning's more conscious intentions. The historical Paracelsus had left a slightly unsavory reputation, but Browning as so often is at least partially engaged in justification and "case-making." Perhaps E. D. H. Johnson is a little nearer the mark, in *The Alien Vision of Victorian Poetry,* when he sees these three works as focussing mainly upon the problem of the modern artist and his failure to communicate—if artist is interpreted broadly to signify any man of original insight. As he lies dying, Paracelsus realizes that mankind cannot be led immediately by men like himself. His quick mind has encompassed too great a revolution too quickly; he can hardly expect to understand and sympathize with the painfully slow and almost blind gropings of the majority of men. As a practical matter, these men will have to be led by men with only a little more vision than themselves. (In part, Browning may be justifying his beloved "Suntreader," who in his lifetime had been as reviled as Paracelsus, and whose fame even then was just beginning to "emerge.") Paracelsus now realizes his deficiencies. But these deficiencies have to some extent been inseparable from the virtues of his quick, *a priori* mind. He could come to understand them only as a result of experience.

The immediate practical failure of Paracelsus was in Browning's eyes no unanswerable argument against the man. With eternity, or an infinite progression of existences, at hand to right the wrongs of the moment, Browning was never a crass pragmatist. He did not have to inform his readers whether Childe Roland slew the giant who emerged from the dark tower; it was sufficient to know that he blew his horn in challenge.

If there is any doubt about Browning's final evaluation of Paracelsus' proud nature, the question can perhaps be settled by considering the final conversion of Festus. Festus has been like the cautious chorus of a Greek tragedy warning the hero against a bold, individualistic course. But from the start he has loved and revered Paracelsus as one greater than himself. At the very close, when outwardly the hero's cause appears most lost, Festus's timid reservations vanish and he avows a full faith. Though he has no comprehension of the intellectual issues involved, the sort of blind instinct which so many of Browning's characters possess guides him; at the critical moment he declares himself to be Paracelsus' disciple.

In the earlier *Pauline* Browning had accepted the common Romantic position that critical thought impaired imaginative belief. If men followed this thought they were worshipping the products of their own mind; in Kantian terms, they were not escaping from the limits of the world of the mere understanding. Only love and imagination could guide them towards something beyond these limits. In *Paracelsus* it is not made wholly clear how much of the hero's final theological insight was attained by the intellectual processes with which he had early identified himself. Presumably quite a bit. Though Browning is very aware of the extent to which intellectual power alienates a man from his fellows, in *Paracelsus* he seems to accept these powers more easily than he had a little earlier. Browning himself will always strike one as primarily a man of instinct, but through most of his life he would probably have defended the intellect in theory. Only towards the end, partly in defiance of materialistic science, does the old anti-intellectualism once more come to the fore.

Sordello and Maturity

SORDELLO, hero of the poem of the same name, is successively poet, lover, and leader of men. As poet he ascends the Platonic ladder of imagination. He starts at the very bottom worshipping the sensuous world—a world vividly described by Browning. Each form of beauty is worshipped for its "proper sake," not scanted as a mere symbol of something beyond. This is as one would expect from a poet who for all his idealism wished to accept the actual. Sordello's devotion to the concrete does not arrest his ascent:

> fresh births of beauty wake
> Fresh homage, every grade is past,
> With every mode of loveliness: then cast
> Inferior idols off their borrowed crown
> Before a coming glory. Up and down
> Runs arrowy fire, while earthly forms combine
> To throb the secret forth; a touch divine—

And the scaled eyeball owns the mystic rod;
Visibly through the garden walketh God.

(I, 496–504.)

Sordello is compared and contrasted with another poet, Eglamour. Eglamour is less a worshipper of the outer world and more a worshipper of art. To him verse is

a temple-worship vague and vast,
A ceremony that withdrew the last
Opposing bolt, looped back the lingering veil,
Which hid the holy place.

(II, 197–200.)

As the description of Eglamour continues, the ironic tone, first suggested when the worship is called "vague," becomes stronger; one wonders if for the moment Browning is agreeing with Immanuel Kant that those who worship art are weaker and more self-centered than those who worship beauty in nature.[8] Eglamour's poems, though more perfectly harmonious than Sordello's, solace chiefly himself and give little help to men in general. Eglamour, the poet-aesthete, is like H. N. Fairchild's picture of the Romantic poet in general, a man who worships the products of the human imagination, chiefly his own. Browning notes, in fact, that even the light which Sordello himself receives from the beauty in nature is essentially light reflected from his own soul. But not being intellectually systematic or strongly critical, Browning does not allow this concession to lead him like Shelley to the verge of a solipsist's despair (or, like Fairchild, to disapproval). In his world the divine fire is running down just as surely as the fire of the human imagination is running up, and there is—at least during these early days—not the slightest suspicion in his mind that the divinity walking visibly in the garden is a mere wishful delusion.

Having ascended to the summit of lonely aspiration, Sordello finds himself for the moment with nowhere further to go. Despondency naturally follows, a paralysis of the will like that which periodically afflicted the hero of *Pauline* and *Paracelsus*. New energy for a further movement forward comes when he returns to Goito, the scene of his childhood. Even more strength comes when he decides to worship a personal image and fall in love with the Lady Palma. This curiously deliberate love affair suggests that Browning himself, who had never yet fallen in love, was half-consciously thinking of doing so by act of will. (Sordello's expectation of renewed energy when, as he says, he places his life under the law of another's being recalls how Wordsworth, tired of his "unchartered freedom," hoped to keep his life "fresh and strong" by submitting to the law of Duty.) Sordello's love affair, as might be expected, is not a notable success; the lady finds a god in her knight more readily than the knight finds a goddess in the lady. The crisis of the maturing hero is still unresolved; once again, more acutely than before, he finds himself alone, deprived of the satisfaction of feeling himself transcended.

This new paralysis is conquered only by a full realization and acceptance of the inevitable. This acceptance Browning sees as the final emergence into maturity: no longer can Sordello worship the truth "veiled" to the capacity of "weak vision," "embodied" so as to "lure" upward a soul still on the lower rungs of the ladder; "stronger vision" can and must endure "unbodied" desire. It can or must, in other words, cease to worship a Grasmere Vale, a Cythna, a Phidian marble, or a Hallam. No longer sustained by sensing another man's "soul above his soul," Sordello must now radiate life from himself to other men rather than receive light from them. He looks down with love upon the men beneath him, becomes a humanitarian, and seeks to aid his people not as a poet but as one more directly involved in the practical world, as warrior and statesman.

Sometimes the Romantic poets were prophets not merely in the sense of uttering metaphysical truths but of foreseeing their own futures. Fortunately not everything in Browning's life turned out quite as here set forth. When he fell in love, he did not have to do so by deliberate decision; he was caught before he knew it. However, when his years as a lover were over, a period of dryness did ensue. Then, moving beyond the limits of private life which had circumscribed his early and middle years, he became a public figure, if not a warrior or statesman at least the god of the Browning Society. In this latter capacity he doubtless gave more light than he received.

It need hardly be added that in public life Sordello still met frustrations. These frustrations did not permanently discourage him but led him to expect more strongly further existences with "new conditions of success," not conditions such as in this world produce "failure." God's ways to men are again justified. All is best though we oft doubt.

The *Essay on Shelley*

IN CANVASSING the psychological problems which a man encounters as he matures, and encounters more severely as he is a man of unusual insight, the three long poems of Browning's apprenticeship had repeatedly developed their discussions in theological terms. Many readers will prefer some of the great poems of Browning's middle years not just because of their artistic superiority but because they appear less theological, more secular and humanistic. Browning's gallery of men and women is a tribute to this earthly life by a man who loved it in its variety and richness; as artist Browning could savor the special quality even of a rogue and villain as well as Chaucer himself. In his finest creative years he often presents clerics and theologizers, but usually in an ironic light. Johannes Agricola, the monk in the Spanish cloister, the bishop ordering his tomb, the monks who reprimand Fra Lippo Lippi, Caliban on the island, even perhaps Bishop Bloughram—all are a humanist's delight, or any man's delight.

But Browning in his middle years is not a secular humanist only. To W. C. DeVane he is insistently the theodicist; to W. O. Raymond he is a Christian humanist.[9] These critics are right in their judgments. Furthermore, the fact that Browning continued to see his poetic creation as developing within a theological framework need not be inferred only from a comprehensive survey of the poems. It is made unmistakably clear in Browning's prose comments on the nature and kinds of poetry in his *Essay on Shelley*.

This essay was written in 1851, just over a decade after the completion of *Sordello*. In it Browning contrasts the "objective poet," such as Shakespeare, who presents life in almost unclassified diversity, without any pronounced selection of materials to support some theological design, with the Romantic poet of vision. Despite the eminence of Shakespeare (and despite his own striving for objectivity), Browning confesses the Romantic poet supplies the stronger need:

> We turn with stronger needs to the genius of an opposite tendency,—the subjective poet of the modern classification. He, gifted like the objective poet with the fuller perception of nature and man, is impelled to embody the thing he perceives, not so much with reference to the many below as to the one above him, the Supreme Intelligence which apprehends all things in their absolute truth,—an ultimate view ever aspired to, if but partially attained, by the poet's own soul. Not what man sees, but what God sees,—the *Ideas* of Plato, seeds of creation lying burningly on the Divine Hand,—it is toward these that he struggles. Not with the combination of humanity in action, but with the primal elements of humanity, he has to do; and he digs where he stands, —preferring to seek them in his own soul as the nearest reflex of

that absolute Mind, according to the intuitions of which he desires to perceive and speak. Such a poet does not deal habitually
with the picturesque groupings and tempestuous tossings of the
forest trees, but with their roots and fibres naked to the chalk
and stone. He does not paint pictures and hang them on the walls,
but rather carries them on the retina of his own eyes: we must
look deep into his human eyes to see those pictures on them. He
is rather a seer, accordingly, than a fashioner, and what he produces will be less a work than an effluence.

A little farther on Browning adds this:

the subjective poet, whose study has been himself, appealing
through himself to the absolute Divine mind, prefers to dwell
upon those external scenic appearances which strike out most
abundantly and uninterruptedly his own light and power, selects
that silence of the earth and sea in which he can best hear the
beatings of his individual heart, and leaves the noisy, complex,
yet imperfect exhibitions of nature in the manifold experience of
man around him, which serve only to distract and suppress the
workings of his own brain.

Later, describing perhaps the change from the eighteenth-century
literature, so rich in observation of men and manners, to the poetry
of the Romantic period, Browning has further praise for the Romantic poet of vision:

There is a time when the general eye has, so to speak, absorbed
its fill of the phenomena around it, whether spiritual or material,
and desires rather to learn the exact significance of what it pos-
sesses than to receive any augmentation of what is possessed.
Then is the opportunity for the poet of loftier vision to lift his
fellows, with their half-apprehensions, up to his own sphere, by
intensifying the import of details and rounding the universal
meaning. The influence of such an achievement will not soon die
out.

But, precisely because this achievement of the poet who freshly
perceives theological truth does not soon die out, the more objective
poet has his uses. Browning says that the fresh insights soon become
hand-me-downs:

Then is the imperative call for the appearance of another sort of
poet, who shall at once replace this intellectual rumination of
food swallowed long ago, by a supply of fresh and living swathe;

getting at new substance by breaking up the assumed wholes into parts of independent and unclassed value, careless of the unknown laws for recombining them (it will be the business of yet another poet to suggest those hereafter), prodigal of objects for men's outer and not inner sight.

The latter are the humanist poets, but Browning sees their delighted concentration on the separate aspects as only a phase of the ever-necessary task which successive generations must face, the rebuilding of theology in terms and images freshly drawn from life itself.

As Professor Raymond has shown, using imagery recurrent in the poet's letters and poems, Browning felt that it was not especially his mission, at his particular juncture, to pierce through the many-colored dome of glass to the pure white light; rather he would note the multiple refracted images of that light which life everywhere affords.[10] These images might be moderately bright and warm—red perhaps or yellow; they might be cold and blue; or they could be a murky brown, all according to the kind of glass through which the full, pure light was transmitted.

Paracelsus had said, in sum, that the man whose intellect has pierced the dome to the whiteness of the full truth beyond, must not scorn such dim and discolored images of truth as the ordinary man's mind supplies him with. Browning was persistently to maintain that the world is a place where the ultimate revelation is accommodated and embodied and veiled, colored so to speak, to come with the range of finite powers of perception. Thus the point of the poem *The Bishop Orders His Tomb* is not just that the speaker is sunk deep in worldliness, but that, amid all the scheming and pushing which have characterized his life, he has still retained a feeble image of goodness in his fondness for the peaceful church of St. Praxed's; also, if he cannot love his old enemy Gandolf, he can still feel some affection for his children and forgive in them a greed not unlike his own. Here, but even more so elsewhere, the fondness of Browning the artist-theologian for difficult cases reminds one of the novels of Graham Green.

But not all the persons and situations which Browning studies refract quite such a dim light as does the bishop. The poems record a hundred moments when his characters catch flashes of varying brightness, sometimes through nature directly, more often through art and music, most frequently through human love. Precisely because life directly encountered offers intimations, Browning is impatient with the lovers in *The Statue and the Bust*, who refuse to encounter life at all. Browning the activist, who in *Paracelsus* praised not the sculptured calm of a snowcapped Mont Blanc but the eruption of a volcano, could justify any sin but apathy. In *Fifine at the Fair* Don Juan himself is portrayed not on a level with the ground but as clinging to a lowly rung of the ladder: he still looks forward to

> some girl by fate reserved
> To give once again the electric snap and spark
> Which prove, when finger finds out finger in the dark
> O' the world, there's fire and life and truth there,
>   link but hands
> And pass the secret on.

(XCI)

To Browning the believer in instinct, as to D. H. Lawrence, the dark gods are still gods. Then of course there are those many Browning characters who from the very incompleteness of this life envision some greater fullness to come. To canvass all the Browning poems which record "anticipations" of the "splendor ever on before" would be to consider almost the entire roster of the poet's works.

Abt Vogler and Saul

INSTEAD OF CATALOGUING a hundred of Browning's moments, it may be wiser to examine carefully a few of the most noteworthy ones. When in his old age the poet was asked by Edmund Gosse to name four of his poems by which he would like to be represented, he chose *Abt Vogler* and *Saul* as examples of his lyric vein.[11] It is not hard to see why these were singled out. In them vision takes on its greatest intensity, the many-colored glass dome between earth and heaven seems to be pierced, for a moment a ray of pure white light comes through. Browning had, after all, conceded that the Shelleyan poetry of vision was the most important. He had also noted that though all poets were both subjective and objective, they were predominantly one or the other and none had yet attained the greatest heights in both modes of poetry. One wonders if in his heart of hearts he felt that in these two poems he had achieved a powerful combination of the personal and visionary with the dramatically objective.

Browning's three early works, especially *Paracelsus* and *Sordello*, are unsatisfactory because they create life too little and discuss it too much. In that fine piece of literary criticism, and alas! self-criticism, *Transcendentalism: A Poem in Twelve Books*, Browning un-

favorably contrasts Jacob Boehme, who wrote about flowers, with
his contemporary John of Halberstadt, the magician, who actually
created them:

> He with his "look you!" vents a brace of rhymes,
> And in there breaks the sudden rose herself,
> Over us, under, round us every side,
> Nay, in and out the tables and the chairs
> And musty volumes, Boehme's book and all,—
> Buries us with a glory, young once more,
> Pouring heaven into this shut house of life.

And again in his old age Browning makes a similar contrast. By then
his own powers had waned; the theological bent is as strong as ever,
but the flashes of vision have been replaced by endless dissertations.
In his *Parleying with Christopher Smart* he remarks humorously that
he is afraid to incorporate into his own poems and lines from Smart's
Song of David; Smart's "glory" would serve only to emphasize the
dullness of his own "gray argument." Even if one admits that ex-
pository poetry is a respectable genre in its own right, one must
grant that it is not Browning's *forte*. He himself must have been
aware of this fact. He probably felt that in *Abt Vogler* and *Saul* he
had created glory and not just talked about it.

   Again, in *Luria* Browning suggests that the "thought" of the
"North" may be needed to give form and permanence to the intuitive "feeling" of the "East," the feeling which senses the nearness
of the divine but which endures only for a moment. In *Abt Vogler*
and *Saul* Browning may have supposed that he had happily combined these two different talents of intellect and emotion.

   It is immediately apparent that *Abt Vogler* embodies a moment's
intense experience of beauty, the beauty, in this case, of art rather
than nature. Like Keats before Phidias's marbles, Abt Vogler while
in the presence of his own music suddenly feels himself face to face
with something quite incommensurable with mortal life as it can be
comprehended by the understanding; he is touched by "a shadow of
a magnitude." This wonderful element dwells within his own spirit
yet seems external to it. In some ways the composer's experience
is similar to the Kantian and Wordsworthian sublime, but the me-
chanics of the experience are different. The sudden transition from
a beauty commensurable with human knowledge to a beauty or sublimity inexplicable and miraculous is effected when Abt Vogler's
conscious creative powers give way to his unconscious ones. At first,
with some prevision of what he is doing, the great extemporizer takes

a theme and starts to build with it a beautiful structure of sound.
Then suddenly, when he has built as beautifully as he consciously
knows how, a power within him comes into play which works won-
drously and without foreknowledge. He becomes like the Shakespeare of Schlegel's and Coleridge's criticism, a "Spinozistic deity, an
omnipresent creativeness," which works from within in such a way
that there is not a fraction of a second's lag between intention and
execution.[12] To Coleridge, and to Schlegel and Schelling, such an
"organic" artist was a living witness to the fact that the basic operation of the human soul is "a repetition in the finite mind of the
eternal act of creation in the infinite I AM." [13] He was peculiarly so
because such an artist as Shakespeare, they supposed, created his
plays according to no predetermined plan or known rules, but had,
so to speak, willed them to be, and there they were. To Browning
Abt Vogler's extemporization is such a witness because—unlike a
poem or a painting—it had not been created in stages, with some lag
between the idea and the final composition. In the case of the poem
or painting,

> *Ye know why the forms are fair, ye hear how the tale is told;*
> *It is all triumphant art, but art in obedience to laws.*

But in the case of the extemporizer in full rapture, we sense the immediate "finger of God, a flash of the will that can." It may be remarked, without detracting from the greatness of Shakespeare, that
musical extemporization is the more dramatic image of Divine creation as this has traditionally been imagined. In Abt Vogler's playing
Browning has discovered the perfect objective correlative to express
the basic Romantic belief in the indwelling Divinity manifested in
the artistic imagination.

  Partly by very reason of this discovery, he has produced a most
striking and complete embodiment of this faith. *Abt Vogler* clearly
incorporates several elements important in earlier Romantic poetry.
Wordsworth, confronting the beauty of nature, suddenly felt the
living presence of a divine force which dwells in the external world
and "in the mind of man," but which is hidden from ordinary awareness. So Abt Vogler suddenly feels a divine power hidden below the
surface of the conscious mind. Also, as the beauty of nature or art
had justified the universe to the Romantics, so the beautiful structure
of sound provides Browning with a justifying image. In this structure individual discords are seen as necessary contributions to the
beauty of the whole. In fact, the music suggests a still more optimistic possibility: that evil may be nothing at all, not fact but absence of

fact, mere "silence implying sound." Lastly, this process of justifying the universe to the imagination is not complete without intimations pointing specifically to man's immortality.

In *Abt Vogler* the intellectual processes which supposedly explain to the understanding the intimating powers of the situation or image are at times clear and on the surface. Among the earlier Romantics such reasoned explanations were usually hinted at or set forth only in prose, in Wordsworth's *Preface*, Shelley's *Defence*, Keats's letter to Bailey. But in this poem of Browning's the final moment of insight is a clearly set forth argument in deductive logic. The musician starts, as any metaphysician must, with certain large assumptions: that the universe is rational, that nothing is purposeless, that nature or God does nothing in vain. Nature or God has, Abt Vogler discovers, when extemporizing on his instrument, given him hidden potentialities of power which are only fleetingly and rather unsatisfactorily made use of in this life. But to grant that God's creation could be so ineffectual is absurd. Therefore this life cannot be the only life; there must be another existence in which this potential will achieve permanent full development and be fully employed. Browning might almost have ended his poem, as geometrical proofs are sometimes concluded, with a *Quod Erat Demonstrandum*.

The other lyric named to Gosse, *Saul*, may be said to take up in its own different way the problem of Wordsworth's *Excursion*. King Saul is suffering from Romantic melancholy and despair. Like Wordsworth's Solitary and Young's Lorenzo, he is incapable of being cheered by any simple optimism. For Browning's implied contention is the same as Wordsworth's expressed one, that in a sensitive man melancholy must ever accompany a failure to believe in immortality. So much of Browning's intention any reader should recognize, though his own personal opinion on the subject may be quite different. Saul's blackness is but a darkening of the greyness which, from similar causes, is settling over the spirits of Browning's classical philosopher Cleon and his modern Englishman of scientific interests in *A Toccata of Galuppi's*.

Through nine sections David tries to cheer Saul by praising, in a mood of reverent gratitude to God the giver, all beauties and wonders of this world and the joy of life itself:

> How good is man's life, the mere living!
>   (ix.)

This is as far as the poem was at first carried. About eight years later Browning continued. Saul has been no more impressed by David's praises than Wordsworth's Solitary had been by the beauty of nature surrounding him. So David renews his efforts and strikes from his harp strains in a higher mood. He says Saul is right to reject the comforts of a merely physical life, and he now praises the life of the spirit: Saul's own spirit, David assures him, will survive in the Israel he has benefited; Israel's sons and daughters will sing his praises in after years. But, as the reader will suspect who remembers Browning's ironic little poem *Earth's Immortalities*, Saul is not cheered by such promises. Suddenly, in a burst of light, a vision so tremendous breaks upon David that he ceases to sing and speaks. This vision is accompanied by a structure of reasoning even more mathematically schematic than that in *Abt Vogler*. God infinitely surpasses David in power, in wisdom, in ninety-nine different ways. Therefore God must infinitely surpass him in love also. But David feels within himself a great love for the despairing king; he would, if he could, give him some gift to complete the imperfect gift of this life. Since God must love Saul even more than David, he also must wish to give Saul the greater gift. But God has infinite power to give what he wishes. Therefore he will give Saul the greater gift. Again one might add *Q.E.D.* Thus David, an Old Testament figure whose environment does not furnish him with any ready-made belief in an afterlife, suddenly and by Browning's typical movement from incompleteness to completeness, receives a powerful intimation of what Browning regarded as one of the greatest parts of Christian revelation. A moment later, by the identical logical movement, an even more astounding truth strikes his soul. He himself, out of his love for the king, would willingly suffer to procure him any gift he needs. But here, in the self-sacrifice of love, God must again excel. In a prophetic moment, foreseeing the twofold Christian mystery of the Incarnation and the Redemption, David addresses God himself:

> "Would I suffer for him that I love? So wouldst thou—
>   so wilt thou!
> So shall crown thee the topmost, ineffablest, uttermost
>   crown—
> And thy love fill infinitude wholly, nor leave up nor down
> One spot for thy creature to stand in! It is by no breath,
> Turn of eye, wave of hand, that salvation joins issue with
>   death!
> As thy Love is discovered almighty, almighty be proved
> Thy power, that exists with and for it, of being Beloved!
> He who did most, shall bear most; the strongest shall stand
>   the most weak.

'T is the weakness in strength, that I cry for! my flesh that
    I seek
In the Godhead! I seek and I find it. O Saul, it shall be
A Face like my face that receives thee; a Man like to me,
Thou shalt love and be loved by, for ever: a Hand like
    this hand
Shall throw open the gates of new life to thee! See the
    Christ stand!"

                                   (xviii.)

All the logical argument which is part of David's vision may seem too heavy a burden for lyric poetry to carry. But Browning has perhaps succeeded as well as John Donne in combining reason and passion. There is, though, an interesting difference between their two accomplishments. Thanks to its mainly anapaestic rhythm (usually an obvious rhythm), *Saul* almost reads itself and its energy and splendor are immediately apparent even before its argument is completely understood. Donne's poems are characteristically the reverse. Their iambics, varied to each turn of thought, do not read themselves; as Coleridge has remarked, they can scarcely be read at all until after their chain of thought has been comprehended.[14] Hence their power and splendor are a final effect more than an initial one.

But in giving so rational a form to what is ostensibly a moment of grace, does Browning run a danger? Some readers may be a little disturbed by the strongly self-assertive character of these poems. This character may be related to their logic; in giving the form of a geometrical argument to a mystical moment, a poet risks the implication that he has himself wholly encompassed and mastered it. It might be possible to imagine Abt Vogler and Saul being rebuked by the voice from the whirlwind, as several persons in the *Book of Job* are rebuked for their confident explanation of divine mysteries. One recent writer on Browning has suggested that as a religious seer he is by temperament too little able to heed the Biblical injunction, "Be still and know that I am God." [15] *Saul* and *Abt Vogler* are impressive poems; precisely how far any such objections will be felt against them is likely to be a matter of theological opinion and of personal taste. It may be said in their defense that they somehow combine with their assertiveness a spirit of reverence and awe at least equally strong—perhaps stronger.

(The reasoning exhibited by these poems, it should be noted, is of one kind only. That this kind can be blended with religious imagination proves nothing about the nineteenth-century conflict between faith and reason. An *a priori* deductive thought in the Platonic tradition has long been an ally of religious belief. The Victorian conflict was between religious belief and the more inductive thinking bred by several centuries of scientific observation of the natural world.)

Both these great lyrics of Browning, despite their outwardly dramatic form, are notably introspective. Keats had sensed his "shadow of a magnitude" in the presence of a work of art created by another; Abt Vogler senses the presence of divinity within his own creative powers. Similarly, while Tennyson had sensed an image of divinity in a man more godlike than himself, young David derives intimations not from Saul but from his own love of Saul. Both of Browning's speakers are apparently to be regarded as fully developed strong souls who can no longer expect to find themselves transcended by their fellow men. They illustrate Browning's contention in the *Essay on Shelley* that a great visionary is one "whose study has been himself, appealing through himself to the absolute Divine mind." Viewed by an unfavorable eye, their introspection may be said to bear out H. N. Fairchild's contentions about the egocentricity of Romantic worship.

The Ring and the Book

THIS PATTERN of the soul's reading its revelation in its own book gives way—in part at least—to more extroverted modes of reverence in *The Ring and the Book*.

Browning's most ambitious work strongly recalls his own favorite Shakespearian play, *King Lear*. In both works the poet's soul and the souls of his characters are burdened by the weight of evil oppressing them, evil everywhere triumphing and seemingly irresistible. In both works this power of evil raises ultimate questions about the nature of the universe. Both works answer these questions in the general fashion outlined many years ago by A. C. Bradley in his *Shakespearian Tragedy*. At terrible cost, good finally re-establishes itself, and this re-establishment gives some precarious grounds for supposing that evil is foreign to the nature of things. Also, as Bradley noted, the tragic action reveals a beauty, a goodness, a nobility in some of the characters which so arouses our admiration that these persons somehow seem superior to any misfortune which may overwhelm them.

So, in *The Ring and the Book*, the characters worth saving (in this work, as sometimes elsewhere, Browning judges harshly) are saved by the flashes of light they see, not in their own characters, but in the characters of others. Caponsacchi, for instance, terms

Pompilia "the glory of life, the beauty of the world, the splendor of heaven," and "food" for his own soul; he says that by finding her he has been rehabilitated spiritually, despite the fact that as a priest he had been trained to find beauty and splendor not in fellow mortals but "at the source, God." Later he addresses his listeners in these words:

> Sirs, how should I be quiet in my grave
> Unless you suffer me wring, drop by drop,
> My brains dry, make a riddance of the drench
> Of minutes with a memory in each
> Recorded motion, breath or look of hers,
> Which poured forth would present you one pure glass,
> Mirror you plain—as God's sea, glassed in gold,
> His saints—the perfect soul Pompilia?
>
> (VI, 1155–62.)

He ends by telling the listeners that Pompilia had filled his soul not with love but with faith:

> it is faith,
> The feeling that there's God, he reigns and rules
> Out of this low world.
>
> (VI, 1193–95.)

Owing to the ambiguity of the word love, Caponsacchi the celibate priest must deny that Pompilia made him feel love. But Browning trusted his readers to know better; the man was filled with love, and, filled with love, had been filled with faith also.

What of Pompilia herself, encompassed by evil and indifference and weakness? Her situation reminds one of the situation of a very different sort of heroine, Shelley's Beatrice Cenci. But Beatrice Cenci is denied all intimations. Not a single beautiful, upright, noble and strong soul comes within her ken. All is black, and in her despair she breaks the Shelleyan and Christian injunction not to oppose evil with evil. Pompilia does not despair. Like Shelley's Cythna in her imprisonment, she is strengthened by her consciousness of the child within her soon to be born. But mainly she is saved by Caponsacchi: his courage delivers her body and flashes light to her soul. Her last words praise him thus:

> Through such souls alone
> God stooping shows sufficient of His light
> For us i'the dark to rise by. And I rise.
>
> (VII, 1843–45.)

Lastly there is the aged Pope. He feels weighed down by the wickedness which the story has revealed, and by the almost universal coldness, baseness, lack of love, and lack of courage. He mourns the death of Pompilia in tones that recall the lament of Shelley at the end of *Alastor:*

> *A faultless creature is destroyed, and sin*
> *Has had its way i'the world where God should rule.*
>
> (X, 1421–22.)

As pastor of Christians, he is disheartened further by the feeling that Christ's birth and death for mankind seem to have availed very little. He ponders the mystery of life in long speculative passages. Ultimately, he holds fast to the instance of Caponsacchi's selfless devotion:

> *What lacks, then, of perfection fit for God*
> *But just the instance which this tale supplies*
> *Of love without a limit? So is strength,*
> *So is intelligence; let love be so,*
> *Unlimited in its self-sacrifice,*
> *Then is the tale true and God shows complete.*
> *Beyond the tale, I reach into the dark,*
> *Feel what I cannot see, and still faith stands.*
> *I can believe this dread machinery*
> *Of sin and sorrow would confound me else.*
>
> (X, 1367–76.)

The Pope goes on to see the dread machinery of this world as the means of developing moral qualities, much as Keats had seen it as a means of soul-building. But that all this soul-building leads to any real goal at all, only such rare loving souls as Caponsacchi seemed to warrant.

Thus *The Ring and the Book* crowns a career of speculation upon faith and the imaginative sources and supplements of faith. The nourishment of faith which is praised in this climactic poem is personal, the goodness discernible in our fellow men, not in impersonal landscape and art. As such it reveals emotional patterns more immediately suggestive of Christianity than the patterns most common in Wordsworth and Keats. The conservatives may find fault with this pattern because it centers the mind and heart too little upon the goodness of Christ, but the truth revealed by the Pope's speech is a real one: it would do men little good to read about Divine love and self-sacrifice in a book if their own experience of the life around them gave them no notion of what they were reading about.

The Ring and the Book, the climax of Browning's theologizing, also recalls the climax of his personal life. As a young man he had had on the wall of the room where he wrote his poems a copy of Caravaggio's "Andromeda." In *Pauline* he had spoken of the maiden in the picture as "she who awaits the snake on the wet beach . . . quite naked and alone"; and he had expressed his faith that some god

> *To save will come in thunder from the stars.*
>
> (l. 667.)

Some years later he himself found a lady defenseless and alone and came like a god from heaven to save her. As Professor DeVane has remarked, this pattern was basic in Browning's thought and life.[16] So, in *The Ring and the Book*, the soul of Pompilia which Caponsacchi reanimates is the soul of Elizabeth Barrett; and the self-sacrificing love of the priest which gives strength to Pompilia and the Pope is Browning's own love. Thus, though *The Ring and the Book* escapes in part from the imaginative focussing on oneself of *Abt Vogler* and *Saul*, it does not escape altogether. It is perhaps hard to imagine any great work of literature which could be said to escape wholly, provided the facts of the author's life are known.

The Face of Christ

AT TIMES Browning seems to have an overwhelming sense of man's being dependent upon his own resources; at such times he does not appear to fit readily into any Christian pattern. Yet the poet's own psychological and intellectual development was such that he had an unusually vivid apprehension of the significance of Christ as traditionally interpreted. In a letter to Ruskin Browning once wrote that the whole problem of poetry was to put "the infinite within the finite." [17] His own poems from *Pauline* onward certainly sustain this thesis. As Browning makes it clear in *A Death in the Desert*, Christ is the answer to this problem: in him the "absolute blaze" of Infinite Truth is

> *reduced to plain historic fact,*
> *Diminished into clearness.*
>
> (ll. 236–37.)

Put another way, Browning in his last years, in writing his *Parleying with Bernard de Mandeville*, expressed his settled conviction that if the Infinite Truth is to be to man more than a negative abstraction, it must be conceived and represented as possessing the attributes of personality. And here the person of Christ was also the answer to Browning's other persistent problem, perhaps the same problem in another form. Again from *Pauline* onward Browning had been haunted by the problem of the essentially worshipful man, insistent upon worshipping personal images, who has reached such a stage of development that he can no longer readily find earthly persons whom he can in all respects revere. In the presence of the figure of Christ as portrayed in the New Testament, even the most mature may still feel themselves transcended. Browning himself, writing in 1876 to a woman who had asked him for an expression of his religious opinions (presumably more direct than the oblique opinions suggested by most of his poetry), cited the remark of Charles Lamb: that if Shakespeare came into the room, all men would rise; but if Christ came into the room, all must kneel.[18]

Even before their marriage, Elizabeth Barrett had urged Browning to seek the same distinction in direct expression as she felt he had already gained in indirect. His *Christmas-Eve and Easter-Day*, published in 1850, was a concession to her wishes. Both halves of the poem combine an intellectual discussion with intensely imagined vision. These visions are not in the full Romantic tradition; in them man's imagination does not discover a transcendental realm, but rather assumes it. The answers to the most ultimate theological questions are taken for granted, and a more or less believing man faces the moral difficulty of putting into practice in his own conduct the divine injunctions which he accepts. Yet no exposition of Browning's transcendentalizing imagination can ignore this work.

In *Christmas-Eve* the poet depicts himself emerging into a dark night from an unlovely service in a Dissenting chapel. All at once the cloud bank is blown back, the moon shines forth, the heavens in their immensity and splendor are bared. (Wordsworth had emerged from the mists atop Snowdon and Arnold spoke of Wordsworth's power to move aside "the cloud of mortal destiny.") Browning has an awed sense of Divinity pervading the entire cosmos and wishes to worship by himself alone, free from the irksome limitations of any sectarian service. In what is almost an excess of glory the skies offer not only the moon but several moon bows; these rise one larger than another, one above another, like the first members in a series of infinite progression. Though Browning offers no explicit comment to such an effect, they symbolize perhaps his own theology of unlimited progression which contrasted with the chapel's one probationary existence followed by a static heaven or hell. But Brown-

ing's feeling of liberation quickly gives way to an equally intense
sense of being overshadowed by a towering figure of Christ. He
cannot see the figure's face, averted perhaps in disapproval; he remembers the words in the New Testament which seem a direct rebuke to any man who would worship alone, or at least to any who
scorns those who worship together:

> "I remember he did say
>   Doubtless that, to the world's end,
> Where two or three did meet and pray,
>   He would be in the midst, their friend."
>   (ll. 443–46; Sect. viii.)

The figure moves away, as though to express displeasure. Browning
calls after, in penitence and prayer, acknowledging his own "folly
and pride." Christ turns back:

> The whole face turned upon me full.
>   I spread myself beneath it,
>   As when the bleacher spreads, to seethe it,
> In cleansing sun, his wool,—
>   Steeps in the flood of noontide whiteness
>   Some defiled, discoloured web—
> So lay I, saturate with brightness.
>   And when the flood appeared to ebb,
>   Lo, I was walking, light and swift.
>   (ll. 487–95; Sect. ix.)

Clinging to Christ's garments, he is carried to Rome, where he witnesses the Christmas service in St. Peter's. Despite the "posturings
and petticoatings" (Browning is assumed to have had High Angli-
cans in mind as well as Roman Catholics), he senses that there is love
in the hearts of the congregation. The poet is then carried to a
Tübingen lecture hall; a wheezing professor is assuring his audience
that though the Christ of the New Testament is not historically true,
one may console oneself with the thought that he is true symbolically. Browning, ever a defender of the historic Christ, feels that
though others may have poisoned the air of religion, the higher
critics have pumped the air out altogether; in their midst he can feel
no more than the "ghost of love." And still the sense of Christ's injunction persists. Browning decides to scurry back into the Dissenting chapel; for all their ungraciousness, the Dissenters are most in
harmony with his beliefs—or, what is likely to be the same thing,
with his childhood image of what worship should be.

The blindly instinctive conviction that the unlovely path is the true path is the same as that expressed in *Childe Roland*. But the main point of *Christmas-Eve* is that it faces the problem already confronted in *Pauline, Paracelsus,* and *Sordello:* that of a spiritual pioneer beyond the line of settlement, the more mature man who would retain a bond of union with his own youth and with his fellow men. For Browning the only solution was at best an unsatisfactory compromise; as he himself says, if earthly solutions were satisfying, what would heaven be for? In his latter days, after returning to England, Browning attended various churches, but only sporadically.

Easter-Day considers another moral problem, the difficulty of heeding Christ's many warnings that man must lose the life of this world in order to find the life of the spirit. Browning's faith is not vivid enough to enable him to forgo the goods of this life which he always found so attractive. He then is presented with a vision of judgment, of heaven and hell, to shock him out of his complacency. Christ speaks to him in an "austere voice":

> *"This world,*
> *This finite life, thou hast preferred,*
> *In disbelief of God's plain word."*
>   (ll. 667–69; Sect. xx.)

The outcome is again a compromise. Browning cannot bring himself to renounce the world, but he has been moved to a sharper realization that its goods are imperfect goods, valuable only as they enable the soul to mount ever higher on the ladder of love. (Similarly, in his best dramatic mode, Browning was to utter through the person of Fra Lippo Lippi his conviction that earthly beauty "means intensely," and through Andrea del Sarto his equally sure, half-contradictory conviction that the most perfect physical beauty is not enough.) At the poem's end Browning is not wholly secure; he wonders whether on judgment day it will be enough to plead that, though unable to renounce the world, he had ever aspired beyond it. However, he does not despair:

> *But Easter-Day breaks! But*
> *Christ rises! Mercy every way*
> *Is infinite,—and who can say?*
>   (ll. 1038–40; Sect. xxxiii.)

The figure of Christ is as vividly present in *Christmas-Eve and Easter-Day* as at the end of each stanza of Thompson's *The Hound of Heaven;* indeed, the impression is inescapable that Browning's

poem afforded Thompson some inspiration. Why then is the completely Christian note of this work so rarely found elsewhere in
Browning's poems? His childhood years apart, Browning appears
most fully a traditional believer during the years with Elizabeth Barrett; after that some readers may sense a decline in belief as well as
in poetic power. W. O. Raymond has noted how the later Browning sometimes resembles the Tübingen professor whose attenuated
religion he deplored.[19] In these last years, when the death of Miss
Egerton-Smith and the current symposium in *The Nineteenth Century* induced him once again to argue at great length the question
of the immortality of the soul, he deliberately leaves Christian revelation aside; in the poem *La Saisiaz* he will give his own answer only,
and this is that man's intellect can prove nothing with certainty and
that man can only hope.[20] Only for a moment, in the earlier part of
the poem, does Browning suggest that man's *Perhaps* may have been
supplemented by God's *Yes:*

> *Mine is but man's truest answer—how were it did God
>   respond?*

(l. 152.)

Browning adds that he will not mimic such Divine response in futile
human speech. As in the case of Tennyson's similar reluctance in *In
Memoriam*, is reverence the only inhibiting force? Is there also an
inner lack of conviction? But Browning's reticence on this point
perhaps had other causes also. There was his well-known reluctance
to express himself directly on deeply personal matters, perhaps reinforced by the similar reluctance of the modern Englishman in general. And there may have been an artist's belief in the autonomy of
art; outside the special domain of hymnology, Browning may have
felt that poetry accomplishes its task best when confined to the
human sphere. This would be in keeping with his notion that God
stands a handbreadth off to give his creatures room to grow. Two
centuries earlier in his *Art Poétique* Boileau had come to similar conclusions; he had decided that even for Christian poets pagan subjects were generally best.

That quality in Browning which often strikes one as a brash self-
confidence is best remembered from his latest poem of all, the *Epilogue* to *Asolando*. As an expression of an old man's courage it will
seem to many readers to be marred by too blatant a self-sufficiency or,
somewhat differently, by a noisy protesting too much. Both a theologian and a humanist might agree in preferring Tennyson's more
modest *Crossing the Bar.* But one ought not to dismiss Browning's

poem out of hand as the expression of two self-centered a religion, nor should one simply deplore its lack of suavity. It is a very human poem and asks only to be understood. Browning's true personality is here finding utterance, but under the pressure of particular external causes. Browning had always been an activist, occasionally inclined to be cocky, persistently governed by images of a hero, semi-divine or human, such as Perseus and Childe Roland. Then in his old age he feels he is confronting the dark tower of an ever-increasing doubt in the world at large and, perhaps, in himself. With something of Childe Roland's loneliness he has persevered to the end and now he must blow his horn in challenge. The assertiveness of the *Epilogue* is not a contradiction of the doubt of *La Saisiaz* but its counterpart.

Yet beneath the reticence and uncertainty, the youthful chapel-goer still persists. There is not only the testimony of Browning's letter to the woman who has asked for his opinion outright. There is even the witnessing of Mrs. Sutherland Orr, who was always somewhat disconcerted when the poet she admired appeared to be less of a freethinker than she herself. Browning had been reading aloud to her an earlier *Epilogue*, that to the volume *Dramatis Personae*. This *Epilogue* had concluded with these lines:

> *That one Face, far from vanish, rather grows,*
> *Or decomposes but to recompose,*
> *Becomes my universe that feels and knows.*

Browning then added these words as a comment: "That face, is the face of Christ. That is how I feel him." [21]

Wordsworth, in his prefatory verses to his celebrated *Ode* as well as in the *Ode* itself, had stated that through all the vicissitudes of adult life and intellectual growth something of the child's insight should persist to unify and nourish. In Browning's case the chief early sympathy had been not with nature but with the Christianity of his youth; the first worship, reinforced by his devotion to his mother, had been directed towards the God of the Chapel. Thus there was never any occasion for a recantation quite like that in Wordsworth's *Elegiac Stanzas*. Both poets display a certain dryness and stoic hardness in their later years. But of the two perhaps Browning could more truly claim that through all the decomposing and recomposing of mental patterns he had best retained his early vision; the child had been the father of the man.

ARNOLD

Something Not Ourselves

SURPRISE MAY BE FELT that Matthew Arnold should be studied in connection with the nineteenth-century poets of intimations. One's sharpest memories of his poetry are likely to be of the final cry in *Dover Beach:*

> Ah, love, let us be true
> To one another! for the world, which seems
> To lie before us like a land of dreams,
> So various, so beautiful, so new,
> Hath really neither joy, nor love, nor light,
> Nor certitude, nor peace, nor help for pain;
> And we are here as on a darkling plain
> Swept with confused alarms of struggle and flight,
> Where ignorant armies clash by night.

There are reasons why *Dover Beach* should be Arnold's most vivid poem. Like many a popular song, it is about love and sadness. It also has a special appeal for certain modern readers whose sensibility is not entirely popular: though it sees the ebbing of the sea of faith as the root cause of modern distress, it neither seeks to buttress the old metaphysical absolutes nor to construct new ones. The merely human remedy of human love is all that is available; and this love, claiming no supernatural kinship with a Heavenly or Divine Love, is such as the modern humanist will approve.

Even if Arnold had made no effort elsewhere to establish a new faith, the fact that he saw the decline of the old faith as the cause of melancholy would make him a figure of interest in such a study as this. But the truth is that he does make such an effort. In this respect *Dover Beach* is not representative of his complete spiritual situation. (There is no reason why a single lyric should be thus complete.) In other poems and in prose Arnold sought somewhat tentatively—and with only very tenuous success—to establish something resembling a metaphysical absolute, a God, an Eternity.

Lionel Trilling, in his chapter on Arnold's religious writings of the 'seventies, sees God or some such postulated Absolute as necessary to Arnold to make his morality operative. Arnold believed, to use his own phrase, that we feel within ourselves "something not ourselves" urging us to perfection. As Trilling says, the objective existence of this generator of a sense of influence is "Arnold's own *Aberglaube* of morality," its postulated superstructure. Also Trilling sees God as necessary to Arnold in another way: "The establishment of God was necessary as a guarantee of the aesthetic life. People who did not need it for metaphysical completeness needed it for Joy." These two necessities for postulating God were, as Trilling notes, related in Arnold's thought: " 'The sense of *life*, of being truly *alive*,' said Arnold, was the reward of right conduct, but it could not be had merely by the performance of duty; it could only be assured by religion, and religion implies a God." [1]

To express Arnold's thoughts in other terms, one might say that he regarded even the adult somewhat as a child who does a task joyfully because he knows his father will approve. Trilling, one gathers, does not experience life in this way, but he notes that Arnold's own grandnephew, Aldous Huxley, after his early modernism, has returned to the older view that a belief in a moral purpose in the universe can make all the difference between "active morality and passive negation," and can flood life with "meaning and energy." [2] By a moral purpose in the universe is here meant a purpose having some existence outside the human mind and heart and will. This relationship between strength and joy on the one hand and metaphysics has already been touched on in these chapters, particularly in the cases of Shelley and Browning. It suggests of course some parallel to the

example of modern communists whose psychology partly resembles
that of the believers in religion; they derive an added strength from
the conviction that in their aspirations and efforts they are not alone
but are cooperating with some ultimate force outside themselves, the
dialectic of history. A hundred years ago many Western believers in
individual freedom and freedom of economic enterprise doubtless
felt that they too were cooperating with their own dialectic of history, the law of inevitable progress by means of the survival of the
fittest. But today many intelligent believers in a more tempered freedom feel themselves wholly on their own. Such perhaps was Carl
Becker, who in the ending of his book *Modern Democracy* stated:

> It is . . . futile to rely upon the saving grace of some transcend-
> ent increasing purpose (a law of nature, or dialectic of history,
> or totalitarian state) to bring us in spite of ourselves to a pre-
> destined good end. For the solution of our difficulties the only
> available purposes are our own, the only available intelligence
> such as we can command.[3]

Though traditional religion could subscribe to most of Becker's first
sentence, it would have reservations about the second. Becker intended this second sentence to be a trumpet call to manly endeavor.
Yet it is not certain that such a philosophy as it expresses is always
invigorating to the masses of men. Matthew Arnold was not certain
that it was invigorating even to the few.

These matters did not have to wait till Arnold's prose writing of
the later years for their working out. More than two decades earlier
Arnold had started to work them out in his poems, in the dramatic
situations and original images appropriate to poetry rather than in the
conceptual language and traditional images suited to prose preaching.

Arnold's early poem *Mycerinus* stresses the close relation between
belief and morality, and between belief and joy and energy. The
oracle tells the young king who is striving hard to be a just ruler
that he has but six years to live. His unjust father had been allotted
a long and secure life. The mystery of such inequitable dispensations
is too great to be borne. The young king exclaims,

> "*Yet surely, O my people, did I deem*
> *Man's justice from the all-just Gods was given;*
> *A light that from some upper fount did beam,*
> *Some better archetype, whose seat was heaven.*"

But he can believe it no longer. There is no perfect, eternal justice
in heaven or anywhere else by which a mortal may be inspired and

with which he may cooperate. Mycerinus loses all hope, all moral energy, and he deliberately embraces a life of sensual pleasure—which he pursues, however, without joy. Arnold consoles himself with the thought that, underneath the din and noise of the last years, the disappointed king may still have remained true to the ideal. This poem, in its youthful directness, reveals how early Arnold was consciously facing one of the problems which was to be of fundamental concern to him all his life. Characteristically he avoids any Browningesque tendency to see in the very imperfection of this world some argument for the existence of another.

Empedocles on Etna again contemplates joy and energy as these are related to belief. Among the best-known passages from this poem are the anti-metaphysical stanzas spoken by the aging philosopher to the accompaniment of the harp. These lines, containing some of the clearest argumentative verse of the nineteenth century, criticize all supernatural religion and urge man to be content with just such a philosophy as the modern humanist holds. The existence of Gods and of a supernatural state which men are destined to attain is denied in terms which attack any imaginative leap from the imperfect to the perfect:

> *Fools! That in man's brief term*
> *He cannot all things view,*
> *Affords no ground to affirm*
> *That there are Gods who do;*
> *Nor does being weary prove that he has where to rest.*
>
> (I, ii.)

And the song ends with a powerful expression of the humanist's philosophy:

> *Is it so small a thing*
> *To have enjoy'd the sun,*
> *To have lived light in the spring,*
> *To have loved, to have thought, to have done;*
> *To have advanced true friends, and beat down baffling foes—*
>
> *That we must feign a bliss*
> *Of doubtful future date,*
> *And, while we dream on this,*
> *Lose all our present state,*
> *And relegate to world yet distant our repose?*

   .   .   .   .

> *But thou, because thou hear'st*
> *Men scoff at Heaven and Fate,*
> *Because the Gods thou fear'st*
> *Fail to make blest thy state,*
> *Tremblest, and wilt not dare to trust the joys there are!*
>
> *I say: Fear not! Life still*
> *Leaves human effort scope.*
> *But, since life teems with ill,*
> *Nurse no extravagant hope;*
> *Because thou must not dream, thou need'st not then despair!*
>
> (II, ii.)

Such passages are too clear to need any elucidation in themselves. But they need to be commented on in their relation to the poem as a whole. So persuasive are these lines that readers are inclined to take them as the expression of Arnold's own whole-hearted beliefs. This they are not. They are rather the expression of a philosophy towards which he was strongly impelled by many currents of the time and by currents within his own nature, but at which he perhaps never completely arrived. It is precisely the internal conflict between the forces urging him towards humanism and those still holding him to vestiges of the old supernaturalism, Christian or Platonic, which is worked out in the play and which must have motivated its composition. This conflict is expressed chiefly by a division within Empedocles himself. These well-known verses are the expression of what might be termed the philosopher's public personality, with its nobility, its courage, its limited assurance. They are delivered to Pausanias for the precise purpose of fortifying him. But immediately Pausanias has departed, we are admitted behind the mask; we see the private soul in all its desperation. This revelation might suggest that there is about the public mask itself a certain hypocrisy. This would be too crude a judgment. It is not so much that Empedocles disbelieves the exhortation which he gives Pausanias; it is rather that it is the most optimistic exhortation to which his intellect can assent. But it leaves his own heart cold:

> *Pausanias is far hence [he says], and that is well,*
> *For I must henceforth speak no more with man.*
> *He hath his lesson too, and that debt's paid;*
> *And the good, learned, friendly, quiet man*
> *May bravelier front his life, and in himself*
> *Find henceforth energy and heart. But I—*

The weary man, the banish'd citizen,
Whose banishment is not his greatest ill,
Whose weariness no energy can reach,
And for whose hurt courage is not the cure—
What should I do with life and living more?

(II, 5–15.)

Still addressing himself, he reveals the death-like cold within:

something has impair'd thy spirit's strength,
And dried its self-sufficing fount of joy.

(II, 21–22.)

What precisely is the "hurt" for which "courage" is not the cure? What the "something" that has impaired the "spirit's strength"? A careful reading discloses that the hurt is of complex origins. Three of the causes may be of special interest here.

First, Empedocles finds that a shallow modern philosophy threatens to extinguish the light of Divinity which earth and man had alike emitted to earlier eyes; he himself must seek refuge in the volcano, the symbol of elemental life:

Ere quite the being of man, ere quite the world
Be disarray'd of their divinity—
Before the soul lose all her solemn joys,
And awe be dead, and hope impossible,
And the soul's deep eternal night come on—
Receive me, hide me, quench me, take me home!

(II, 31–36.)

So several of the Romantics had lamented that the one-sided development of the mere understanding reduced the world to a mechanism, mere inert atoms pushed around according to the laws of gravity and motion, devoid of indwelling life. Better to be a pagan, Wordsworth had said, one who sees gods in rivers and oceans, than to see the external world as dead. So the speaker in Browning's *Pauline* felt that when everything appeared to be understood by the intellect, nothing remains of which one can be in awe.

Secondly, Empedocles' own intellectuality and intellectual eminence have isolated him from the ordinary companionship and the simple joys of his fellows; he is a "naked, eternally restless mind"; and he is "weary" of his "unloved preeminence." In this state he appears to Callicles as "sad" and "proud," even as Browning's Paracelsus had appeared to Festus. (In both poems, written by Arnold

and Browning while they were still comparatively young, a reader
senses the prolongation of the Byronic note.) Browning had in his
still earlier *Pauline* evinced a tentative sense of guilt aroused by the
pride of intellectual adventure. So Arnold, in a poem earlier than
Empedocles, had expressed a similar feeling; in *Stagirius* he had
prayed:

> *When the soul, growing clearer,*
>   *Sees God no nearer;*
> *When the soul, mounting higher,*
>   *To God comes no nigher;*
> *But the arch-fiend Pride*
> *Mounts at her side,*
> *Foiling her high emprise,*
> *Sealing her eagle eyes,*
> *And, when she fain would soar,*
> *Makes idols to adore,*
> *Changing the pure emotion*
> *Of her high devotion,*
> *To a skin-deep sense*
> *Of her own eloquence;*
> *Strong to deceive, strong to enslave—*
>   *Save, oh! save.*

Professor Fairchild could scarcely have expressed better his own
evaluation of the high-aspiring Romantic imaginative effort. A few
years later in *Empedocles*, however, Arnold has come, as Browning
had come in *Paracelsus*, to feel less disturbed by the accusation of
pride; he appears rather to be accepting as a tragic fact that something resembling pride and an accompanying loneliness were the
inevitable lot of a certain type of mind at certain stages of intellectual
development.

Lastly, Empedocles' despair is further deepened by the failure of
his own pioneering mind to lead him to any point where he may rest
in full, immediate possession of Absolute Truth; he envisions probationary existence after probationary existence, in each of which
men will still be the slaves and prisoners of the forms of "Thought"
and "Mind":

> *And they [Thought and Mind] will be our lords, as*
>   *they are now;*
> *And keep us prisoners of our consciousness,*
> *And never let us clasp and feel the All*
> *But through their forms, and modes, and stifling veils.*

And we shall be unsatisfied as now;
And we shall feel the agony of thirst,
The ineffable longing for the life of life
Baffled for ever.

(II, 351–58.)

Immanuel Kant, as this study has already noted, had seen man
similarly imprisoned by the forms of the understanding. Man's escape,
in Kant's view, was to be effected in two stages. First, man recognized that some principle within him freely submits to a moral law
distinct from the natural laws of the physical world. Secondly, his
imagination could then carry him to some higher cosmic principle,
some "supersensible substrate." Arnold's Empedocles performs much
the same escape in the same stages. First, he apprehends his own
moral vitality by recognizing that he has never grown "easy" within
the bonds which mind imposes; he has never "loved" darkness nor
"sophisticated" truth. With this assurance of a moral life within
himself, his imagination can now succeed where it has earlier failed;
his last words, as he is about to jump into the fires of Etna, show
that just for a moment—perhaps no longer than one of Wordsworth's
flashings of a shield—he feels he is embracing life:

—Ah, boil up, ye vapours!
Leap and roar, thou sea of fire!
My soul glows to meet you.
Ere it flag, ere the mists
Of despondency and gloom
Rush over it again,
Receive me, save me!

(II, 410–16.)

Empedocles' problem had been his spiritual loneliness, and for one
climactic moment his imagination tells him that at the source of
things is companionship or union; thanks to the imagination, he can
feel that what he has been aspiring towards is not a subjective fantasy
but a reality. For Empedocles' embracing of the physical elements is
not to be taken literally. The significance of the end is that the
philosopher becomes the creative poet. He is a creative poet in the
grand Romantic tradition: his highest moment of creation is a moment of vision. Poetry turns out to be, as Wordsworth in his *Preface*
said it was, "the first and last of all knowledge," "the upholder and
preserver" of the human spirit.

Of course, in Empedocles' vision the high Romantic imagination
appears desperately tenuous; if it achieves any faith at all, it does so

most precariously. Compared with the ancient philosopher's final hope, even that of Shelley at the end of *Adonais* seems massively secure.

Walter E. Houghton, who has finally given *Empedocles on Etna* the careful and sympathetic study which it merits, agrees with this present interpretation in regarding the ending as a triumph of sorts. Yet he disagrees also.[4] He is sympathetic to the anti-transcendental humanism of the speech to Pausanias and finds no contradiction between this exhortation to trust in human life alone and the final embracing of some cosmic vitality; he comments upon the ability of the philosopher to escape the trammels of intellect and "to return to his mother earth and share in her joyful, creative life." Professor Houghton is therefore at some pains to explain away Arnold's assertion, made some years after the writing of the poem, that the philosophy imparted to the disciple is not one to live by and that it is in fact refuted by the dramatic action of the poem itself. He believes that Arnold had early accepted this humanism and only began to reject it later when he was "intent upon preaching a new Christianity." Presumably the basic contrast is assumed to be between a philosophy of *earth*, which Professor Houghton applauds, and a philosophy of the Christian *heaven* which is to be dismissed as a mere myth. There is certainly some basis in the poem for this interpretation. Yet perhaps it might be more fundamentally true to say that the chief contrast is between man alone and man in alliance with some cosmic force. Precisely one of the things that was new in Arnold's "new Christianity," if it is to be called such, is its extreme chariness in assigning any objective reality to the traditional heaven. What it demanded of its devotees in the way of faith was merely that they have a sense of some Influence other than, perhaps prior to, the mere working out of mechanical law—the something other than ourselves working for Righteousness. Empedocles had told Pausanias simply to place his faith in human life; he himself a moment later shows that for him this is not enough, that he craves to penetrate to some inner mystery, not just to life but to the "life of life" as he terms it. This is the equivalent of Arnold's later Influence. To some theists such an Influence may seem little better than no God at all. But to Arnold it was important. It was important not just when he was writing his later books upon religion, but from the very beginning of his poetic career.

In his comments on the drama Professor Houghton feels compelled, because of his own interpretation of its significance, to justify what he thinks is the somewhat unvital, unimpassioned formality of tone in the sermon to Pausanias—and yet, in the end he still wishes the sermon had been given more dramatic life. But perhaps these lines, in their clear rejection of supernaturalism, were intended to have the dry lucidity of intellect and to lack the living power which derives from the imagination. In the discussion of Wordsworth in the earlier part of this book it was suggested that the imaginative apprehension of the vital was perhaps basic to all Wordsworth's other more distinctly transcendentalizing apprehensions. So the entire drama of *Empedocles*, as distinct from the few stanzas addressed to the disciple, suggests that the chief crisis to Arnold, at its fundamental or initial stage, was not in the choice between earth and heaven, or between pantheism and Christianity, but between mechanism and a vitalism which is at least potentially an idealism. If life (or spirit) is a mere occasional, almost accidental byproduct of a universe which is essentially no more than an aggregate of inert atoms, operating according to those blind laws of the scientific understanding which Tennyson in *In Memoriam* found so unsatisfying as the ultimate explanation of things—if such is the case, then human life is indeed a lonely fact and the philosophy recommended to Pausanias is all that man has to help him make the most of it. If, on the other hand, imagination is to be our proper guide, then we may feel (as Coleridge and Wordsworth would have us feel) that life is of the very essence of the universe. The way is then open for us to decide at some later date between pantheism and theism, as Coleridge was impelled to do and ultimately Wordsworth also. Or one may hedge and compromise as Arnold did and simply trust in the Influence. But in either case, having chosen imagination rather than the physicist's reason, the human being feels less lonely in the cosmos, less an alien than before.

The Sublime and the Beautiful

ACTUALLY, Empedocles' feelings at this point represent but one of two poles between which Arnold's sensibility appears to oscillate. Empedocles' imagination as it embraces the elements of nature seems to be embracing some inner divine life. Two of Arnold's poems, *In Harmony with Nature* and *Morality*, appear to deny any such possibility. They affirm, almost with joy, that there is nothing in nature that is ours, that between nature and man is a great cleavage. They can discover in nature no image of that ultimate reality to which we are akin and towards which we aspire.

The paradox is an old one. Christianity had traditionally been willing to point to the beauty of nature as a revelation of the glory of God; but it had maintained that it was really in man's soul that we find God's image and likeness. Similarly, Kant had been willing to assert that the beautiful in nature and in art perhaps afforded some intimation of a divinity behind the material world which was in harmony with our nature; but right afterwards he had maintained that in the sublime we sense the true abyss between matter and spirit and our essential kinship with the world of spirit: the beautiful tells us that nature can image the ultimate truth; the sublime tells us it cannot. Perhaps in intellectual matters as in moral ones virtue lies in the mean. Christianity had traditionally hovered between the intellectually opposite poles of dualism and monism. Kant hovered there also. And so does Arnold.

These two poles correspond to those two sides of Arnold's nature, the Hebraistic and the Hellenistic. Arnold himself, in *Culture and Anarchy*, urges his countrymen to give themselves a little less wholly to the moral struggle which he felt was the Hebraist's lot, to be less convinced that the only truth was the personal struggle against sin, and to allow themselves to think that there might be some wisdom in the Hellenist's less combative, more detached quest for a certain wholeness and harmony. But it is a critical commonplace that Arnold himself was by nature as much a Hebraist as a Hellenist. He did not denounce the fundamental discontent of the Hebraist with things as they are; rather he upheld it. But he thought that it must be kept from narrowness and fanaticism by the opposite urges of the Hellenist to be sure that it was in fact seeing things as they are, and to enjoy as good in themselves whatever examples of fullness and harmony this world might briefly afford.

Corresponding to these two opposite but complementary urges of the human spirit, Arnold's poems show us two different moments of imaginative vision. In *Morality* Arnold contrasts Nature's "free, light, cheerful" air with man's "struggling, task'd morality." Here Nature may be said to be a Hellenist. Arnold wonders whether her freedom and cheerfulness are a rebuke to man's discontent. But the real truth he believes is quite the contrary, as Nature's reply reveals:

> "*Ah, child!*" *she cries,* "*that strife divine,*
> *Whence was it, for it is not mine?*
>
> "*There is no effort on* my *brow—*
> *I do not strive, I do not weep;*
>
> *I rush with the swift spheres and glow*
> *In joy, and when I will, I sleep.*

Yet that severe, that earnest air,
I saw, I felt it once—but where?

"I knew not yet the gauge of time,
Nor wore the manacles of space;
I felt it in some other clime,
I saw it in some other place.
'Twas when the heavenly house I trod,
And lay upon the breast of God."

(Nothing in nature, Kant had said, was truly sublime; sublimity is in man's soul.) Here Arnold would appear to be pushing Hebraism to its farthest limits. When Browning had expressed hope that he might "fight on, fare ever,/ There as here," he had regarded striving as the lot merely of humanity, in this world and the next. Arnold regards it as the lot of God himself. Traditional theology, deriving in part from Greek notions of the Idea as perfect in itself, as an Unmoved Mover, might at first seem to dissent from Arnold's view. But Plato himself in the *Timaeus* perhaps offers Arnold some support. And so does Christianity with its God-Man toiling and suffering for men.

In the *Lines Written in Kensington Gardens* Nature is as calm and untroubled as in *Morality*. But now God himself is also calm rather than striving. In a Hellenist's moment of vision the poet's imagination sees the peace in nature as the image of the Divine peace:

Here at my feet what wonders pass,
What endless, active life is here!
What blowing daisies, fragrant grass!
An air-stirr'd forest, fresh and clear.

Scarce fresher is the mountain-sod
Where the tired angler lies, stretch'd out,
And, eased of basket and of rod,
Counts his day's spoil, the spotted trout.

In the huge world, which roars hard by,
Be others happy if they can!
But in my helpless cradle I
Was breathed on by the rural Pan.

I, on men's impious uproar hurl'd,
Think often, as I hear them rave,
That peace has left the upper world
And now keeps only in the grave.

Yet here is peace forever new!
When I who watch them am away,
Still all things in this glade go through
The changes of their quiet day.

Then to their happy rest they pass!
The flowers upclose, the birds are fed,
The night comes down upon the grass,
The child sleeps warmly in his bed.

Calm soul of all things! make it mine
To feel, amid the city's jar,
That there abides a peace of thine,
Man did not make, and cannot mar.

The will to neither strive nor cry,
The power to feel with others give!
Calm, calm me more! nor let me die
Before I have begun to live.

Of course the striving of London, outside the calm of the gardens, was not precisely the striving Arnold had in mind when he wrote *Morality*. But the opposition between the moods of the two poems, though not total, is real enough. Which poem expresses Arnold's truest thoughts? One might as well ask which are true, Blake's *Songs of Innocence* or his *Songs of Experience*. Both presumably, but neither wholly.

Though man in his thinking is likely to be stretched between two poles, he is never content thus. On one occasion, recorded in *A Summer Night*, Arnold saw an image which, though somehow including the two different impulses, was not torn between them but united them into one wholeness. The image was that of the heavens, Hellenist in their beauty and serenity, Hebraist in their constant useful activity. Arnold is echoing Wordsworth's tribute to the heavens in his *Ode to Duty*, and possibly also Keats's description of the moon at its "priest-like" task of moving the cleansing tides around earth's shores:

Plainness and clearness without shadow of stain!
Clearness divine!
Ye heavens, whose pure dark regions have no sign
Of languor, though so calm, and, though so great,
Are yet untroubled and unpassionate;
Who, though so noble, share in the world's toil,
And, though so task'd, keep free from dust and soil!

. . . I will rather say that you remain
A world above man's head, to let him see
How boundless might his soul's horizons be,
How vast, yet of what clear transparency!
How it were good to abide there, and breathe free;
How fair a lot to fill
Is left to each man still!

Work may be man's lot in higher spheres as well as here, but if the work in such a sphere is quite as stupefying and narrowing and soiling as, earlier in the poem, Arnold had said it usually is here, one might well exclaim in Browning's words, "What's a heaven for!" But the image of the night skies fortifies Arnold by giving him a warrant that a fuller, a more harmonious state is not an impossible dream. From this warrant should come perseverance in moral endeavor and, Arnold would hope, joy.

Immortality

So FAR we have examined principally those moments when Arnold, or one of his characters, imagines some life or some state of being at the heart of the universe roughly comparable to the God of traditional thought. The questions of the existence of God and the immortality of the soul are likely to be very closely related: having imagined some more perfect being or life, man naturally thinks of the possibility for himself of a fuller union with that being or life. As has just been seen, the poem *A Summer Night,* illustrates the closeness of the two ideas. The moon and the heavens tell Arnold of some more harmonious mode of existence; then he immediately thinks of man's own future in relation to this existence:

How it were good to abide there, and breathe free;
How fair a lot to fill
Is left to each man still!

Yet those who know Arnold best would probably agree that in the last two lines he was not thinking specifically of immortality in any traditional sense; if he had anything very definite in mind, it was perhaps chiefly man's opportunity for development in the life he is living right now.

It will be instructive to examine more fully Arnold's feelings upon the question of immortality and to look at some of the poems in which this immortality is touched upon. Arnold is in general more reluctant to canvass this question explicitly than Shelley, Tennyson, or Browning. The indefiniteness with which he touches the matter when he touches it at all makes him seem less traditional, closer to the scepticism of the modern humanist.

There is one important difference between Arnold's feeling about what may be called the existence of God and his feeling about personal immortality. He usually felt that something equivalent to the old belief in God was essential to his own spiritual well-being. He felt that a belief in the immortality of the soul, more particularly an immortality of reward and punishment, was necessary to the moral life of the simpler sort of men. Persons in Arnold's situation have existed in almost all times, detached by their critical intellect from the traditional imagery of an afterlife, and themselves motivated as much by a thirst for harmony or perfection as by hope of worldly reward or fear of punishment. They are likely to arrive at some compromise similar to that of the ancient Stoics and others: they may imagine the soul as a spark of the Divine light that pervades the universe, destined to return after death to the eternal source of light; or as a spark of fire destined to return to the eternal flame. Such imagery does not absolutely preclude the possibility of some continuation of individuality, but it shows little interest in it. Some who prefer such imagery may point to its greater unselfishness, its suitability to those who in their earthly existence have been more engaged in forwarding the general welfare than in pushing their own fortunes. Perhaps such natures are more concerned with the reality of the ideal and with our kinship with the ideal, with our own semi-divinity so to speak, than with immortality as generally conceived. Wordsworth in the *Prelude* and the *Ode* is thus concerned with Divinity and our own semi-divinity, and Shelley everywhere and Browning often. But Shelley, along with what one might call his intense philosophical desire, had at the same time some narrower feelings, an intense horror of personal extinction. Something of this narrower feeling shows in Wordsworth and Tennyson, and in Browning at times. It makes them seem more traditional than Arnold, in whom such a feeling is scarcely to be detected. Of course, Shelley's horror of individual extinction was compounded by his extreme sensitivity to what seemed undeserved individual suffering. Arnold was not wholly without such sensitivity but it was not dominant in his thought.

Arnold's *Thyrsis* reveals very well his attitude on these matters. At first the poem may seem to consider only the question of the reality of the ideal. The question of immortality is not touched upon until the end and then only fancifully. But since the poem is partly about the death of Clough, it was perhaps implicit from the beginning.

In the opening stanzas of *Thyrsis* Arnold's imagination grasps at what was one of his most cherished images of ideal perfection, the Oxfordshire countryside. This image is for him a source of hope in the midst of near despair. So much is the poem a struggle between hope and despair that one is forcefully reminded of Shelley. Arnold's problem is Shelley's—and similar to Wordsworth's in the Intimations *Ode:* how amid the harshness of the world and its numbing tasks to keep the ideal alive in one's soul. It is kept alive in Arnold's by a return to the physical beauty of his old haunts. When Arnold laments "Too rare, too rare, grow now my visits here," he is lamenting not merely the rareness of pleasure and peace, but the rareness of reinforcements to his faith. In the absence of these reinforcements despondency threatens to overcome him, a despondency dull rather than anguished:

> And strange and vain the earthly turmoil grows,
> And near and real the charm of thy repose, [*Clough's*]
> And night as welcome as a friend would fall.
>
> (ll. 148–50.)

These lines do not express quite the *contemptus mundi* of the medieval moralists, but a deep moral lassitude. Arnold could not take life's struggle seriously because it seemed "strange and vain." It seemed vain because the ideal towards which one battled appeared at times illusory; and so death was to be welcomed not as a victory but as a surcease. But the Oxfordshire countryside testified to Arnold, as the Vale of Grasmere to Wordsworth, of an ideal reality. To it he returns to drink, as Wordsworth would say, "as at a fountain."

At first Arnold fears that this fountain may have lost its restorative powers. Much has changed. Fields once full of wild flowers have been torn up by the plow. Secluded nooks are now desecrated. Most disturbingly, the Fyfield elm, associated by Arnold and Clough with the scholar-gypsy and his eternal quest, is not to be seen. These crumblings of the outer image may only hasten that crumbling of the inner ideal which has been going on within Arnold:

> That single elm-tree bright
> Against the west—I miss it! is it gone?
> We prized it dearly; while it stood, we said,
> Our friend, the Gipsy-Scholar, was not dead;
> While the tree lived, he in these fields lived on.
>
> (ll. 26–30.)

The images and symbols which have been built into the fabric of his spiritual life have gone, and there is danger that now the life itself will go too. So, according to Proust, spiritual vitality had ebbed in the painter Elstir when, in his old age, a change of fashion in feminine beauty and in women's clothes abruptly swept away a set of images which he had spent a lifetime idealizing. And there had been Wordsworth's response in his later years to the threat of a railway being built through the Lake District; the response was so intense because the railway threatened an image which had become an inextricable part of that not too sturdy structure, Wordsworth's latter-day faith. And now we see Arnold trying to recapture a faith. Suddenly he succeeds, tenuously. The tree is sighted. The imagination seizes the tree's persistence as proof that the scholar-gipsy still lives on. And Arnold's imagination is now able to think of his departed friend Clough not as sunk in the sleep of night, but enjoying a "happier air" as he wanders in "the great Mother's train divine." He can even imagine Clough addressing him in these words:

> Why faintest thou? I wander'd till I died.
> Roam on! The light we sought is shining still.
> Dost thou ask proof? Our tree yet crowns the hill,
> Our Scholar travels yet the loved hill-side.
>
> (ll. 237-40.)

The primary emphasis is upon the assurance that the ideal itself persists; a suggestion of a future life is there also but weakened by its connection with the wholly fanciful earthly immortality of the gipsy.

Equally indicative of Arnold's feelings are the closing lines of *Sohrab and Rustum*. The burden of the mystery which remains to be lifted after Rustum has killed his son is a heavy one. By stressing the nobility and beauty of the young man's character beyond anything found in his sources, Arnold has in some ways increased this burden— why should one so fine, so full of promise, be snatched away so soon? The very youthfulness of Sohrab, like Clough's comparative youthfulness at the time of his death, insists more strongly upon an answer to the question of immortality than did Arnold's usual experience of the evils of this world. The imagination seems to demand some continuity more urgently than it does when a man has lived out a longer span. So Arnold, when he comes to end his tale, adds the image of the Oxus River, beside whose waters the fatal combat had taken place:

> But the majestic river floated on,
> Out of the mist and hum of that low land,

Into the frosty starlight, and there moved,
Rejoicing, through the hush'd Chorasmian waste,
Under the solitary moon;—he flow'd
Right for the polar star, past Orgunjè,
Brimming, and bright, and large; then sands begin
To hem his watery march, and dam his streams,
And split his currents; that for many a league
The shorn and parcell'd Oxus strains along
Through beds of sand and matted rushy isles—
Oxus, forgetting the bright speed he had
In his high mountain-cradle in Pamere,
A foil'd circuitous wanderer—till at last
The long'd-for dash of waves is heard, and wide
His luminous home of waters opens, bright
And tranquil, from whose floor the new-bathed stars
Emerge, and shine upon the Aral Sea.

Something more is being accomplished in this passage than is effected by those touches of nature's beauty with which Thomas Hardy and A. E. Housman relieve their gloom. Arnold is suggesting an allegory with some traditional overtones. The river is the river of human life, the narrow passages in which the river nearly strangles is death, and the "luminous home of waters," bright and tranquil, is the sea of eternity—as it is in Wordsworth's *Ode*. Also the stars, though not particularly suggesting the persistence of individuality (since the river is the prime symbol of individual life), inevitably recall the star in *Adonais*. Most particularly, since the stars are "new-bathed," they recall the ending of *Lycidas*, the most orthodox of this series of elegies:

Weep no more, woful Shepherds, weep no more,
For Lycidas, your sorrow, is not dead,
Sunk though he be beneath the watry floor,
So sinks the day-star in the Ocean bed,
And yet anon repairs his drooping head,
And tricks his beams, and with new-spangled Ore,
Flames in the forehead of the morning sky.

But the main image, that of the river returning to the sea and perhaps being lost in it, is not particularly suited to suggest notions of continuing individuality. Without such a notion the logical mind, working with traditional categories, might ask how the demands of justice are to be answered. But poetry's appeal is not to the logical mind alone. Arnold's final image is intended to satisfy the imagination, and in this task it meets with some success. The image of the river finding its way to the sea is a favorite of Arnold's; he makes notable use of it in *The Buried Life* and *The Future*, and in *The Future* he makes quite explicit the correspondence between the sea and the "Infinite." [5]

The fate of all rivers when they reach the sea is the same. However, nearly all rivers do reach the sea. It is ironic that Arnold should, as he undoubtedly does, have a fondness for an image that makes no discrimination between the sheep and the goats. In his own way Arnold could be an even sterner judge than traditional religion. His sonnet *Immortality* speaks contemptuously of those who find consolation in the thought of another life because they are depressed and worn out in spirit:

> *No, no! the energy of life may be*
> *Kept on after the grave, but not begun;*
> *And he who flagg'd not in the earthly strife,*
>
> *From strength to strength advancing—only he,*
> *His soul well-knit, and all his battles won,*
> *Mounts, and that hardly, to eternal life.*

So Browning had also prized active energy, and he too could at times sound equally severe—though his Paracelsus had foreseen some sort of universal salvation and though Abt Vogler was sure that there "shall never be one lost good."

Personal Relationships

A FAR BETTER KNOWN POEM which shows the same Hebraist's admiration for moral energy and similarly relates it to immortality is *Rugby Chapel*, Arnold's tribute to his father. Though Thomas Arnold may have had a certain calm and poise greater than his more sceptical son ever knew, he is generally thought of as a valiant combatant rather than a serene philosopher. As such Arnold celebrates him. In fitting tribute the elegy places greatest emphasis upon the moral power and endurance necessary if one is to be saved. Thomas Arnold is praised for possessing a surplus of this strength; he has both persevered himself on the long climb to the "City of God" and brought others along with him, ever assisting the weak and pressing the stragglers back into the column of march. But, as is usual in Arnold's poetry, the principal question is not whether men will reach the ideal but whether the ideal exists. Here men like his father supply an affirma-

tive answer by very reason of their divine energy; they themselves
are images of the very Divinity towards which they are urging us:

> *Servants of God! —or sons*
> *Shall I not call you? . . .*
>
> *. . . in such hour of need*
> *Of our fainting, dispirited race,*
> *Ye, like angels, appear,*
> *Radiant with ardour divine!*
> *Beacons of hope, ye appear!*
> *Languor is not in your heart,*
> *Weakness is not in your word,*
> *Weariness not on your brow.*
> (ll. 162–63; 188–95.)

For the moment the great human problem is not seen as narrow
fanaticism or ignorance, but as lassitude and despair caused by lack
of belief. By giving imaginative reality to the ideal heroic men can
inspire others with some of their own strength. Along with his power
to give substance to notions of deity, Arnold's father gives substance
to notions of the great men of the past:

> *. . . through thee I believe*
> *In the noble and great who are gone;*
> *Pure souls honour'd and blest*
> *By former ages, who else—*
> *Such, so soulless, so poor,*
> *Is the race of men whom I see—*
> *Seem'd but a dream of the heart,*
> *Seem'd but a cry of desire.*
> (ll. 145–52.)

Once again, as in the cases of Browning's Pompilia and his Pope and
of Shelley's Beatrice Cenci, hope depends on belief and belief revives
or fades according to whether a god-like hero appears or fails to
appear.

Supreme moments of personal relationship more to the taste of
the Hellenist in Arnold are recorded in *The Buried Life*. In love between man and woman, according to this poem, we fleetingly experience some fragment of an ultimate fullness and serenity. It is
important here to distinguish between *The Buried Life* and *Dover
Beach*. *Dover Beach* acclaims love simply because its joy and peace
were the best this world can offer; it makes no claim that these are

images of a greater joy and peace. But in *The Buried Life* the perfection which lovers know in the inner, private world of their love is taken as a hint of the existence of some ultimate Perfection. In the usual course of living, says Arnold, the soul is so involved in the false shows of this world that it never knows its own deepest nature:

> *Only—but this is rare—*
> *When a belovèd hand is laid in ours,*
> *When, jaded with the rush and glare*
> *Of the interminable hours,*
> *Our eyes can in another's eyes read clear,*
> *When our world-deafen'd ear*
> *Is by the tones of a loved voice caress'd—*
> *A bolt is shot back somewhere in the breast,*
> *And a lost pulse of feeling stirs again.*
> *The eye sinks inward, and the heart lies plain,*
> *And what we mean, we say, and what we would, we know.*
> *A man becomes aware of his life's flow,*
> *And hears its winding murmur; and he sees*
> *The meadows where it glides, the sun, the breeze.*
>
> *And there arrives a lull in the hot race*
> *Wherein he doth forever chase*
> *That flying and elusive shadow, rest.*
> *An air of coolness plays upon his face,*
> *And an unwonted calm pervades his breast.*
> *And then he thinks he knows*
> *The hills where his life rose,*
> *And the sea where it goes.*

In the older and more conventional kind of Platonizing love-poetry, the lover finds images of perfection in something exterior to himself, in the lady's physical beauty or in her beauty of soul. Arnold's poem in its special "interiorness," in finding perfection only in the shared inward moment of mutual feeling, may seem today to be more immediately the product of fresh experience—like some of the love poems of Donne and Browning and like Rosetti's *Silent Noon*. Despite this freshness, however, Arnold is left in his usual uncertainty; he can only say that he "thinks" he knows his soul's true home. This uncertainty is further emphasized by the note of Platonizing nostalgia already familiar in Wordsworth's *Ode* and occasionally in Tennyson; the ideal, if it exists, is something fading out behind us rather than something looming up ahead.

Thomas Arnold in the very assurance of his activity may well have possessed some of the calm fullness which his son cherished. But the dominant moods of *Rugby Chapel* and *The Buried Life* remain quite different from each other. Did Arnold ever find in one person whom he encountered an image such as he believed *A Summer Night* describes, which could satisfy equally both sides of his nature? Once perhaps yes, when, as *East London* records, he met a clergyman in the slums. Thanks to a living faith this clergyman was able, as Arnold was convinced man should be able, to be at once engaged in the struggle and serene:

> '*Twas August, and the fierce sun overhead*
> *Smote on the squalid streets of Bethnal Green,*
> *And the pale weaver, through his windows seen*
> *In Spitalfields, look'd thrice dispirited.*
>
> *I met a preacher there I knew, and said:*
> *"Ill and o'erwork'd, how fare you in this scene?"—*
> *"Bravely!" said he; "for I of late have been*
> *Much cheer'd with thoughts of Christ,* the living bread."
>
> *O human soul! as long as thou canst so*
> *Set up a mark of everlasting light,*
> *Above the howling senses' ebb and flow,*
>
> *To cheer thee, and to right thee if thou roam—*
> *Not with lost toil thou labourest through the night!*
> *Thou mak'st the heaven thou hop'st indeed thy home.*

This sonnet is an interesting tribute by one who did not quite believe to one who did.

The last two lines of the poem reveal one of Arnold's most characteristic attitudes. They all but ignore the question of immortality and exalt that inner security and strength which will redeem human life here and now. The kingdom of heaven—as Arnold, who knew his Scripture very well, was fond of pointing out—is within us. Since Arnold's time orthodoxy itself has been increasingly affected by what is sometimes called the existential point of view.

Arnold himself sought, amid the somewhat less dispiriting circumstances of his own life, to set up some mark above the howling senses: but for this mark he seems to have relied less upon "Christ, the living bread" than upon such images as were offered by the Oxfordshire countryside; the grand style of Homer, noble and serene; the grand style of Milton, noble and severe.[6]

Poetry the Ever-surer Stay

ARNOLD THE LITERARY CRITIC is famous for his insistence that in great poetry the human race of the future would find an ever-surer stay. What precisely did he believe that great poetry could offer? The question cannot be fully answered here, but one or two facts may be noted.

As Wordsworth's Tintern Abbey *Lines* reveal, the unintelligible complexity of life can sometimes be felt to be the greatest part of its burden. Arnold proposed great poetry as a means of lifting this burden. This proposal is made most clearly in his inaugural address as Professor of Poetry at Oxford titled "On the Modern Element in Literature." [7] Here uncertainty, multifariousness, and incomprehensibility are seen as constituting the chief difficulty of modern life. In this address as elsewhere Arnold expresses considerable faith in the intellect; a richer and truer set of ideas will make life more understandable and help produce "that noble serenity which always accompanies a true insight." The great poetry which Arnold hopes will once again be written must have ideas adequate to our present complexity.

But a reading of all Arnold's criticism reveals another aspect to his dictum that poetry is a criticism of life. Besides applying ideas to life, great poetry by mere virtue of its fullness and harmony is a criticism of the incompleteness and discord of daily existence. Homer and Sophocles did not have a stock of ideas sufficient to the needs of the nineteenth century, but in their works Arnold found solace and strength. What Homer and Sophocles did offer to the imagination were poised works incorporating into their harmonious totalities a reasonable portion (though by no means all) of human life's complexities. So the image of Grasmere Vale had for Wordsworth incorporated much of man's daily living into a noble harmony "complete in itself," into a "unity entire."

To Wordsworth the harmonies of landscape existed in at least partial independence of the human mind. So for Arnold must the harmonies of great poetry. In his 1853 *Preface* he stressed the desirability of a poetry with a more externalized objectivity than Romantic poetic poetry usually possessed. That his own poetry usually failed to achieve this ideal only increases the ideal's significance. Arnold sensed a dangerous morbidity in Romantic introspection; a merely confessional and self-revealing poetry could never fulfill poetry's great mission. One might suppose that in his theory of poetry, by

insisting on the objective independence and unity of a poem, Arnold
was unconsciously trying to solve the Romantic dilemma: was an
ultimate harmony nothing but the dream of desire, the object of the
never-to-be-assuaged "eternal Passion, eternal Pain" of Arnold's
Philomela, or was it something existing independently of our wishes?
was there a "something not ourselves" making for unity? Thus the
beauty of great poetry offered to him at least semi-transcendental
hints, as beauty had offered hints to his Romantic predecessors. In
his address at Oxford he claimed that Sophocles offers not only a picture of life as observed by an active, mature, free, and intelligent
man, but a picture "idealized and glorified by the grace and light
shed . . . by the noblest poetic feeling." The "grand style" which
he extolled was very largely a means of achieving this glorification.
And this glory achieved, as the address *Milton* makes clear, is to save
men by being an objectified revelation of some actually existent excellence and perfection ever on before. In short, in Arnold's philosophy it played at least part of the role which the Incarnation plays in
traditional Christianity.[8]

Taking the Omen

IN REVIEWING the key images of Arnold's poetry one may note
that they are more varied and interesting than they are powerful.
They do not have sufficient strength to induce even a temporary belief in Arnold himself, as landscapes seem occasionally to have done
in Wordsworth's case.

This comparative weakness of Arnold's intimations resembles the
uncertainty which he deplored in his friend Clough. Lionel Trilling
and Louis Bonnerot have commented so ably on this relationship that
little need be said.[9] In brief, Arnold feared to remain too closely
knit to Clough because in him he found his own weakness in more
pronounced form. For instance, he wrote to Clough:

> You certainly do not seem to me sufficiently to desire and earn-
> estly strive towards—assured knowledge—activity—happiness. You
> are too content to *fluctuate*—to be ever learning, never coming to
> the knowledge of the truth. That is why, with you, I feel it neces-
> sary to stiffen myself—and hold fast my rudder.[10]

This uncertainty in Clough need have posed no threat to one more
certain in himself. It is not that Arnold is uncertain everywhere.
Arnold the prose writer, the literary, social, and political critic, is

sure enough of himself. But Arnold's poetry, like so much of the great poetry of the century, deals very often with more ultimate matters. And here Arnold the poet, the private soul as opposed to the public critic, is revealed in the very candid poems to be deeply uncertain. In one way only may it be said that he did not fluctuate: he was always an idealist. But he was often an idealist by default only; to be anything else would to him have been intolerable.

Yet the strength of Arnold's idealism is constantly threatened by the unsteadiness of his notions about the best ways by which a man may apprehend the eternal Idea, the Platonic One. As any Platonist knows, and any poet and semanticist, it is to be apprehended by images. But the great images of traditional religion, though not so alien to Arnold as to Shelley, were not to be accepted easily, naturally, unselfconsciously, as something given. He once wrote to Clough: "There is a God, but he is not well conceived of by all." [11] If one is always conscious of the inadequacy of the terms in which traditional ideals are expressed, the ideals at times can seem as tentative as the terms. The result in Arnold's case was that he was forced to discover his own images, so to speak.

Yet Arnold was fully aware of the disadvantages of creating one's own images in these matters. His general sympathy was with the Anglican Establishment, with all its defects, rather than with the smaller, more original sects and the new cults. He was eloquent in pointing out the deficiencies of the new, ready-made religion of a certain Miss Cobbe, and in telling us that not in such individual confections was to be found the depth and breadth and grandeur and authority of the great religions of history.[12] But in his own case, a strongly developed critical sense seems to have cut him off from much of the permanent imagery of the New Testament, which has always remained the core of Christianity. He could on occasion use this imagery with some unction when addressing a wide audience. But in his own interior life he could not use it so well; he was in a position not so different from Miss Cobbe's.

All this uncertainty about modes of apprehension and expression, infecting with uncertainty the very ideal to be apprehended, inevitably produced a poetry lacking in that poised assurance which was Arnold's self-appointed goal. And this poetry lacked also that joy which Arnold often associated with this assurance. As Trilling has noted, Arnold acknowledged that religion was necessary for joy, for "the sense of *life*, of being fully *alive*." Joy and a sense of being fully alive were not to be found in Clough's poetry, harried as he was by a painfully conscientious intellect from one tentative formulation to another. How could such a spirit produce a poetry with

that "pure serene" which Keats found in Homer and Arnold drank
deeply of from the same source? It could not produce even that
somewhat less serene certainty afforded by the grand style of Milton.
Strongly critical in spirit though Milton was, he was working in an
earlier age before the old inherited certainty had been dissipated.
Hence, though one may not often find in him a fullness of joy, there
is yet at least the "assured knowledge—activity" that Arnold missed
in Clough.[13]

Arnold has himself acknowledged that his own poetry falls short
precisely in this matter of poised assurance. He wrote to Clough:

> I am glad you like the Gipsy Scholar—but what does it *do* for
> you? Homer *animates*—Shakespeare *animates*—in its poor way I
> think Sohrab and Rustum *animates*—the Gipsy Scholar at best
> awakens a pleasing melancholy. But this is not what we want.
>
> *The complaining millions of men*
> *Darken in labour and pain—*
>
> what they want is something to *animate* and *ennoble* them—not
> merely to add zest to their melancholy and grace to their dreams.
> —I believe a feeling of this kind is the basis of my nature—and of
> my poetics.[14]

The terms which Arnold applies to *The Scholar-Gipsy*, though one
may not regard them as so wholly damaging as Arnold does, apply
to Arnold's poetry generally. Even of *Sohrab and Rustum* one can at
best make but a partial exception.

Arnold's explicit devotion to joy and life and assurance, here
found in a comparatively early letter to Clough, is not an early phase
of his thinking only. Trilling's chapter, "Joy Whose Grounds Are
True," is a discussion of the later theological writings. And in the
later critical writings the same devotion is expressed in his evaluation of the great Romantics. As Trilling says, Wordsworth takes
superiority over Byron in Arnold's estimation by right of his power
of joy and consolation, his ability to be that ever-surer stay which
Arnold and Wordsworth alike thought poetry should be. In Trilling's words:

> the sense of the supernal which Wordsworth conveyed, with
> which, indeed, Wordsworth had expressly sought to bring com-
> fort to souls sterilized by the Revolution, was what Arnold sought
> in the highest poetry. Wordsworth spoke of imagination but
> always of imagination as against critical intellect and always of

imagination as carrying the imaginer to meaning, to awe, to union. Neither French poetry nor the English poetry of the 18th century, so much influenced by France, had, in Arnold's sense, imagination.[15]

But, with a more strongly critical bias than Wordsworth, and living at a later date, Arnold is not carried by his imagination to anything better than the most tentative meaning, awe, union.

At times Arnold's tentativeness may seem to be no more than a matter of technique, of such prosaic, anti-climactic, unvatic procedures as we witness in *Dover Beach* when the poet tells us, "we / Find also in the sound a thought." But the technique is not unsure, it is simply honest. The outer tentativeness is the proper expression of an inner tentativeness, of that dialogue of the mind with itself which Arnold found so characteristic of the modern age and from which, like Keats, he could find a welcome escape in the unselfconsciousness and "pure serene" of Homer. The climax of *The Buried Life*, as has already been remarked, can assert no more than,

> *And then he thinks he knows*
> *The hills where his life rose,*
> *And the sea where it goes.*

And at the highest moment in *Thyrsis*, when Arnold once again catches sight of the elm, he says, "I take the omen!" In this one line the great difference between Wordsworth's intimations and Arnold's images is sharply apparent. Wordsworth writes as one who has known a mystical rapture: he does not himself decide to find a thought or take an omen; a thought or omen is unmistakably forced upon him. He accepts some faith because the evidences seem compulsive, not merely because he has long desired to find some faith. The sense of being wholly at the disposition of some superior power is well conveyed in those lines of *The Prelude* which describe his feelings in the dawn amid the mountains after the all-night dance:

> *I made no vows, but vows*
> *Were there made for me; bond unknown to me*
> *Was given, that I should be, else sinning greatly,*
> *A dedicated spirit.*
> (*Prelude*, IV, 341–44; IV, 334–37.)

In Wordsworth not only does man reach up; some greater spirit reaches down. But Arnold's poetry is like Shelley's, though far less intense: if any flash is vouchsafed, it is often after such despondency and anguish that there must always lurk, in the poet's own mind, the suspicion that the answer was not really received but conjured up by longing. Because Wordsworth had many powerful passages free of this tentativeness, and because a certain metaphysical assurance carried over from his mystical moments to his poems generally, Wordsworth was for Arnold the greatest of the nineteenth-century English poets. In later years Arnold would still have assented to his early judgment, in *Memorial Verses*, that Wordsworth was best able to shed

> *On spirits that had long been dead,*
> *Spirits dried up and closely furl'd,*
> *The freshness of the early world;*

that he was best fitted to move aside "The cloud of mortal destiny."

Another way of pointing up this same difference between Arnold and Wordsworth is to note that many of Arnold's most memorable images, despite their elegance and their applicability, are often merely illustrative. They express, often perfectly, the directions of a highly self-conscious thought. To Wordsworth and to Keats the intensely imaginative moment of insight was the primary fact, the irrefutable experience of the total man. Any self-conscious attempts to relate the experience to sets of metaphysical ideas, in letters and prefaces or in the poems themselves, were perhaps tentative; but the experience itself—whatever it meant—was certain.

Modern Instances:

YEATS/STEVENS/ELIOT

THOUGH THIS STUDY of the transcendentalizing imagination has concentrated upon poets of the nineteenth century, it would be misleading to end with Arnold. The old impulses show themselves very much alive in our own time. Particularly interesting are the cases of Yeats, Stevens, and Eliot. Yeats inclined like young Keats to the ultra-Romantic view that the soul can create its own immortality. Stevens like a good Romantic extolled the exercise of imagination as the highest good but long resisted the notion that it tells us anything of God or eternity.[1] In the end both poets' subjectivism and agnosticism yielded more ground than has been generally realized. Eliot's conversion, much earlier and going all the way to orthodox Christianity, was the literary sensation of two continents. What is less widely understood is that Eliot acknowledges both in his poetry and his prose that a tempered Romantic faith in the natural imagination is a necessary pre-condition of religious belief.

Of developments between the great Victorians and the poets after the first World War little will be said here. In the latest generation of nineteenth-century writers there is often some relaxation of the tensions which characterized Tennyson, Browning, and Arnold. The more extreme disciples of art for art's sake slake their thirst for the absolute by domesticating it in the work of art itself; art is

226

sufficient in itself and is not made the basis of any theory which will aid man to understand his own predicament or reconcile him to the disturbing world-view created by an advance in intellect. Art is less a solution than an escape. Likewise some of the poets of this period might be said to have half-domesticated the absolute in the Roman Catholic Church and in these also the imaginative strain is diminished.

But such relaxations were not universal. To Hardy, for example, the evils of this life were a constant and unevadable fact. Nature, when it was beautiful, might briefly mitigate. The beauty of his own art, which somehow encompasses and incorporates the evil, could perhaps console. But the consolation was not strong enough to support an optimistic philosophy. At the beginning of the nineteenth century the Romantic poets had been able to share at least for a moment the joy of the linnets, skylarks, and nightingales which they heard singing in spring and summer; at the century's end Hardy hears an old thrush in mid-winter and can find nothing to explain its joy:

> *So little cause for carollings*
> *Of such ecstatic sound*
> *Was written on terrestrial things*
> *Afar or nigh around,*
> *That I could think there trembled through*
> *His happy good-night air*
> *Some blessed Hope, whereof he knew*
> *And I was unaware.*
> (*The Darkling Thrush.*)

Arnold's imagination at the end of *Thyrsis* may have supplied him with only a fanciful omen, but at least he decided to "take" it. Hardy says that he "could think" some good was portended, but apparently he does not. After the turn of the century, in his old age, Hardy was to continue his confrontation of evil with perhaps some diminution of his pessimism.

Yeats

YEATS in his youth was influenced by French symbolism. In his study *The Heritage of Symbolism* C. M. Bowra has discussed the symbolist movement as an attempt of the imagination to supply some Absolute to take the place of traditional religion. He sees in this movement a course of development not unlike that which this study has sought to trace in English poetry. Baudelaire, a progenitor of the movement, was in this respect like Wordsworth: he felt that the imagination not only created but received. As Baudelaire says in his sonnet *Correspondances:*

> La Nature est un temple où des vivant piliers
> Laissent parfois sortir des confuses paroles;
>   L'Homme y passe à travers des forêts de symboles
>   Qui l'observent avec des regards familiers.

His correspondencies are like that pre-established harmony, that exquisite fitting of the external world and the human mind to each other which Wordsworth had noted; like the Platonist, as he goes about the world, he feels that he is seeing or hearing something he had seen or heard before. Then, with the passage of time in France, there is an increasing tendency towards art for art's sake. With more self-conscious theorizing than their English counterparts, the later French poets begin to apotheosize the poem itself: the supreme imaginative act is the creation of the work of art and this work is regarded as absolute in itself more than as an intimation of something beyond. This whole movement is part of Yeats's background.

In Yeats's early poetry the idealizing imagination expresses itself in misty evocations of the heroes and heroines of Celtic legend, creatures of an unearthly strangeness. The poet shows a strong inclination to escape reality and its evils; the image of the island in *The Lake Isle of Innisfree* encompasses far less of the life of humanity than Wordsworth's Vale of Grasmere. The early poem *The Lover Tells of the Rose in his Heart* shows Yeats burdened less by the philosophically unintelligible than by the aesthetically distasteful:

> All things uncomely and broken, all things worn out and old,
> The cry of a child in the roadway, the creak of a lumbering
>   cart,
> The heavy steps of the ploughman, splashing the wintry
>   mould,
> Are wronging your image that blossoms a rose in the deeps of
>   my heart.
>
> The wrong of unshapely things is a wrong too great to be
>   told;
> I hunger to build them anew and sit on a green knoll apart,
> With the earth and the sky and the water, re-made, like a
>   casket of gold,
> For my dreams of your image that blossoms a rose in the deeps
>   of my heart.

Some of this aestheticism had been present in Wordsworth. One of the important things about Grasmere Vale was that it provided a setting for life in which nothing was inharmonious to the senses. But this valley was a refuge, a justifying image, to a poet who had already contemplated the sufferings and injustices of life far more intensely than young Yeats had yet done—and one who had never been so delicate as to wish to dispense with the creak of a cart or the heavy tramp of a plowman.

This early poetry of Yeats strikes us as merely unreal rather than transcendental. Yet some kind of transcendentalizing pressures long continued to work in the poet's imagination. The early closeness to the Celtic sense of another world was succeeded by the interest in dreams, spiritualism, the occult, and a rather occultist neoplatonism.

Starting a few years before 1910, Yeats's poetry takes on a new realism as he becomes more deeply involved in the actual struggles of contemporary Irish life and, it would seem also, in the sexual life of an adult. Yet at the same time the simplest lines in his new style can effortlessly invest the real persons he writes about with a more than life-size stature, an epic dignity, an immortal symbolic value. He also records with a new sharpness non-human images, but these likewise may hint at something which the poet's everyday reality lacks. The "mysterious, beautiful" birds in *The Wild Swans of Coole*, like the figures of Keats's urn, bespeak an eternity of passion and vigor:

> *Unwearied still, lover by lover,*
> *They paddle in the cold*
> *Companionable streams or climb the air;*
> *Their hearts have not grown old;*
> *Passion and conquest, wander where they will,*
> *Attend upon them still.*

The lake itself, as described in *Coole and Ballylee, 1931*, suggests a justice and a rightness which modern life does not offer:

> *so lovely that it sets right*
> *Which knowledge or its lack had set awry.*

The aristocratic Georgian houses in *Nineteen Hundred and Nineteen* and the ceremonious life they still sheltered seem symbols of permanence in an age of confusion and change; they are

> *Protected from the circle of the moon,*
> *That pitches common things about.*

It was inevitable that to the poet who had wished to remake the world like a casket of gold, art itself would appear as an efficacious talisman against evil and decay. In *Sailing to Byzantium* Yeats hopes that the sages who have wrought in the world of intellect or imagination will enable him to escape the ravages of the world of flesh and gather him "into the artifice of eternity"; this artifice is imagined as a mechanical golden bird:

> *Once out of nature I shall never take*
> *My bodily form from any natural thing,*
> *But such a form as Grecian goldsmiths make*
> *Of hammered gold and gold enamelling*
> *To keep a drowsy Emperor awake;*
> *Or set upon a golden bough to sing*
> *To lords and ladies of Byzantium*
> *Of what is past, or passing, or to come.*

And in the poem *Byzantium*, desiring a remedy not just against decay but against the confusing duality and unintelligibility of human life, Yeats again has recourse to the golden bird and, along with it, to other works of Byzantine artifice:

> *Marbles of the dancing floor*
> *Break bitter furies of complexity,*

and

> *A starlit or a moonlit dome disdains*
> *All that man is,*
> *All mere complexities,*
> *The fury and the mire of human veins.*

These last lines particularly recall Shelley's contemplation of the serene and lofty splendor of Mont Blanc. From these same lines G. Wilson Knight has taken the title of his book *The Starlit Dome*, in which he studies as "eternity symbols" the pleasure dome that rises above the river of time in *Kubla Khan* and a host of other Romantic domes and related images. (In most of the earlier poems the word dome means simply a lofty and splendid edifice and not the more restricted architectural component which the word signifies today.)

One of Yeats's most notable efforts to discover a possible unity and wholeness amid the dualities of human life is his poem *Among School Children*. He takes one of his symbols of unity, the tree, from nature, and the other, the dance, from the borderland between nature and art:

> *Labour is blossoming and dancing where*
> *The body is not bruised to pleasure soul,*

Nor beauty born out of its own despair,
Nor blear-eyed wisdom out of midnight oil.
O chestnut tree, great rooted blossomer,
Are you the leaf, the blossom, or the bole?
O body swayed to music, O brightening glance,
How can we tell the dancer from the dance?

Keats, like Yeats, had sometimes felt strongly that a natural harmony of human life can be spoilt by such a "fierce miscreed" as this poem ascribes to Maud Gonne. He would have admired these lines.

But Yeats recognizes after all some difficulties in the way of achieving within the limits of this life the wholeness which the blossoming tree represents. His imagination extends itself as easily as that of young Keats into some transcendental realm beyond: we "worship" such images as the tree, he tells us, because they "symbolize" all "heavenly glory." The question is, in what fashion does Yeats conceive of this heavenly glory? The two Byzantium poems, from this same period, are concerned with much the same theme. Yet neither of these urgently compels us to consider seriously some such objectively real eternity as Platonism and Christianity generally suppose to exist. Both may be read mainly as the expression of an old man's defiant delight in the continued use of his imagination and intellect. We the readers may experience delight simply because two such tersely splendid poems exist amidst the democratic flatness of our age and all its nerveless, wordy prose.

The truth is that Yeats's philosophy in these years is so subjective, so focussed upon the powers of original genius rather than upon any power which might have created that genius, that the whole question of belief as traditionally understood becomes almost irrelevant. Like Blake and Shelley in certain phases, Yeats adopts a Berkeleian subjective idealism without Berkeley's distinct and separate God; thus he emphasizes what the mind can create rather than what it can receive. In his first version of *A Vision* he made the Blakean prophecy that after the year 1927 "Men will no longer separate the idea of God from that of human genius, of human productivity in all its forms." [2] Eternity if it exists will have something of the quality of human artifice, like the golden nightingale of Byzantium. In his introduction to the *Oxford Book of Modern Verse* Yeats said that "soul must become its own betrayer, its own deliverer, the mirror turn lamp." As Keats had written to Bailey, whether or not essential beauty existed before the artist imagined it, it exists after. Even as Keats had proposed that we imagine our own Elysian condition

into being, so Yeats in the poem *The Tower* proposes that his soul
be its own deliverer in this same pleasant fashion:

> *I mock Plotinus' thought*
> *And cry in Plato's teeth,*
> *Death and life were not*
> *Till man made up the whole,*
> *Made lock, stock and barrel*
> *Out of his bitter soul,*
> *Aye, sun and moon and star, all,*
> *And, further add to that*
> *That, being dead, we rise,*
> *Dream and so create*
> *Translunar Paradise.*
> *I have prepared my peace*
> *With learned Italian things*
> *And the proud stones of Greece,*
> *Poet's imaginings*
> *And memories of love,*
> *Memories of the words of women,*
> *All those things whereof*
> *Man makes a superhuman*
> *Mirror-resembling dream.*

Yeats's statement that the mirror will turn lamp supplied M. H.
Abrams with the title of his book *The Mirror and the Lamp*, which
studies the Romantic change from the older, more objective view
of the power of imagination to newer, more subjective views. The
emphasis shifts from the mind receiving light to belief that it gener-
ates its own light. Yet during the 1920's, when Yeats's subjective
philosophy was at its height, he wrote one poem, *Stream and Sun at
Glendalough*, in which the lamp for the moment condescends to be
a mirror also. The poem is less a deliberately created imaginative experience in its own right, like the *Ode on a Grecian Urn*, than the
record of an unsought moment of imaginative sensitivity which has
been granted to the poet before he even considered writing the
poem. As a result of this unsought experience Yeats says that the
soul briefly seems to be its own deliverer, but the careful description
of the event itself implies that there has in fact been some such interaction as Wordsworth celebrated between beauty received and
beauty lent by the mind itself. And the beauty received has in this
instance been from the world of nature rather than from that of art:

Through intricate motions ran
Stream and gliding sun
And all my heart seemed gay:
Some stupid thing that I had done
Made my attention stray.

Repentance keeps the heart impure;
But what am I that dare
Fancy that I can
Better conduct myself or have more
Sense than a common man?

What motion of the sun or stream
Or eyelid shot the gleam
That pierced my body through?
That made me live like those that seem
Self-born, born anew?

In Yeats's *Last Poems* little remains of the old thirst for such idealities as his imagination had long conjured up. Yet, the naturalism, admirable in its vigor, is perhaps a little too insistent, as though a pressure of some kind were still subconsciously at work. In his own Byronic way, Yeats is still wearing one of those "masks" of which Richard Ellmann has written.[3] The striking fact about these last years, however, is that the time of the triumph of naturalism may also be the time when Yeats is closest to religious belief in the usual sense. As Professor Ellmann has seen Yeats's development, the last pages of the revised *Vision*, completed during these years, virtually admit the inadequacy of that vast man-made machinery which Yeats had elaborately erected to explain and supplement the world and its history. This final subsidence of the will-to-create is, in effect, a return to more usual views, and the return involves both a gain and loss of freedom. Human freedom to act within the framework of history is restored, but the freedom to create one's own deity and, by implication, one's own "Translunar Paradise" is forgone. This latter freedom, as Keats had suspected long ago, had been sensed in the end to be but a "Purgatory blind." Professor Ellmann describes Yeats's final shift in these words:

Only at this point do we realize that Yeats, after building up a system over three hundred pages, in the last two pages sets up that system's anti-self. All the determinism or quasi-determinism of *A Vision* is abruptly confronted with the Thirteenth Cycle which is able to alter everything, and suddenly free will, liberty,

and deity pour back into the universe. This revolt against his
father's scepticism and against his own is complete at last, though
it brought him to no church. God had forced His way ineluecta-
bly into Yeats's mind:

> Then my delivered soul shall learn
> A darker knowledge and in hatred turn
> From every thought of God mankind has had.
> Thought is a garment and the soul's a bride
> That cannot in that trash and tinsel hide:
> In hating God she may creep close to God.
>
> At stroke of midnight soul cannot endure
> A bodily or mental furniture.
> What can she take until her Master give!
> Where can she look until He make the show!
> What can she know until He bid her know!
> How can she know till in her blood He live!

Looking back over Yeats's work, we can see that such a God was
always likely to come out of it; the 'Eternal Darkness' and the
'great journey-man' were among his antecedents, but until now
He had been as much as possible disregarded and His power
undermined. He is the God of unwilling belief.[4]

About a week before his death Yeats read aloud to his wife and
a few friends his final poem *The Black Tower*. In it Yeats expresses
a definite confidence that the soul's "Master" will indeed come. In
dramatic situation and in some details of imagery *The Black Tower*
is strikingly reminiscent of a poem of Arnold's considered before, the
Stanzas from the Grande Chartreuse. But Yeats's poem is more concentrated and vivid, free of that plaintive elegance which Arnold
sometimes regretted in his own poetry, and strong in an indomitable
expectation. In Arnold's stanzas a last remnant of believers and would-
be believers, regarded as fools by the world at large, huddle together beneath the wall of the abbey where they have been raised:
committed from youth to an other-worldly ideal, they cannot be
lured away to join the hunting party of pleasure seekers or the still
more attractive cavalcade of the ambitious, with their "banners" and
"bugle-music." In Yeats's poem an old tower is the central symbol
rather than an abbey. As is usual in his poetry, the tower is a symbol of the contemplative life, perhaps a recollection, as F. A. C.
Wilson notes, of Plotinus's "old watchtower beaten by storms"
which directs man away from mundane concerns towards the eternal

ideal.[5] Despite all their hardships the garrison besieged within the tower will not surrender; they are "oath-bound men." The "banners" of materialism advance to "bribe or threaten"; the foes whisper to them that they are besotted to remain loyal to a king who "died long ago." The garrison cook suddenly swears that he hears the "king's great horn." The soldiers call the cook a lying fool; they cannot believe that deliverance is immediately at hand. But they hold out none the less, with blind faith in an ultimate release.

Stevens

WALLACE STEVENS SPECULATES persistently upon the significance of imagination and varies his views with a highly developed awareness and a light heart. If any one view is central to his thought it is that of the modern humanist worshipper of art, from the traditional point of view an atheist or at least an agnostic. He feels himself to be at the portal of a new age and upon this portal is inscribed a new profession of faith: "No longer do I believe that there is any mystic muse . . . I am myself part of what is real, and it is my own speech and the strength of it, this only, that I hear or ever shall." [6] The artistic imagination is important to him in the first instance, not because it offers an analogy to any divine imagination which created the world but because it provides us "with precious portents of our own powers." [7] In this new age, presumably, those older divisions of philosophy known as theology and ontology, with their explicit reference to some ultimate reality independent of the human mind, are both reduced to psychology only. Evaluated in terms of its psychological effects, art offers man a "justification," [8] a "purification"; it is "akin to mysticism"; thus, Stevens says, "in an age in which disbelief is so profoundly prevalent or, if not disbelief, indifference to questions of belief, poetry and painting, and the arts of life in general, are, in their measure, a compensation for what has been lost. Men feel that imagination is the next greatest power to faith; the reigning prince." [9]

A work of art can accomplish its "justification," can lighten what Stevens calls the "heaviness of the world," [10] in much the same way as a landscape could at times lift the "burden of the mystery" for Wordsworth or Shelley—by its perfection of form and by its being thoroughly penetrated by life or spirit or light. Stevens thus expresses his satisfaction after seeing an exhibition of paintings by the modern artist Villon:

I was immediately conscious of the presence of the enchantments
of the intelligence in all his prismatic material. A woman lying in
a hammock was transformed into a complex of planes and tones,
radiant, vaporous, exact. A tea-pot and a cup or two took their
place in a reality composed wholly of things unreal. These works
were *deliciae* of the spirit as distinguished from *delectationes* of
the senses and this because one found in them the labor of calculation, the appetite for perfection.[11]

Radiant, vaporous, its earthly solidity transfigured—thus it was that
the landscape seen from the Euganean Hills had appeared to Shelley;
in fortunate moments the vales of the Lake District had taken on
the same appearance before Wordsworth's eyes, and as an arrangement of forms the hills of Grasmere were at all times deeply satisfying.

But this brief summary does not take into consideration the ways
in which Stevens' philosophy came into being; its nuances and conscious ironies; and its final relaxation, from what Stevens himself
humorously calls an "insatiable" egotism,[12] into something a little
closer to the worshipful attitude of tradition, an awed awareness of
some greater power.

The early poem *The Comedian as the Letter C*, in a humorous,
grotesque style not unlike that sometimes employed by Browning,
describes how the young poet Crispin deliberately embarks upon a
voyage. He wishes to depart from the land of finished harmonies,
from a region already spiritualized by the traditional Romantic imagination, to land more strident and raw, to sail beyond "Bordeaux"
to "Yucatan." Crispin's motives are partly the same as those which
had impelled young Browning to create a fresh sensibility of his
own: the old sensibility must inevitably come to him second-hand; to
be strongly affected by it would be to submit to a "drenching" of
one's own life by "stale lives." Our modern poet in his youthful
vigor welcomes the opportunity to create a "colony" of his own in
a new disorderly world. But Stevens goes farther in his reaction than
Browning. In an imagery which anticipates Aldous Huxley's criticism of Wordsworth, he states his belief that a harsh sun, strong
colors, rank vegetation, and "parrot-squawks" may present a truer
picture of reality than the "passionately niggling" song of the "nightingale." The Romantic imagination may be a deceptive "moonlight"
which, by toning down the harshness of life, gives man a false sense
of some "blissful liaison between himself and his environment." Unlike Shelley and Tennyson, Stevens is not abashed by the possibility
that the ultimate nature of the universe may not derive from any-

thing so accordant with our desires as a spirit of love. Browning himself had also regarded his fresh assessment of life as a testing of the Romantic-Christian view, but he was not inclined to consider seriously that this view, when tested, might be found wanting.

The Comedian is a brilliantly subtle revelation and, in view of Stevens' development, a prescient one. Though written in the first flush of his belated poetic career, when his mind seems buoyantly free to receive fresh impressions, the poem confesses that the shades of the prison house are already closing in. The world at large in its rawness, altogether ununified by the poetic spirit, is proving too much to assimilate. Stevens has already become not a man looking outward but an "introspective voyager." He retreats from the wild tropics of Yucatan to a middle region of the "Carolinas." There he shuts himself in a "hermitage" and cossets his "prismy blonde," who symbolizes the richly sensuous world of his quite ordinary and comfortable everyday life. Upon her he begets four daughters who are simply "personae" of himself—the various fancies and imaginings which his mind can beget upon the sensuous world. Such are his satisfactions with his rather passive concubine and his somewhat more lively young "chits," that his "quotidian" life with them "saps" his philosopher's ambition to discover meaning. His little fancies, though delightful, do not solve the world or penetrate to its core, but leave it still the same "insoluble lump." Stevens' diagnosis of his own case is quite right. As a poet he is in many ways not open to all the influences of life but very much the elegant and introspective hermit. He succeeds in excluding from his poetry any strong traditional sense of a cosmic being who might interfere with the rapt attention with which he listens to his own voice, and also in shutting out all his fellow human beings as well. Like a still-life artist, arranging and rearranging mute objects in interesting patterns, he purifies his aesthetic response from contamination by the welter of men's hopes and despairs and of their relations with one another. Indeed, when one considers the immense effort of Wordsworth and Keats and Shelley to comprehend within the imaginative processes of their art the suffering and injustice of the world, it is hard not to smile (as Stevens himself perhaps smiles) at the bold assurance of young Crispin that he was developing a broader and tougher aesthetic than his Romantic predecessors. In one respect, however, it should be noted that the poem does not fully foresee the future: in the years to come the philosopher's speculative instincts, far from weakening, develop more and more strongly until at times they predominate over the sensuous perceptions and imaginative processes which they are supposed to be contemplating.

It was Stevens' freely shifting, agnostic mind which made such protracted speculation possible. On the one hand he argues eloquently in his poem *Sunday Morning* against the lady's need to believe in some "imperishable bliss." In the last stanza he presents life as we know it as a casual episode on a minor planet, cut off, "unsponsored" by any central principle of life as our own earth and solar system are cut off by unbridgeable vastnesses of space:

> *We hear, upon that water without sound,*
> *A voice that cries, "The tomb in Palestine*
> *Is not the porch of spirits lingering.*
> *It is the grave of Jesus where he lay."*
> *We live in an old chaos of the sun,*
> *Or old dependency of day and night,*
> *Or island solitude, unsponsored, free,*
> *Of that wide water, inescapable.*
> *Deer walk upon our mountains, and the quail*
> *Whistle about us their spontaneous cries;*
> *Sweet berries ripen in the wilderness;*
> *And, in the isolation of the sky,*
> *At evening, casual flocks of pigeons make*
> *Ambiguous undulations as they sink,*
> *Downward to darkness, on extended wings.*

Yet if it is true that we make pamphlets out of our debates with others and poems out of our debates with ourselves, the lady and her immortal longings may represent a very faint residuum within the poet himself. In the exquisite dying fall of the final lines the "ambiguous undulations" of the birds' wings seem almost to constitute an uncertain symbol, a glancing recognition that there may be something beyond the apparent fact, perhaps even some principle capable of resisting the downward sinking. In another well-known early poem, the *Anecdote of the Jar*, there is another basic ambiguity of feeling, in this instance quite explicitly acknowledged. As becomes a man who said that our own voice, such as we hear it in works of art, is all that we can or ever will hear, Stevens praises the jar for taming the wilderness of Tennessee and furnishing us with a focal point of dignity. But he is ironically aware that devotion to art may stifle our awareness of such life as may be present in the world itself:

> *It took dominion everywhere.*
> *The jar was gray and bare.*
> *It did not give of bird or bush,*
> *Like nothing else in Tennessee.*

Also, even in *The Comedian as the Letter C*, at the same time that Stevens had refused to take for granted that the world was already harmonized by some spirit other than man's, or had any meaning other than what man's mind may choose to give it, he had yet conceded that when tested the shapeless "prose" world might "wear a poem's guise at last." In that case, possibly, the "blissful liaison" which religious and Romantic imaginations set up between man and the universe would after all not be an "evasion" or mere "minor meeting," but indeed man's "chief motive, first delight." In that event "Triton's horn," that voice akin to his own which Wordsworth had heard in nature, would no longer be dismissed as "hallucinating" or "negligible," as the mere "unavoidable" but meaningless "shadow of himself" which man's mind projects onto the outer world.[13]

For years to come Stevens continues to hold half at bay traditional notions of an intentionally harmonized and meaningful universe. The speculations continue, insistent but inconclusive. Yet, like Keats, though without Keats's anguish, Stevens remains a "teased spirit." The possibility of some harmonious solution, valid not only personally but cosmically, will from time to time make itself felt. The very power of artistic creation will itself suggest, as it did to Kant and his followers and to Coleridge, the existence of some analogous power greater than itself: in one of his essays, Stevens describes his dim but tantalizing apprehensions in these words:

> To describe it by exaggerating it, he [the poet] shares the transformation, not to say the apotheosis, accomplished by the poem. It must be this experience that makes him think of poetry as possibly a phase of metaphysics; and it must be this experience that teases him with the sense of possibility of a remote, a mystical *vis* or *noeud vital*.[14]

In *Notes Toward a Supreme Fiction*, though the general emphasis is upon the necessity of man's creating his own means of worship, almost his own object of worship, Stevens also describes occasions of a more traditional sort of mystical awareness, times when, as Keats had also noted, we feel this life is a sleep in the midst of which we have momentarily awakened and glimpsed some reality beyond. In *Sunday Morning*, in a moment of full sensuous content, the lady had spoken of the "need" for some immortal bliss. But in this later poem there is no mention of a sense of need: the earthly perfection, of itself as it were, suggests something loftier. The moment is more like a grace given than a vision created by one's own imagination:

> *Perhaps there are times of inherent excellence,*

As when the cock crows on the left and all
Is well, incalculable balances,
At which a kind of Swiss perfection comes

And a familiar music of the machine
Sets up its Schwärmerei, not balances
That we achieve, but balances that happen,

As a man and woman meet and love forthwith.
Perhaps there are moments of awakening,
Extreme, fortuitous, personal, in which

We more than awaken, sit on the edge of sleep,
As on an elevation, and behold
The academies like structures in a mist.

The half ironic imagery of the first lines suggests the slight embarrassment which a modernist must feel upon making such admissions. In the lines which follow, the "elevation" delicately recalls such hills of vision as those from which Spenser's Red Crosse Knight and Bunyan's pilgrims had beheld the Heavenly City; the "academies like structures in a mist" evoke some traditional, Platonic metaphysic of the sort which Stevens was usually inclined to forgo and which he here sees only as a hazy and uncertain hypothesis.

Stevens' final volume of poems is titled *The Rock* in allusion to his early statement that life without imagination is a rock of earth and that it is imagination only which impregnates it with leaf and flower and fruit. This view is essentially the same as that of the man who can hear no voice but his own, whose fanciful creations, instinct with the life of his own mind, were the only portentous signals he would ever receive. But the ironies of the *Anecdote of the Jar* had early exposed the paradox of this position, since the jar in Tennessee had seemed to kill more life than it created. In *The Rock*, which Stevens regards as a turning "downward toward finality," there is some subsiding of the pressure to impregnate life with the poet's own fancy; as Professor Roy Harvey Pearce has noted, Stevens is trying to arrive at a more objective assessment of reality by imagining imagination away.[15] In other words, he is attempting to take out of life the elegant jars which his imagination has put into it, in order to see what "Tennessee" by itself is really like.

The results of this more receptive attitude are a freer and fuller flowering of traditional apprehension long half suppressed. The poem *To an Old Philosopher in Rome* is still a celebration of the power of the mind to create its own cosmos; but at the same time Stevens sees the dying philosopher as about

> *To join a hovering excellence, to escape*
> *From fire and be part only of that of which*
> *Fire is the symbol: the celestial possible.*

No matter how these lines, reminiscent of Eliot's *Four Quartets*, are interpreted, they differ strikingly from the sinking "downward into darkness" in the "old chaos of the sun" at the end of *Sunday Morning*. It is almost as though Stevens' lifelong emphasis upon things of the "spirit," for all its narrow aestheticism, is threatening to pay off at last in ways he had not earlier foreseen. In another poem, *Notes on Moonlight*, the universe is again apprehended as religion and idealistic philosophy had apprehended it, and as Wordsworth had viewed it most particularly in the Prospectus to *The Excursion*, as a pre-established harmony. The beauty of the moonlight is no longer feared as an evasion. It tells Stevens that life is not a mere episode in an essentially inert cosmos; the heavens themselves, Wordsworth's "one galaxy of life and joy," are so apprehended that Stevens makes a profession of imaginative faith:

> *this warm, wide, weatherless quietude*
> *Is active with a power, an inherent life,*
> *In spite of the mere objectiveness of things . . .*

The "one moonlight, the various universe," capable of generating this sense of liaison, are now "intended . . . to be seen"; the cosmic "purpose" which it reveals may be logically "absurd," but it is "Certain and ever more fresh. Ah! Certain, for sure . . ."

The affirmations of *The Rock* reach their climax appropriately enough in the last poem of all, *Not Ideas About the Thing But the Thing Itself*. The "Thing Itself" is the world outside the mind, as it is independently of the order which the mind seeks to impose; in short, it is Tennessee but Tennessee now apprehended in a new way. Stevens had earlier, in one of his prose essays, commented upon the teasing nature of certain aspects of the natural world, such as the sky, which seem to be poetry of themselves.[16] At the time he was inclined to explain away this mysterious quality, as a good logical positivist might, as the mere chance result of some childhood experience long forgotten. Now in his final poem Stevens is himself presented as if by chance with a whole aggregate of such natural symbols, of the very sort cherished by the naturally religious imagination—the waking from sleep, the song of an unseen bird, the end of winter, the end of night, the dawn, the sun. These stanzas, despite Stevens' customary well-bred restraint, dramatize something very like a mystical experience; the images of the last lines are even permitted to suggest the quality of Dante's *Paradiso:*

> *At earliest ending of winter*
> *In March, a scrawny cry from outside*
> *Seemed like a sound in his mind.*
>
> *He knew that he heard it,*
> *A bird's cry, at daylight or before,*
> *In the early March wind.*
>
> *The sun was rising at six,*
> *No longer a battered panâche above snow . . .*
> *It would have been outside.*
>
> *It was not the vast ventriloquism*
> *Of sleep's faded papier-mâché . . .*
> *The sun was coming from outside.*
>
> *That scrawny cry—it was*
> *A chorister whose c preceded the choir.*
> *It was part of the colossal sun,*
>
> *Surrounded by its choral rings,*
> *Still far away. It was like*
> *A new knowledge of reality.*

Thus does the solipsist, the "introspective voyager," escape at last
from the little hermitage into which he had shut himself with his
"prismy" but mute "blonde," to listen to the sound of his own voice
and beget "personae" of his own mind. The man who had thought
that the portents of his own powers were the only portents he would
ever know, now acknowledges receiving the portent of a universal
power. This harbinger of a great chorus is not, as it had seemed to
him during his long "sleep," merely a sound within his own mind,
something which man, by an unconscious ventriloquism, wrongly
ascribes to the world at large. This final awakening from sleep is
a fuller realization of those earlier, more tentative awakenings when
he thought he glimpsed academies in the mist. Although Stevens, unlike Shelley, had never been appalled at the possibility that there
might be no escape from solipsism, this last poem, in its reiterated,
almost unbelieving "outside . . . from outside," expresses a trembling joy at his final release from long immurement. The sense of
liaison which when first intimated to the younger poet by moonlight
had seemed a possible evasion, can now sustain the full light of the
sun, can even be reinforced by it. Stevens had once said that art is

the "violence from within that protects us from the violence from without."[17] In his closing poem art turns out to be celebration of a great harmony existing independently of his own imagination yet singing in unity with that imagination, and intended so to sing.[18] The "Supreme Fiction" has now become a revelation.

Traditionalists are perhaps fond of seeking out instances of death-bed conversions. It is important not to claim too much. In theology Stevens has in *The Rock* come a long way from his position in the final stanza of *Sunday Morning*. Yet his final, joyous sense of a living cosmic power, to which by anthropomorphic analogy he ascribes "purpose" and "intent," is not much more than young Crispin had foreseen years before when he had conceded that the wilderness of the world might "wear a poem's guise at last," and that a sense of some central harmonizing power, if indeed such existed, would be man's "chief motive, first delight." Stevens likewise must have felt that his own Bergsonian vitalism was different in important ways from the theism of the orthodox. And in the realm of "ecclesiology" the poet remained the unregenerate individualist to the end, happy in his condition. He explains his position in the poem *St. Armorer's Church from the Outside*. The once splendid church, symbol of traditional religion and ecclesiastical organization, appears deserted and decaying. By its side, in the churchyard, is a small chapel, symbol of the imaginative beliefs which each man erects for himself. This chapel remains ever fresh because it is always being renewed. In it each man "walks and does as he lives and likes."

Eliot

T. S. ELIOT's USE of the ecstatic moment, usually a moment of beauty, has received some attention. Leonard Unger focussed upon a particular aspect of the subject a number of years ago in his article, "T. S. Eliot's Rose Garden: A Persistent Theme."[19] F. O. Matthiessen treated the subject broadly and sympathetically in the chapter on the *Four Quartets* in his book *The Achievement of T. S. Eliot*. Yet one suspects that the basic insights which these and other studies contain are still not understood by many persons generally well-informed upon modern literature. A brief résumé will be attempted here in the light of such question as the present study has posed.

Eliot from the very beginning evinced a sensibility fuller and closer to that of religion than Yeats and Stevens. He shows little of the early tendency to escape from the drabness of life around him into a Celtic twilight or an abstract or at least unconcerned art. From

Prufrock through *The Waste Land* he presented scenes of everyday existence in all its enervated futility or its brutish sordidness; he presented them with some scorn perhaps, with a little more pity and sympathy, and most of all with a compressed vividness which inaugurated a new poetic era. Admittedly in *The Waste Land* he used the richness and perfection of art as a criticism of everyday life: Spenser's line about Sweet Thames is set against the rat with its slimy belly, the dull canal, and the gashouse. But more than in the cases of Yeats and Stevens one senses from the beginning a strong moral concern mingling with the aesthete's fastidious distaste or evasion: life should perhaps be more beautiful, but it should certainly be infused with some loftier purpose. The recollections of Eastern and Western religious writings used to summon the Waste Land to repentance affirm Eliot's bond with tradition. The ominous thunder suggests that something more cosmic than one individual prophet is giving warning; the hope of rain suggests that some greater-than-human agency will make the barren life fruitful.

In *Ash Wednesday* Eliot's partially anticipated conversion to religion is becoming a fact. The first section of the poem shows him in an anguish of repentance; overwhelmed by his awe for eternity, he seeks to cast off all affections of a man living in time: ambition, pride of knowledge, even love of the beauty of nature. This last he renounces

> *Because I cannot drink*
> *There, where trees flower, and springs flow, for there is*
> *   nothing again*
>
> *Because I know that time is always time*
> *And place is always and only place.*

In the third section the effort of renunciation must be repeated. As he struggles up a Platonic staircase towards eternity he must somehow succeed in passing a bay window which opens on a distractingly lovely scene of May flowering and music and love. In the sixth section he half rebels; he wonders whether he must wholly forget the ecstatic moments recollected from youth:

> *Wavering between the profit and the loss*
> *In this brief transit where the dreams cross*
> *The dreamcrossed twilight between birth and dying*
> *(Bless me father) though I do not wish to wish these things*
> *From the wide window towards the granite shore*
> *The white sails still fly seaward, seaward flying*
> *Unbroken wings*

And the lost heart stiffens and rejoices
In the lost lilac and the lost sea voices
And the weak spirit quickens to rebel
For the bent golden-rod and the lost sea smell
Quickens to recover
The cry of quail and the whirling plover
And the blind eye creates
The empty forms between the ivory gates
And smell renews the salt savour of the sandy earth

This is the time of tension between dying and birth.

The poem ends with the tension still unresolved. While trying to submit to the divine will, Eliot hopes that religious aspiration need not cut him off wholly from those recollections at which his heart "stiffens and rejoices":

Sister, mother
And spirit of the river, spirit of the sea,
Suffer me not to be separated.

Eliot is seeking to hold together the supernatural and the natural, to keep open a way between the religious life and the energy and joy of natural life, to preserve that imaginative bond between adulthood and the ecstasies of youth which Wordsworth said can and must be maintained. The internal separation which he dreads is very similar to that which Keats dreaded as the possible result of attachment to an ideal goal. Eliot's poem also offers an obvious parallel to Browning's *Easter-Day*, though Browning had sought to save more than just the ecstatic moments of the natural life.

In *Marina* Eliot appears to have found some of the oneness he was seeking. He feels that certain recollected images have their important uses. He is struck by the undying persistence of certain moments of beauty:

What seas what shores what grey rocks and what islands
What water lapping the bow
And scent of pine and the woodthrush singing through the fog
What images return.

He then lists those things which produce "Death": savagery, vanity, self-satisfied torpor, brutish sensuality. These are less persistent; they

Are become unsubstantial, reduced by a wind,
A breath of pine, and the woodsong fog
By this grace dissolved in place.

He continues:

> *What is this face, less clear and clearer*
> *The pulse in the arm, less strong and stronger—*
> *Given or lent? more distant than stars and nearer than the eye*
>
> *Whispers and small laughter between leaves and hurrying*
> *   feet*
> *Under sleep, where all the waters meet.*

The eternal, more distant than the star, is not distant only; it is also, he says, near at hand in time, a "grace dissolved in place." The secret laughter under the leaves seems to have been such a moment of grace, an early sense of sexual attraction, as Leonard Unger maintains; it has taken on permanent imaginative significance for Eliot, as a similar moment had done for Dante. In the next section of the poem Eliot perhaps recalls a summer day off the New England coast many years before. He feels himself sailing in a leaking ship towards an unknown reality ahead, a reality symbolized by those very things which had stirred him as a child:

> *What seas what shores what granite islands towards my*
> *   timbers*
> *And woodthrush calling through the fog*
> *My daughter.*

These early natural images must be cherished; they seem the only fitting means of giving imaginative substance to the categories of the poet's transcendental philosophy, of filling "the empty forms between the ivory gates." In his recognition of the important role of memory in his religious sensibility, Eliot here resembles Wordsworth: not just beauty itself but the persistence of beauty in the mind is responsible for the sense of portent. In Eliot's case, however, no actual return seems to have been required.

In his essay *Dante* in 1929 Eliot had expressed his belief in the possibility of such an early impulse to sexual love as Dante records in the *Vita Nuova*. Furthermore, he agrees in giving to such a moment and other similar ones Dante's Platonic-Christian interpretation: their final cause is "the attraction towards God."

The same faith in the value of images, especially of images as they live again in the memory, is expressed in the *Four Quartets*. Eliot's sense of the imperfection of the world is as strong as ever, as is his insistence upon renunciation and repentance. The Eternity which is our proper goal can, however, be symbolized by art: in *Burnt Norton* Eliot says,

> *only by the form, the pattern,*
> *Can words or music reach*
> *The stillness, as a Chinese jar still*
> *Moves perpetually in its stillness.*

But static images and images of art are not dominant. Much more fully in this same poem Eliot goes back in memory to youthful experiences, as to a rose garden where children are hidden in the shrubbery and where the empty pool for a moment seems to fill up quietly with living water. A cloud then passes over and he discovers that the waters have disappeared, because "human kind / Cannot bear very much reality." *The Dry Salvages* returns to the same theme: only the saints, the poet says, truly apprehend the intersection of the timeless with time; but certain experiences give ordinary men hints:

> *For most of us, there is only the unattended*
> *Moment, the moment, in and out of time,*
> *The distraction fit, lost in a shaft of sunlight,*
> *The wild thyme unseen, or winter lightning*
> *Or the waterfall, or music heard so deeply*
> *That it is not heard at all, but you are the music*
> *While the music lasts. There are only hints and guesses,*
> *Hints followed by guesses; and the rest*
> *Is prayer, observance, discipline, thought and action.*

(Keats has been charged with indulgence, while Eliot renounces. Yet the configuration of the intensely imaginative moment can be the same for both. Keats's insistently present yet hidden flowers in the *Ode to a Nightingale* are parallel to Eliot's "wild thyme unseen" and so is the unseen nightingale itself; they resemble also the joyous children present in their heard laughter but concealed by the shrubbery from the eye. Also, Keats had heard the nightingale as Eliot says music can be heard, so deeply that it is not heard at all; and he had extolled in the *Ode on a Grecian Urn* an inverted but similar experience, not hearing music at all so that it can be imagined more intensely.) Despite the tentativeness of these elusive moments, Eliot now proceeds to claim for them the most sacred character: they are fleeting revelations of what Christianity has preached as the eternal made temporal in Christ:

> *The hint half guessed, the gift half understood, is Incarnation.*
> *Here the impossible union*
> *Of spheres of existence is actual,*
> *Here the past and future*
> *Are conquered, and reconciled.*

The end of *Little Gidding*, the last of the four quartets, variously suggests Platonism, Wordsworth's Ode, and Christ's injunction to become again "as little children"; in preparation for the ultimate reconciliation of eternity, Eliot tells us, we must somehow work back in our own nature to the joy and innocence of childhood:

> *We shall not cease from exploration*
> *And the end of all exploring*
> *Will be to arrive where we started*
> *And know the place for the first time.*
> *Through the unknown, remembered gate*
> *When the last of earth left to discover*
> *Is that which was the beginning;*
> *At the source of the longest river*
> *The voice of the hidden waterfall*
> *And the children in the apple-tree*
> *Not known, because not looked for*
> *But heard, half-heard, in the stillness*
> *Between two waves of the sea.*
> *Quick now, here, now, always—*
> *A condition of complete simplicity*
> *(Costing not less than everything)*
> *And all shall be well and*
> *All manner of things shall be well*
> *When the tongues of the flame are in-folded*
> *Into the crowned knot of fire*
> *And the fire and the rose are one.*

Despite their great differences, Wordsworth and Eliot, the two poets who at the beginnings of the nineteenth and twentieth centuries seemed to sweep away the old and usher in the new, reveal in spiritual matters a profound kinship of which we are not always aware.[20] They both emphasize simplicity, childhood, a divine life present "here, now," which occasionally flashes forth and reveals itself to the uncorrupted consciousness. Neither poet was necessarily averse to the idea of a deliberate quest, but both felt the importance to belief of moments of a more relaxed receptivity when one is not "forever seeking"; the intimation comes to Wordsworth most potently in times of "wise passiveness," to the heart "that watches and receives"; and to Eliot it comes in the "unattended moment" when "not looked for." Moreover, Wordsworth, like both Eliot and Keats, had been aware of the unusual imaginative power of a "hidden" source of beauty and harmony: as a boy he had listened with wonder to the voice of the always unseen cuckoo; under the four yew-trees of Borrodale he had imagined the shapes of Fear and Hope and Death listening, in "mute repose," to the "mountain flood / Murmuring from Glaramara's inmost caves"; and, most of all, on the top of Snowdon he had listened in awe as the "one voice" of "innumerable torrents" came up to him from the dark depths hidden below the cloud. Why should imagination find such situations so mysteriously moving? Are they perhaps analogs of the cosmic situation as a Platonic Christianity views it: behind the appearances of things is a hidden glory and life which may one day be revealed fully to the mind's eye, a glory which for the present time may not be known clearly but may be felt with that peculiar intimate poignancy which sound and scent from unseen sources can somehow evoke. Perhaps, in the words of the Tintern Abbey *Lines*, they suggest that "more deep seclusion" of the "hidden God," the *deus absconditus* of tradition.

The Ennobling Interchange

SHAKESPEAREAN *fish swam the sea, far away from land;*
Romantic fish swam in nets coming to the hand;
What are all those fish that lie gasping on the strand?

Yeats's lines, titled *Three Movements*, express his sense of the impoverishment of modern men, their displacement from their proper
environment. Poets, like Shakespeare, are likely to feel that their
environment of heaven and earth contains more things than are
dreamt of in a materialist philosophy. They are likely to worship
images they know not why, and then perhaps to conclude that they
have worshipped them because things visible and temporal image
things invisible and eternal. In the past century and a half, in an
effort to remedy the impoverishment of which Yeats speaks, the
most serious of the poets with striking uniformity have trusted the
imagination to discover some revelation. Browning in *Paracelsus* said
that men have

> *August anticipations, symbols, types*
> *Of a dim splendor ever on before.*
> (V, 775-76.)

Mallarmé, at first glance so very dissimilar to Browning, believed essentially that the object of poetry was not to depict the shell of life around us but to recreate the flashes from eternity that came through this shell.[1]

It is quite possible to concede that men use images drawn from material objects or situations as symbols, and yet to deny that these images are, inherently, of themselves, symbols; in other words, to maintain that images can tell men nothing about the ultimate nature of the universe, only about the impulses of their own hearts. Shelley, of all the great nineteenth-century English poets, was most haunted by the sense that such might be the case. But, like the other poets, he had his periods of faith when images seemed natural symbols of the sort he desired.

The ultimate assumption behind this faith is a philosophical equivalent of the religious belief in a Divine Providence: the universe is accepted as the product of beneficent design, of a pre-established harmony such as the idealist tradition has assumed to exist between the human spirit and the world in which its lot is cast. This is the harmony which Wordsworth celebrated in the closing passage of *The Recluse* (the same lines which were later used to introduce *The Excursion*):

> *How exquisitely the individual Mind*
> *(And the progressive powers perhaps no less*
> *Of the whole species) to the external World*
> *Is fitted:—and how exquisitely too—*
> *Theme this but little heard of among men—*
> *The external World is fitted to the Mind.*

The argument from design was once commonly accepted as one of the great proofs of the existence of God. In recent centuries many philosophers have found the argument defective. But the poets, when they accept images as something given rather than as something which they have pressed into service, are in effect still accepting a form of the old argument. As we have noted earlier, Immanuel Kant, one of the most notable rejectors of any theological reasoning based upon the designs and purposes which the scientific understanding discovers in the material world, tentatively accepts almost the same argument with respect to beauty; we are not justified, he feels, in drawing any metaphysical conclusions from the perfect mechanism of the flower, but from its beauty we may be. Similarly many poets have seen beauty as a grace that hovers over the mere mechanism of the universe. This grace or glory is apparently unnecessary to the purely physical order of the world; it is accepted as the proper nourishment of man's spirit.

When man's imagination is in proper relationship to the universe and its pre-established harmony (when he is neither a fish in a net nor a fish on the strand), then—says Wordsworth—he achieves "spiritual dignity"; this dignity is both established and maintained by a proper "balance,"

> an ennobling interchange
> Of action from without and from within;
> The excellence, pure function, and best power
> Both of the object seen, and eye that sees.
> (The Prelude, XII, 376–79; XIII, 375–78.)

These lines, already commented upon earlier, express the heart of the Wordsworthian faith. More than a century after they were written, Wallace Stevens suggested that the modern "disappearance of nobility" might be no more than a "maladjustment between the imagination and reality," and he actually uses the word "interchange" to describe the relationship between the two.[2] Wordsworth believed that the proper balance or adjustment had been disturbed in his time, partly by crass greed and materialism, partly by the pride of intellect which "murders to dissect." And so Stevens in our own day has commented upon the dangerous power of intellect to dissolve external reality into a mere collection of concepts and, finally, turning inwards, to dissolve man's sense of his own inner reality.[3] The basic agreement between these two very different poets commands attention.

Stevens' comments at times suggest that he despairs of man's recapturing this lost dignity, of being able once again to balance his own desire for spiritual dignity with a sense of some spiritual dignity outside himself. In the poem *Esthétique du Mal,* Stevens claims

> The greatest poverty is not to live
> In a physical world, to feel that one's desire
> Is too difficult to tell from despair.
> (Section XV.)

Of course there is no doubt that Stevens could live in a physical world in the simplest sense. But to feel his desire fully satisfied he had to feel that this world in some way corresponded to what he himself termed man's "rage" for order and meaning. Puzzled as he was by epistemological problems, he seldom felt himself to be living amid such a universal order until the period when he wrote his final poems. Yvor Winters has described Stevens' art as no more than the "mitigation of his own loneliness"; [4] and in a curious way one often feels that this is so despite his cheerful tone. So much of his poetry builds no substantial bridge between himself and the natural and human world about him, though the possibility of building such a bridge was the theme of his work from first to last. Stevens' description of the poverty, so like despair, of not being able to live in a physical world, reminds one of certain moments in the writings of Shelley. In one of his essays, Stevens the "introspective voyager" uses the figure of Narcissus to express the relationship between the "ego and reality": Narcissus looks into the stream and sees only his own reflection there.[5] The same image had been used by Shelley in *Alastor* to express his solipsist's despair.

Stevens writes—very attractively—of the poet who sits in the "radiant and productive atmosphere, which is his life, surrounded not only by double characters and metaphysicians, but by many men and many kinds of men, by many women and many children, and many kinds of women and children." [6] Parts of this description suggest perhaps the half-metaphysical dreams of Keats's Endymion, or even the aspiration of Stevens' lady on Sunday morning. Other parts suggest the warm, radiant humanity of the simple society in which Endymion lives, or the glittering naturalism which Stevens opposes to the lady's desires. The description also breathes the spirit of the happy and very human naturalism of the French Impressionist painters. For this naturalism Stevens had much sympathy and admiration, but the fact of the matter is that his own poetry does not often exhibit its equivalent. In this poetry, as in the life of Endymion and in the history of modern painting, the mood of naturalism could not long be sustained. Intellectually half-convinced that "it is my own speech and the strength of it, this only, that I hear or ever shall," [7] Stevens' poems sometimes resemble the works of painters since Cézanne who have ceased to celebrate the poetry which artists in the past have often found more or less inherent in the world around them, and to have moved instead towards the new reality which he congratulates modern art upon achieving, that "modern reality" which is "a reality of decreation, in which our revelations are not the revelations of belief, but the precious portents of our own powers." [8] Furthermore, the "metaphysicians" that hover over the natural world in Stevens' work and at times all but obliterate this world, often seem less the products of imaginative creativity than of philosophical speculation. Despite the fact that he tells the artist at one point not to be too enslaved to intellectual truth, it would seem that he himself was very conscious of the intellectual developments of recent times as these have deprived artists of the older belief in the supernatural and hence determined their peculiar modern milieu.[9]

If we remain strictly within the non-supernatural limits which these developments have supposedly set down for us, are we to be deprived as we are in much of modern art of the natural world also? Somewhat before Stevens' time another poet chanted that God was dead and that we hear no voices but our own. The result was to be the coming of man into his freedom, the fulfilling of his own proper nature. But the truth was again ironic: by no other nineteenth-century poet is the human so de-humanized and the natural world so deprived of a life and identity of its own as by Swinburne when he incorporates both into the all-else-obliterating cadences of his verse. As has been suggested before, the naturalism and the supernaturalism which Stevens sets at odds in *Sunday Morning* may in fact be supplementary to each other, in somewhat the same way as Browning thought they were and as Eliot in *Marina* decided they must be.

A quarter of a century ago, in an essay "The Personal Heresy in Criticism," C. S. Lewis made a spirited attack upon the solipsist theory of such modernists as Stevens sometimes shows himself to be:

The personal dogma [Lewis writes] springs from an inability which most moderns feel to make up their mind between two alternatives. A materialist, and a spiritual, theory of the universe are both equally fatal to it; but in the coming and going of the mind between the two it finds its opportunity. For the typical modern critic is usually a half-hearted materialist. He accepts, or thinks he accepts, that picture of the world which popularized science gives him. He thinks that everything except the buzzing electrons is subjective fancy; and he therefore believes that all poetry must come out of the poet's head and express (of course) his pure, uncontaminated, undivided 'personality,' because outside the poet's head there is nothing but the interplay of blind forces. But he forgets that if materialism is true there is nothing else inside the poet's head either. For a consistent materialism, the poetless poetry [a meaningful harmony inherent in the nature of things] for which I contend, and the most seemingly self-expressive 'human document,' are equally the accidental result of impersonal and irrational causes. And if this is so, if the sensation (Professor Housman has told us about it) which we call 'enjoying poetry' in no case betokens that we are really in the presence of purpose and spirituality, then there is no foothold left for the personal heresy. All poetry will indeed *suggest* something more than the collision of blind forces: but the suggestion will, in every case alike, be false. And why should this false suggestion arise from the movements in the things we call brains rather than from any other movements? It is just as likely to arise from historical accidents of language, or from printers' errors. If, on the other hand, something like Theism or Platonism or Absolute Idealism is true—if the universe is not blind or mechanical, then equally the human individual can have no monopoly on producing poetry. For on this view all is designed, all is significant. The poetry produced by impersonal causes is not illusory. The Muse may speak through any instrument she chooses.

Surely the dilemma is plain. Either there is significance in the whole process of things as well as in human activity, or there is no significance in human activity itself. It is an idle dream, at once cowardly and arrogant, that we can withdraw the human soul, as a mere epiphenomenon, from a universe of idiotic force, and yet hope, after that, to find for her some *faubourg* where she can keep a mock court in exile. You cannot have it both ways. If the world is meaningless, then so are we; if we mean something, we do not mean alone. Embrace either alternative, and you are free of the personal heresy.[10]

In Wordsworth's view we avoid despair, the despair of the solipsist's exile, by realizing and partly fulfilling some of our desires in the affections of human life and in the images of nature, and especially in such images of man and nature existing in harmonious splendor as the Wye valley and Grasmere afforded. Thus we *discover* as well as create comprehensive images of cosmic order which we can cherish. In the proper "interchange" which Wordsworth's poetry celebrates, we sometimes do both simultaneously. By this means we sense the "one life within us and abroad." [11] In other words, while Wordsworth would agree with Stevens that we should live fully in the physical world, he would add that we must live also in the intrinsically imaginative world afforded by the life within us and around us. When we do this, he believes we are ennobled by sensing two facts more or less concurrently: the superiority of some element within ourselves to the mere physical flux, and the kinship of that element to the greater force which forever breathes form and life into this flux. Stevens himself, notwithstanding isolated statements to the contrary, had never wholly rejected this philosophic position and came in the end to affirm his own very temperate version of it.

To live in such an imaginative world as Wordsworth believed in may be difficult to many modern men for purely topographical reasons. They dwell in cities where the works of man are virtually all that they see; at night the light which man has made blanks out the very stars themselves and an aggregation of light such as that at Times Square is the greatest "galaxy of life and joy" they ever know. Hence their eyes are not "fed," as Wordsworth believed they should be, with images which unconsciously impress them with a sense of man's living his life in harmony with some great scheme not of his own making.

But to live in such an imaginative world may be difficult for logical reasons also. For those whose critical intellect is strongly developed, such living seems to require as a necessary condition of its being some of that very faith which it is supposed to develop. A Wordsworthian could only reply that some such faith, though it may be weakened by unfavorable conditions, is almost a natural endowment of mankind. Even Stevens himself, in supposing that the present condition of many moderns may be the result of a "maladjustment," implies the earlier existence of some happier and more normal condition. Indeed, the peculiarly modern man with his peculiarly modern dilemmas may loom larger in the discussions of intellectuals than in the world of ordinary men and women. Many of these ordinary men and women, even as late as the middle of our century, may be assumed to experience still some of the older and happier interchange.

It should be noted that excessive intellectuality may be attended by the loss of one's natural birthright even when the philosophy pursued is supposedly the opposite of the scientific and mechanical. Coleridge the idealist philosopher, who in *Dejection* wrote that there was little left for him other than "by abstruse research to steal / From my own nature all the natural man,"—this Coleridge as distinct from the poet who had written the Conversation Poems and the redemption scene in *The Ancient Mariner*, persuaded Wordsworth to adopt for the last stanzas of the Intimations *Ode* a metaphysic which comes close to denying the existence of any inherent poetry in the natural world. But Wordsworth was never one to permit himself to be pushed by systematic logic to conclusions which did violence to his deepest instincts. The epistemology of the later stanzas of the *Ode* he would not have regarded as a rejection of that of the earlier stanzas, but rather as a reciprocating adjustment of the mind to the earlier conditions. The "balance" which he speaks of in the last books of *The Prelude* is rather like an interaction between the two epistemologies, between our intuitive sense of the beauty of the world and our intuitive sense of the sublimity of our own spirit. These two senses live together, one dominating at one time and the other at another, in a condition of "interchangeable supremacy."

So much for the one form of imbalance, when the impulses from within dominate too persistently and all but obliterate the impulses from without, so as to deprive this world—human as well as natural— of its vital life and independent reality. In any situation where a proper balance is the desirable state, the imbalance may presumably be in either direction. Wordsworth himself affords an example of an imbalance opposite to the one which we have been considering. Wordsworth believed that at one period in his youth his own appetite for external images of order had been excessive. He was right. He also believed, when he was writing the last part of *The Prelude*, that his undue craving had been brought under control, that his own internal imaginative powers had been sufficiently strengthened to require less external support. What he fails to note is that he had conquered his spirit's craving to be "fed" through the eye by surrendering to it; once he had settled at Grasmere he was supplying the eye day after day, year after year, with the one scene which he found most satisfying. The initial effects of this constant gratification were beneficial; Wordsworth experienced at first a period of comparative calm such as each man is perhaps entitled to from time to time. And for several years he continued to write great poetry. The poetry soon deteriorated, however, and the calm was succeeded by a certain aridity. The excess of beauty around him was probably not the principal cause of the deterioration, but it may well have been a contributing cause. Wordsworth acknowledges in *The Prelude* that when he was first living away from the grandeur of the Lake District, amid the flats of Cambridgeshire, he had felt "awaken'd, summon'd, rous'd, constrain'd" by the absence of external grandeur to use his own inner powers to supply the deficiency.[12] And when he visited Bartholomew Fair in London and recovered from the initial shock to his sensibility caused by its visual chaos, a miniature of the "unmanageable sight" afforded by the great city itself, he felt similarly aroused to search for some underlying harmony not immediately apparent.[13] Contrariwise, in *The Recluse* Wordsworth praises the power of Grasmere Vale to

> soothe
> *And steal away, and for a while deceive,*
> *And lap in pleasing rest, and bear us on*
> *Without desire in full complacency,*
> *Contemplating perfection absolute*
> *And entertained as in a placid sleep.*
>
> (ll. 303–8.)

Every man is benefited by periods of rest and restoration. But one so sensitive to visual effects as Wordsworth was perhaps running a risk in remaining permanently amid such overwhelming beauty; the "full complacency" and "placid sleep" might last too long. He says that the vale offers the soul not only an image but also a "habit" of eternity and God. A habit of eternity and God is perhaps not a good thing for a mere mortal. It is better for the active painter to visit the Louvre than to live there. It is better for the active Christian occasionally to attend splendid services in a Cathedral than to be there morning and evening of each day and three times on Sunday. Somewhere between starvation and surfeiting there is a mean.

Epilogue by an Amateur Theologian

THE CURRENT FASHION for theologically oriented criticism sometimes takes injudicious forms. Many readers of literature dislike attempts to confine its free and varied insights within the limits of a system of thought too abstract, too neat, too rigid. Such readers, in the case of a study like the present one, will find the most vital material in those chapters which constitute the body of the book: there in the presentations of the central imaginative developments of the actual poets themselves, not in theoretical conclusions drawn therefrom, they will find living truth. In an important sense they are right. But the generalizing faculty will assert itself and within limits it should be allowed a hearing. In this instance, where the literature surveyed has so persistently raised metaphysical questions, some theological discussion is inevitable. Moreover theology, which should presumably serve to deepen man's insight more than to restrict it, usually raises questions of moral and humanistic interest which even the most secular minds will find meaningful.

Three main elements of the old religion, the beliefs in a personal Deity, in Divine Providence, and in the immortality of the soul, were not always equally missed by the poets in the Romantic tradition; a poet's imagination would often seek to supply the lack of one belief more than another. But the truth may be that all three beliefs are bound up together; they are imaginatively of a piece. The belief in Divine Providence is bound up with the idea that the supreme force in the universe is like a father who sees what his children need and provides it. The belief in personal immortality, in the human soul's ability to exist independently of one particular body, is bound up with the notion of a Creator who transcends his creation, somewhat as a human being transcends his own creations; if the supreme force is regarded as inherent only, as no more than a mere *anima mundi*, it is difficult to regard the human spirit as any more than a mere *anima corporis*. As has been suggested, the sheer impossibility of Shelley's viewing the supreme force as a father or as a person of any sort, explains in part the sense of strain which many detect in his imaginative creations and the recurring note of desperation. The quieter desperation which Keats's poems and letters reveal from time to time may be partly owing to a similar cause, though in his case even more than in Shelley's much may be properly ascribed to the tragic circumstances of the poet's life. Conversely, it was Browning, in his middle years the most buoyant in faith of the great poets of the century, who most vividly expressed the wonder of the belief in a cosmic creative force which is like man himself. Browning's Karshish is deeply stirred by the possibility that the incarnation of deity, which the early Christians claimed had just occurred, gave evidence that such a force existed:

> So, through the thunder comes a human voice
> Saying, "O heart I made, a heart beats here!
> Face, my hands fashioned, see it in myself!
> Thou hast no power nor mayst conceive of mine,
> But love I gave thee, with myself to love,
> And thou must love me who have died for thee."
>   (*An Epistle*, ll. 306–12.)

Browning's David, in *Saul*, as the belief in a personal Deity comes to him with unusual power and with new implications, and as the belief in human immortality comes to him as a concomitant of the same imaginative vision, expresses more wonder still. Unlike Karshish, who is deterred by a materialistic and scientific rationalism, he can accept the vision.

Between the doctrinaire materialist like Karshish and the Romantic poet the *a priori* disagreements are so complete that fruitful discussion is difficult. Until some momentous experience changes one or the other, they must agree to disagree. But Romanticism and the religious orthodoxy of such a critic as H. N. Fairchild have important presuppositions in common. A short dialogue between the two points of view may be one way to examine certain basic problems.

If Romantic individualism carried to its final development comes to so clear a dead end in the solipsism of the modern poet who hears no voice but his own, does this show that individualism is wholly unsound? If this solipsism is the natural *reductio ad absurdum* of several centuries of intellectual and imaginative effort, of Protestantism and religious liberalism, does this absurd end not prove that the whole progression was radically in error? Professor Fairchild's studies are more imposing than some of the more ardent admirers of Romanticism have been willing to concede. But it may be pointed out that the end has not in fact been reached by mere logical reduction. It has been reached by the introduction of a new factor. This factor is the decision to give up the search for ultimate metaphysical truth. No matter how much the search of most of the great nineteenth-century poets was modified by the realization that all man's metaphysical apprehensions must be inadequate and must vary in form from age to age, it remained the great search still. It ceases to be so only when men decide that any such central truth is but illusion, and when they therefore no longer seek to relate their own apprehensions to some such larger truth. There have been men in all times who believe they have made this last break, and the reasons which have urged them to do so are understandable. But as the instance of Stevens shows, a poet more perhaps than some other men finds it difficult to break completely.

What of the orthodox objection that the poets in the Romantic tradition, when seeking by the powers of their own imagination to penetrate to those mysteries which Christ has revealed, are guilty of pride? Even a conservative may feel that the Judaeo-Christian and the Greek warnings against independent thought are to be construed as warnings of danger rather than as absolute prohibitions. Again, some orthodox reasoning implies that the story of the Fall of Man records a historic fact rather than a moral insight. The historic fact is that the long emergence of the human race is more like a rise, and that most of the rise occurred before the advent of Christianity. Christ, who said that he came not to destroy the old law but to complete or perfect it, has at times been regarded even by the orthodox as completing such natural theologies as man's own imagination had already suggested. Indeed, when Wordsworth hoped to supply the lack of natural reverence and natural religion in some of his contemporaries, he was doing no more than seeking to restore to them some of the full humanity which many of Christ's hearers must have possessed in Judaea two thousand years ago. The Romantic appeal to the imagination and the heart can be regarded as a step from rationalism back towards traditional religion rather than as another step away. It was regarded as such by Coleridge and perhaps, with more serious reservations, by Newman himself.

Lack of reverence is likely to include a lack of reverence for self, of self-respect. Among the Romantics, Wordsworth and Shelley were especially aware of the harmful effects of such a lack and they hoped that their poetry would teach men a due reverence for their own nature. Orthodoxy may sense a danger in the methods which Wordsworth and Shelley used to this end, but the pursuit itself was not altogether misguided. If men are to strive to act as befits children of God, they must presumably be convinced that they are children of God, that they are—in Pascal's terms—of royal birth. Religion may find it more desirable to persuade men of their worth than of their worthlessness.

But men should be persuaded of their sinfulness also, the objector may say. The Romantics in their reaction against prescriptive authoritarianism sometimes went to extremes. But to judge from the New Testament, Christ did not convince men of their sinfulness merely by holding up a high standard of conduct and showing how this had not been achieved (though this was part of the gospel), but by offering men in his own person an image of perfection, by bringing men love and showing them hope. Now it was the general conviction of the Romantic poets that they themselves were often addressing not sinning Christians, men flagrantly violating principles in which they firmly believed, but men indifferently good or even virtuous but paralysed by a lack of hope. Dante placed such men in Limbo, living as they had lived on earth, without serious moral defect but "in desire without hope." The Romantics themselves lived in desire and sought to assure themselves and their readers of hope. Only with some basis of hope is conviction of sin, in the religious sense, possible. Coleridge shows an understanding of the problem in *The Ancient Mariner:* up to the turning point of the action the mariner has felt only sterile remorse; then, when the beauty of the sea creatures offers a vision, a moment's insight into some spirit of goodness in the universe against which he has acted, the mariner's remorse becomes fruitful repentance.

Orthodoxy may perhaps concede that poets can strengthen men's natural insights and virtues, but it may also urge them to take more cognizance of the special supernatural revelation of the Christian religion. But this cognizance, which the hymn writer displays easily within the conventions of his form, the original poet can often show only with the greatest difficulty or indirection. Elizabeth Barrett, who was not an especially original poet, could not fully understand her husband's difficulty. But long before the nineteenth century, in the France of Louis XIV, Christian writers had wondered whether literature must not do its work more or less independently of the partly incommensurable facts of religion. Still earlier, in the Middle Ages, Chaucer evaluated human life thus independently in his *Troilus and Criseyde*. The author of the powerful French prose story of Lancelot and Guinevere did the same: the final seclusion of the queen in a nunnery and of her knight in a hermitage is but an epilogue; the imaginative working out of the story itself has already brought the writer and the actors and the readers to essentially the same judgments as the epilogue seeks to reinforce. In comparable fashion, medieval theologians with the aid of Aristotle had sought to develop natural theology and natural ethics as far as they felt they could be carried. The Romantic poets have considerable precedent for seeking to evaluate life and death independently. It could even be said that only by so doing could they do what it may be the peculiar task of literature to perform.

Besides C. S. Lewis other modern men of letters writing from a generally orthodox and conservative position may be cited as recognizing to some extent a connection between the faith in the imagination of the natural man which is so conspicuous a part of Romanticism and the faith of the religious believer. D. G. James in his *Scepticism and Poetry* remarks that "the ship of poetry must . . . suffer shipwreck at the entrance to the harbor." [14] By this he means that the secular imagination must always fail ultimately to resolve the enigmas and contradictions of life in any stable and satisfying fashion. In emphasizing the failure he is at one with Professor Fairchild, but in supposing that the imagination may lead one to the very verge of truth, he may be revealing what Fairchild might regard as unsound sympathies. Professor James's general contention both in this book and in the later *Romantic Comedy* is, as has already been noted, that imagination leads not to belief or disbelief but to a state of tension between the two—hence the importance of Keats to his discussion in both volumes. Again, as has already been noted, Allen Tate in *On the Limits of Poetry*, a book whose very title suggests a fundamental agreement with James, is probably reaffirming this agreement when he says that the *Ode to a Nightingale* "at least tries to say everything that poetry can say"; at the same time his essay upon Keats as a whole suggests more sympathy than Fairchild feels with this attempt to push poetry to its utmost bounds.[15] Basil Willey's opinion may be cited for the second time because it is an unusually clear statement of the respect which an orthodox writer may show towards the efforts of the poetic imagination to resolve the enigmas of life independently of the revelations of religion; after noting that literature lives generally on the level of nature, not of grace, Professor Willey makes these observations upon *In Memoriam:*

> It goes behind Christianity, or passes it by, confronting the preliminary question of whether there can be any religious interpretation of life at all. What made the poem acceptable even to

Christian readers in the Victorian age was that having, though with diffidence and humility, vindicated the believing temper, accepted the reasons of the heart, Tennyson had opened the door which gave access to Christian territory.[16]

And so T. S. Eliot in 1941 defended the naturally imaginative philosophy of Kipling's Sussex stories: "It is not a Christian vision, but it is at least a pagan vision—a contradiction of the materialist view: it is the insight into the harmony of nature which must be reestablished if the truly Christian imagination is to be recovered by Christians." [17] In some such fashion Wordsworth had praised the Greek poetic imagination which had peopled the seashore with "Proteus rising from the sea" and "old Triton" blowing his wreathèd horn, and he had himself undertaken to people the English landscape with "Presences" and "Powers" and the "Souls of lonely places." Eliot's comment upon Kipling is in fact but an application to criticism of the relation between the natural and the supernatural which Eliot himself, in *Mariana* and *Four Quartets*, had seen emerging in his own life. If made consistently, this application implies some qualification of Eliot's earlier inclusion of Wordsworth (along with Shelley), among "the great heretics of all time" [18]—except of course that in terming a man a heretic one is conceding to him a certain oblique kinship with whatever orthodoxy one has in mind. The truth is that Eliot's view of Kipling's imagination, like Willey's of Tennyson's, closely parallels the view which Wordsworth came to take of his own poetic mission.

Professor Fairchild's sweeping indictment of the human self-will evident in the entire intellectual movement since the Middle Ages leaves one with the impression that his view of the earlier period is as "enchanted" as his view of the later is disenchanted, a fact which is hard to believe of one whose criticism is so often interspersed with passages of sharply tonic realism.[19] The human pride which has been exhibited since the Renaissance was amply anticipated in the Middle Ages by the worldly pride of some ambitious churchmen and the intellectual pride of many Schoolmen, both vehemently denounced at the time by men of intensely religious spirit. That these two forms of pride were corrupting religion from within rather than weakening it from without would seem, from the orthodox point of view, to constitute at best but a dubious advantage.

In the lives of poets within the Romantic tradition Fairchild everywhere discovers evidence of self-will, near the surface or deeply covered. As one of the manifestations of Romantic egotism, Fairchild notes that the poets' notions of the Supreme Power are created very much in their own image. This perception is important but not completely devastating. The orthodox themselves cannot entirely escape the same limitation: even a proper concentration upon the person of Christ only partly liberates a man from egocentricity since his own personality and his experience largely determine which passages in the New Testament will impress him most deeply and how. Employing the same sort of psychological insight with the same destructive intent, Professor Fairchild relishes in Betty Miller's *Robert Browning* the disclosures of what would usually be regarded as the inner weaknesses of the poet's personality.[20] But whereas Mrs. Miller cannot help acknowledging the curious strength with which these weaknesses are combined, Fairchild feels he has further evidence that Browning's boasted faith is no more than a mask. Where the inner secrets of the personalities are known, might not an unfriendly critic make a somewhat similar charge against the orthodox themselves, suggesting that their strong reliance on the Church was no more than a compensation, their ambition for her success no more than a transferred egotism. Fairchild's dissections of character are memorable and emphasize an important part of the total truth, but the knife with which he cuts deeply may be made to cut in other directions. The sort of dissection he performs so well has been performed by Lytton Strachey on no less a subject than the great Cardinal Manning himself.

One can concede Fairchild's rightness in pointing to the many sad effects since the Renaissance of men's rebelliousness and intellectual self-assurance, and yet feel that he has neglected to mention the benefits. The assertiveness which makes a man's children less submissive than his dog is not entirely a defect. A society consisting entirely of completely submissive churchgoers is as unthinkable as one in which all children were completely pliable to their parents' will. In the New Testament narrative, the Father actually gave the prodigal son his inheritance and allowed him to spend it as he saw fit. The story, be it noted, is primarily that of the son who went astray rather than of the one who remained at home. And so the story of literature is more likely to be that of poets who went out to see the world for themselves than of those who did not. Yet if one is as highly sensitized as Professor Fairchild to the dangers of Romantic self-will, one might almost charge Christ himself with an insidious sentimental bias when he makes the character of the prodigal dramatically a little more interesting, more sympathetic, than that of his brother.

But in the long succession of Romantic prodigals, it might be maintained, many never returned to their father's house, and finally the modern humanists have become convinced that there is no house but their own. Yet the poets studied here were for the most part serious seekers. Professor Fairchild regrets the extreme seriousness of all the Romantics other than Byron, but this seriousness usually saves them from what Fairchild would probably regard as the supreme degradation—a dilettantish enjoyment of their own sensitivity to "the human predicament," an emotion sometimes so satisfying in itself as to preclude any serious search for a solution. If Arnold more frequently than the others sometimes comes close to exhibiting this attitude, he is—as a result of his strong moralistic inclinations—the quickest to condemn himself.[21] In general the poets' passionate natures kept them true to their quest. When one considers Keats's *Fall of Hyperion* and Shelley's *Triumph of Life* and his growing appreciation of Dante, it is hard not to suspect that even the two who died youngest were moving in the direction of such traditional wisdom as Professor Fairchild would approve.

In support of Professor Fairchild's point of view one should at least mention Frederick L. Jones's suggestion—not pressed very insistently—that Wordsworth may in fact have prevented Shelley from becoming a Christian.[22] In his early essay *On Life* Shelley had decided that there might be only two logical alternatives, Christianity and atheism. Then he read Wordsworth's Intimations *Ode* and wrote his own *Hymn to Intellectual Beauty*. Wordsworth, in short, had suggested a third possibility, reliance on the mystic insight of one's own imagination. Here, of course, is precisely the gravamen of Fairchild's charge against Romanticism: it offers some of the satisfactions of faith without necessitating any surrender of the sense of self-sufficiency. This position satisfies human vanity in itself and it is rendered more attractive by the poetic glamor in which the great poets manage to invest it. But it is difficult to believe that Shelley was on the verge of conversion when he wrote *On Life*, or that he could have been brought to it by mere force of logic. One cannot forget the power that he had already demonstrated to spiritualize and poeticize his peculiar brand of "atheism," so that it became, if not wholly satisfying to his imagination, at least not unattractive. An even greater obstacle was his massive conviction that organized Christianity was part of the vast established fabric of privilege and oppression which he was dedicated to opposing. The history of religion offers so many astonishing examples of a sudden *volte-face* that it would be rash to exclude Professor Jones's suggestion out of hand, especially in view of the insistence with which Shelley's imagination pressed toward that very worship of a person which the Enlightenment denied him. Yet it would be more natural to suppose that he responded to Wordsworth's *Ode* and then to Platonism in general because these were what he was ready for. Then, if he had been destined at all to confess the merits of traditional religion, it would have been only after his burning ability to go *through* a certain phase of experience, his increasingly sharp sense of the uncertainty of all things temporal, and the increasing realism brought about by his accumulated experience—only after these might have caused him, as they caused Wordsworth, to lose some though not all of his Romantic faith in imagination.

Romantic faith is, to Professor Fairchild, an "illusioned" view of life and one can agree with him so far as to grant that the natural development from Romantic faith to Christianity must proceed through at least partial disillusionment. Between the expansive faith of the Romantics in their youth and the acceptance of Eliot's *Four Quartets* lies a Wasteland. But one should note also that before there can be disillusionment there must be "illusion"; the *Four Quartets* did not emerge from realism and disillusionment alone but from the state of tension Eliot had earlier exhibited between these attitudes and the "Romantic" pressures so clearly evident in the nostalgically beautiful tags of poetry interspersed amidst the dry realism of his most famous work.

Lastly, there is the implication in Professor Fairchild's writing that the pervasive melancholy of the Romantics is in itself strong evidence of theological error. But the melancholy—perhaps over-emphasized—need not suggest that they have been working entirely in the wrong direction, merely that they have not proceeded far enough. Moreover, the bleakness recurring in the lives of Keats and Shelley, dominating Wordsworth's middle and later life, and de-tectable perhaps in Browning's later years, has its counterpart in the very orthodox Newman. Newman compared himself to a pane of glass which remains cold itself while transmitting warmth to others.[23] Men of wide culture like Newman or of unusually complex aware-ness like Keats are perhaps susceptible to melancholy whatever their belief. They cannot commit themselves so totally as the uncritical. The energy of persons uncritically committed is indispensable, but so also, in its different way, as a check against fanaticism and narrow-ness of any sort, is the greater freedom of mind of those who must, as it were, commit themselves afresh each day because each day they realize afresh the force of the objections.

Ironically enough the aridity of Wordsworth's middle and later years has seemed to some to be evidence of quite a contrary sort. In the past some liberals have at least half suggested that the drying up of Wordsworth's creative powers is evidence of the wrongness of the religious (as well as the social) conservatism towards which he was moving. But such matters are always very complex. Also, some special significance may be discovered in the fact that Wordsworth was, as Coleridge believed, very much a philosopher-poet. Besides worshipping images, he speculated upon his response to them. By 1805 the speculative system by which he sought to explain the mysteries of life was essentially complete. He had been seeking some final truth and, during the years 1805 to 1810 he must have come to feel that he understood about as much as men are likely to understand. Insofar as the poetic impulse had been an urge to explain the universe, it was natural that this impulse should no longer be so strongly felt.[24]

So it was with Browning also. He had, in his youth, felt himself closer to traditional religion than Wordsworth. He too, however, found it necessary to correlate the Christianity to which he acknowledged a certain allegiance with his own imaginative apprehensions of life: of good and evil, hope and despair, beauty and love and lack of beauty and love. The correlation was sufficiently complete by the time he finished *The Ring and the Book*. He might have done better at this time to have stopped habitual composition and to have written only when the impulse was irresistible. Shakespeare himself, after writing his last plays in which critics have seen imaginative suggestions of redemption, retired to Stratford.

In short, if the nineteenth-century poets, even more than most, are best suited to expressing truth emerging in their own minds rather than truth fully emerged, the drying up of the creative impulse may be construed as reflecting not the inadequacy but the comparative adequacy of the truth discovered.

Perhaps such writers as Wordsworth or Browning or Shakespeare are inherently less likely to go on producing interesting poetry than such men as Yeats and Stevens, who search but appear through most of their lives to find less—or at least find less which, because of its agreement with a central tradition, has an air of conclusiveness. Such a notion may explain why painters more commonly than poets continue creating with undiminished freshness. If Joseph Wood Krutch is right and all art is, in the broadest sense, an effort to justify the universe, it may be supposed that painting by itself from its very nature is not likely to do so with any appearance of finality; it must inevitably omit so much of human experience. Yet Leibniz and other philosophers in the Platonic tradition suggest why the painter's quest can exert so powerful a fascination: the nature of the universe, according to idealism, is such that even the smallest particles reflect something of the One, the Divine origin; thus a Cézanne or a Matisse can go on year after year breaking up the world into elements of

form and color and putting these together again in fresh ways, and
the elements being what they are and the human mind being what it
is, the finished products may always suggest however dimly something deeply satisfying, something of cosmic significance—Stevens'
vis or *noeud vital*. The painter and his admirer are forever surprised,
as by a continuous miracle. Wordsworth in his youth, ever admiring
effects of scenery and ever craving new effects, had resembled many
painters: he had been like a child turning a kaleidoscope, always
excited that at each new turn an interesting pattern emerged. The
analogy is in keeping with traditional idealist thought, since according to this idealism the universe, like the kaleidoscope, is constructed
of mirrors.

Yet Wordsworth did not turn the kaleidoscope indefinitely. He
used all his powers in an effort to understand why a pattern was
always discernible. His attempt was a worthy one. But in any such
adventure the joy of the quest and the joy of discovery are likely
to be followed by a reaction. The decline in a poet's creativity which
may attend such a reaction may be greater precisely because what
has been discovered, as distinct from the route by which the discovery has been reached, turns out to be broadly traditional rather than
original and personal.

But though a conservative might wish to defend Wordsworth's
general movement of thought, particularly against a doctrinaire agnostic, some reservations about the later poetry are almost inevitable.
Wordsworth's early vital apprehensions of man and nature, which
decline so rapidly after 1800, have sometimes been deplored for their
heterodoxy. But the loss may be an impoverishment not only humanly but religiously. If instead of losing them the poet had been
able to transpose them into a new key, his later religion might seem
less forlorn. Here as always the poet's imagery reveals the inner
change. At the end of the *Excursion*, finished in 1814, is a description
of Grasmere Vale which contrasts sharply with Wordsworth's earlier
scenes and with comparable images in other poets. The occasion is
an evening of "extraordinary splendor." But the poet is not strongly
aware of any vital force immediately at hand. The rich light is reflected from the clouds down to the lake and from the lake back
to the clouds, but the sun itself has set. The landscape, illuminated
by the "unapparent fount of glory," may at first seem a noble Christian emblem. It may be noted again that the birdsongs which moved
other poets so powerfully came from unseen birds, the memorable
fragrances from invisible flowers and thyme. But the difference is as
notable as the similarity. The sunken sun is far more remote than the
hidden bird. Also, Wordsworth had always been most susceptible to

visual images; this fact is in keeping with his contemplative nature. Yet the contemplative steadiness which had early been the distinctive character of his poetry in the course of time becomes the distinctive vice. The later poems urgently need more of the immediacy and intimacy which auditory and olfactory images can convey. They need some of Eliot's

> *Hidden laughter*
> *Of children in the foliage*
> *Quick now, here, now, always—*
> *(Burnt Norton*, V.)

The problem as Eliot saw it—and as Wordsworth saw it—was not to become "separated," not to lose all connection between vivid early apprehension and later philosophic and religious conviction. But Wordsworth's later life is too far separated from the energies of his youth, and his later eternity seems too remote from his time. His later religion is too tired: it is too narrowly based upon a merely passive sense of duty, upon a too patient resignation to the sufferings of mankind, and a longing for an immortality which will release us from mortal perplexities—upon orthodox virtues, in short, but virtues somehow a little too far removed from the joy of which Wordsworth had had so much to say. Eliot's religion may be based a little more firmly upon the central Christian doctrine of Incarnation, a doctrine which Eliot in keeping with tradition interprets as signifying not only a remote historic event but an ever-present fact. Platonism and a Christianity based upon Incarnation, despite their resemblances when viewed from a distance, when experienced closely are significantly different: this difference will be especially apparent when the Platonism is strongly colored by an imagery which puts the temporal in too uncreative a role, as a mere reflection or inactive mirroring of the eternal.[25]

It is possible to view in another way also the difficult later years of a poet whose life has been a metaphysical quest. If the search for truth has been a principal motive, the *raison d'être* of his poetic career, what course still remains open once he feels that his imaginative efforts have brought him to his goal? Browning as a young man had shown a prophetic insight into the problem. His poet-hero Sordello after reaching the truth by contemplation enters upon a period of sterility; his cure is a life of action, an endeavor to serve his fellow men as a humanitarian and statesman. And so Tennyson in *The Ancient Sage* had emphasized that vision is not enough, that "Virtue must shape itself in Deed." It is not easy to picture just what sort of more active and self-sacrificing life Wordsworth or Brown-

ing might have led in their later years. At the critical juncture in
their lives they were a little old to have become doctors and perhaps
gone to Africa as Albert Schweitzer has done. Indeed, a great many
reasons can be cited to explain why they did precisely what they
did. For one, the somewhat paralyzing tradition of the society in
which they lived assumed that just to be a gentleman and a poet was
enough. For another, Wordsworth must have felt that he needed
to write more poems to help support his family. Both poets, furthermore, had made immense imaginative efforts and may have experienced a certain psychic exhaustion. The whole question may be
dismissed simply by saying that it is too much to expect a great poet
to be a saint also. But if the religion at which a poet believes he has
arrived is a very urgent religion, if it was begun by one who symbolically washed his disciples' feet and gave his life for his fellow-
men, the poet's later years are likely to be tinged with sadness if they
are devoted principally to a rather redundant literary activity.
Browning himself in *Prospice* said that on the balance sheet of life
he owed an "arrears" of "pain, darkness, and cold"; he had nurtured
his imagination in the heroic tradition and the most he had ever
done, apart from his writing, was to rescue the woman he loved and
marry her. T. S. Eliot, in *Four Quartets*, arriving at the same difficult point, notes that "action" and "observance" still remain to be
accomplished. The sort of religious observance to which Eliot probably refers, and for which Wordsworth and Browning had in practice little use, is in itself a mode of action. By means of it the poet
may unite, in a commitment of the whole person, with men and
women from whom he appears widely separated by the terms of
his thought and the vocabulary of his imagination. In *The Cocktail
Party*, of course, Eliot's Celia, young and ardent, feels herself irre-
sistibly summoned to some action beyond and above ordinary observance, and she goes to her martyr's death among the savages. This
part of the play's ending has left many playgoers a little uncomfort-
able, just as Eliot doubtless intended it should do. He was willing to
take the risk since he believed the issue to be important. Keats in
The Fall of Hyperion and Tennyson in *The Palace of Art* had felt
the same urgency. When one thinks of Tennyson's palace one is
reminded of Wordsworth secluded in his northern Vale. As early
as 1800, in *The Recluse*, "Home at Grasmere," he had described his
vale in terms that suggest the richness and perfection of art. One
can at least wish that he had once or twice, for periods of six months
or a year, taken a sabbatical from his long sabbatical and lived in
Liverpool or Manchester or in London, that "hell" to his eye and

ear. Few critics have valued Wordsworth more highly than Matthew Arnold, but there is some truth in Arnold's charge that Wordsworth averted his eyes "from half of human fate." [26] At the end of *The Recluse*, Wordsworth trusted that with Nature's beauty to strengthen him he might not lose the hope of better worlds to come when he heard

> *the fierce confederate storm*
> *Of sorrow, barricadoed evermore*
> *Within the walls of cities.*

But when he wrote this poem he had been living at his chosen abode for a few months only, and had already noted the ability of the valley "to deceive," to induce "complacency" and "sleep." A few quotations to the contrary can be cited, but there is little doubt that increasingly over the next fifty years remaining to him he heard this voice of the cities' sorrow too faintly, from too great a distance.

Yet it is time to return to the larger question of Romantic self-will, to the tendency of poets, like the Prodigal Son, to wish to explore life for themselves. Even if orthodoxy urges a certain surrender, not merely of physical comfort but of imaginative and intellectual independence, where the imagination and intellect have made little original effort, there can be little significant surrender. The divine revelation which orthodoxy believes in, like the natural revelation which Wordsworth celebrated, must presumably involve some interchange and alternation between activity and passivity. According to Christianity itself, the special revelation which it cherishes was vouchsafed only after centuries of that "wrestling with God" which the Old Testament records, and the individual believer and the Romantic poet alike may both repeat in their personal lives some of the experience of the race.

Again, where there has been no powerful sense of earthly beauty, this beauty cannot be effectively used (or sacrificed) in the achieving of a loftier goal. The earlier discussion of Browning has already noted the religious truism that the thought of heavenly joy means little to one who has had no vivid experience of its earthly counterpart. Truisms like this are what original poets infuse with new life and vigor. The experiences of beauty and joy are what the Romantic poets most seriously explore, and they explore them precisely as they intimate some truth of great significance. Wordsworth in his later years often seems to have lost more of his early joy than he has succeeded in preserving and transmuting to some higher use. Yet C. S. Lewis, the modern apologist for orthodoxy, uses as the title of his spiritual autobiography the words which begin one of the best of Wordsworth's later sonnets, *Surprized by Joy*. Lewis does not seek to explain the exact nature of the connection between his early moments of imaginative ecstasy and the later joy of his own religious conversion, but he is convinced that the connection exists: the later, with a steadier happiness, seems to fulfill what the earlier had promised. Wordsworth in his *Ode*, lamenting that the early intensity has been lost, has some difficulty persuading himself and his readers that such a satisfying fulfillment has come to pass in his own life. But he is convinced that in the proper course of things it should come to pass.

NOTES

BIBLIOGRAPHY

INDEX

NOTES

Notes to Chapter i

1. Letter to George and Thomas Keats, 13 January 1818. The *Ode* is quoted four times in the letters and, according to Houghton's *Life*, was a favorite poem.

2. *The Major English Romantic Poets*, ed. Clarence D. Thorpe, Carlos Baker, Bennett Weaver, pp. 193–99.

3. Basil Willey, *Nineteenth Century Studies*, p. 30. This work and its successor, *More Nineteenth Century Studies*, set forth clearly the philosophical and religious positions of a number of writers, including Coleridge, Newman, Tennyson, and Matthew Arnold.

4. For a suggestive discussion of unconscious Platonism in poetry, see the Introduction to *The Myths of Plato*, tr. J. A. Stewart. With particular reference to the relation between religion and Platonism in Wordsworth, see Edith Batho, *The Later Wordsworth* and two books by W. R. Inge: *Studies in English Mystics* and *The Platonic Tradition in English Thought*.

5. The passage on Hope in Pope's *Essay on Man* is part of the background here.

6. *The Necessary Angel*, p. 30 and elsewhere.

7. "A Reading of Keats," in *On the Limits of Poetry*, pp. 165–84.

8. John Crowe Ransom, "William Wordsworth: Notes Towards an Understanding of Poetry," in *Wordsworth: Centenary Studies*, ed. G. T. Dunklin, pp. 104–5.

9. This question will be canvassed again in the last chapter. F. R. Tennant in the article "Deism" in the *Encyclopedia Britannica* (1956) expresses the belief that the one lasting contribution of deism to theological thought was its affirmation of the truth that revealed religion presupposes natural religion; Tennant believes that this fact was overlooked in much of the nineteenth-century conservative theological reaction against the Enlightenment. Of course natural religion in its long history has been something much wider and deeper than the highly rational religion favored by many deists; it has often inclined more towards pantheism than towards the rationalistic view of God as an absentee landlord or the builder of a perpetual motion machine so perfect that it needs no further

supervision. Nor should natural religion be identified with "naturism," a term sometimes used to designate the attempt to explain or explain away all religion on purely material grounds. Traditional theology has in general opposed not natural religion but the claim that natural religion by itself is sufficient.

10. Something of the variety of the age may be gleaned from two books by Basil Willey: *Seventeenth Century Background* and *Eighteenth Century Background*.

11. Relevant here is the critique of the dangers of intellectual abstraction which is a recurrent theme in the writings of A. N. Whitehead. See especially his lengthy comments on the value of Wordsworth's concrete intuitions of truth in Chapter 5 of *Science and the Modern World* and Charles G. Hoffmann's article, "Whitehead's Philosophy of Nature and Romantic Poetry," *Journal of Aesthetics*, X (1952), 258–63. See also a useful book of some years back, S. F. Gingerich's *Essays in the Romantic Poets*.

12. *The Mystery of Keats*, p. 229.

13. Behind Locke's work, of course, was that of Hobbes.

14. The italics are my own.

15. See sections iii–viii of the Introduction to the *Critique of Judgment* for Kant's observations on the unifying function of aesthetic judgment, particularly section viii for comments on "the supersensible substrate." Section 59 expresses the opinion that beauty is a "symbol" of the good and notes the deficiencies of deism. This part of Kant's thought is perhaps less familiar to American scholars today than it might have been over half a century ago before the influence of German idealism had so greatly declined. It is covered in all serious studies of what might be called the aestheticometaphysical thought of Kant, Schelling, and Hegel. See especially John Watson, *Schelling's Transcendental Idealism*. This aspect of Kantianism may seem most strange to those familiar chiefly with the *Critique of Pure Reason*. This first critique, which undermines all dogmatism, whether of the idealist or the materialist, is well suited to the modern sceptical temper. But it is far from expressing the whole of Kant. In the later *Critique of Judgment*, though the philosopher persists in some of the "hedging" which is appropriate to his *critical* technique, and which is perhaps a mark of his seriousness, he yet emerges as something of a secret Platonist after all, undermining from within the position of complete metaphysical scepticism. It was this last critique which was the point of departure for much of Schelling and Hegel, including their exaltation of art and of the imaginative faculty by which art is created. When Hegel appears to drop Kant's last reservations, when he becomes an *absolute* rather than a *critical* idealist, he admittedly loses touch with the Kantian spirit and with the sympathies of many moderns. See the three essays on aesthetics in *The Heritage of Kant*, ed. G. T. Whitney and

D. F. Bowers, and also W. K. Wimsatt, Jr. and Cleanth Brooks, *Literary Criticism: A Short History*, which reveals a familiarity with the mysteries of German *hochphilosophie* not often found among literary scholars in the English-speaking world. See also the extensive comments on Addison, Kant, Wordsworth, and Coleridge in E. F. Carritt, *The Theory of Beauty*.

16. Kant seems to have had a decided preference in these matters. He regarded an "immediate interest" in the beauty of nature as the mark of a "good soul"; he does not say the same for love of art, apparently because he felt this was less likely to be "immediate" or pure and more likely to be corrupted by the vanities of connoisseurship. See Section 42 of the *Critique of Judgment*. —On the other hand, the modern theologian Paul Tillich, who is perhaps somewhat in the tradition post-Kantian German thought, can praise with all the fervor of Browning's Fra Lippo Lippi the ability of art to reveal the Divine beauty to man. I have come across this opinion of Tillich's only in a newspaper article: "One Moment of Beauty," in the "Parade" section of the *St. Louis Post-Dispatch* (Sept. 25, 1955), p. 2. But Tillich's interest in art is well known.

17. For three poets, Wordsworth, Shelley, and Keats, David Perkins' *The Quest for Permanence*, published since this chapter was written, now performs this task admirably.

18. *The Romantic Comedy*, pp. 3-9.

19. The Bishop's book was, of course, the occasion of Wordsworth's youthful *Letter to the Bishop of Llandaff*—which the poet prudently did not publish.

20. A particularly strong statement of this idea (perhaps too strong) is found in John Jones's *The Egotistical Sublime*, pp. 49, 168.

21. W. H. Auden's *The Enchafèd Flood; or, The Romantic Iconography of the Sea*, for all its suggestiveness, has the same defects of its qualities as Miss Bodkin's study. Perhaps the present writer is temperamentally unfitted fully to appreciate studies of the collective unconscious.

22. Arthur Symons, *The Romantic Movement in English Poetry*.

23. It might be argued that no one should venture statements about Blake who has not spent years studying him. A reader who wishes to form his own opinion justly, besides reading Blake himself with care, should read some of the works which show a fuller sympathy with his accomplishment: S. F. Damon, *William Blake: His Philosophy and Symbols*; J. Middleton Murry, *William Blake*; Northrop Frye, *Fearful Symmetry*; David V. Erdman, *Blake, Prophet Against Empire* (this last chiefly political); Mark Schorer, *William Blake: The Politics of Vision*. But logically it should be possible to have considerable respect for Blake's thought without regarding the Prophetic Books as artistically successful. D. G. James (*The Romantic Comedy*, p. 29.) attributes Blake's artistic failures in part

to his falling "between the two stools of mythology and allegory." This judgment seems sound.

24. See also the most detailed study of Kubla's dome as an eternity symbol: Dorothy F. Mercer, "The Symbolism of *Kubla Khan*," *Journal of Aesthetics*, XII (1953), 44–66. As a discussion of the poem this article is somewhat unbalanced by its elaborate exploration of all the ways in which Boehme's theory of the reconciliation of opposites may have influenced Coleridge. However, the analysis of Boehme is suggestive in itself and interesting to anyone concerned with the origins and character of Coleridge's philosophy.

25. See Miss Mercer's article just cited and James V. Baker, *The Sacred River: Coleridge's Theory of Imagination*, pp. 129–36. Among the older studies which present this aspect of Coleridge's thought are the introduction to Shawcross's edition of the *Biographia Literaria* and Alice D. Snyder, *The Critical Principle of the Reconciliation of Opposites as Employed by Coleridge*.

26. *Appendix* to *The Statesman's Manual: The Complete Works of Samuel Taylor Coleridge*, ed. Shedd, I, 466. This passage is cited by James V. Baker, *op. cit.*, p. 156. No matter how far the search for unconscious symbols may sometimes lead criticism astray, this practice is not likely to be checked even by Miss Schneider's eloquent warning against the dangers of such a method.

27. Chapter XIII of the *Biographia Literaria* is the *locus classicus* here. In this instance especially a knowledge of Kant, influential though he was, is not quite adequate; a student should be acquainted with Schelling also if he is to understand in its historical context Coleridge's famous statement: "The primary Imagination I hold to be the living power and prime agent of all human perception, and as a repetition in the finite mind of the eternal act of creation in the infinite I AM. The secondary imagination [the creator of works of art] I consider as an echo of the former, coexisting with the conscious will, yet still identical with the primary in the *kind* of its agency, and differing only in *degree*, and in the *mode* of its operation." Coleridge later felt that Schelling's "Transcendental Idealism" was little better than pantheism, that it failed to distinguish sharply enough between God and his creation. Probably for this reason the phrase "as a repetition in the finite mind of the eternal act of creation in the infinite I AM" was crossed out in a copy of the *Biographia* in which Sara Coleridge discovered marginal comments by the author himself. But D. G. James rightly notes a certain continuity between Coleridge's thoughts on "imagination" before 1817 and his thoughts after 1817 on "reason" as the organ of metaphysical insight. See D. G. James' essay, "The Thought of Coleridge," in *The Major English Romantic Poets*, ed. Clarence D. Thorpe, Carlos Baker, Bennett Weaver, and his chapter on Newman and Coleridge in *The Romantic Comedy*.

28. Frank Kermode, *Romantic Image*, pp. 162–63. See the book's index for comments upon Coleridge and the German philosophers, and upon Blake, Wordsworth, Shelley, Keats, Tennyson, and Arnold.

29. Professor Foster's work is being reviewed just as this book is going through its final preparation for the press, and I have not yet had time to read it.

Notes to Chapter ii

1. This scheme, though evolved directly from the study of Wordsworth himself, bears some resemblance to that cited in Chapter i, which was proposed many years ago for the study of Wordsworth and other Romantics by S. F. Gingerich in his *Essays in the Romantic Poets*.

2. This point is not made in the well-known Vienna lectures but in the earlier Berlin lectures: *Vorlesungen über Schöne Litteratur und Kunst*, I, 98. Yet Coleridge, who had read only the Vienna lectures, immediately applied Schlegel's term "organic unity" to the freedom of the individual from determination as well as to the freedom of the work of art from prescriptive principle.

3. *English Poetry and its Contribution to the Knowledge of a Creative Principle*, with a preface by T. S. Eliot.

4. *The Prelude*, XI, 223–305.

5. *The Mind of a Poet*. Havens' chapter "Antirationalism," cited earlier, is relevant here. Wordsworth's life and his theology are naturally intimately connected; since the emphasis in this present study is often theological, any of its insights may be usefully supplemented by reading critics whose interest is more strongly psychological or biographical. Of many such only two of the more recent need be cited here: F. W. Bateson, *Wordsworth: A Re-interpretation* (Second Edition) and Donald E. Hayden, *After Conflict, Quiet*.

6. In this chapter I have quoted from the 1805 version of *The Prelude*, ed. de Selincourt, since our concern is primarily with Wordsworth's thoughts and feelings just about the turn of the century, as expressed in their freshest form; the first citation of book and line number will always be from this version, the second from the regular version. In most of the passages quoted the difference is slight, if any at all.

7. See M. H. Abrams, "The Correspondent Breeze: A Romantic Metaphor," *Kenyon Review*, XIX (1957), 113–30.

8. Note also that when Wordsworth is praising Nature as the restorer of Imagination later in *The Prelude*, he cites especially the wind, the roaring waters, and the lights and shadows that marched and countermarched upon the hills (XI, 138–48; XII, 93–103).

9. John Ruskin, in whom the love of beauty and the love of justice appeared at times as conflicting impulses, finally decided (like a good Platonist) that ultimately the two impulses were one. See the discussion of Ruskin in Katherine Gilbert and Helmut Kuhn, *A History of Aesthetics*, p. 414.

10. "The Tragic Fallacy" in *The Modern Temper*, p. 125.

11. Speaking of the central purpose of Wordsworth's poetry, George M. Meyer says: "That purpose, quite simply, is to 'justify the ways of God to man,'" *Wordsworth: An Appreciation, Tulane Studies in English*, III, 11.

12. *The Mind of a Poet*, p. 2.

13. This discussion of the *Lines* is largely a transcription from an article by the author, an article from which this entire book might be said to have developed: "*Tintern Abbey* Revisited," *PMLA*, LXV (March, 1950), 154–62.

14. N. P. Stallknecht (*Strange Seas of Thought*, pp. 14–15.) notes how interpenetration or "interfusion" is strikingly imaged to Wordsworth by the landscape which *The Prelude* describes his having witnessed during the crossing of the Alps. Stallknecht further discusses this important aspect of Wordsworth's thought (p. 65 and pp. 81–86.) and compares it rightly with what Whitehead has to say in *Science and the Modern World* about the valuable truth to be found in Wordsworth's perception of reality. See later in this chapter the discussion of the images of interpenetration which Wordsworth discovered at Grasmere and on the top of Snowdon, and in this and the last chapter the sections titled "The Ennobling Interchange." Havens (*The Mind of a Poet*, p. 240.) notes how for Wordsworth the imagination was the faculty which makes "limits vanish." *The Infinite* as Wordsworth writes of it suggested to him not only the absence of external limits to the universe but the softening of harsh internal distinctions so that nothing is completely isolated from anything else or from the whole. The successful work of art, as Wordsworth saw it, was that in which the creative imagination duplicated in the microcosm of the work that "infinity" which the imagination, half-creating, half-perceiving, was aware of in the greater world. Cf. Coleridge's whole doctrine of imagination, expressed in the *Biographia* and elsewhere, of the imagination as faculty of totality which perceives and creates things *together*, the parts and the whole mutually modifying each other, in contrast to the understanding which perceives things as separates. See J. V. Baker, *The Sacred River*, pp. 113–51, and all other adequate discussions of Coleridge's doctrine.

15. *Sämmtliche Werke*, Jubiläumsausgabe, XXX, 9.

16. *Coleridge's Shakespearean Criticism*, ed. Raysor, I, 4–5.

17. *The Great Chain of Being*, p. 11.

18. *Wordsworth's Imagery: A Study in Poetic Vision*, p. 58.

19. See the statement by Thomas Arnold, Wordsworth's friend and neighbor, quoted by Basil Willey, *Nineteenth Century Studies*, p. 71: "The girdling of the mountains round the valley of our home is as apt an image as any earthly thing can be of the encircling of the everlasting arms, warding off evil and showering all good." How much less protected, more exposed, were the spiritual sensibilities of the son Matthew Arnold on the beach at Dover at low tide, by "the vast edges drear / And naked shingles of the world"!

20. Apropos of Wordsworth's inclination to view Grasmere Vale as a "temple," as something like a work of art, it may be relevant to suggest a possible connection between art and landscape. In his Preface to the *Lyrical Ballads*—as has already been noted—Wordsworth had commented upon the justificatory power of meter, the ability of its ordered patterns to make a tragic tale more bearable; so the grandly harmonious and permanent architectonics of the vale, underlying the scene of human life which its fields and farms and village afforded, no doubt helped to blend the more discordant tones of life into a "still, sad music." If discord and impermanence were to Wordsworth two of the great evils of human life, the artistic form of a poem and the form of the vale could in somewhat similar fashion help to remedy both. See the remarks which John Crowe Ransom has made apropos of the structure of meter and which might almost equally well apply to Wordsworth's sense of the structure of the valley which he made his home ("Humanism at Chicago," *Kenyon Review*, XIV [1952], 658-59): "There is but one big construct left in the poem, and it is entirely visible and audible: the metered one, within which all the words of the poem dutifully assume their places though they may be very busy at other things. The rhythm of the meter envelops the two other objects, like an atmosphere, a constraint and a blessing too. For it is sounding all the time; it is a low-grade music making an elemental, cosmic, and eternal object. Very diffidently I venture to construe it. I think the meters are an apt imitation of the Platonic Ideas, and in permeating our two other worlds permit us to have them *sub specie aeternitatis*. For the worst thing about those two worlds is that the objects and the arrangements we sense so exquisitely and cherish so deeply are doomed; they are mortal. That awareness is never withheld from us in the poem, but quite the contrary. Nor is there any possible human equivalent for them, really, in a world of Platonic Ideas. But still that world has the distinction of being the world of the immortals, and we like to sense its presence." To be as sensitive in spirit as Wordsworth to the physical configurations and movements in nature is unusual perhaps, but it was doubtless this sensitivity rather than mere acuteness of the physical senses of sight or hearing which Wordsworth had in mind

when he said in the 1800 *Preface* that the poet should be a man of more than usual "organic sensibility."

21. In the chapter on Keats I shall suggest that orthodox Christianity, in refusing to regard physical matter as evil and holding to the doctrine of a resurrection of the "body" in some glorified form, is more holistic in its sensibility than, say, Manichaeanism or some aspects of Platonism.

22. D. G. James (*Scepticism and Poetry*, pp. 134–37.) discusses this matter in a passage rich in poetic and psychological insight, and perhaps indirectly of religious insight also: "Yet by the very power of embodying it [conflict], poetry is also a kind of transcendence of it, a catharsis whereby conflict is denied a power of controlling disturbance and is pushed out from the centre of personality; and whereby it is not merely suffered but beheld as from a 'central peace subsisting at the heart of agitation.' . . . The imagination fails to see in human life a wholeness in the contemplation of which it can rest. The moral experience, which is the human experience, is necessarily incomplete, and demands for its completion something other than morality. The imagination, we have seen, is not suborned to morality; it stands outside of the life of the will and the endless conflict to which the will is bound. Only through it do we obtain deliverance from the hopeless task of morality, the failure in which the will is rooted, and stability whereby we are armed against the failures and chances of the life of action. And in its contemplation of human life and its unavoidable tragedy, it seeks also the perception of that which lies beyond the moral state. In its vivid apprehension of human life it fails to discover unity and harmony, and therefore carries within itself the dream of a perfection which is impossible to human life. In the greatest poets we can see how, perceiving the insoluble conflict of human life, they turn to the dream of 'unknown modes of being.' This transcendent activity of the imagination is, we have noted, a condition of health in the moral life and saves morality from the dangers natural to it. Yet morality itself cannot have enjoyment of that dream, for it is a dream of what is not a moral state. And the imagination in its turn can but enjoy it as a dream, though it be a dream of compelling power, and wait patiently upon it. 'Adam's dream,' wrote Keats, 'will do here.'"
—The two phrases about the "central peace" and the "unknown modes of being" are, of course, from Wordsworth. See also N. P. Stallknecht (*Strange Seas of Thought*, p. 194) apropos of *The Prelude*, XIII, 105 ff.: "The life of the imagination brings with it, then, freedom from unruly desire and establishes the soul as a Power which recognizes its own nature and is thus oriented to the universe."

23. The "viewless realms," the goal of the spirit's soaring in the early *Descriptive Sketches*, are a foreshadowing of the later "worlds / To which the heaven of heavens is but a veil" in the final lines of *The Recluse* used as the prospectus of *The Excursion*. George M. Meyer (*Wordsworth's Formative Years, University of Michigan Publications in Language and Literature*, XX, 254.) cites the line "if this be but a vain belief" as be-

tokening Wordsworth's doubts, even as early as the Tintern Abbey *Lines*, of the possibility of a complete naturalism. The unity of Wordsworth is the theme of the study by Mary E. Burton, *The One Wordsworth*, as it is also to some extent of Edith Batho's *The Later Wordsworth*. G. M. Harper's biography of the poet, for all its excellence, perhaps errs in the encouragement it gives to the notion of two Wordsworths; see also H. l'A. Fausset's *The Lost Leader* and Herbert Read's *Wordsworth*.

24. H. N. Fairchild in volume III of his *Religious Trends* is a case in point.

25. See note 22 of this chapter, which quotes D. G. James's passage ending with the citation of Keats's phrase 'Adam's dream.' Besides the passages from Wordsworth just quoted in this paragraph, see also *The Prelude*, II, 367–71; II, 348–52:

> *Oft in those moments such a holy calm*
> *Did overspread my soul, that I forgot*
> *That I had bodily eyes, and what I saw*
> *Appeared like something in myself, a dream*
> *Or prospect of the mind.*

26. "The Eye on the Object in the Poetry of Wordsworth," in *Wordsworth: Centenary Studies*, ed. G. T. Dunklin, pp. 23–42.

27. In *The Mind of a Poet* and in Chapter V, "Visionary Dreariness," of *Scepticism and Poetry*.

28. *Strange Seas of Thought*, pp. 227–36, in the discussion of what Stallknecht terms Wordsworth's "democratic fallacy."

29. One recent work, W. K. Wimsatt, Jr. and Cleanth Brooks' *Literary Criticism: A Short History*, makes clear the special character of the Kantian sublime and calls attention (p. 108) to the one section of the Longinian treatise in which Kant is clearly anticipated: "Take the Longinus of *Peri Hupsous*, Chapter XXXV, alone ('Wherefore not even the entire universe suffices for the thought and contemplation within the reach of the human mind, but our imaginations often pass beyond the bounds of space . . .'), and we have a very good start toward the 'sublime' in Kant's *Critique of Judgment* in 1790." Wimsatt and Brooks' entire Chapter XVIII, "Imagination: Wordsworth and Coleridge," is helpful here. See also E. F. Carritt on Addison, Kant, and Wordsworth in *The Theory of Beauty;* Clarence D. Thorpe, "Coleridge on the Sublime," in *Wordsworth and Coleridge: Studies in Honor of George M. Harper*, ed. Earl L. Griggs; W. J. Hipple, Jr., *The Beautiful, the Sublime, & the Picturesque in Eighteenth-Century British Aesthetic Theory;* and, especially, two very recent studies, Ernest Lee Tuveson's *The Imagination as a Means of Grace* and Marjorie Hope Nicolson's *Mountain Gloom and Mountain Glory: The Development of the Aesthetics of the Infinite*. Iris Murdoch, in "The Sublime and the Beautiful Revisited," *Yale Review*, XLIX, 247–71, briefly discusses Kant's conception of the sublime as an

introduction to her plea that modern novelists devote themselves less to the cult of isolation and see whether it is still not possible to write novels which create a sense of an abundance of vitalities, to portray life as a scene of many persons commingled.

30. Wordworth's letter to Dorothy shortly after crossing the pass reports the experience in a much simpler and more traditional way: "Among the more awful scenes of the Alps I had not a thought of man, or a single created being, my whole soul was turned to him who produced the terrible majesty before us." (Letter reprinted by de Selincourt in his first edition of the early version of *The Prelude*, pp. 279–80.) This statement bears at least one important resemblance to the account in *The Prelude:* by implication the poet's consciousness, in passing beyond all created being, is passing beyond the mountains themselves. The fact that Wordsworth's youthful poem *Descriptive Sketches* omits the crossing of the Alps suggests that this experience had not yet been digested, that the poet was perhaps half aware that his statements to his sister were not enough.

31. See Bennett Weaver, "Wordsworth's *Prelude:* The Poetic Function of Memory," *Studies in Philology*, XXXIV (1937), 552–63; and Georges Poulet, "Timelessness and Romanticism," *Journal of the History of Ideas*, XVI (1954), 3–22.

32. Denis Saurat (*Modern French Literature*, p. 136) has well described these Proustian moments.

33. Wordsworth's massive grounding in the poetry of the eighteenth century, including of course Young's *Night Thoughts* on "life, death, and immortality," is well exhibited in Abbie F. Potts' *Wordsworth's "Prelude."*

34. F. W. Bateson (*Wordsworth: A Re-interpretation*, p. 68.) is too harsh in his opinion of the latter part of this poem.

35. *The Prelude*, XI, 385; XII, 326.

36. T. M. Raysor ("The Themes of Immortality and Natural Piety in Wordsworth's Immortality Ode," *PMLA*, LXIX (1954), 861–75) takes up the question of the possible logical conflict between Wordsworth's emphasis on the soul's partaking of the infinite, the boundless, and his orthodox inclination to regard the soul as always destined to preserve the limits of an individual identity. He concludes, I think rightly, that despite all his emphasis on the former, Wordsworth tends always to retain much of the latter. I have not myself stressed this conflict, which was not a conflict to the poet himself. One image in *The Prelude* seems to combine suggestions of both:

> *I love a public road: few sights there are*
> *That please me more; such object hath had power*
> *O'er my imagination since the dawn*

Of childhood, when its disappearing line,
Seen daily afar off, on one bare steep
Beyond the limits which my feet had trod
Was like a guide into eternity,
At least to things unknown and without bound.
                    (XII, 145–52; XIII, 143–52.)

The individual road, an image of the individual being, stretches beyond the horizons of this life, is lost to our sight as it progresses ever onward into landscapes of boundless possibility, but it remains the same road still. But see also the passage quoted in the final section of this chapter, *The Prelude*, VIII, 624–40; VIII, 476–94.

37. Bennett Weaver attacked the idea that Wordsworth turns his back on human misery in his article, "The Property of Fortitude," *Studies in Philology*, XXXVII (1940), 610–31. See also D. G. James chapter "Visionary Dreariness" in *Scepticism and Poetry*. Arnold's charge, in his *Stanzas in Memory of the Author of 'Obermann,'* that Wordsworth diverted his eyes from "half of human fate" presumably refers to his turning his back on the cities and the new class of industrial workers.

38. See *The Recluse*, especially lines 290–355.

39. Marjorie Hope Nicolson, *Mountain Gloom and Mountain Glory: The Development of the Aesthetics of the Infinite*, pp. 384–93, notes that the Romantics felt a less sharp distinction between the beautiful and the terrible than their eighteenth-century predecessors, and that for Wordsworth especially the two often merge, as inseparable parts of one experience, into what the poet himself termed a "tranquil sublimity."

40. *The Prelude*, XIII, 1–65; XIV, 1–66. David Ferry, in his recent book *The Limits of Mortality: An Essay on Wordsworth's Major Poems*, believes in effect that after about 1805 the "supremacy" was not "interchangeable" enough: that Wordsworth's mystical sense of the "calm of blessed eternity," like too brilliant moonlight, blanked out earthly values, that the aloofness always discernible developed into a "hatred of life." Ferry believes that Wordsworth earlier shared Coleridge's [and Browning's] "sacramental" view, accepting human life as a divinely ordained field for soul-making, but that with the passage of years this view was overwhelmed by his mystical, anti-materialist view. Professor Ferry's beautifully written book, with its multitude of sensitive explications, is a pleasure to read. It stresses and stresses again, so as to leave an indelible impression, the strain of austerity in the poet's character, a trait at times unattractive and disadvantageous even from a moral point of view. Yet Ferry's searching exploration of an important part of Wordsworth's imagery reminds me of an amusing paper read by Mark Schorer about a dozen years ago at the English Institute. Professor Schorer had gleaned from Jane Austen's novels a host of half-dead metaphors which revealed

how thoroughly her style is pervaded by an imagery of calculation. Loyal Janeites, including perhaps Schorer himself, cannot deny that their idol valued prudence very highly, but they have only to return to the novels themselves to discover that she is not such an inhuman monster as a highly selective examination of her imagery may suggest.

Professor Ferry (pp. 169–71) places great stress upon the Snowdon passage and feels that by its inherent denial of life it tragically mars the ending of a great poem designed as an acceptance of life. Here is one of the few places in which Ferry's special emphasis, his admitted *parti pris*, leads him into a distinct misreading. He exaggerates out of all proportion any sense of recoil which Wordsworth may have felt in response to the "abysmal, gloomy, breathing place" which opened through the sea of clouds at his feet, the space through which mounted

> *the roar of waters, torrents, streams*
> *Innumerable, roaring with one voice!*
> *Heard over earth and sea, and, in that hour,*
> *For so it seemed, felt by the starry heavens.*

The streams and falls of his native mountains were always a symbol for Wordsworth of the mysterious sources of life present upon the earth about him, and within himself; here, as usual, he harkens to their voices with a mingled awe and delight—as the ecstatic tone of these last lines suggests. The sense of mystery is heightened by the fact that the torrents are invisible in the darkness below the cloud, and that their voices rise up through so gloomy an opening; but the awe and delight are thereby intensified rather than diminished. The phrase "shaped for admiration and delight" is admittedly found only in the 1805 version.

Another book published since these chapters were written, David Perkins' *The Quest for Permanence*, agrees at least in part with Professor Ferry's view of the later Wordsworth. Perkins' last chapter on Wordsworth is titled "The Withdrawal" in marked contrast with the title "The Acceptance of Process" given to the last chapter on Keats. *The Prelude* is throughout, and most explicitly in the last chapter, an acceptance of process, though a careful reader can find—as might be expected in so complex a poem from so complex a poet—some of those unconscious reservations stressed by Ferry. Regardless of Wordsworth's attitude towards process, it is true that the combination of his temperament and his circumstances did not in his later years provide him with enough process, enough new developments; there was too much stasis; his later struggles were too much a mere holding action.

Viewing the matter in another way, one may suggest the same deep, intense, inner turbulence, viewed sympathetically by such critic-biographers as F. W. Bateson and Donald E. Hayden, persisted into the later years, though more suppressed and more controlled. Hence the same compulsion persisted to value the ideal of serenity. Yet Wordsworth was still withal the poet who had viewed the starry heavens as "one great galaxy of life and joy." As strong a charge for denying life might be brought against Yeats in his equally passionate later days. It was Yeats who dreamed of escaping anguish by being re-incarnated as a mechanical nightingale; it was he who in his poem *Byzantium* worshipped the cold moonlit dome because it "disdained" all man's complexity, who cherished the geometric marble floor because it "broke" the perplexity that flesh and blood are heirs to.

Notes to Chapter iii

1. *The English Romantic Poets: A Review of Research*, ed. T. M. Raysor, cites many writers on both sides of this question. Those who are less conscious of a change in Shelley and see rather considerable uniformity of thought first to last are at least partially right. For though it seems that some impulses of thought grew stronger and others weaker, they can almost all be discovered present at any period. Those who cherish the non-transcendental Shelley can find passages to their liking even in the last years. Likewise those who like better the final stanzas of *Adonais* can find Shelley soaring as early as 1812 in *The Retrospect:*

> And early I learned to scorn
> The chains of clay that bound a soul
> Panting to seize the wings of morn,
> And where its vital fires were born
> To soar, and spurn the cold control
> Which the vile slaves of earthly night
> Would twine around its struggling flight.

These lines and the almost equally early lines 188-89 of *Queen Mab* should not be dismissed by the student of Shelley as mere facile poetic figures; they represent too essential a part of their author's personality. In support of my own feeling that Shelley moved towards a theistic position, I cite only Carlos Baker in *Shelley's Major Poetry* and in his contribution to *The Major English Romantic Poets*, ed. C. D. Thorpe and others.

2. Shelley's opinion is found in his Preface to his *History of a Six Weeks Tour* (1817), in which the poem first appeared. Leavis's opinion is in *Revaluation*, p. 213. Earl R. Wasserman, in the chapter on *Mont Blanc* in his recent book *The Subtler Language*, does not agree with Shelley or Professor Leavis. He finds the poem a highly organized one in which philosophical speculations and imaginative responses advance dialectically to an inevitable, more or less Berkeleian conclusion.

3. "The One 'Mont Blanc,'" *Keats-Shelley Journal*, IV (1955), 55-56.

4. "The Meaning of Shelley's 'Mont Blanc,'" *PMLA*, LXII (1947), 1046-50.

5. *Poetical Works*, ed. Woodberry, p. 639, note on line 96 of *Mont Blanc*.

6. *Rehabilitations and Other Essays*, p. 28.

7. *Prometheus Unbound, University of Michigan Publications in Language and Literature*, XXVII.

8. *Prometheus Unbound*, II, iii, 13 and II, ii, 17. The grove, which was "curtained out from heaven's wide blue" except for a cleft through which a star occasionally shone, reminds one of Keats's grove in the *Ode to a Nightingale*, where there is "no light / Save what from heaven is with the breezes blown / Through verdurous glooms and winding mossy ways." Both groves express the theological beliefs or feelings of the two poets— that they received only brief and flickering indications that beyond this world Heaven's light was indeed shining.

9. Bennett Weaver, *op. cit.*, p. 6. Professor Weaver's study called my attention to the two passages just cited.

10. *Paradise Lost*, I, 17.

11. George Santayana, *The Winds of Doctrine*, pp. 167–68, remarks, "Shelley's earthly paradise, as described in *Prometheus* and in *Epipsychidion*, is too festival-like, too much of a mere culmination, not to be fugitive: it cries aloud to be translated into a changeless and metaphysical heaven, which to Shelley's mind could be nothing but the realm of Platonic ideas, where 'life, like a dome of many-coloured glass,' no longer 'stains the white radiance of eternity.'"

12. Cf. Ellsworth Barnard, *Shelley's Religion*, pp. 264–66: "It will doubtless seem strange that Shelley, a rebel almost from his cradle, to the end of his life a passionate crusader in the cause of liberty, and a preacher of the doctrine that, except for hatred of others, self-contempt is perhaps the greatest sin, should not have felt that man's salvation lies wholly with himself. But here again it must be remembered that according to Shelley's view there are two selves; and what most men call the self—that is, the personality—is an illusion that stands between the higher self and the divine Spirit to which the higher self is akin, and with which it strives to be united. And the business of poetry, Shelley believes, is not with the personal self, but with the 'self' that is common to all men. 'A poet participates in the eternal, the infinite, and the one.'" It is not the practice here to cite all the works that are concerned more with the poet's thought than with his imagination (insofar as these are separable), but Barnard's whole book is useful. The chapters "God" and "Life, Death, and Eternity" bring together dozens of quotations from the poems and prose which cannot be cited here. If the result is sometimes confusing, this fact is only a sign of Barnard's completeness. There may be some truth in Barnard's contention (p. 163) that the conflicts within Shelley's

theological position are no greater than in any theological position. Religious positions are likely to be a practical reconciliation of the theoretically irreconcilable.

13. R. H. Fogle, *The Imagery of Keats and Shelley*, p. 123, comments on Shelley's "fusion": "Shelley, indeed, merges and interfuses different orders of sensation in response to his yearning, both philosophical and temperamental, for Unity. Beyond and above the Many, the perplexing variety of things, lies the One, simple, perfect, complete, 'an elemental subtlety like light.'" As an example of fusion and final unity, Fogle quotes (p. 127) the lines from this passage about the air-dissolved star mingling light and fragrance and the final line about the interpenetration of light.

14. Besides Ellsworth Barnard and many other commentators, see especially B. P. Kurtz, *The Pursuit of Death*.

15. Letter of January 2, 1812, in *Letters*, ed. Ingpen, I, 205.

16. See Eliot's preface to Leone Vivante's *English Poetry and Its Contribution to the Knowledge of a Creative Principle*.

17. *Rehabilitations and other Essays*.

18. Letter of November 24, 1811, in *Letters*, I, 174. See also letter of June 20, 1811, *Letters*, I, 99.

19. Letter of April 10, 1822, in *Letters*, II, 953–54. Shelley is slightly misquoting (though not misunderstanding) lines, from the unpublished *Prelude*, which Wordsworth published separately under the title *French Revolution*.

20. See B. P. Kurtz, *The Pursuit of Death*.

21. "A Study of *Alastor*," *Kent State University Publications*, Series II, 1954.

22. "*Adonais:* Progressive Revelation as a Poetic Mode," *ELH*, XXI (1954), 274–326.

23. A careful reader of this chapter in manuscript has pointed out that the fate of the critic is different from that of Keats even without any hypothetical afterlife, since the critic is shamed. In this case, presumably, the triumphal close might be given a mere humanist's interpretation: Keats is to be rewarded by poetic glory. But this solution has already been dismissed as inadequate a few stanzas earlier. Here one comes face to face with a basic difficulty in deciding upon an interpretation of Shelley. In his poems, as in those of Keats, a modern non-theological humanist finds so very much which resembles his own views that he is tempted to assume a more complete agreement than exists. I have just quoted from the letter to Gisborne, written even later than *Adonais*, in which Shelley termed "demoniacal" the notion that men find their hap-

piness in this world or not at all. Most orthodox Christians who have admired Shelley have been content to recognize, despite all the resemblances, that Shelley in basic ways differed from themselves. Perhaps humanists should recognize a comparable distinction between Shelley's ideas and their own.

24. R. H. Fogle, *The Imagery of Keats and Shelley* notes (p. 123) the tendency of Shelley's images "to culminate in abstraction." Such a culmination is in accord with what Fogle (p. 219) notes as the whole effort of Shelley's language "to grasp and express an unseen and unobtainable truth." See the further comment on the same page: "To this restlessness of aspiration is to be attributed both his virtue and his defect: fierce power and a wearying lack of repose." Cf. also David Perkins, *The Quest for Permanence*, especially pp. 166–70.

25. E. J. Trelawny, *Records of Shelley, Byron, and the Author*, p. 80, quoted by Barnard, *Shelley's Religion*, p. 161. S. C. W. has applied the apt phrase "sceptical idealism" to Shelley, in a review of an article on *Alastor*, in *Philological Quarterly*, XXXIV (1955), 121.

26. *Shelley's Religion*, p. 62.

27. Prologues to *Queen Mab* and *The Revolt of Islam*.

28. Letter to Gisborne, June 18, 1922, *Letters*, II, 976.

29. The Preface to *The Cenci*.

30. Albert Gerard, in "*Alastor*, or the Spirit of Solipsism," *Philological Quarterly*, XXXIII (April, 1954), 164–77, sees Shelley's dilemma as a concomitant of his modified Berkeleianism. K. N. Cameron, reviewing J. A. Notopoulos's *The Platonism of Shelley* in *Philological Quarterly*, XXIX (April, 1950), 125, notes the Berkeleianism of *Mont Blanc*. So also does Earl R. Wasserman in his discussion of the poem in his book *The Subtler Language*, though he does not concede the perplexity which some others find in the poem and which Shelley in due time appears to have found himself.

31. See Robert A. Wishart, "*Alastor*, ll. 645–58," *Explicator*, XII (November, 1953), #11, for comments on two other points of light different from those which the poet sees when looking into the pool. Both sets of points were undoubtedly allied in Shelley's imagination.

32. Nowhere is that "man-centered" aspect of Shelley's faith (such as Professor Fairchild so strongly objects to) more vividly expressed than in this already cited stanza xlvii of *Adonais*:

> *Who mourns for Adonais? Oh, come forth,*
> *Fond wretch! and know thyself and him aright.*
> *Clasp with thy panting soul the pendulous Earth,*
> *As from a centre, dart thy spirit's light*

NOTES TO PAGES 101-111

> *Beyond all worlds, until its spacious might*
> *Satiate the void circumference.*

Yet, as this chapter and Barnard's book have tried to show, Shelley's imaginative sensibility sometimes reveals the opposite or complementary instinct to focus upon something outside and above man. But this latter instinct was continuously inhibited. The title of the article already cited, "Alastor, or the Spirit of Solipsism," is well phrased: the point of the poem is not just that its hero is alone in the usual human sense, but that his imagination is alone in the cosmos.

33. See passage already cited, *Revaluation*, p. 213, in which Leavis contrasts the supposed scatteredness of Shelley's *Mont Blanc* with the "collectedness" of Wordsworth's passage on crossing the Alps.

34. I have not yet, as this manuscript goes to press, digested Milton Wilson's book, *Shelley's Later Poetry: A Study of the Prophetic Imagination*, nor Desmond King-Hele's, *Shelley: The Thought and the Work*.

Notes to Chapter iv

1. Amy Lowell, *John Keats*.

2. H. W. Garrod, *Keats*.

3. H. N. Fairchild, *Religious Trends in English Poetry*, III.

4. Clarence D. Thorpe, *The Mind of John Keats*; Douglas Bush, *Mythology and the Romantic Tradition in English Poetry*; D. G. James, *Scepticism and Poetry*, *The Romantic Comedy*, and *Three Odes of Keats*; R. H. Fogle, *The Imagery of Keats and Shelley*.

5. Allen Tate, "A Reading of Keats," *On the Limits of Poetry*, p. 177.

6. C. L. Finney, *The Evolution of Keats's Poetry*, Chapter 7.

7. J. Middleton Murry, *The Mystery of Keats*.

8. R. D. Havens, "Unreconciled Opposites in Keats," *Philological Quarterly*, XIV (1939), 289.

9. Cf. Shelley's similar cherishing of the sense of "mystery" allied to beauty, as expressed in the *Hymn to Intellectual Beauty*: "aught that for its grace may be / Dear, and yet dearer for its mystery."

Keats's aesthetic response to mountains with lakes would appear from his letters to have been as strong as his response to the sea, and likewise to have included a large element of wonder which somehow half-resolved his perplexities over man's fate. He wrote thus, June 25–27, 1818, to his brother Tom, speaking of Windermere: "the two views we had of it are of the most noble tenderness—they can never fade away—they make one forget the divisions of life; age, youth, poverty and riches; and refine one's sensual vision into a sort of north star which can never cease to be open-lidded over the wonders of the great Power."

Marjorie Hope Nicolson's book, *Mountain Gloom and Mountain Glory*, shows how frequently in the eighteenth century men felt that an acquaintance with the sublimer works of nature created on a grand scale, whether mountains or the new stellar regions being explored by astronomy, went hand in hand with a wider and deeper spiritual sensitivity; both aspects of expanding consciousness were evidence of man's "elastic soul." Edward Young's *Night Thoughts* is as one might expect Professor Nicolson's prime example of the astronomical sublime.

10. Cf. Shelley's *Adonais* (lii): "Rome's azure sky, / Flowers, ruins, statues, music, words, are weak / The glory they transfuse with fitting truth to speak."

11. Cf. also Newell Ford's book, *The Prefigurative Imagination of John Keats*. Professor Ford's study preceded Wasserman's and can still be read with interest, though in my opinion it exaggerates the extent to which Keats expected the prefigurings to be realized within the span of this life, and is too reluctant to concede how frequently they are viewed as anticipating an Elysian hereafter.

12. See the passage, cited in Chapter I from Kant's *Critique of Judgment*, section 59.

13. F. R. Leavis, *Revaluation*, p. 213, already cited in earlier chapters.

14. W. P. Ker, *Form and Style in Poetry*, p. 121.

15. *Biographia Literaria*, end of chapter 13.

16. Cleanth Brooks, "Keats's Sylvan Historian," *The Well Wrought Urn*.

17. Wordsworth's sonnet *Upon the Sight of a Beautiful Picture*, beginning "Praised be the Art." Wordsworth's comments are usually printed therewith.

18. R. H. Fogle, "Keats's *Ode to a Nightingale*," *PMLA*, LXVIII (1953), 211-22.

19. C. L. Finney, *The Evolution of Keats's Poetry*, chapter 7; Clarence D. Thorpe, *The Mind of John Keats*, p. 135.

20. Letter no. 302, 28 September 1820—actually September 30, as Rollins' note remarks.

21. "A reading of Keats," *On the Limits of Poetry*, p. 168.

22. *Scepticism and Poetry*, and also *The Romantic Comedy*.

23. Earl R. Wasserman, *The Finer Tone*, p. 183.

24. Especially Earl R. Wasserman, *op. cit.*

25. F. R. Leavis, *Revaluation*, p. 244.

26. Byron has commented with effective coarseness upon what he disliked most in Keats, a tendency deliberately to goad the imagination to ecstasy. (L. A. Marchand, *Byron*, p. 886.) There is point in Byron's accusation, yet it ignores the complexity of the interchange which usually took place between Keats's imagination and the object. It is amusing that the stone should be cast by the author of such a deliberate emotional indulgence, such a determined sentimental journey, as *Childe Harold's Pilgrimage*.

27. David Perkins, in *The Quest for Permanence*, titles his last chapter on Keats "The Acceptance of Process."

28. *Biographia Literaria*, Chapter 12.

Notes to Chapter v

1. Hallam Tennyson, *Alfred Lord Tennyson: A Memoir*, I, 43-44.

2. Basil Willey, in his chapter on Tennyson in *More Nineteenth Century Studies*, discusses Tennyson's evolutionary thought. See also W. R. Rutland, "Tennyson and the Theory of Evolution," *Essays and Studies by Members of the English Association*, 1940, and Douglas Bush, *Science and English Poetry*.

3. In *"In Memoriam," Selected Essays* (1950), pp. 252-53.

4. For a discussion of Tennyson's theology, his ideas on God and immortality, see E. H. Sneath, *The Mind of Tennyson*, and Sir Charles Tennyson, *Six Tennyson Essays*.

5. Introduction to *Poems of Alfred Lord Tennyson*, pp. xviii-xix.

6. *Mythology and the Romantic Tradition in English Poetry*, p. 227.

7. *A Commentary on Tennyson's In Memoriam*.

8. *More Nineteenth Century Studies*, pp. 95-98.

9. *Ibid.*, p. 85.

10. [Herbert] Marshall McLuhan, in "The Aesthetic Moment in Landscape Poetry," *English Institute Essays*, 1951, discusses those occasions when the poets from the Romantics to T. S. Eliot experienced an "unexpected transport from the realm of time to eternity" (p. 175). He contrasts the exterior landscapes from Thompson to Tennyson with the "interior" landscapes of Poe, Baudelaire, and Rimbaud. When he refers, however, to Tennyson's "manipulating an external environment as a means of evoking art emotion" (p. 168), he seems perhaps to suggest that the unexpected transport is entirely a subjective experience in no way the result of the environment; thus he would preclude in Tennyson's case any that sense of "ennobling interchange" to which Wordsworth assigned such momentous importance. Perhaps some recognition of this inter-

change is to be inferred in other parts of Professor McLuhan's very compressed paper.

11. In *More Nineteenth Century Studies* (p. 63), Willey notes, as others must have done before, that Hallam in a way completed Tennyson by possessing precisely some of the virtues which Tennyson lacked.

12. *Ibid.*, pp. 96–98; this famous section of *In Memoriam* is also discussed by E. B. Mattes in *In Memoriam: The Way of a Soul*, pp. 49–53.

13. Basil Willey, *More Nineteenth Century Studies*, p. 56, connects Tennyson's generally "believing temper" and his trustfulness with his prolonged close relationship with his mother.

14. *"In Memoriam," Selected Essays.*

15. *More Nineteenth Century Studies*, p. 81. For a very favorable recent appreciation of *In Memoriam*, see John D. Rosenberg, "The Two Kingdoms of *In Memoriam*," *Journal of English and Germanic Philology*, LVIII (1959), 229–40: Rosenberg regards the "synthesis" of ideas in the poem, though not without inconsistencies, as more "daring, persuasive, and eloquent" than any attempted since. See also the final pages of G. M. Young's "The Age of Tennyson," in *Critical Essays on the Poetry of Tennyson*, ed. John Killham. If Tennyson were living today he would presumably be attracted by the syntheses of scientific and religious awareness offered by Lecomte du Noüy and Teilhard de Chardin.

16. Such an opinion, partly explicit and partly implicit only, may be gathered from T. S. Eliot's essay *"In Memoriam"*; the judgment is a natural one to make and I am perhaps remembering another writer's expression of it.

17. *Tennyson*, pp. 61–65.

18. Quoted by Sir Charles Tennyson, *Six Tennyson Essays*, p. 115.

19. Introduction to Alfred Tennyson, *Selected Poems*, ed. Herbert Marshall McLuhan. McLuhan cites Hallam's views.

20. Basil Willey, *More Nineteenth Century Studies*, pp. 57–60, discusses the great importance to Tennyson's imagination of his early years in the Lincolnshire Wolds, and at the same time he relates much that is false in Tennyson's taste to those false Victorian recreations of Gothic such as were frequently erected at this time amidst what remained of idyllic England, like the neo-Gothic improvements which Tennyson's wealthy brother was happily engaged in at Bayons Manor: "The oncoming world is raw and hideous: very well, let us pretend that the old order is unchanging, that the feudal hierarchy persists, that landed property, not industrial capital, still controls politics and society! A decaying order is never so fanatically upheld as when it is touched by the finger of death. And this pattern of life, this notion of success, of what it is worth while

to do with money, a pattern so blatantly visible at Bayons, runs through the whole fabric of upper- and middle-class Victorian life and thought. It is important for the understanding of literature that such things should be remembered, because it was with such patterns in mind, or buried in the subconsciousness, that part of the literature of the Victorian age was written. Tennyson's own pageantry was more unsubstantial, but Camelot, the city of shadowy palaces, is his Bayons none the less."

Tennyson of course fared much better in his celebration of the beauties of nature than in his creation of Camelot; indeed, upon this theme he is a wonderful poet indeed. His power here, according to G. M. Young ("The Age of Tennyson," *Critical Essays on the Poetry of Tennyson*, ed. John Killham, p. 31.), accounts in large part for his replacing James Thomson after the midpoint of the last century as the favorite poet of the British middle class: "The public of which I am speaking, Tennyson's public, was becoming, in spirit, suburban: a country-bred stock, entangled in a way of life which it had not learned to control, was instinctively fighting for breath. And for sixty years its poet was there, flashing on it in phrases of faultless precision, pictures of the world from which it was exiled and in which it yearned to keep at least an imaginary footing."

21. W. W. Robson, in "The Dilemma of Tennyson," *Critical Essays on the Poetry of Tennyson*, ed. John Killham, p. 159, finds Tennyson's manner too self-conscious; he grants the poet's seriousness and intelligence but finds his style still essentially "the style of a minor poet"—and of "the most un-strenuous, lonely, and poignant of poets." Yet Tennyson's instinctive will to religious belief was essentially optimistic, very much like Browning's. This is why it seems right to me to ascribe his somewhat ennervated manner to factors other than the Victorian religious crisis.

Notes to Chapter vi

1. See W. C. DeVane, *A Browning Handbook* (1955), pp. 45-46, for an account of the incident; and Griffin and Minchin, *The Life of Robert Browning*, pp. 59-60, for a reprint of Mill's observations.

2. *Robert Browning: A Portrait*. This particular theme is almost continuous through the first part of the book.

3. See W. C. DeVane, *A Browning Handbook*, p. 244.

4. *Ibid.*, p. 483.

5. So the imagination was to be the "Necessary Angel" to Wallace Stevens, mediating between earth and a wholly fanciful heaven; see Chapter viii below.

6. W. O. Raymond, *The Infinite Moment and Other Essays in Robert Browning*, p. 164, notes Aprile's similarity to Shelley. Speaking of the

hero of Pauline, of Paracelsus, and Sordello, Raymond suggests (p. 160) that all three faced the problem of adjusting "the infinite aspiration and towering ambitions of genius" to the "finite conditions and limitations of life."

7. *Ibid.*, p. 163.

8. See the passage (already cited above) in *The Critique of Judgment*, Section 42.

9. W. O. Raymond, " 'The Jewelled Bow': A Study in Browning's Imagery and Humanism," *PMLA*, LXX (1955), 115–31.

10. *Ibid.*

11. W. C. DeVane, *A Browning Handbook*, p. 292.

12. For the passage on Shakespeare as the Spinozistic Deity, see Coleridge's *Works*, ed. Shedd, VI, 312; for the passage on the simultaneity of intention and execution see Coleridge's *Shakespearian Criticism*, ed. T. M. Raysor, I, 224. The latter passage is virtually translated from Schlegel.

13. *Biographia Literaria*, Chapter XIII. Emerson R. Marks, in his "Browning's *Abt Vogler, 43–56*," *Explicator*, XVI, item 29, relates this poem to the general Romantic emphasis upon the unaccountability of beauty: Browning speaks of taking three sounds and making not a fourth sound but a "star"; Coleridge speaks of beauty's emerging as a "tertium aliquid." Henry Charles Duffin, in his *Amphibian: A Reconsideration of Browning*, pp. 291 ff., denies the highest rank as a lyric poet to Browning precisely because he feels the poet lacks the ability, possessed at times by Tennyson, to take his images and his cadences and weave them into a pattern of magical grace suggestive of some extra-terrestrial dimension.

14. *Coleridge on the Seventeenth Century*, ed. Roberta Florence Brinkley, pp. 519–21.

15. H. C. Duffin, "Mysticism in Browning," *Hibbert Journal*, LIII (1955), 372–75.

16. *A Browning Handbook*, p. 44.

17. *The Works of John Ruskin*, XXXVI, xxxiv.

18. *Letters*, ed. Hood, pp. 171–72.

19. *The Infinite Moment*, p. 43.

20. H. N. Fairchild, "*La Saisiaz* and *The Nineteenth Century*," *MP*, XLVIII (1950), 104–11, makes the point that the omission of Christian arguments was in fact quite voluntary on Browning's part and not, as has sometimes been supposed, required by the terms of the symposium.

21. Mrs. Sutherland Orr, "The Religious Opinions of Robert Browning," *Contemporary Review*, December, 1891, p. 880.

H. N. Fairchild, in *Religious Trends in English Poetry*, IV, 145, quotes from the same article Mrs. Orr's statement that Browning conceded that Christianity might be a "fiction" and then added, "But I am none the less convinced that the life and death of Christ, as Christians apprehend them, supply something which their humanity requires, and that it is true for them." Since this study is primarily concerned with patterns of imaginative belief rather than with religious beliefs as these are usually understood, I have in this chapter confined myself largely to a sympathetic presentation of what these patterns were in Browning's case. H. N. Fairchild sharply distinguishes between orthodoxy and the subjective Christianity of Browning and other assenters to the Victorian compromise. More will be said upon this topic in the final chapter. Logically this subjectivism or "Tübingenism," towards which Browning's faith tends (despite his scornful rejection of Renan and Strauss) may be said to resemble Shelley's frequent tendency to solipsism. If the dangers of subjectivism have not been made the theme of this chapter as much as they were of the chapter on Shelley, the reason may be that Browning, unlike Shelley, was not often pushed to the verge of despair by the fear that his own imaginative aspirations had no objective validity; Browning had more steadily that faith in imagination which Shelley had only during happier periods. Perhaps relevant to Browning's greater philosophic stability was the fact that he did not plague himself with the epistemological question of whether the beauty of the blooming pear tree which he saw in April and which delighted him had any objective validity; he quite naturally and with deplorable lack of philosophical sophistication, assumed Wordworth's "ennobling interchange" between our outer and inner worlds to be reality. Professor Fairchild agrees with R. D. Altick's "The Private Life of Robert Browning," *Yale Review*, XLI (1952), 247–62, that psychological insecurity rather than psychological security was the basic fact of Browning's life, that the security was a mask or created personality. There is naturally a sort of truth in what both writers say, but again I have chosen to postpone till the final chapter any further comments on the religious questions raised by this "split" in Browning's personality—a split which is probably not such an unusual one.

Joseph E. Baker, "Religious Implications in Browning's Poetry," *Philological Quarterly*, XXXVI (1957), 436–52, offers a resumé of a number of writers who have found Browning too earth-bound, too much a worshipper of mere energy, to be taken seriously as a religious poet. He himself finds Browning too insistently cheerful to be a true follower of the "man of sorrows, acquainted with grief." In view of the New Testament parable enjoining us from trying to root out the tares from the field of growing wheat, Professor Baker is perhaps unfortunate in his phrasing when he objects to Browning's not wanting to pull the "weeds" out of the garden.

Notes to Chapter vii

1. *Matthew Arnold*, p. 352. The entire chapter "Joy Whose Grounds Are True" is excellent. Some critics write as though there were "two Arnolds"—like the hypothetical "two Wordsworths." But Trilling's study sees the final very tentative, very qualified affirmation of a highly subjective religion not as a betrayal of the earlier agnosticism but as the resolution of a tension which had always been present.

2. *Ibid.*, p. 346.

3. *Modern Democracy*, p. 100.

4. Walter E. Houghton, "Arnold's 'Empedocles on Etna,'" *Victorian Studies*, I (1957-8), 311-36.

5. The final image of *Sohrab and Rustum* is one of those studied by Maud Bodkin, *Archetypal Patterns in Poetry*, pp. 65-68. Note also the imagery of the sea in Wordsworth's Intimations *Ode* and in sonnet XXXIII in his River Duddon series; in the latter the river which had been turbulent near its source is finally "Prepared, in peace of heart, in calm of mind / And soul, to mingle with Eternity." Donald E. Hayden, in his *After Conflict, Quiet*, p. 47, notes the ironic fact that the sea, which in Wordsworth was to become an orthodox symbol to reconcile "the problems of mutability," had originally in the Letter to the *Bishop of Llandaff* been the symbol of oblivion—as in Byron's *Childe Harold*. (So, in the case of Arnold, the reconciling sea of *Sohrab and Rustum* had been the "unplumb'd salt, estranging sea" in *To Marguerite—Continued*.) Henry Vaughan, though the last lines of *To Night* had shown him eager to shed the burdens of individuality ("O for that Night when I in Him / May live invisible and dim!"), in *The Waterfall* sees the stream rising from its "rocky grave" beneath the fall and then running a "longer course more bright and brave" before finally reaching the "sea of light" from which it came. This brighter, braver, longer course between death and eternity might seem to correspond less to what Tennyson in *In Memoriam* called the "early Heaven" of standard Protestant theology than to Tennyson and Browning's own private theology envisioning a succession of higher states. Vaughan and his two great Victorian successors might presumably be compared to the Catholics in their insistence on a Purgatory, provided this Purgatory is viewed more as a state of active growth than of mere passive punishment.

6. Apropos of Arnold's feeling for the symbolic value of the Scholar Gypsy's countryside, Louis Bonnerot remarks, I think perceptively (*Matthew Arnold, Poète*, p. 488.): "Dans *Thyrsis* et *The Scholar Gypsy*, la pastorale est non seulement l'aspect idéal d'Oxford et de sa jeunesse, mais encore . . . l'équivalent de ce 'paradis révélé' dont, selon Baude-

laire, la vertu de la Poésie est de nous assurer la jouissance 'immédiate-ment, sur cette terre même.' " The suggestions of Baudelaire to which Bonnerot refers are similar to those thoughts in Keats's letters, so frequently reflected in his poetry, that the poetic imagination provides us here and now with a foretaste of Elysium.

7. This important essay has not been easily get-at-able; it has been available in the selection from Arnold titled simply *Essays* (London, 1914). Now, however, it is found in the first volume of *The Complete Prose Works of Matthew Arnold*, ed. R. H. Super.

8. The resemblance to Keats's view of the urn is clear, as it is also to the attitude towards art expressed by Wordsworth—in more traditional terms—in the sonnet *Upon the Sight of a Beautiful Picture*, where he praises the art which gives "To one brief moment caught from fleeting time / The appropriate calm of blest eternity." Arnold's response to art as the mediator between the real and the ideal also corresponds to that of such post-Kantian idealists as Schelling and Hegel, though Arnold would naturally dispense with the elaborate metaphysical *system* of thought which is so characteristic of these men.

9. Trilling, *Matthew Arnold*; Bonnerot, *Matthew Arnold, Poète*, especially p. 470.

10. *The Letters of Matthew Arnold to Arthur Hugh Clough*, ed. H. F. Lowry, p. 146.

11. *Ibid.*, p. 87.

12. In "The Function of Criticism at the Present Time," *Essays in Criticism: First Series*.

13. *The Letters of Matthew Arnold to Arthur Clough*, ed. H. F. Lowry, p. 146.

14. *Ibid.*

15. *Matthew Arnold*, p. 377. See Wordsworth's meditation in *The Prelude* (XIII, 66–119; XIV, 67–129), ascribed to his night on the peak of Snowdon, upon the joyous "consciousness of whom we are" which habitually infuses the life of the man in proper imaginative relationship with his environment. In the later version of *The Prelude* the "whom" is capitalized.

Notes to Chapter viii

1. That Stevens is "centrally in the Romantic tradition" is affirmed by Northrop Frye in "The Realistic Oriole: A Study of Wallace Stevens," *Hudson Review* (1957), X, 353–70. Stevens himself, like the Imagists and other moderns, is inclined to use the word "Romantic" in a pejorative

sense, as signifying the indulgence in sentiment divorced from imaginative precision. Just as this book is going to print a student has called my attention to the useful article by J. V. Cunningham, "The Poetry of Wallace Stevens," *Poetry*, LXXV (1949), 149–65.

2. *A Vision* (1925), p. 215.

3. *Yeats: The Man and the Masks.*

4. *Ibid.*, pp. 283–84.

5. F. A. C. Wilson, *W. B. Yeats and Tradition*, pp. 223–30.

6. *The Necessary Angel*, p. 60.

7. *Ibid.*, p. 175.

8. *Ibid.*, p. 50.

9. *Ibid.*, p. 169.

10. *Ibid.*, p. 63.

11. *Ibid.*, p. 166.

12. "The Comedian as the Letter C," *Collected Poems*, p. 30.

13. "The Comedian as the Letter C," Sections I and III. Hi Simon's article, " 'The Comedian as the Letter C': Its Sense and Its Significance," *Southern Review*, V (1940), 453–68, was written before the later poetry and the essays made interpretation a little easier. Despite the poem's earthy tone, important parts of *The Comedian* ascend to that rarefied zone where epistemology, aesthetics, and theology overlap. One difficulty may have been that Simon interpreted "Triton" and his perhaps "hallucinating" horn as symbols simply of the "variableness of the sea" instead of expressions of the imagination's power to sense a divinity within the natural world—the divinity which is precisely Wordsworth's subject in his sonnet on Triton beginning "The world is too much with us."

14. *The Necessary Angel*, p. 49.

15. "Stevens Posthumous," *International Literary Annual*, II (1959), 65–89. See also Stevens' "The Plain Sense of Things," *Collected Poems*, p. 503.

16. *The Necessary Angel*, p. 59.

17. *Ibid.*, p. 36.

18. Northrop Frye, "The Realistic Oriole: A Study of Wallace Stevens," *Hudson Review*, X (1957), 370, remarks: "It was persistence that transformed the tropical lushness of *Harmonium* into the austere clairvoyance of *The Rock*, the luxurious demon into the necessary angel, and rounded out a vision of major scope and intensity." In part yes, but one wonders

if there is not another explanation also. R. P. Blackmur, in "The Substance that Prevails," *Kenyon Review*, XVII (1955), pp. 100 and 107, applies the term "dandyism" to Stevens' insistence upon being "deeply involved but uncommitted." After so many decades of uncommitted intensity, when he was himself an old man, Stevens may simply have found this philosophic position exhausting. Yeats's last days are another case in point.

19. *Southern Review*, VII (1941-2), 667-89. This essay is collected with another by the same author in *T. S. Eliot: A Selected Critique*, ed. Leonard Unger.

20. See also an article by the present author, "The Romantic Tradition: Wordsworth and T. S. Eliot," *Bucknell Review*, VIII (December, 1959), 277-86.

Notes to Chapter ix

1. The phrasing is that of Denis Saurat, *Modern French Literature*, p. 25.

2. *The Necessary Angel*, pp. 33, 169.

3. So I interpret the quotations from Professors Joad and Richards on pages 25 and 18 of *The Necessary Angel*, where the general advance of intellect is apparently being viewed as one of the forces in our modern environment which imagination must counteract.

4. *In Defense of Reason*, p. 57.

5. *The Necessary Angel*, p. 79.

6. *Ibid.*, p. 62.

7. *Ibid.*, p. 63.

8. *Ibid.*, p. 175.

9. *Ibid.*, p. 33, where Stevens says, "We have been a little insane about the truth. We have had an obsession." I do not wish to minimize the power of life itself, even without the help of philosophy, to perplex us. But in Stevens' case philosophy played an unusually large role. He himself cited the subjective aspects of Kant in support of his own subjectivist position (*The Necessary Angel*, p. 56.); he may have been another disciple who never got beyond *The Critique of Pure Reason*. That he read widely in philosophers since Kant is apparent in both his prose and verse. He expressly notes that his own insistence upon the merely subjective value of imagination enables his faith to "escape destruction at the hand of the logical positivists" (*The Necessary Angel*, pp. 138-39). Perhaps there are others like myself, who prefer poetry to epistemological analysis and wish that so very gifted a poet as Stevens had never read the philosophers at all; or at least one wishes, as one does in long stretches

of *The Prelude,* that the philosophy had been kept separate and written down in prose. It is hard at times when reading the poems between *Harmonium* and *The Rock,* not to think of Coleridge's unhappy description of himself in *Dejection:*

> And haply by abstruse research to steal
> From my own nature all the natural man—
> This was my sole resource, my only plan:
> Till that which suits a part infects the whole,
> And now is almost grown the habit of my soul.

10. "The Personal Heresy in Criticism," *Essays and Studies by Members of the English Association,* XIX (1933), 27-28. Professor Lewis's essay was provoked in part by E. M. W. Tillyard's *Milton,* and there is a rebuttal by Tillyard in the succeeding issue of *Essays and Studies.*

11. Coleridge, *The Aeolian Harp.*

12. *The Prelude,* III, 108-18; III, 108-24.

13. *Ibid.,* VII, 695-740; VII, 722-71. This interesting and not wholly clear passage virtually identifies London's visual disorder and lack of visual wholeness with the city's moral disorder which struck Wordsworth with equal force and more or less simultaneously: in both respects he found it difficult in London to achieve among the multifarious "little things" that "under-sense of greatest" which his favorite landscapes and the simpler lives of their inhabitants so powerfully supplied.

14. *Scepticism and Poetry,* p. 265.

15. "A Reading of Keats," *On the Limits of Poetry,* p. 168.

16. *More Nineteenth Century Studies,* p. 81.

17. *On Poetry and Poets,* p. 250.

18. *The Use of Poetry and the Use of Criticism,* p. 91.

19. Fairchild's indictment is found in its most comprehensive, concentrated, and eloquent form in the final chapter of his *Religious Trends in English Poetry,* III. The immediately succeeding discussion is most closely pertinent to these pages.

20. See *Religious Trends in English Poetry,* IV, 135-36, where he also cites an article which brings further argument and evidence in support of his view of the poet, R. D. Altick's "The Private Life of Robert Browning," *Yale Review,* XLI (1952), 247-62.

21. *The Letters of Matthew Arnold to Arthur Hugh Clough,* ed. H. F. Lowry, pp. 145-46.

22. "Shelley's *On Life,*" *PMLA* (1947), 774-83.

23. *Letters and Correspondence of J. H. Newman,* ed. Anne Mozely, I, 416. The admission is from Newman's year of crisis, but one wonders whether he might not sometimes have felt this same way in later years also.

24. Graham Hough, *The Romantic Poets,* p. 93, notes that the end of the significant part of Wordsworth's poetic creation coincided with the completion of his philosophical development.

25. In *The Egotistical Sublime,* p. 49, John Jones states somewhat emphatically that Wordsworth's conversion to Christianity came not through a sense of "sin and glory" but through "wanhope" or "colorless despair"; that he does not embrace it but is forced to it by the exclusion of alternatives. One should, however, read Edith Batho's full and sympathetic account, *The Later Wordsworth.*

26. In *Stanzas in Memory of the Author of "Obermann."*

(With a few exceptions, this bibliography lists only such works as are cited or referred to in the text.)

General Works and Studies of Several Poets

Abrams, M. H. "The Correspondent Breeze: A Romantic Metaphor," *Kenyon Review*, XIX (1957), 113–30.

——. *The Mirror and the Lamp: Romantic Theory and the Critical Tradition.* New York, 1953.

Auden, W. H. *The Enchafèd Flood; or, The Romantic Iconography of the Sea.* New York, 1950.

Beach, Joseph Warren. *The Concept of Nature in Nineteenth-Century English Poetry.* New York, 1936.

Bloom, Harold. *The Visionary Company: A Study of English Romantic Poetry.* Garden City, N.Y., 1961.

Bodkin, Maud. *Archetypal Patterns in Poetry: Psychological Studies of Imagination.* London, 1934.

——. *Studies of Type-images in Poetry, Religion, and Philosophy.* London, 1951.

Bowra, C. M. *The Heritage of Symbolism.* London, 1943.

——. *The Romantic Imagination.* Cambridge, Mass., 1949.

Bush, Douglas. *Mythology and the Romantic Tradition in English Poetry.* New York, 1937.

——. *Science and English Poetry.* New York, 1950.

Carritt, E. F. *The Theory of Beauty.* London, 1928.

Fairchild, H. N. *Religious Trends in English Poetry.* 4 vols. New York, 1939–1957.

Faverty, Frederic E., ed. *The Victorian Poets: A Guide to Research.* Cambridge, Mass., 1956.

Foster, Richard. *The New Romantics: A Reappraisal of the New Criticism.* Bloomington, Ind., 1962.

Gilbert, Katherine E., and Helmut Kuhn. *A History of Aesthetics.* New York, 1939.

Gingerich, S. F. *Essays in the Romantic Poets.* New York, 1924.

Goethe, Johann Wolfgang von. *Sämmtliche Werke*, Jubiläums-ausgabe. Stuttgart & Berlin, 1902–1907.

Hartman, Geoffrey. *The Unmediated Vision: An Interpretation of Wordsworth, Hopkins, Rilke, and Valéry.*

Hipple, W. J., Jr. *The Beautiful, the Sublime, and the Picturesque in Eighteenth-Century British Poetic Theory.* Carbondale, Ill., 1957.

Hoffmann, Charles G. "Whitehead's Philosophy of Nature and Romantic Poetry," *Journal of Aesthetics and Art Criticism,* X (1952), 258–63.

Hough, Graham. *The English Romantic Poets.* London, 1953.

Inge, W. R. *The Platonic Tradition in English Religious Thought.* New York, 1926.

———. *Studies in English Mystics.* London, 1906.

James, D. G. *The Romantic Comedy.* London, 1948.

———. *Scepticism and Poetry: An Essay on the Poetic Imagination.* London, 1937.

Johnson, E. D. H. *The Alien Vision: Sources of the Poetic Imagination in Tennyson, Browning, and Arnold.* Princeton, 1952.

Kant, Immanuel. *Critique of Judgment,* trans. with an introd. by J. H. Bernard. New York, 1951.

———. *Critique of Judgement,* trans. with several introductory essays, notes, and analytical index, by James Creed Meredith. Oxford, 1911.

Ker, W. P. *Form and Style in Poetry,* ed. by R. W. Chambers. London, 1928.

Kermode, Frank. *Romantic Image.* London, 1957.

Knight, G. Wilson. *The Starlit Dome: Studies in the Poetry of Vision.* London, New York, 1941.

Krutch, Joseph Wood. *The Modern Temper: A Study and a Confession.* New York, 1929.

Leavis, F. R. *Revaluation: Tradition and Development in English Poetry.* New York, 1947.

Lecomte du Noüy, Pierre. *Human Destiny.* New York, 1947.

Lewis, C. S. "The Personal Heresy in Criticism," *Essays and Studies,* XIX (1933), 7–28.

———. *Surprized by Joy.* London, 1955.

Lovejoy, A. O. *The Great Chain of Being: A Study of the History of an Idea.* Cambridge, Mass., 1936.

Monk, Samuel Holt. *The Sublime: A Study of Critical Theories in XVIII-century England, with a new preface by the author.* Ann Arbor, 1960.

Murdoch, Iris. "The Sublime and the Beautiful Revisited," *Yale Review,* XLIX (1959–60), 247–71.

Nicolson, Marjorie Hope. *Mountain Gloom and Mountain Glory: The Development of the Aesthetics of the Infinite.* Ithaca, 1959.

Peckham, Morse. "Towards a Theory of Romanticism," *PMLA,* LXVI (1951), 3–23.

Perkins, David. *The Quest for Permanence: The Symbolism of Wordsworth, Shelley, and Keats.* Cambridge, Mass., 1959.

Poulet, Georges. "Timelessness and Romanticism," *Journal of the History of Ideas,* XVI (1954), 3–22.

Plato. *The Myths of Plato,* originally trans. and introd. by J. A. Stewart, now ed. and newly introd. by G. R. Levy. Carbondale, Ill., 1960.

Ransom, John Crowe. "Humanism at Chicago," *Kenyon Review*, XIV (1952), 647-59.

Raysor, Thomas M., ed. *The English Romantic Poets: A Review of Research*, revised edition. New York, 1956.

Roppen, Georg. *Evolution and Poetic Belief: A Study in Some Victorian and Modern Writers*. Oslo, 1956.

Santayana, George. *Winds of Doctrine: Studies in Contemporary Opinion*. New York, London, 1913.

Saurat, Denis. *Modern French Literature, 1870-1940*. New York, 1946.

Schlegel, A. W. von. *Vorlesungen über Schöne Litteratur und Kunst*. Heilbronn, 1884.

Shaftesbury, Anthony Ashley Cooper, 3rd Earl of. *Characteristicks of Men, Manners, Opinions, Times*. London, 1711.

Symons, Arthur. *The Romantic Movement in English Poetry*. New York, 1909.

Teilhard de Chardin, Pierre. *The Phenomenon of Man*, with an introd. by Julian Huxley, trans. by Bernard Wall. New York, 1959.

Tennant, F. R. "Deism," *Encyclopedia Britannica*, 1956.

Thorpe, Clarence D., ed. *The Major English Romantic Poets: A Symposium in Reappraisal*. Carbondale, Ill., 1957.

Tillich, Paul. "One Moment of Beauty," the "Parade" section, p. 2, *St. Louis Post-Dispatch*, September 25, 1955.

Tuveson, Ernest Lee. *The Imagination as a Means of Grace: Locke and the Aesthetics of Romanticism*, Berkeley, 1960.

Vivante, Leone. *English Poetry and its Contribution to the Knowledge of a Creative Principle*, with a preface by T. S. Eliot. London, 1950.

Watson, John. *Schelling's Transcendental Idealism: A Critical Exposition*. Chicago, 1882.

Whitehead, Alfred North. *Science and the Modern World*, New York, 1925.

Whitney, George, and David F. Bowers, ed. *The Heritage of Kant*, Princeton, 1939.

Willey, Basil. *The Eighteenth Century Background: Studies on the Idea of Nature in the Thought of the Period*. London, 1940.

———. *More Nineteenth Century Studies: A Group of Honest Doubters*. London, 1956.

———. *Nineteenth Century Studies, Coleridge to Matthew Arnold*. New York, 1949.

———. *Seventeenth Century Background*. London, 1934.

Wimsatt, W. K., Jr., and Cleanth Brooks. *Literary Criticism: A Short History*. New York, 1957.

Studies of Individual Poets and Works by These Poets

ARNOLD

Arnold, Matthew. *The Complete Prose Works of Matthew Arnold*, ed.
R. H. Super. Ann Arbor, 1960——.

——. *The Letters of Matthew Arnold to Arthur Hugh Clough*, ed.
H. F. Lowry. London, New York, 1932.

——. *Poetical Works*, ed. by C. B. Tinker and H. F. Lowry. London,
New York, 1950.

Bonnerot, Louis. *Matthew Arnold, Poète: Essai de Biographie Psycho-
logique*. Paris, 1947.

Houghton, Walter E. "Arnold's 'Empedocles on Etna,' " *Victorian Studies*, I (1957–1958), 311–36.

Robbins, William. *The Ethical Idealism of Matthew Arnold: A Study of
the Nature and Sources of his Moral and Religious Ideas*. London, 1959.

Trilling, Lionel. *Matthew Arnold*, 2nd ed. New York, 1949.

BLAKE

Damon, S. F. *William Blake: His Philosophy and Symbols*. New York,
1947.

Erdman, David V. *Blake, Prophet Against Empire*. Princeton, 1954.

Frye, Northrop. *Fearful Symmetry: A Study of William Blake*. Princeton, 1947.

Murry, J. Middleton. *William Blake*. London, 1933.

Schorer, Mark. *William Blake: The Politics of Vision*. New York, 1946.

BROWNING

Altick, R. D. "The Private Life of Robert Browning," *Yale Review*, XLI
(1952), 252–67.

Badger, Kingsbury. " 'See the Christ Stand!': Browning's Religion" (Boston University), *Studies in English*, I (1955–56), 53–73.

Baker, Joseph E. "Religious Implications in Browning's Poetry," *Philological Quarterly*, XXXVI (1957), 436–52.

Browning, Robert. "An Essay on Shelley," see Appendix to *The Complete Poetical Works of Browning*, ed. Horace E. Scudder. Boston, 1895.

——. *Letters of Robert Browning*, collected by Thomas J. Wise, ed. by
Thurman L. Hood. New Haven, 1933.

——. *The Works of Robert Browning*, ed. F. G. Kenyon. London, 1912.

DeVane, William C. *A Browning Handbook*, 2nd ed. New York, 1955.

Duffin, Henry Charles. *Amphibian: A Reconsideration of Browning*.
London, 1956.

——. "Mysticism in Browning," *Hibbert Journal*, LIII (1955), 372–75.

Fairchild, H. N. "*La Saisiaz* and *The Nineteenth Century*," *Modern Philology*, XVIII (1950), 104–11.

Griffin, W. Hall, and H. C. Minchin. *The Life of Robert Browning.*
London, 1910.

Marks, Emerson. "Browning's *Abt Vogler*, 43–56," *Explicator*, XVI
(1957–58), item 29.

Miller, Betty. *Robert Browning: A Portrait.* London, 1952.

Orr, Alexandra L. (Mrs. Sutherland). "The Religious Opinions of Robert
Browning," *Contemporary Review* (1891), pp. 876–91.

Raymond, W. O. *The Infinite Moment and Other Essays in Robert
Browning.* Toronto, 1950.

———. "'The Jewelled Bow': A Study in Browning's Imagery of Humanism," *PMLA*, LXXI (1955), 115–31.

COLERIDGE

Baker, James V. *The Sacred River: Coleridge's Theory of Imagination.*
Baton Rouge, 1957.

Benziger, James. "Organic Unity: Leibniz to Coleridge," *PMLA*, LXVI
(1951), 24–48.

Coleridge, S. T. *Biographia Literaria*, ed. with an Introduction by J. Shawcross. Oxford, 1907.

———. *Coleridge's Shakespearean Criticism*, ed. T. M. Raysor. Cambridge,
Mass., 1930.

———. *The Complete Works of Samuel Taylor Coleridge*, ed. Professor
Shedd. New York, 1853.

James, D. G. "The Thought of Coleridge," in *The Major English Romantic Poets*, ed. Clarence D. Thorpe, Carlos Baker, Bennett Weaver.
Carbondale, Ill., 1957.

Mercer, Dorothy F. "The Symbolism of Kubla Khan," *Journal of Aesthetics*, XII (1953), 44–66.

Thorpe, C. D. "Coleridge on the Sublime," in *Wordsworth and Coleridge: Studies in Honor of George M. Harper*, ed. Earl L. Griggs.
Princeton, 1939.

T. S. ELIOT

Benziger, James. "The Romantic Tradition: Wordsworth and T. S. Eliot,"
Bucknell Review, VIII (1959), 277–86.

Eliot, T. S. *Complete Poems and Plays.* New York, 1952.

———. *On Poetry and Poets.* London, 1957.

———. *Selected Essays.* New York, 1950.

———. *The Use of Poetry and the Use of Criticism.* Cambridge, Mass.,
1933.

Kenner, Hugh. *The Invisible Poet: T. S. Eliot.* New York, 1959.

Matthiessen, F. O. *The Achievement of T. S. Eliot*, with a chapter on
Eliot's later work by C. L. Barber. New York, 1958.

Smith, Grover, Jr. *T. S. Eliot's Poetry and Plays: A Study in Sources and
Meaning.* Chicago, 1956.

Unger, Leonard, ed. *T. S. Eliot: A Selected Critique.* New York, 1948.

Unger, Leonard. "T. S. Eliot's Rose Garden: A Persistent Theme," *Southern Review*, VII (1942), 667–89. (Reprinted in collection just listed.)

KEATS

Bostetter, Edward E., "The Eagle and the Truth: Keats and the Problem of Belief," *Journal of Aesthetics and Art Criticism*, XVI (1957–58), 362–72.

Brooks, Cleanth, "Keats's Sylvan Historian," in *The Well Wrought Urn*. New York, 1947.

Finney, C. L. *The Evolution of Keats's Poetry*. Cambridge, Mass., 1936.

Fogle, R. H. *The Imagery of Keats and Shelley*. Chapel Hill, 1949.

———. "Keats's *Ode to a Nightingale*," *PMLA*, LXVIII (1953), 211–22.

Ford, Newell F. *The Prefigurative Imagination of John Keats: A Study of the Beauty-Truth Identification and its Implications*. Stanford, 1951.

Garrod, H. W. *Keats*. Oxford, 1926.

Havens, R. D. "Unreconciled Opposites in Keats," *Philological Quarterly*, XIV (1935), 289–300.

Houghton, Richard Monckton Milnes, Lord. *Life and Letters of John Keats*, Introd. by R. Lynd. New York, 1954.

James, D. G. *Three Odes of Keats*.

Keats, John. *The Letters of John Keats*, ed. H. E. Rollins. Cambridge, Mass., 1958.

———. *Poetical Works*, ed. by H. W. Garrod. 2nd ed. Oxford, 1958.

Lowell, Amy. *John Keats*. Boston and New York, 1925.

Murry, J. Middleton. *The Mystery of Keats*. New York, 1949.

Tate, Allen. "A Reading of Keats," in *On the Limits of Poetry: Selected Essays, 1928–1948*. New York, 1948.

Thorpe, Clarence D. *The Mind of John Keats*. New York, 1926.

Wasserman, Earl R. *The Finer Tone: Keats' Major Poems*. Baltimore, 1953.

SHELLEY

Baker, Carlos H. *Shelley's Major Poetry: The Fabric of a Vision*. Princeton, 1948.

Barnard, Ellsworth. *Shelley's Religion*. Minneapolis, 1937.

Fogle, Richard H. *The Imagery of Keats and Shelley*. Chapel Hill, 1949.

Gerard, Albert. "*Alastor*, or the Spirit of Solipsism," *Philological Quarterly*, XXXIII (April, 1954), 164–77.

Hildebrand, W. H. "A Study of *Alastor*," *Kent State University Publications*, Series I (1954).

Jones, Frederick L. "Shelley's *On Life*," *PMLA*, LXII (1947), 774–83.

Kapstein, I. J. "The Meaning of Shelley's 'Mont Blanc,'" *PMLA*, LXII (1947), 1046–50.

King-Hele, Desmond. *Shelley: The Thought and the Work*. London, 1960.

Kurtz, B. P. *The Pursuit of Death: A Study of Shelley's Poetry*. New York, 1933.

Lewis, C. S. *Rehabilitations and Other Essays*. London, New York, 1930.

Notopoulos, J. A. *The Platonism of Shelley*. Durham, N. C., 1949.

Shelley, Percy Bysshe. *The Complete Poetical Works of Percy Bysshe Shelley*, ed. George E. Woodberry. Boston, New York, 1901.

———. *The Letters of Percy Bysshe Shelley*, collected and ed. by Roger Ingpen. London, 1909.

Trelawny, E. J. *The Last Days of Shelley and Byron; Being the Complete Text of Trelawny's "Recollections,"* ed. by J. F. Monpurgo, New York, 1952.

Vivian, Charles H. "The One 'Mont Blanc,'" *Keats-Shelley Journal*, IV (1955), 55–65.

Wasserman, Earl R. *"Adonais:* Progressive Revelation as a Poetic Mode," *ELH*, XXI (1954), 274–326. (See also in next item.)

———. *The Subtler Language*. Baltimore, 1959.

Weaver, Bennett. *"Prometheus Unbound," University of Michigan Publications in Language and Literature*, XXVII, Ann Arbor, 1957.

White, Newman Ivy. *Shelley*. New York, 1940.

Wilson, Milton T. *Shelley's Later Poetry: A Study of His Prophetic Imagination*. New York, 1959.

Wishart, Robert A. *"Alastor,* ll. 645–658," *Explicator*, XII (1953), no. 11.

WALLACE STEVENS

Blackmur, R. P. "The Substance that Prevails," *Kenyon Review*, XVII (1955), 94–110.

Cunningham, J. V. "The Poetry of Wallace Stevens," *Poetry*, LXXV (1949), 149–65.

Frye, Northrop. "The Realistic Oriole: A Study of Wallace Stevens," *Hudson Review*, X (1957), 353–70.

Munson, Gorham. "The Dandyism of Wallace Stevens," *Dial*, LXXIX (1925), 413–17.

O'Connor, William Van. *The Shaping Spirit: A Study of Wallace Stevens*. Chicago, 1950.

Pack, Paul. *Wallace Stevens: An Approach to his Poetry and Thought*. New Brunswick, N. J., 1958.

Pearce, Roy Harvey. "Stevens Posthumous," *International Literary Annual*, II (1959), 65–89.

Simon, Hi. "The Comedian as the Letter C," *Southern Review*, V (1940), 453–68.

Stevens, Wallace. *Collected Poems*. New York, 1954.

———. *The Necessary Angel: Essays on Reality and the Imagination*. New York, 1951.

———. *Opus Posthumous*, ed. with an Introduction by Samuel French Morse. New York, 1957.

Tindall, William York. *Wallace Stevens* (University of Minnesota Pamphlets on American Writers, no. 11). Minneapolis, 1961.
Winters, Yvor. "The Hedonist's Progress," in *The Anatomy of Nonsense.* Norfolk, Conn., 1943. Reprinted in *In Defense of Reason.* New York, 1947.
———. *Primitivism and Decadence.* New York, 1937. Reprinted in *In Defense of Reason.* New York, 1947.

TENNYSON

Auden, W. H. Introduction to *A Selection from the Poems of Alfred, Lord Tennyson,* selected . . . by W. H. Auden. Garden City, N. Y., 1944.
Baum, Paull Franklin. *Tennyson Sixty Years After.* Chapel Hill, 1941.
Bradley, A. C. *A Commentary on Tennyson's In Memoriam.* London, 1901.
Buckley, Jerome H. *Tennyson: The Growth of a Poet.* Cambridge, Mass., 1960.
Bush, Douglas. *Science and English Poetry.* New York, 1950.
Fausset, Hugh l'Anson. *Tennyson.* London, 1929.
Hough, Graham. "The Natural Theology of *In Memoriam*," *Review of English Studies,* XXIII (1947), 244–56.
Killham, John, ed. *Critical Essays on the Poetry of Tennyson.* London, 1960.
Masterman, C. F. G. *Tennyson as a Religious Teacher.* London, 1900.
Mattes, E. B. *In Memoriam: The Way of a Soul.* New York, 1951.
McLuhan, [Herbert] Marshall. "The Aesthetic Moment in Landscape Poetry," *English Institute Essays* (1951).
———. Introduction to Alfred Tennyson, *Selected Poetry,* ed. by Herbert Marshall McLuhan. New York, 1956.
Potter, George R. "Tennyson and the Biological Theory of Mutability in Species," *Philological Quarterly,* XVI (1937), 321–43.
Rosenberg, John D. "The Two Kingdoms in *In Memoriam*," *Journal of English and Germanic Philology,* LVIII (1959), 229–40.
Rutland, W. R. "Tennyson and the Theory of Evolution," *Essays and Studies by Members of the English Association* (1940).
Sneath, E. H. *The Mind of Tennyson: His Thoughts on God, Freedom, and Immortality.* London, 1900.
Tennyson, Alfred, Lord. *The Complete Poetical Works of Tennyson,* ed. W. J. Rolfe. Boston, New York, 1898.
Tennyson, Sir Charles. *Six Tennyson Essays.* London, 1954.
Tennyson, Hallam. *Alfred, Lord Tennyson: A Memoir.* London, 1905.
Willey, Basil. *More Nineteenth Century Studies: A Group of Honest Doubters.* London, 1956.

WORDSWORTH

Bateson, F. W. *Wordsworth: A Re-interpretation*, 2nd ed. London, 1956.

Batho, Edith. *The Later Wordsworth*. New York; Cambridge, England, 1933.

Benziger, James. "*Tintern Abbey* Revisited," *PMLA*, LXV (1950),154–62.

Burton, Mary E. *The One Wordsworth*. Chapel Hill, 1942.

Fausset, Hugh l'Anson. *The Lost Leader: A Study of Wordsworth*. London, 1933.

Ferry, David. *The Limits of Mortality: An Essay on Wordsworth's Major Poems*. Middletown, Conn., 1950.

Geen, Elizabeth. "The Concept of Grace in Wordsworth's Poetry," *PMLA*, LVIII (1943), 689–715.

Harper, George M. *William Wordsworth*. New York, 1929.

Havens, R. D. *The Mind of a Poet: A Study of Wordsworth's Thought with Particular Reference to the Prelude*. Baltimore, 1941.

Hayden, D. E. *After Conflict, Quiet: A Study of Wordworth's Poetry in Relation to his Life and Letters*. New York, 1951.

Jones, John. *The Egotistical Sublime: A History of Wordsworth's Imagination*. London, 1954.

Lacey, Norman. *Wordsworth's View of Nature and its Ethical Consequences*. Cambridge, England, 1948.

Logan, James Venable. *Wordsworthian Criticism: A Guide and Bibliography*. Columbus, 1947.

Marsh, Florence. *Wordsworth's Imagery: A Study in Poetic Vision*. New Haven, 1952.

Martin, Arthur D. *The Religion of Wordsworth*. London, 1936.

Meyer, George W. *Wordsworth: An Appreciation, Tulane Studies in English*, III, 5–31. New Orleans, 1952.

———. *Wordsworth's Formative Years, University of Michigan Publications in Language and Literature*, XX. Ann Arbor, 1943.

Pottle, F. A. "The Eye on the Object in the Poetry of Wordsworth," in *Wordsworth: Centenary Studies*, ed. Gilbert T. Dunklin. Princeton, 1951.

Potts, Abbie F. *Wordsworth's "Prelude": A Study of its Literary Form*. Ithaca, 1953.

Rader, Milton M. *Presiding Ideas in Wordsworth's Poetry, University of Washington Publications in Language and Literature*, VIII, no. 2. Seattle, 1931.

Ransom, John Crowe. "William Wordsworth: Notes Towards an Understanding of Poetry," in *Wordsworth: Centenary Studies*, ed. Gilbert T. Dunklin. Princeton, 1951.

Raysor, T. M. "The Themes of Immortality and Natural Piety in Wordsworth's Immortality Ode," *PMLA*, LXIX (1954), 861–75.

Read, Herbert. *Wordsworth*. New York, 1931.

Stallknecht, Newton P. *Strange Seas of Thought: William Wordsworth's Philosophy of Man and Nature*, 2nd ed. Bloomington, 1958.

Weaver, Bennett. "The Property of Fortitude," *Studies in Philology*, XXXVII (1940), 616–31.

———. "Wordsworth's *Prelude:* The Poetic Function of Memory," *Studies in Philology*, XXXIV (1937), 552–63.

Wordsworth, William. *Guide to the Lakes,* with an Introduction by Ernest de Selincourt. London, 1906.

———. *The Poetical Works of William Wordsworth,* ed. by Ernest de Selincourt. Oxford, 1940.

———. *The Prelude,* ed. by Ernest de Selincourt, 2nd ed. rev. by Helen Darbishire. Oxford, 1959.

YEATS

Ellmann, Richard. *The Identity of Yeats.* New York, 1954.

———. *Yeats: The Man and the Masks.* New York, 1948.

Moore, Virginia. *The Unicorn: William Butler Yeats' Search for Reality.* New York, 1954.

Wilson, F. A. C. *W. B. Yeats and Tradition.* London, 1958.

Yeats, W. B. *A Vision.* London, 1925.

———. *The Variorum Edition of the Poems of W. B. Yeats,* ed. by Peter Allt and Russell K. Alspach. New York, 1957.

INDEX

Adams, Henry: 135
Addison, Joseph: 53, 137
Aestheticism: 229, 241, 243. *See also* Art-for-art's-sake
Agnosticism: 226. See also *Scepticism*
Akenside, Mark: 174
Aristotle: 262
Arnold, Matthew: finds Wordsworth's sense of supernal more valuable than Goethe's wisdom or Byron's force, 5–6; thought poetry would replace religion, 6; convinced that joyous, active life required faith in cosmic force, other than human mind, that worked for perfection, 198–201; *Empedocles* dramatizes internal conflict between his humanism and his fading belief in Divinity, 201–6; hero's suffering ascribed to rationalism, loneliness of an intellectual, and Kantian inability to penetrate beyond shifting forms of mind to some Absolute, 203–5; at death momentarily escapes solipsism by Kantian reliance on moral instinct and imagination, 205; contrast between Arnold's Hebraist "sublime" poems in which sense of moral activity separates him from nature, and Hellenist ones in which nature's beauty intimates Divine serenity, 207–10; in *A Summer Night* the heavens intimate possibility of condition at once "tasked" yet free and serene, 210–11; inclined to view such a condition as goal to be reached in this life, 211; thought idea of immortality more useful to men in general than to himself, 213; end of *Thyrsis* intimates "reality of the ideal" more than immortality, 213–14; yet at end of *Sohrab* wrongs of time righted to imagination when strangled river Oxus breaks through to the shining sea from which stars arise "new-bathed," 214–15; fondness for such imagery, 216; sonnet posits eternal life for the very strong only,

Arnold, Matthew (*Cont.*):
216; Arnold's father as an image of radiant Divine energy helping men to the Heavenly City, 217; joy of lovers possible intimation of state from which we come and to which return, 218; tasked but serene priest in *East London* makes "heaven" he hopes for his "home" here and now, 219; in own life the great restorative images were Oxfordshire countryside and "grand style" of great poetry, 220; in such poetry's assurance and nobility, even more than in its ideas, men must trust, 219–20; yet uncertainty as to how ideal to be apprehended infected own poetry, as he knew, 223–24; hence appreciation of Wordsworth's assurance and sense of supernal as warranting "joy," 225; Arnold's poetic images elegantly illustrative of moods and ideas discussed, but imaginative moments lack power of summons not-to-be-denied, 224–25; mentioned, 11, 104, 117, 118, 134, 151, 162, 226, 227, 234, 271
—*The Buried Life*, 216–17, 224; *Culture & Anarchy*, 208; *Dover Beach*, 198–99, 217, 224; *East London*, 219; *Empedocles*, 201–7; *The Future*, 216; *Immortality*, 216; *Lines Written in Kensington Gardens*, 209; *Memorial Verses*, 5, 8; *Milton*, 221; *Morality*, 207, 208; *Mycerinus*, 117, 201; *On the Modern Element in Literature*, 220; *On Translating Homer*, 163; *Philomela*, 221; *Preface of 1853*; *Rugby Chapel*, 216; *The Scholar-Gipsy*, 223; *Sohrab & Rustum*, 163, 214–16, 223; *Stagirius*, 204; *Stanzas from the Grande Chartreuse*, 8, 234; *A Summer Night*, 210, 219; *Thyrsis*, 212–14, 224, 227
Arnold, Thomas: 216–17, 219
Art: stimulus to supernal imaginings, 18–19; justificatory function, 37; truth to individual aspects of experi-